Inside Windows NT Workstation

George Eckel

New Riders Publishing, Indianapolis, Indiana

Inside Windows NT Workstation

By George Eckel

Published by:
New Riders Publishing
201 West 103rd Street
Indianapolis, IN 46290 USA

Copyright © 1996 by New Riders Publishing

Printed in the United States of America 1 2 3 4 5 6 7 8 9 0

CIP data available upon request

Warning and Disclaimer

This book is designed to provide information about Windows NT Workstation. Every effort has been made to make this book as complete and as accurate as possible, but no warranty or fitness is implied.

The information is provided on an "as is" basis. The author(s) and New Riders Publishing shall have neither liability nor responsibility to any person or entity with respect to any loss or damages arising from the information contained in this book or from the use of the disks or programs that may accompany it.

Publisher	*Don Fowley*
Publishing Manager	*Emmett Dulaney*
Marketing Manager	*Ray Robinson*
Managing Editor	*Carla Hall*

Aquistions Editor
Mary Foote

Development Editor
Ian Sheeler

Project Editor
Laura Frey

Copy Editor
David Bradford

Associate Marketing Manager
Tamara Apple

Acquisitions Coordinator
Stacia Mellinger

Publisher's Assistant
Karen Opal

Cover Designer
Sandra Schroeder

Book Designer
Sandra Schroeder

Production Manager
Kelly Dobbs

Production Team Supervisor
Laurie Casey

Graphic Image Specialists
Clint Lahnen
Laura Robbins
Craig Small
Todd Wente

Production Team
Heather Butler
Angela Calvert
Kim Cofer
Tricia Flodder
David Garratt
Erika Millen
Beth Rago
Erich Richter
Christine Tyner
Karen Walsh

Indexer
Ginny Bess

Production Analysts
Jason Hand
Bobbi Satterfield

About the Author

George Eckel has worked on a number of books for Macmillan Publishing, including *Memory Management for All of Us, Inside Windows NT,* and *Inside Unix.* As a professional writer, George has worked as a consultant for Hewlett-Packard, Sun Microsystems, Informix, AT&T, Time-Warner, and Silicon Graphics, Inc. Presently, he is part of the core team that developed and demonstrated the world's first interactive television, and is running a consulting business for companies setting up services on the Internet. You can reach him at geckel@warp.engr.sgi.com, or 510-820-5243.

George is the father to three children: Madeline, Nathalie, and Genevieve, and happy jusband of Shirlee, whose patience and support helped make this book possible.

Trademark Acknowledgments

All terms mentioned in this book that are known to be trademarks or service marks have been appropriately capitalized. New Riders Publishing cannot attest to the accuracy of this information. Use of a term in this book should not be regarded as affecting the validity of any trademark or service mark.

Acknowledgments

George Eckel would like to thank everyone who worked so hard to make this book possible.

Contents at a Glance

Table of Contents

Introduction

When Microsoft released version 3.0 of the Windows operating system in 1990, PC users entered an entirely new world of computing. They were freed from the constraints imposed by the MS-DOS operating system and the underlying architecture of the original IBM PC (a computer originally conceived when no one thought that any computer user would need more than 64 KB of RAM).

In this new "Windows" world, PC users took advantage of all the memory their computers could access. Proportionally spaced fonts, a wide range of video and printer options, and updated screen graphics came to every desktop as a part of the operating system. Each user had a WYSIWYG (what-you-see-is-what-you-get) display, and could be reasonably assured that what was on the screen was what would print on paper. This was a brave and exciting new world.

With the introduction of version 3.1 of Windows, Microsoft updated these features and added a new font technology, more memory-management capabilities, integrated multimedia features, and advanced object-oriented data management. Shortly after Windows 3.1 appeared, Windows for Workgroups added peer-to-peer networking features to the Windows environment. The Windows world expanded greatly, becoming doubly exciting.

Windows NT 3.1 was similar to Windows for Workgroups in that it was designed to operate in a networked environment. NT, however, was created to compete with client/server giant, Unix. Windows NT tried to incorporate all of Unix's features while maintaining an easy-to-use, familiar interface, For example, Windows NT introduced several security features: logon accounts; user privileges; and a new, optimized file system (known as the NT File System, or NTFS) that enables file-level security control and better data recovery.

In addition, Windows NT is not intended just for the PC. Although the initial release of Windows NT runs on the Intel 80x86 hardware platform, versions also are available for Alpha- and MIPS-based computers.

Windows NT 3.51 adds yet another platform on which Windows NT can run: PowerPC. It also adds support for PCMCIA cards; cards that fit into laptop computers and act as modems, disk controllers, and more.

Version 3.51 also strives to solve the problem of unearthing hidden windows by including a new library called Common Controls. This library adds to the windows widget set tabs. Tabs appear just like the tabs on manila folders. Five tabs in one window, for example, provide instant access to all five, tabbed screens, regardless of how deeply they are buried.

Version 3.51 also improves multimedia performance; an aspect of applications that has become popular.

Available with Windows NT Workstation 3.51 is the graphical interface first introduced by Windows 95. In Windows NT this interface is called Windows NT Explorer. *Inside Windows NT Workstation* is the first book to show you Windows NT Explorer. Explorer is not supported by Microsoft. You can download it for free from Microsoft. Microsoft has made Explorer public so that developers can use it and discover its bugs before version 4.0 of Windows NT Workstation premieres. Explorer is the only interface for Windows NT Workstation version 4.0.

Inside Windows NT Workstation prepares the experienced user of a command-line-based operating system, such as MS-DOS, OS/2, or Unix, to productively enter the world of Windows NT. It helps you to make the shift from the command-line environment to the milieu of the graphical user interface quickly and easily.

Inside Windows NT Workstation teaches you the basics of the Windows graphical user interface, helping you to acquire the new working habits that such an interface demands of you. It also shortens your learning curve by introducing you to the advanced features that Windows NT offers a user of software written for Windows NT itself, Windows 3.1, MS-DOS, OS/2, PowerPC, and POSIX.

This book is also for the experienced Windows and Windows NT user making the transition to the latest version of Windows NT. This book describes all the new features implemented by this new version of Windows NT.

Most of all, *Inside Windows NT Workstation* is for real-world users of computer systems. It approaches the operating system from the point of view of the person who actually uses a computer to accomplish the tasks that make up the working day.

Many Windows NT books take a very high-level approach to explaining the complexities of the new Windows NT environment. *Inside Windows NT Workstation,* on the other hand, understands that you have a job to do and that you want to learn as much about Windows NT as you need to in order to get your work done.

With an operating system that offers the complexities that Windows NT offers, understanding the *Inside Windows NT Workstation* point of view is essential. Users easily can get lost by trying all the new features and capabilities, and can be intimidated by the sheer scale and power of Windows NT.

Inside Windows NT Workstation can serve as your guide to the part of the operating system that you use to accomplish work, placing all the new features and capabilities into your working perspective. *Inside Windows NT Workstation* not only shows you how to get up to speed quickly, but, more importantly, how to get your work done as efficiently as possible.

How This Book Is Different from Most Windows NT Books

Inside Windows NT Workstation is the first book about Windows NT that describes NT's new interface, Explorer. The screen shots and feature descriptions in this book not only apply to version 3.51, but also the newest version of Windows NT Workstation, version 4.0. Instead of reading other books that stick to the interface used in version 3.5, this book catapults you into the future. *Inside Windows NT Workstation* is your key to placing yourself at the forefront of Windows NT's technology and feature set.

Inside Windows NT Workstation is designed and written to accommodate the way you work. The authors and editors at New Riders Publishing know that you do not have a great deal of time to learn Windows NT, and that you are anxious to begin using Windows NT to help you become more productive in your daily work.

This book, therefore, does not lead you through endless exercises in every Windows NT function, and it does not waste your time by repeating clearly obvious information. Each chapter introduces you to an important group of related Windows concepts and functions, and quickly shows you how these aspects of Windows NT relate to your computer system.

The chapters also lead you through the basic steps you must follow to incorporate each new concept and function into your own computing work. This book's tutorials are fast-paced; they help you to become productive in the shortest time possible after you understand the concepts and functions involved.

Later in this introduction, you will find descriptions of each of this book's sections and chapters. You also will find descriptions of other Windows and Windows NT books available from New Riders Publishing.

Who Should Read This Book?

Inside Windows NT Workstation is written for two types of readers: experienced users of a command-line operating system (DOS, OS/2, or Unix), and experienced Windows users who want to upgrade to Windows NT.

The Benefits of This Book for New Windows NT Users

If you are entirely new to the world of Windows NT, *Inside Windows NT Workstation* takes your needs seriously. Many Windows NT books are available, ranging from very basic books to advanced, specialized books for experienced users and software developers. Only a few Windows NT books, however, make a genuine effort to present information with comprehensive explanations, practical examples, and a minimum of hand-holding.

Because of the depth of the topic discussions and the breadth of the topic coverage in *Inside Windows NT Workstation,* you can use it both as a means of getting started and as a reference long after you have mastered the Windows NT interface.

This book's sections on DOS, OS/2, PowerPC, and POSIX applications are a valuable resource if you want to move existing command-line applications to the Windows NT environment. Windows NT provides a sound platform for most of your existing applications, even those that require exclusive use of the computer's resources (such as memory, serial ports, and graphics). In fact, your existing applications might run even better under Windows NT.

Experienced Windows Users Moving to Windows NT

If you fall into the second group of readers for whom *Inside Windows NT Workstation* is written, you are an experienced user of an earlier version of Windows or Windows NT. You have either upgraded to the latest version of Windows NT, or you are considering making the upgrade. This book introduces you to the capabilities that are new to Windows NT. You can learn how to apply the latest enhancements to your own computing work without relearning the Windows concepts and functions you already know through your own experience.

The Benefits of This Book for Experienced Windows Users

In contrast to other books on Windows NT, *Inside Windows NT Workstation* emphasizes practical examples that demonstrate the subject material without belaboring the point. You should work through as many examples as you like, and feel free to experiment. As you already know, Windows keeps you from damaging anything in the process.

If you already are an experienced Windows user, you will benefit by learning about Windows NT's new interface, Explorer. You might want to skim many of the chapters that introduce features, like the Control Panel, that you already know. Look, instead, for the discussions of the differences between Windows NT and other versions of Windows or Windows NT. Checking chapter headings for unfamiliar information and figures for unfamiliar screens shows you where the new material is. When you note unfamiliar information, slow down and read it carefully.

How This Book Is Organized

Inside Windows NT Workstation is organized into five logical parts. Each part dissects some aspect of Windows NT, and carefully documents what you need to know to get your work done.

Each part contains several chapters that discuss certain topics in sufficient depth to provide a solid foundation for your use of Windows NT. Skip over any chapters or parts of chapters that are obvious to you or irrelevant to your requirements.

Part One: Migrating to Windows NT: Concepts and Installation

This section provides the basis for users moving to Windows NT from other operating systems such as DOS or OS/2. These eight chapters discuss everything from the overall design of Windows NT to installation and setup.

Chapter 1, "What's New in this Release of NT Workstation."

Chapter 2, "Exploring the Road to Windows NT," gives a brief history of Windows NT and discusses the long road that led to the initial release of Windows NT.

Chapter 3, "Revealing the Windows NT Operating System," explains the basic differences between Windows NT and other operating systems.

Chapter 4, "Migrating from Windows 3.1 or Windows 95," provides a guide for the experienced Windows 3.1 or 3.0 user. Although Windows NT is superficially very similar to previous versions of Windows, important differences exist.

Chapter 5, "Comparing Windows NT and Windows 95," describes the differences between the two operating systems and provides a guideline for those people choosing one of the two to use.

Chapter 6, "Installing Windows NT 3.51," is a guide to the job of installing Windows NT on the end-user workstation. The many installation options are described in detail to aid you as you perform this important task.

Chapter 7, "Troubleshooting Installation Problems," provide a variety of helpful tips that can help you overcome the problems you might encounter when installing Windows NT.

Chapter 8, "Optimizing Windows NT," describes how you can get the optimum performance from your computer that is running Windows NT.

Part Two: Managing the Windows NT Desktop

This section, consisting of five chapters, takes a practical approach to learning everything you need to become productive with NT.

Chapter 9, "Exploring Windows NT New Interface," is most useful to new Windows users. Even experienced Windows users, however, will be introduced to the many differences between Windows NT and earlier versions of Windows.

Chapter 10, "Mastering the Windows NT Application Groups," provides insight into using the basic Windows utilities.

Chapter 11, "Configuring and Customizing the Windows NT Desktop," describes the steps necessary to customize Windows NT to suit your particular work style.

Chapter 12, "Using Windows NT Applets," describes the new Windows NT mini-applications that are not included in earlier versions of Windows.

Chapter 13, "Printing and Managing Fonts," tells you how to use the Windows NT Print Manager and TrueType fonts under Windows NT.

Part Three: Creating Solutions through Integration

This section explores one of the most exciting aspects of Windows NT. It offers unexcelled capabilities to run "foreign" applications from OS/2, DOS, and Unix systems. No other operating system offers such flexibility right out of the box. You will enjoy reading Microsoft's solution to the problem of porting your existing applications to Windows NT.

Chapter 14, "Running DOS, OS/2, and POSIX Applications," provides the background necessary to move your applications from your old operating system to Windows NT.

Chapter 15, "Exchanging Data between Windows Applications," explains the exciting capability to exchange data and information between applications.

Chapter 16, "Using Object Linking and Embedding," explains the Windows NT implementation of OLE. Experienced Windows users will recognize the value of OLE and will be interested in seeing how to exploit this capability in Windows NT.

Part Four: Managing the Windows NT Network

This section explains the way Windows NT implements peer-to-peer networking.

Chapter 17, "Exploring Networking with Windows NT," describes the Windows NT approach to networking.

Chapter 18, "Using the Remote Access Service," describes how to connect to a remote workstation and network and work just as though they were working directly on the remote workstation in the remote network.

Chapter 19, "Understanding the System Registry," explains how the NT System Registry works for system administrators.

Chapter 20, "Exploring the Windows NT Advanced Server," briefly examines Windows NT's fit as an enterprise computing platform. The advanced security and fault-tolerant features of Windows NT are important parts of Microsoft's strategy for moving Windows NT into more and more corporate environments.

Part Five: Appendices

Appendix A, "Creating an Answer File," gives you a sample answer file that you can use to perform an unattended Windows NT installation.

Appendix B, "Learning How to Perform Basic Tasks with Windows NT."

Conventions Used in This Book

Throughout this book, certain conventions are used to help you distinguish the various elements of Windows, MS-DOS, OS/2, POSIX, their system files, and sample data. Before you look ahead, you should spend a moment examining these conventions:

◆ Shortcut keys normally are found in the text where appropriate. In most applications, for example, Shift+Ins is the shortcut key for the **P**aste command.

◆ Key combinations appear in the following format:

Key1+Key2: When you see a plus sign (+) between key names, you should hold down the first key while pressing the second key. Then release both keys.

◆ On-screen, Windows NT underlines the letters of some menu names, filenames, and options names. For example, the File menu is displayed on-screen as **F**ile. The underlined letter is the letter you can type to choose that command or option. In this book, however, such letters are displayed in bold, underlined type for emphasis: **F**ile.

◆ Information you type is in **boldface**. This applies to individual letters and numbers, as well as to text strings. This convention, however, does not apply to special keys, such as Enter, Esc, or Ctrl.

◆ Text that is displayed on-screen but which is not part of Windows NT or a Windows application, such as command prompts and messages, appears in a `special typeface`.

Special Text Used in This Book

Throughout this book, you find examples of special text. These passages have been given special treatment so that you can instantly recognize their significance and easily find them for future reference.

Notes, Tips, and Warnings

Inside Windows NT Workstation features many special sidebars, which are set apart from the normal text by icons. This book includes three distinct types of sidebars: "Notes," "Tips," and "Warnings."

Note A Note includes extra information that you should find useful, but which complements the discussion at hand instead of being a direct part of it. A note might describe special situations that can arise when you use Windows NT under certain circumstances and tell you what steps to take when such situations arise. Notes also tell you how to avoid problems with your software and hardware.

Tip A Tip provides you with quick instructions for getting the most from your Windows NT system as you follow the steps outlined in the general discussion. A tip might show you how to speed up a procedure, how to perform one of many time-saving and system-enhancing techniques, or how to take advantage of an advanced feature of Windows NT.

Stop A Warning tells you when a procedure may be dangerous that is, when you run the risk of losing data, locking your system, or even damaging your hardware. Warnings generally tell you how to avoid such losses, or describe the steps you can take to remedy them.

New Riders Publishing

The staff of New Riders Publishing is committed to bringing you the very best in computer reference material. Each New Riders book is the result of months of work by authors and staff who research and refine the information contained within its covers.

As part of this commitment to you, the NRP reader, New Riders invites your input. Please let us know if you enjoy this book, if you have trouble with the information and examples presented, or if you have a suggestion for the next edition.

Please note, though: New Riders staff cannot serve as a technical resource for Windows NT or for related questions about software- or hardware-related problems. Please refer to the documentation that accompanies Windows NT or to the applications' Help systems.

If you have a question or comment about any New Riders book, there are several ways to contact New Riders Publishing. We will respond to as many readers as we can. Your name, address, or phone number will never become part of a mailing list or be used for any purpose other than to help us continue to bring you the best books possible. You can write us at the following address:

New Riders Publishing
Attn: Publisher
201 W. 103rd Street
Indianapolis, IN 46290

If you prefer, you can fax New Riders Publishing at (317) 581-4670.

You can send electronic mail to New Riders at the following Internet address:

edulaney@newriders.mcp.com

NRP is an imprint of Macmillan Computer Publishing. To obtain a catalog or information, or to purchase any Macmillan Computer Publishing book, call (800) 428-5331.

Thank you for selecting *Inside Windows NT Workstation*!

Part I

Migrating to Windows NT: Concepts and Installation

C H A P T E R

1

What's New in This Release of NT Workstation

The introduction of Windows NT 3.1 was exciting. It made high-end features, such as security, available to small companies and individuals. The newest version of Windows NT, however, is even more exciting because it adds new features, upgrades old functionality, runs on more platforms, and incorporates a powerful, flexible GUI interface, called Windows NT Explorer.

This chapter explains all of the new and revised features of Windows NT, except for Windows NT Explorer; an entire chapter (Chapter 9) is devoted to the interface upgrade. The features mentioned in this chapter are amplified in the remaining chapters in this book.

For those of you who are new to Windows NT Workstation, the final section of this chapter provides an overview of the entire Windows NT Workstation product.

New Features in Windows NT Workstation

The new version of Windows NT is more powerful and more versatile than the previous version. This section takes a look at all of the new features and changes.

Dropping Compatibility with 5.25 Inch Drives

In the past, when you ran Setup to install Windows NT, you were allowed to use 5.25 or 3.5 inch floppy disks to create an emergency disk to retain the configuration information your system needs should you ever uninstall Windows NT or find that you cannot boot your computer. Now, however, Windows NT no longer enables you to use 5.25 inch floppy disks.

Many software manufacturers are dropping their support for 5.25 inch floppy disks. If you have a 5.25 inch drive, it probably came packaged with your 3.5 inch drive, or you have one to retain compatibility with older applications distributed on 5.25 inch disks. Support is waning for these drives because they hold less data than 3.5 inch drives and their flimsiness makes them more vulnerable to damage.

Chances are that the new restriction of not using 5.25 inch floppies will not be a problem for you. If, for some reason, your system only has 5.25 inch drives, you should consider purchasing a 3.5 inch drive.

If you cannot buy a 3.5 inch drive, you have one other alternative for saving the configuration data. Instead of saving the configuration information on floppy drives, Windows NT can save the information to the hard disk.

Using the hard disk to store the emergency information is the only alternative when installing Windows NT on many workstations across a network. Network installation occurs remotely. Networked computers often do not have floppy drives or, even if they do, Setup does not generate floppy disks with the emergency information for each workstation. The downsides of this alternative are that the saved, emergency information consumes space on your hard drive, and if you are running a standalone computer, you might not be able to access the emergency information if you find that you cannot boot your disk.

To save the configuration information on the hard drive, you use the win /b command at the command prompt if your computer is currently running MS-DOS. If you are upgrading an older version of Windows NT, you use the command winnt32 /b.

Using Unattended Mode for Setup

Installing or upgrading an operating system often means waiting for files to expand and copy to the hard drive. Now, Windows NT gives you the option to install or upgrade to the latest version of Windows NT without being there! It is called unattended Setup.

If you have installed or upgraded Windows NT in the past, you know that Setup asks you a number of questions along the way. Unattended Setup does not avoid those questions; it requires that you put the answers to those questions in a file, called answer file. This means that there is some preparation needed for using the unattended mode of Setup. It does not make sense to spend a lot of time making an answer file if you are only installing Windows NT on one or two computers. On the other hand, if you have to make new installations on five or more computers, the unattended mode of Setup can save you a lot of time.

Installing Windows NT using the unattended mode has two consequences. First, because you are not present, you cannot supply floppy disks when Windows NT asks for them when it wants to make emergency disks. Consequently, the emergency information that normally would be copied to a floppy disk is saved on the hard disk. This action requires additional disk space.

Second, in unattended Setup mode, Setup does not check to see whether your Pentium chip suffers from a floating point error. If you want to check for yourself, run the pentnt command.

Upgrading to a Newer Version of Windows NT

If you are just upgrading to a newer version of Windows NT, the unattended Setup mode can save you time when you upgrade one or more computers because you do not have to create an answer file. Windows NT can use the information installed already on your computer.

To use the unattended mode when upgrading Windows NT, use the /u switch with the winnt32 command, as follows:

```
> winnt32  /u
```

where the /u switch stands for "unattended."

Performing an Unattended Installation

To use the unattended installation feature, you must perform the following tasks:

1. Place the Windows NT Workstation (or Server) software distribution files on a server. (The server and workstation files must be in different directories if they are on the same server.)

2. Create an Answer file. Appendix A gives you a template for creating an Answer file. Refer to it for detailed instructions.

3. Establish a connection between the server holding the software distribution and the computer where Windows NT Workstation will be installed.

4. Initiate the Setup application.

Setup runs its normal course using the supplied answer file to set up each computer's correct configuration. When you return to your computer, Windows NT should be fully installed.

Correcting Floating-Point Division Errors

You might remember the predicament Intel was in when people discovered that some Pentium chips had been shipped with imperfections. Under specific, fairly rare circumstances, the Pentium chip would make an error in its calculations.

Windows NT Setup now has the capability to determine if your Pentium chip has the floating-point division error. If Setup determines that your Pentium chip is flawed, you have two options:

◆ Do nothing and trust that the chances of your applications suffering from this flaw are remote.

◆ Disable floating-point division on the Pentium chip.

If you do nothing about the error and the applications you run are typically not heavy number-crunchers, such as statistical applications or 3D graphics rendering engines, you probably will never encounter the Pentium chip flaw.

If you choose to disable floating-point division on the Pentium chip, Windows NT performs floating-point division using software instead of the flawed hardware.

If you do not disable floating-point division in the hardware during Setup, you can disable it after running Setup by using the pentnt command.

For more information about correcting the floating-point error, see the section, "Detecting Pentium Errors," later in this chapter.

New Windows Functionality

Windows NT now supports Common Controls, so a great many of the windows you are used to using—File Manager, Print Manager, Clipboard Viewer, Command Prompt, Chat, CD Player, Media Player, and Sound Recorder—have changed. Common Controls is a library of new window widgets. The most notable of the new widgets are the following:

◆ tabbed dialog boxes

◆ context sensitive help buttons

◆ tools tips

The following sections describe each of these new features.

Using Tabbed Dialog Boxes

In the past, when you had a number of screens that related to one another, they all could be summoned as individual windows either appearing sequentially or all together. Going back and forth in a sequential presentation of windows was burdensome, as was unlayering the window you wanted from the heap of windows.

The Common Controls library now supports tabbed dialog boxes. Each screen appears like a file folder sporting a tab on the top or side, as shown in figure 1.1.

Figure 1.1

The tabbed dialog window.

The tabs at the top of the window enable you to see and have immediate access to all of the windows. Windows presented together using tabs are always related. If you are using Scheduler+, the tabs allow you to schedule your appointments, read the tasks you must complete, and set up reminders. Clicking on a tab moves its window to the top of all the windows. As you can see, this is a much cleaner presentation of related screens.

Getting Context-Sensitive Help

You can still display help information about specific windows by clicking on a Help button in a window, by pressing F1, or by searching through the Help index.

The Common Controls library adds two new ways of receiving help:

◆ Clicking on a window object with the secondary mouse button

◆ Clicking on a question button with the primary mouse button

When a window appears with a question mark in the upper right corner, you can display pop-up information about objects on the window by using the following procedure.

1. In a Dialog box where a question mark appears in the upper right hand corner, use the secondary mouse button to click on a window.

   A pop-up window with the words, "What's This?" appears as shown in figure 1.2.

Figure 1.2

The pop-up Help screen.

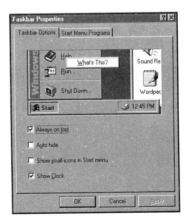

2. Use the primary mouse button to click on the What's This pop-up window. Context-sensitive help displays.

You can also display context-sensitive help using the following procedure.

1. Use the primary mouse button to click on the question mark button. The mouse cursor changes to a question mark.

2. Use the question mark cursor to click on a window object with the primary mouse button.

   Pop-up, context-sensitive help displays about the object you clicked on.

Either of these means of getting help are much more streamlined than the bother you went through when you opened a help window and searched through the list of help topics for the one you wanted.

Using Tools Tips

Although developers do their best, sometimes the graphics on toolbar buttons are confusing. To help remedy this problem, the Common Controls library now includes Tools Tips. Tools Tips display a pop-up help windows that describes the functions of the buttons in the toolbar, as shown in figure 1.3.

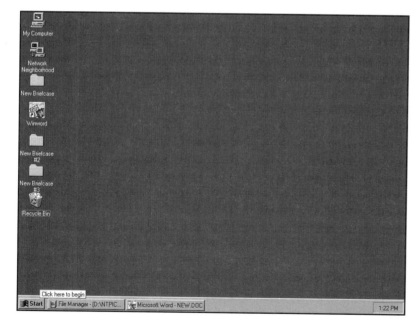

Figure 1.3

Tool Tips.

Tools Tips automatically display when a pointing device, usually a mouse cursor, goes on top of a toolbar button. To dismiss the pop-up window, you just move the mouse cursor off of the toolbar button.

Using the New Help System

In addition to the question mark in windows that enables you to display context-sensitive information, the Help system provides more detailed help than you receive with the context-sensitive information. The Help system in Windows NT has been revised to match the Help system in Windows 95. The purpose of the Help window remains the same: find the topic about which you want to learn.

If you used the Help system in NT version 3.x, you remember the rather clumsy interface that required you to choose an indexed topic in one window and then choose a subtopic in a second window. Windows NT Explorer allows full-text searches. It does not, however, support the search indexes (the files using the extension .IND) to perform full-text searches.

The new Help system supports full-text searches using the Help systems that came with Windows 3.x, Windows for Workgroups 3.x, and Windows NT 3.x whether or not the indexes were compiled for use with full-text searches. The first time you perform a full-text search, Windows NT Explorer compiles a full-text word list (*.FTS) file.

The new Help window uses three tabs: Contents, Index, and Find, as shown in figure 1.4.

Figure 1.4

New Help Window.

The following sections explain how to use the Index and Find tabs.

Using the Index Tab

The Index tab has two options: either you type in a word in the text entry field to see if there is a match in the index field, or you just scroll through the index entries to see if an entry matches your needs.

You do not use the text entry field to enter phrases or even complete words. Typing "libraries," for example, would miss the index entry, "library." For that reason it is better to enter just the first several letters of the word as search criteria.

Using the Find Tab

The Index tab allows you to type a word, or partial word, in the text entry field and see whether or not the word has any matches in the Help index. A full-text search, on the other hand, is a much more exhaustive search. When you type a word or phrase in the text entry field in the Find tab, Explorer searches through the Help files, not just the index entries, for matches.

Help files consist of words other than just Help text. For example, Help files contain annotations. When you first perform a full-text search, Explorer asks how many of the different types of words in the Help file you want to search through. According to your choice, Explorer compiles a file of the words you selected.

Explorer gives you three options for the kinds of searches you can perform:

◆ **Minimize database size (recommended).** Allows full-text searches of words, not phrases.

◆ **Maximize search capabilities.** Allows full-text searches of words, phrases, matching phrases, untitled topics, annotated, or bookmarked topics.

◆ **Customize search capabilities.** Allows you to determine how much of the maximum search capabilities you want to use.

Your search choice determines what you can type in the text entry field in the Find tab. If you build the minimum database, for example, you can only enter single words in the text entry field.

Supporting PCMCIA Cards

Windows NT Workstation now supports certain PCMCIA (a type of bus) modem cards, small computer system interface (SCSI) cards, network adapter cards, and hard disk cards.

To detect one of these cards, first install Windows NT Workstation, shut down the system, insert the PCMCIA card, and then restart the system.

You can confirm the detection of PCMCIA cards by looking in the Registry. For example, if you added a SCSI PCMCIA card, look for the following line in the Registry:

```
HKEY_LOCAL_MACHINE\HARDWARE\DEVICEMAP\SCSI
```

To view the Registry, double-click on the REGEDT32.EXE application found in the system32 directory in the File Manager. Windows NT displays the Registry Editor.

 Stop You should only look at the Registry. Changing it may render your system unusable.

Using Online Books

The new utility, Books Online, allows you to read Windows NT Workstation manuals online (and Windows NT Server manuals, if you also purchased Windows NT Server). The advantage of reading manuals online is that you can use hyperlinks to find information.

If you made a new installation of Windows NT Workstation (or Server), Setup places the Books Online icon in the Main application group. If, however, you upgraded from a previous version of Windows NT Workstation, the Books Online utility is installed but the icon is not added to the Main application group. You can still use Books Online by typing ntbooks at the command prompt. Otherwise, you can associate the executable, ntbooks, with an icon.

Using Search Mechanisms

The Books Online utility, shown in figure 1.5, has three tabs: Contents, Index, and Find.

Figure 1.5

The Books Online utility.

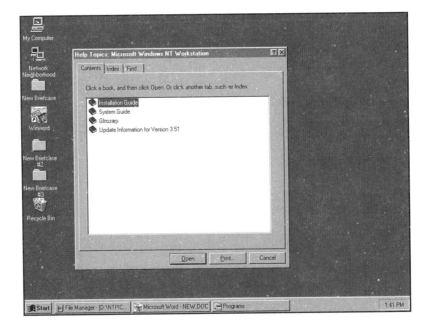

The first tab, Contents, lists the manual set. When you double-click on one of the books, Books Online displays the chapters in the book. When you double-click on one of the chapters, Books Online displays headings in the chapter. When you double-click on a heading, Books Online displays subheadings.

You can display as much or as little of a table of contents as you want using the Contents tab.

The Index tab displays the composite index of all of the books in the book set, as shown in figure 1.6.

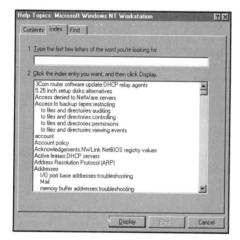

Figure 1.6

The Index tab.

Double-clicking on one of the entries in the index takes you to that page in the manual set.

The Index tab also provides a text entry field so that you can type the first few letters of a word to find in the index. If Books Online finds a match in the index, it scrolls to that entry and highlights it.

The third tab, Find, shown in figure 1.7, allows you to search through the composite Help topics of the book set.

You type a word, or partial word, about which you want to learn in the text entry field. If Books Online finds a match, it highlights and displays the help topic in the list of Help topics.

Figure 1.7

The Find tab.

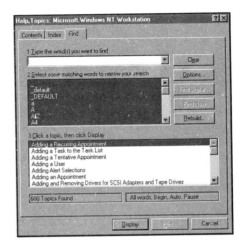

Using the Console

The Console window allows you to set the characteristics of windows that appear in Windows NT Workstation. The tabs in the Console window are as follows:

◆ **General Settings.** Sets such things as the cursor size, the display size of a window, and the size of the command buffer (see fig. 1.8).

Figure 1.8

The General Settings tab.

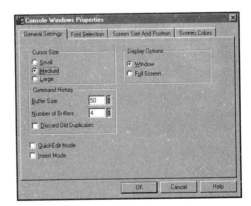

◆ **Font Selection.** Sets the size and fonts of the text in windows. Figure 1.9 shows the Font Selection tab.

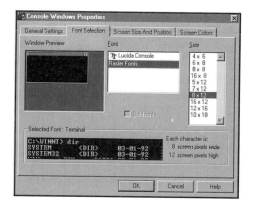

Figure 1.9

The Font Selection tab.

◆ **Screen Size And Position.** Sets the buffer size, window size, and window position on the screen. Figure 1.10 shows the Screen Size And Position tab.

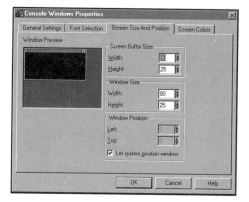

Figure 1.10

The Screen Size And Position tab.

The buffer size is the amount of memory reserved for display. It is measured in the number of characters wide by the number of characters high.

The screen size is also measured by the number of characters wide by the number of characters high. You cannot have the screen size exceed the buffer size. You can, however, have the buffer size exceed the screen size. In that case, windows will display with a scroll bar so that all of the screen buffer can be viewed. The most common setting, however, is for the screen size and buffer size to be the same.

The window position section specifies where you want windows to display. You can either specify the location on the screen of the top, left corner of every window when it opens or you can let the system place the window where it sees fit. The only drawback about specifying the location of where all windows will open is that windows open directly on top of one another. For the purpose of access windows, it is usually better to cascade the windows. In that case, letting the system determine the position of windows is a good choice.

◆ **Screen Colors.** Sets the foreground and background colors for screen text and pop-up menus. Figure 1.11 shows the Screen Colors tab.

Figure 1.11

The Screen Colors tab.

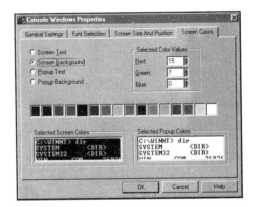

The procedure for defining the colors is simple: you choose the object you want to set the color for, and then you select the color. The sample displays in the Screen Colors tab enables you to review your color selections.

Detecting Pentium Errors

Some Pentium chips produce an error when performing floating-point division. Although encountering the error is rare, it remains a possibility.

When you install Windows NT Workstation, Setup automatically checks to see if your computer has a Pentium chip and if it is defective. If so, it asks if you want to disable floating-point division on the chip or to ignore the error. If you choose to disable floating-point division on the chip, Windows NT Workstation emulates the floating-point division using a software algorithm.

If you perform an unattended installation, or if you install Windows NT Workstation over a network, Setup does not try to detect the Pentium defect because no one is there to make the decision of whether or not to disregard the Pentium defect.

You can, however, look for the Pentium error yourself by typing pentnt at the command prompt. The command takes two parameters: -c and -f. You use the -c parameter if you want Windows NT to disable floating-point division on the chip only if it finds a defect in the Pentium chip. The -f option forces Windows NT to disable floating-point division on the chip regardless of whether or not there is a defect in the Pentium chip. If you run pentnt without either parameter, Windows NT asks whether or not you want to disable floating-point division on the chip.

Using the Compact Utility

The Compact utility sets the compression status of a directory and actually compresses or decompresses files on NTFS partitions. This utility is not compatible with the compression utilities supplied with MS-DOS, including DriveSpace(TM) and DoubleSpace(R).

When you specify that a directory is a compressed directory, files currently in the directory retain their compressed (or uncompressed) status. When new files are moved to a compressed directory, however, they are compressed.

Specifying that a directory is uncompressed simply disables the compressed status. Files in uncompressed directories retain their current compressed (or uncompressed) status, and compressed files moved to a uncompressed directory are not uncompressed.

The compact utility takes a variety of parameters. To compress the files in a directory and its subdirectory, and set the status of the directory and subdirectories as compressed, type the following command:

```
> compact /c/s
```

To remove the compression status from a directory, use the following command:

```
> compact /u C:\temp
```

where *temp* is the directory you want to decompress.

Revisions to Programs in Previous Versions

Windows NT Workstation upgrades a number of programs and features in older versions. This section takes a look at all of the revisions.

Setting the Properties in Command Prompt Windows

When you click on the Command Prompt icon in the Main application group, Windows NT displays a window with a command prompt, as shown in figure 1.12.

Figure 1.12

The Command Prompt window.

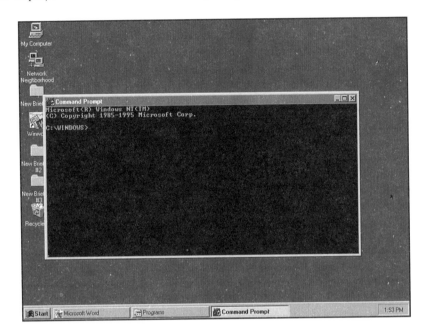

New in this version of Windows NT is the addition of the Properties option in the Control menu. You display the Control menu by single-clicking on the icon to the extreme left in the Title bar.

When you click on the Properties option, Windows NT Explorer displays the Command Prompt Properties window, as shown in figure 1.12. The tabs are the same, and the contents of the tabs are the same as in the Console Properties window. Some of the characteristics you can modify include the following:

◆ Fore- and background colors of screen text and pop-up menus

◆ Font style and size

◆ Screen size

◆ Screen buffer

◆ Position of the window

For more information about setting any of these characteristics in the Command Prompt window, see the discussion in the section, "Using the Console."

Changes to Commands

In version 3.*x*, you could use the format command to create a high performance file system (HPFS) in a partition. In the current version of Windows NT, the format command will no longer create HPFS partitions.

Note A partition is a section of a hard drive. Many hard drives have only one partition. You can, however, split a hard drive into more than one partition and use a different file system in each, for example, NTFS and HPFS.

The TCP/IP command, route, has a new parameter, -p. This parameter makes an IP route persistent. When used with the add command, you can preserve the IP route even across system restarts.

Specifying Trays for Postscript Printers

Windows NT now allows you to specify the paper in the printer's tray you want to use. You specify the paper using the Printer Manager (located on the Main application group). When you click on the Setup button in the Printer Manager, the Printer Setup window displays, as shown in figure 1.13.

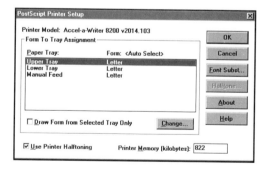

Figure 1.13

The Printer Setup window.

Click on the tray whose paper you want to specify. When you click on the Change button, the Change Form Assignment window opens, as shown in figure 1.14.

Figure 1.14

The Change Form Assignment window.

Clicking on one of the entries in the list of paper types specifies the kind of paper NT should expect to find in the selected tray.

Setting the Maximum Size of the Registry

The Registry is the place where many environment variables are defined. The Registry is a very powerful tool, but its commands and syntax are obscure. It is best to leave the Registry alone.

The Registry can grow in size as a result of installing new applications or adding new user and group accounts.

You can specify the maximum size of the Registry in the Virtual Memory window. The last text entry field on the window sets the maximum size for the Registry. The default Registry size is 25% of the size of the swap file.

Changes to the Schedule Service

You use the Schedule service to execute an action at a specified time. You might use it, for example, to do unattended system backups in the middle of the night when no one will be bothered.

In the previous version of NT, cmd was loaded by default by the Schedule service. It is no longer loaded by default. You must, however, include cmd when using the following commands: dir, copy, and > or >>, for example:

```
cmd /c dir >d:\backup.out
cmd /c d: & cd directoryName > file.out
```

If you use the at command with redirection or conditional processing, include the command in quotes, for example:

```
at 18:00 "cmd.exe /d dir > c:\logFiles
```

Changing Sound Formats

Windows NT Workstation has added the Properties option to the File menu in the Sound Recorder. When you click on that option, Windows NT displays the Properties for Sound window.

In this window you can select the sound file whose format you want to convert. After selecting a sound file, you click on the Convert Now button. Windows NT displays the Sound Selection window.

In the Sound Selection window you specify the sound format you want the sound file converted to.

Saving Telnet Log Data

Windows NT Workstation is now able to save all screen output that transpires during a Telnet session in a log file.

 Note In a Telnet session, your computer connects to a remote computer over telephone lines through a modem. A window opens on your computer but it acts as though it were a window on the remote computer. You can perform all command line tasks, such as making directories and listing files. You can only have one display, however. This restriction means that you cannot execute an application on the command line and expect to see the application on your machine (because the application does not run inside that window).

To record all screen output during a Telnet session, click on the Start Logging option in the Terminal menu of the Telnet window.

When you click on the Start Logging option, Windows NT asks you to specify a log file to send screen output to.

Clicking on the Stop Logging option terminates the logging screen output to the log file.

Changes to the Uninterruptible Power Supply Application

The value of an uninterruptible power supply (UPS) is that it can shut down the system gracefully when it detects an interruption in the power supply.

In previous versions of Windows NT, the administrator could specify that UPS could close any dialog boxes on the screen if a power outage occurred. Dialog boxes are a problem in time-critical activities because the Dialog box can wait forever for the user to input information and therefore make a graceful system shutdown impossible.

Windows NT no longer provides the facility for UPS to close dialog boxes.

Changes in Logon Script Execution

An administrator can determine whether or not a logon script a user has runs sequentially or concurrently with the system letting the user on. A logon script typically maps network drives and copies files that applications in the Startup application group can use.

New to Windows NT is the checkbox on the User Profile Editor window labeled as Wait For Logon Script To Complete Before Starting. When this checkbox is checked, the user's logon scripts must complete before the applications in the Startup application group are run. If the checkbox is unchecked, user scripts can run at the same time that applications in the Startup application group are run.

Multimedia Performance Upgrades

The latest version of Windows NT Workstation incorporates a list of multimedia upgrades. The following list gives you some indication of the changes.

◆ The video capture is faster because an intermediate step in the capture-to-disk operation was eliminated.

◆ The display control interface (DCI) that enables applications to write directly to the display video buffer is now supported by Windows NT Workstation. The display driver must support DCI for this to work. If it does, video playback is often smoother.

◆ The Audio Compression Manager (ACM) no longer loads audio codecs into processes that do not use audio. This feature reduces the amount of memory required by the ACM.

◆ The throughput of the musical instrument digital interface (MIDI) has been improved by moving some of the MIDI code into the kernel.

◆ The Sound Recorder can now support audio codecs that do not record and compress audio in real-time.

◆ The Media Player now supports the following list of new parameters:

  ◆ **/open** allows you to open a specific file.

  ◆ **/play** allows you to play a specified file.

  ◆ **/close** closes a specified media file after it has been played (using the /play parameter).

  ◆ **/embedding** executes as an OLE server.

  ◆ **/wave** allows you to open a wave (.WAV) file.

  ◆ **/midi** allows you to open a midi file.

  ◆ **/vfw** allows you to open a VFW file.

The following sections explain these enhancements in more detail.

CD Player Enhancements

In the latest version of Windows NT, you can use the Preferences dialog box in the CD Player to continue playing a CD even though you terminate the CD Player application.

The same dialog box also allows you to include a 5 to 15 second introduction to a track on the CD.

In addition to running CD Player using its icon, you can execute CD Player from the command line. To play a CD, you use the command

```
> cdplayer /play
```

If you want to play just a specific list of tracks on the CD use the following command. When you use the /track switch, CD Player displays a dialog box so that you can choose the track to play.

```
> cdplayer /track
```

If you want to specify a single track to play on the command line, you use the following syntax:

```
> cdplayer /play d:\track04.cda
```

This command plays track four found on the CD in the D drive. Track files have the extension .cda.

If you want to play a listof tracks, use the following syntax:

```
> cdplayer /play /track d:\track04.cda d:\track02.cda d:\track09.cda
d:\track01.cda
```

This command plays tracks 4, 2, 9, and 1 (in that order) on the CD in drive D.

Windows NT Workstation Product Overview

The chapter up to this point has described the changes in the latest version of Windows NT Workstation. For users who are new to Windows NT, the following product description provides an overview of the technical features of Windows NT.

Supporting Applications

The following features describe the application support that Windows NT provides:

- ◆ Application support for the following types of applications:
  - ◆ 32-bit Windows, including all Win32(r), Windows 95, and Win32s(r)-based applications
  - ◆ 16-bit MS-DOS
  - ◆ 16-bit Windows
  - ◆ 16-bit OS/2 (r)
  - ◆ POSIX 1003.1-based applications
- ◆ Isolated memory spaces for 16-bit applications
- ◆ Preemptive multitasking for 16- and 32- bit applications
- ◆ OLE implementation between all 16- and 32-bit Windows applications
- ◆ 16-bit fax application support

◆ Asynchronous I/O queue for message handling to improve performance

◆ Structured exception handling makes troubleshooting easier.

As you can see, NT provides sophisticated application support.

Supporting Networks

The following features describe the network support that Windows NT provides:

◆ Client Telnet and FTP applications.

◆ Peer-to-peer and FTP server functionality.

◆ Support for the 15 network protocols, including NetWare, TCP/IP (which includes DHCP, WINS, PPP, and SLIP), DLC, DCE RPC, IPX/SPX, and NetBEUI.

◆ Numerous network utilities, including finger, ftp, arp, hostname, ipconfig, lpq, lpr, nbstat, ping, netstat, rcp, rexec, route, rsh, tftp, and tracert.

NT supports all of the major networking features that you need.

Supporting Remote Access

The following features describe the remote access service support that Windows NT provides:

◆ Dial-in from a remote computer to any workstation.

◆ Dial-out to remote machines including Internet servers.

◆ Dial-in using the Remote Access Service (RAS) to remote NetWare servers.

◆ TCP/IP, IPX/SPX, and NetBEUI provide full network operations.

These features allow sophisticated remote user dialup and dialback.

Supporting Communications

The following features describe the communications support that Windows NT provides:

◆ Includes the e-mail application, Microsoft Mail.

◆ Includes the scheduling application, Scheduler+, that can look across a network at other people's schedules, for example, to arrange meeting times.

◆ Includes Microsoft Mail postoffice, so that a workstation can function as a mail server.

◆ NetDDE, WINCHAT, and NET MESSAGE can be used to communicate across a network.

NT supports all of the standard network communications tools that you might like to use.

Supporting Security

The following features describe the communications support that Windows NT provides:

◆ User ID and password provides user account and local workstation security.

◆ Lockout based on numerous failed login attempts provides account and local workstation security.

◆ C2 security level.

◆ Security provided on a per file and per directory basis using the NTFS file system.

◆ Network security is provided using credentials in a question/response protocol.

NT's security system is elaborate and powerful. It provides adequate protection of your system and files.

Supporting Multimedia

The following features describe the multimedia support that Windows NT provides:

◆ Provides OpenGL APIs for three dimensional graphics.

◆ Provides Video for Windows 1.1 16- and 32-bit APIs.

◆ Includes the Multimedia Extensions included in Windows 3.1.

As multimedia continues to skyrocket, these APIs make sure that even the hardiest of multimedia applications will be supported in NT.

Supporting Utilities

The following features describe the utilities support that Windows NT provides:

- ◆ NTFS file system provides file compression.

- ◆ User Manager provides user administration and security.

- ◆ Disk Administrator configures graphical disks.

- ◆ Diagnostics performs tests on basic system operations.

- ◆ Performance Monitor measures the performance of any local or networked computers.

- ◆ Tape backup utility allows easy backup for information on drives.

- ◆ Unlimited Power Supply (UPS) allows the computer to shutdown gracefully in the event of a power outage.

- ◆ Event Viewer displays log files that record various kinds of events.

- ◆ The Registry Editor manages configuration settings.

- ◆ FAT, HPFS, and NTFS file systems support long (greater than eight characters) file names.

These utilities make NT easier to run, provide greater security, and give you sophisticated configuration flexibility.

Supporting Remote Management

The following features describe the remote management support that Windows NT provides:

- ◆ Utilities, including Performance Monitor, Service Controller, Event Viewer, and the Registry Editor, work across a network.

- ◆ Dial-out to remote machines is supported.

- ◆ Dial-in to any workstation is supported.

These utilities provide administrators with the tools they need to work across a network.

Supporting Setup and Installation

The following features describe the setup and installation support that Windows NT provides:

- ◆ Recognizes and configures most hardware automatically.

- ◆ Supports using scripts for automated installations.

- ◆ Allows OS/2 users to upgrade to Windows NT because it supports HPFS file systems.

- ◆ User can review all network protocols, bindings, and services.

Setup automation takes much of the tediousness out of NT's installation.

Summary

In this chapter you looked at all of the new features available in the latest version of Windows NT Workstation, and at all of the revisions made to existing features. Some of the most notable changes are the new interface, Windows NT Explorer, and Windows NT support for the PowerPC platform and for PCMCIA cards used in laptop computers.

At the end of the chapter you looked at a complete description of the technical features of the latest version of Windows NT Workstation.

Exploring the Road to Windows NT

Windows NT's conceptual roots stretch back to the beginnings of Unix in 1969. Windows NT developers have tried to incorporate into Windows NT all the major innovations in user interfaces and operating systems that have transpired since then. This chapter provides you with an understanding of the ways in which Windows NT has been shaped, including the following:

♦ Understanding OS/2's lack of success

♦ Developing Windows NT

♦ Reviewing the evolution of Windows NT

By the end of the chapter, you will see where many of the ideas come from that are engineered into NT.

Understanding OS/2's Lack of Success

In the mid-1980s, Microsoft and IBM developed an operating system so superior to DOS that it was to become the dominant operating system of the 1980s and 1990s. They called it Operating System 2, or OS/2.

Incorporated into OS/2 were many of the features that make Unix so powerful, including multitasking, multiprocessing, multithreading, and 32-bit addressing. An operating system with such prowess easily should have overshadowed the offerings of DOS and Windows. At least, that's what Microsoft and IBM thought.

History had a different ending to the story, however. OS/2 sales were meager, at best. The third version of Windows took off like fireworks and banished OS/2 to obscurity. Why?

The developers of OS/2 made a fundamental miscalculation when they created their product. The microprocessor at the leading edge of technology for the 1980s desktop was the 80286—not a speed demon by today's standards. The desktop operating system had to be large, much larger than DOS or Windows to realize the power of Unix. So, in their effort to make a large operating system run as fast as possible on a slow platform, Microsoft and IBM developers chose to write OS/2 in assembly language.

Assembly language, unlike C, Pascal, and other higher-level languages, manipulates data in the CPU and memory.

The problem with assembly language, however, is that it is not portable; that is, it must be written for specific processors—the 80286, in this case. As technological innovations advanced and microprocessors came and went, the 80286 was left behind (and with it, OS/2). Software developers never took to OS/2.

With a new version of software necessary for each new microprocessor, OS/2 applications required a lot of work to maintain. For that reason, OS/2 never enjoyed the number of applications that were written for DOS or Windows.

 Note Assembly language is only one step up from machine code: zeros and ones. At that level, the way the chip works is central to the assembly language code. If different chips work in different ways, the assembly language program must account for the differences. In this way, one assembly language's program cannot run on different processors.

Although Microsoft enjoyed moderate success with Windows 2.0, they knew that with more powerful processors, more powerful applications, and higher user expectations

on the horizon, Windows needed to be replaced. People were turning to Unix to fulfill their needs for a complex networking, multitasking, multiprocessing, and secure operating system.

Microsoft developers knew they had to create an operating system for the future that offered the power of Unix. The sales figures told them that OS/2 would not be that system. So in 1988, Microsoft hired David Cutler to create a new operating system— the operating system for the nineties.

Developing Windows NT with David Cutler

David Cutler was project director at DEC in the 1980s for a variety of products, including the very successful VMS operating system. In 1985, DEC assigned him the task of developing a super operating system, called Prism, that was to supersede VMS and Ultrix, DEC's flavor of Unix. After three years of work, however, DEC decided to cancel Prism because it was incompatible with the company's proprietary products, that is, products that only run on DEC machines.

DEC's cancellation of Prism hit Cutler like a bomb. He immediately gave his 180-person staff a one-month furlough. During that month he weighed his options. Although entrepreneurs offered him money to begin his own company, he refused their offers because he didn't aspire to running a company. He wanted, instead, to create a great operating system.

OS/2 was released in 1987, and by 1988 it was clear to Microsoft that OS/2 was floundering. Bill Gates, cofounder of Microsoft, learned of Cutler's situation at DEC and began to court him for Microsoft.

Microsoft released Windows 2.0 in 1988. It was better than the first version. For example, it enabled windows to overlap rather than tile but it in no way approximated the sophistication of the Apple's Macintosh graphical user interface (GUI).

Microsoft aggressively enlisted the services of developers to create applications for Windows. It also leaked word about what would be included in version 3.0. The rumors about version 3.0 excited developers; it sounded as if Windows would finally catch up to the Macintosh interface.

Attracted by the marketing might of Microsoft and the promise of Windows 3.0, Cutler left DEC for Microsoft. Although Cutler began work on Windows NT in 1988,

Windows NT reflects his three years of work on Prism. Also, many of DEC's contract software engineers and programmers followed Cutler to Microsoft. So not only did Microsoft get three years of research paid for by DEC, but they also got an entire core of programmers who, during those three years, had grown expert at designing operating systems.

Determining Primary Marketing Requirements

From the fall of 1988 until early in 1989, David Cutler and his core group of engineers defined the primary marketing requirements for Windows NT. These requirements were as follows:

◆ **Portability.** Everyone had learned from OS/2's downfall about the danger of making an operating system that wasn't portable across a variety of processors. Windows NT had to move easily between many processor architectures.

◆ **Multiprocessing.** Computers that use more than one processor were becoming more common in the marketplace. Because few operating systems at the time took advantage of multiple processors, developers decided that Windows NT had to offer multiprocessing.

Windows NT wasn't just for high-end computers, however. Not only did Windows NT have to take advantage of multiprocessing, the same applications that work on multiprocessing machines had to work on single-processor computers.

◆ **Networking.** The number of desktop computers skyrocketed in the eighties. Gone forever was the dominance of the single mainframe computer that served an entire company. Because sharing files among isolated desktop computers was a problem, companies began using networks to tie together computers so that users could share information and system resources.

With networking, users also could take advantage of distributed computing. Instead of making networking a third-party, add-on facility, Windows NT developers decided to make it part of the operating system.

◆ **POSIX compatibility.** POSIX is an acronym for Portable Operating System Interface based on Unix. The Institute of Electrical and Electronics Engineers (IEEE) created the POSIX standard, number 1003.1, in 1988 to encourage vendors to standardize the Unix-type interface so that applications could be portable across operating systems.

POSIX is one of the U.S. government's procurement requirements. Because the government represents the single largest potential buyer for Windows NT, developers decided to provide a POSIX environment.

◆ **Security.** If Microsoft considered the government an important potential buyer of Windows NT, a government-approved security system had to be part of Windows NT. The first release of Windows NT qualified for a class C2 security rating.

The government has seven classes of security; class A is the highest. The C2 rating allows for ownership of objects, restricted read/write/execution of those objects, and restricted system access. Plans for later versions of Windows NT include satisfying class B2 security requirements.

Class B2 security requires Windows NT to recognize user and process security levels (such as Secret and Top Secret), and to support compartments (groups of users that are entirely isolated from other users).

Originally, the new technology (Windows NT) operating system was to look and work like OS/2. That was understandable, considering the investment Microsoft had already made in OS/2. By the late 1980s, however, it was not hard to figure out that Windows NT should look more like Windows than OS/2.

Instead of making one Windows operating system obsolete in favor of another, Microsoft decided to develop a family of Windows operating systems, each with its unique user profile. Windows 3.*x* is for individual users, Windows for Workgroups is for small businesses, and Windows NT is for users who need a multitasking environment, and large organizations that need the benefit of NT's security features (see fig. 2.1).

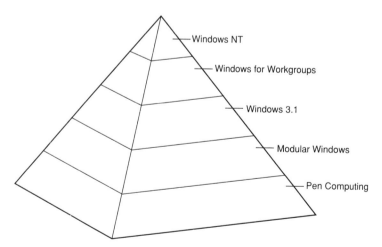

Windows NT

Windows for Workgroups

Windows 3.1

Modular Windows

Pen Computing

Figure 2.1

The Windows family.

Other new members of the Windows family include Windows for Pen Computing, which is used for pen-input devices; and Modular Windows, which is designed for consumer hardware interfaces. All members of the Windows family have the same look; all provide different features.

Understanding Software Design Goals

With a product as complex as Windows NT, planning was an absolute necessity before the programmers could begin to write the code. Developers resolved many design conflicts and answered many questions by defining software design goals. The goals were as follows:

◆ **Flexibility.** Windows NT had to be easily modifiable to accommodate changing hardware and software requirements. Consequently, NT runs on 16- and 32-bit operating systems.

◆ **Portability.** Windows NT had to satisfy the marketing goal of being applicable to a wide variety of system architectures. Consequently, NT runs on a variety of platforms, including MIPS, Alpha, and *x*86.

◆ **Stability.** In a networking environment, it is crucial that applications not crash the operating system. Windows NT had to isolate the kernel from user applications and, at the same time, monitor any attempts, inadvertent or otherwise, to compromise the security and normal functioning of the system.

◆ **Compatibility.** Microsoft's trump card in catapulting Windows NT past Unix and OS/2 in sales was the number of Windows applications already sold. By enabling Windows 3.*x* applications to run on Windows NT, Windows NT automatically would be supported by programs already in the marketplace and in the office. Thus, users and businesses did not have to buy all new software, or learn new systems and applications.

ote Although the 16-bit Windows applications do not run as fast as Win32 applications, companies can get most of the power of Windows NT and be up and running with it for only the cost of the operating system.

◆ **Speed.** Given all the other goals, Windows NT had to run as quickly as possible on all platforms.

The rest of this section examines the way developers sought to accomplish these goals.

Flexibility

With the continuous introduction of new hardware devices, such as scanners and CD ROM drives, Windows NT developers wanted to make the job of modifying Windows NT to accommodate these changes as easy as possible. Their solution to the problem was to develop a unique operating system design that put some of the operating system in user mode.

Windows NT consists of two basic parts, the privileged Executive and the nonprivileged protected subsystems. The concept of privilege derives from processors, which have two modes of operation: privileged, called kernel mode, and nonprivileged, called user mode.

 Note In an operating system, the kernel is the core portion that performs the most essential tasks, such as controlling the time an application has with the CPU.

In *user mode*, certain commands and memory addresses are inaccessible; in *kernel mode*, all machine commands and memory addresses are accessible (see fig. 2.2).

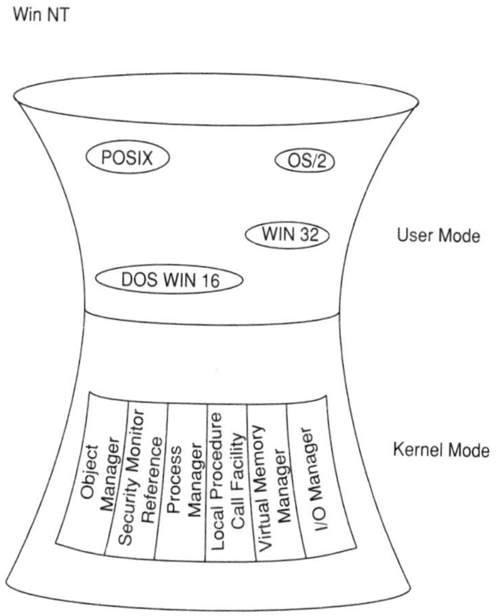

Figure 2.2

User and kernel mode modularity.

Windows NT's Executive, which runs in kernel mode, provides elemental services. It relies on the protected subsystems running in user mode to provide additional capabilities, including operating system APIs.

By dividing the operating system in this way, Microsoft can leave Windows NT's Executive alone and simply add or replace an entire protected subsystem as a unit. This modular approach to revising the software clearly limits the lines of code that need revision, and isolates the changes from the rest of the system so that the rest of the system can remain up and running and free of bugs.

Note   An application programming interface (API) is a library of routines and services, each built from low-level operating system commands, which accomplish common tasks. For example, an interactive TV API might have a function, called display() that displays a frame of video. Rather than dealing with the intricacies of the frame buffer, a developer can simply call the display() function.

In addition to splitting up Windows NT into both kernel and user modes, Windows NT developers included the following additional features to make it flexible:

◆ **Executive modularity.** Developers used a modular approach when designing the Executive (see fig. 2.1). Each of these modules, such as the virtual memory manager and the object manager, interact with one another only through kernel interfaces.

   This design makes it easy to upgrade or add new functionality. Instead of working on the entire kernel a programmer can simply replace a module.

◆ **System resource modularity.** Windows NT treats all system resources as objects. All objects are manipulated by the same set of object services. Adding or subtracting objects, therefore, does not affect the other objects. To add new hardware functionality to Windows NT, you simply add a new object to the system.

◆ **Service modularity.** Remote procedure calls (RPCs) enable applications to use services anywhere in the network. By adding new services to one machine in the network, they become available to all other machines. For example, a media delivery service running on one machine can be accessed and used by a remote workstation to play a movie.

◆ **Driver modularity.** The Windows NT I/O consists, in part, of a number of drivers. To add new file systems, hardware devices, and networks, you simply add to the I/O new file system drivers, device drivers, or transport drivers, respectively.

In an effort to keep things modular, NT engineers tried to make adding on to the system easy. Rather than rebuilding everything in the Kernel, by keeping things modular, engineers can simply add on to what already works.

Portability

Although an operating system can be rewritten for any processor or configuration, a system is considered *portable* only if it is easy to do so. Developers used the following guidelines to make Windows NT portable:

◆ **Use high-level languages.** To make a system portable across many processors, you must write the code in a language that all the processors understand. High-level languages, such as C, are standardized without regard to the processors on which they run.

Microsoft chose to write Windows NT in C. (A small portion, including the graphical user interface and portions of the networking interface, is written in C++.) Only those very few operations that needed maximum speed, such as precision-integer arithmetic, were written in assembly language. Developers isolated the assembly language code in well-defined modules so they could easily change them.

◆ **Minimize hardware-dependent code.** Code that directly manipulates hardware, such as registers, is inevitably dependent on the machinery. By eliminating or minimizing as much of this code as possible, you can make the system more portable.

◆ **Isolate hardware-dependent code.** Some of the code in an operating system must be hardware-dependent. By placing this code in well-defined modules, revising the code for different processors is easy, and bugs do not spread throughout the system.

Not only did Windows NT developers isolate hardware-dependent code, they also isolated platform-dependent code in a dynamic link library called the hardware abstraction layer (HAL). Vendors sometimes build different platforms around the same processor, such as the MIPS R4000. The low-level code in HAL makes the differences between platforms invisible to the higher-level operating system code.

Stability

Windows NT developers considered two facets of stability. First, Windows NT had to anticipate, prevent (if possible), and respond effectively to errors, both in software and hardware. Second, the operating system had to be impervious to user applications that, intentionally or not, might damage or crash the system. Microsoft developers made Windows NT stable in the following ways:

◆ **Error handling.** Windows NT uses a method known as structured-exception handling for detecting and dealing with errors. When the operating system or the hardware detects errors, the kernel switches control to the exception handler, which responds to the error and prevents user programs from either malfunctioning or from damaging the operating system.

◆ **Windows NTFS.** Developers created a new file system, called new technology file system (NTFS), which enables Windows NT to recover from virtually any kind of disk crash. It works by storing information in more than one place.

◆ **Security.** The security system helps eliminate or limit damage caused by users.

◆ **Isolated APIs.** By making each API a separate, protected subsystem, a crash in one cannot affect the others.

◆ **Virtual memory manager.** The Executive's virtual memory manager swaps programs between disk and RAM. It assures that one application's memory addresses don't overlap another's.

These safeguards make NT extremely reliable and secure.

Compatibility

Compatibility refers to an operating system's capability to run applications that were designed for earlier versions of the operating system (or for other operating systems). Compatibility is one of Windows NT's most unique features and greatest strengths.

 Note When you purchase an operating system, you usually must use only those applications written for it. With Windows NT, however, you can run most DOS, Windows, character-based POSIX, and OS/2 applications as well as Windows NT applications.

There are two levels of compatibility: binary and source-level. The difference between the two is determined by whether or not an application must be recompiled before it runs on a different operating system.

If the machine language in the executable file of the application works on the different operating system, the operating system is considered binary compatible because the machine code, which is binary, is the same in different operating systems. If the application must be recompiled before it can work on the new operating system, the system is considered source-level compatible, because it is the source code, not the executable code, that is the same.

Note Because recompiling inevitably introduces bugs in the application, binary compatibility is highly preferable to source-level compatibility.

The processor on which an operating system runs determines whether or not the operating system is binary compatible. Different processors generally use different machine-language command sets. Processors within a family, such as Intel's *x86* processors, often can achieve binary compatibility with applications. Processors from different makers can achieve binary compatibility only if the makers provide an emulation program that translates the machine language code of the executable application from one processor to another. Without that translation software, developers must recompile, relink, and debug the application for the new processor.

On Intel processors, Windows NT provides binary compatibility with existing Microsoft applications, including MS-DOS, 16-bit Windows, OS/2, and LAN Manager. On MIPS RISC processors, Windows NT provides binary compatibility with MS-DOS, 16-bit Windows, and LAN Manager (with emulation). Windows NT provides source-level compatibility for POSIX applications.

Windows NT also is compatible with a number of different file systems, including FAT (MS-DOS), HPFS (OS/2), CDFS (CD-ROM), and Windows NTFS (Windows NT).

Speed

The speed of an application is both hardware- and software-dependent. The faster a microprocessor is, the faster the application executes. The better the operating system is, the more it can take advantage of the faster microprocessor. For example, the 80486 is a 32-bit chip. Sixteen-bit applications, however, generally move information only 16 bits at a time, even on 32-bit processors. The 32-bit applications move twice that amount in the same time. Thus, Win32 applications run roughly twice as fast as 16-bit Windows applications.

The developers of Windows NT maximized its execution speed in the following ways:

◆ **Performance testing.** Developers carefully optimized each part of the system that influenced the execution speed of Windows NT, including system calls and page faults.

◆ **Local procedure call.** The protected subsystems that provide the operating system APIs communicate frequently with one another and with their client applications. To make these communications move as quickly as possible, Microsoft incorporated a local procedure call (a fast message-passing facility) in the operating system.

◆ **System services.** When Microsoft engineers created the protected subsystems that provide the operating system APIs, they determined which system service calls were used most often, and then maximized their execution speed.

◆ **Networking.** Networking is a central feature of Windows NT. To make Windows NT run quickly, components of the networking software were included in Windows NT's Executive.

Speed is the crucial factor in any operating system's evaluation. NT engineers knew that and made fast execution their goal. Sixteen-bit Windows 3.*x* programs never quite ran as fast in NT as they did under Windows 3.*x*, but as 32-bit applications come to dominate the market, applications running under Windows 95 and Windows NT will run at approximately the same speed.

Reviewing the Evolution of Windows NT

It is difficult to say exactly where Windows NT began. Here are some of the milestones in the generation of the ideas that went into Windows NT:

◆ **1969.** Ken Thompson at Bell Labs writes Unix, which is a time-sharing, multitasking operating system that enables his DEC PDP-7 to support several users at once. Unix sets the standard by which people judge all other high-end operating systems for the next 25 years. Microsoft incorporates Unix's multitasking, multiprocessing, networking, platform-independent, and security features into Windows NT.

◆ **1973.** Xerox's Palo Alto Research Center (PARC) designs a radically different kind of operating system for a computer: the Alto (and its successor, the Bravo). Neither are commercially produced.

Instead of using an arcane command-language interface, like those of Unix and DOS, PARC uses high-resolution monitors to show a desktop with pictures of file folders, mail, and in-and-out baskets. They name these graphical elements icons, and use a mouse to manipulate them. They create a laser printer called Dover, which enables them to print WYSIWYG (what-you-see-is-what-you-get) documents.

The graphical user interface of Windows NT derives directly from the applications started at PARC.

◆ During the same time period at PARC, researchers create a way to share system resources, such as laser printers, among users. They use coaxial cable to support

data throughput of 10 megabits per second, which is 10,000 times faster than current phone lines can support (1,200 bits per second). They call the linkage between computers a local area network, and name their version Ethernet.

Note   Today, Microsoft considers networking so integral to the design of Windows NT that developers decide to put part of the network programming into Windows NT's Executive.

◆ **1975.** Bill Gates and Paul Allen, undergraduates at Harvard, enter a contest to write a BASIC programming language for the first personal computer, the Altair. It uses an 8088 chip with 4 KB of RAM. Allen writes an emulator that simulates the 8088 chip on Harvard's PDP-10 mainframe. Gates writes the BASIC language for the Altair. Together they win the contest.

Note   Today, Microsoft uses an emulator, called the virtual DOS machine (VDM), to enable DOS and 16-bit Windows applications to run in Windows NT.

◆ **1979.** Steve Jobs sees the Alto computer and decides that Apple's next computer, the Lisa, will use a graphical user interface. Only a few months later, Bill Gates visits PARC, and makes a commitment to a graphical user interface that he calls Windows.

◆ **1983.** Microsoft and IBM start work on an operating system to replace DOS. They incorporate into the new operating system many ideas borrowed from Unix, such as multitasking, multiprocessing, multithreading, and 32-bit addressing. Bill Gates expects this to be the next super operating system. Microsoft calls it OS/2.

◆ **1985.** David Cutler begins work on a super operating system for DEC called Prism. After three years of work, DEC cancels Prism.

◆ **1987.** Microsoft releases OS/2. It flops. Gates realizes that Microsoft must create a new super operating system, called Windows NT, which will capitalize on the research done for OS/2.

◆ **1988.** Bill Gates succeeds in bringing Cutler and a core group of engineers to Microsoft. Cutler uses his three years of research at DEC to devise Windows NT.

Microsoft releases Windows 2.0. Sales go well, and Microsoft leaks rumors about version 3.0. IBM and Gates announce a renewed effort to support OS/2.

Microsoft changes direction, abandons OS/2, and pours its energy into developing Windows 3.1 and Windows NT. Microsoft managers decide that Windows NT should look like Windows, not OS/2.

◆ **1990.** Microsoft spends $18 million to market Windows 3.0. Sales exceed wildest expectations. Finally, Windows approaches the graphical user interface started by PARC and successfully implemented on the Macintosh.

◆ **1993.** Microsoft introduces Windows NT 3.1.

◆ **1994.** Microsoft revises Windows NT to version 3.5.

◆ **1995.** Microsoft adds three functions and fixes some bugs and calls the version, Windows NT 3.51.

Microsoft spends $20 million to market Windows 95.

Microsoft makes available, but does not support, the Windows 95 interface for use with Windows NT. The new version of Windows NT is called 4.0. The interface itself is called Windows NT Explorer.

NT was originally written to challenge Unix. NT was to have the power of Unix with the ease of use provided by a GUI interface. In the client/server world, Unix continues to dominate. That might change, however, for three reasons:

◆ Windows NT now can run transparently on four platforms. When developers write an NT application, they know it automatically runs on four platforms which means, a larger market, lower development costs, and high profit potential.

◆ The 3.*x* interface was easy to use because it was graphical, but it was small compared to the Unix GUIs, such as Solaris and Motif. Windows NT Explorer bears a strong resemblance to both Solaris and Motif. Finally, Windows NT has an interface that is intuitive and powerful.

◆ Windows 3.*x* and Windows 95 are the de facto standard operating systems for PCs. OS/2 has some market share, but it is small compared to Windows. Because so many people are familiar with Windows, and because Windows NT and Windows 95 have essentially the same interface, there are vast numbers of people who already know how to work in the Windows NT Explorer environment. This is not the case, however, for Unix GUIs, and the Unix command line. Although Unix has its staunch supporters, and should remain a vital part of the industry, Windows NT is bound to gain more market share.

When Windows 95 and NT Workstation finally merge in the years ahead, there will be a vast number of 95/NT users. At that time, NT will be used by more people than Unix.

Summary

Like many great creations, Windows NT stands on the shoulders of its predecessors. Microsoft engineers, benefiting from 25 years of operating-system evolution, bundled the best parts of Unix, Prism, OS/2, Windows, and object-oriented programming into one single package: Windows NT.

The power of Windows NT rivals that of Unix, and its ease of use matches that of Windows. The well-defined, interchangeable parts of the protected subsystems in user mode (and of the Executive kernel mode) make Windows NT easy to upgrade.

Revealing the Windows NT Operating System

Windows NT has the potential of being the best of two worlds: a popular graphical environment for end users, and a full-fledged 32-bit operating system every bit as powerful as Unix. Although the heart of this book is devoted to the end-user aspects of Windows NT, this chapter looks under the hood to examine the core architecture of the Windows NT operating system.

This chapter is technical in nature, but it offers something for everyone. Operating system neophytes should not be scared away. Most of the discussion is intended as an introduction to such concepts as 32-bit processing, preemptive multitasking, and peer-to-peer networking. In reading this, you can get a better grasp of what Windows NT is really all about.

For those well versed in operating systems, you will find the discussion substantive in its examination of Windows NT's underlying architecture. Moreover, if you have experience with OS/2 or Unix, the last part of this chapter will be particularly interesting to you as it compares Windows NT with these two operating systems.

This chapter focuses on the following subjects:

◆ Windows NT's 32-bit architecture

◆ Multitasking

◆ Multithreading

◆ Multiprocessing

◆ Windows NT subsystems

◆ Windows NT networking

◆ System security

◆ The way Windows NT works with your existing applications

◆ Windows NT versus other 32-bit operating systems

Understanding Windows NT's 32-Bit Architecture

If you read about Windows NT in any computer magazine, the term 32-bit operating system usually surfaces somewhere. What exactly is a 32-bit operating system? To answer that question, this section looks at Windows NT's 32-bit addressing and 32-bit processing capabilities.

32-Bit Addressing

Before looking at Windows NT's 32-bit addressing, take a look back at the world of DOS, Windows 3.1, and Windows 95. DOS was developed in the early 1980s for 8088 and 8086 chips. These 16-bit chips had a limited number of memory addresses that they could access.

 Note   Like your home address, a memory address defines a specific location. In computer memory, this address defines the location of a byte of information.

When computers were sold with 128 KB, 256 KB, and 512 KB of random-access memory (RAM), an address space of 1 MB seemed like an ocean of memory. To accommodate the memory requirements of hardware such as video boards and

network cards, developers agreed to segment the 1M of memory in the following way: the first 640 KB were reserved for the operating system and its applications, and the remaining 360 KB were divided into 64 KB sections, called *pages*, each having a different purpose. A system with this address structure is known as a segment-addressing system.

An address space of 640 KB seemed more than ample for applications. That was true until personal computers found their way into business applications, such as spreadsheets and database management systems. Because only a limited amount of data can fit into 640 KB of memory, spreadsheets and databases were limited in size. This created a problem for all but the smallest of companies. In a short time, 640 KB changed from an ocean of memory to a barrier with which programmers and users alike have had to deal.

The 80386 chip was the first to implement a linear (nonsegmented) 32-bit address space. In theory, applications did not have to be crammed into the first 640 KB of RAM. The reality, however, was that the 32-bit address space was incompatible with applications written for the older processors. Therefore, to remain compatible with these applications, the 386 chip ran in real mode, which enabled the 386 to function like a fast 8086.

Developers also enabled the 386 chip to run in another mode, called protected mode, in which memory was accessed in a linear address space. Protected mode also prevented one application's data from occupying the address space of another application's data. Although this was an advance, the DOS 640 KB barrier still proved a big impediment to the development of more sophisticated applications.

 Note   Although other modes have also been created, DOS and Windows 3.1 programmers still labor to circumvent the 640 KB barrier.

Windows 95 is an environment, not an operating system. It rides on top of DOS. Many functions that Windows performs take place through DOS. The original aim of Windows 95 engineers was to get rid of DOS altogether. That goal was not met; however, many strides were taken in that direction. Many of the limitations of DOS are overcome in Windows 95, such as memory limitations and the size of filenames. Although Windows 95 still rides on DOS, the new DOS is not as restricting as that which supported Windows 3.1.

Windows NT, like other 32-bit operating systems (such as OS/2 and Unix), leaves these artificially imposed barriers far behind. Because it is a true linear-addressing system, it takes better advantage of 386, 486, and Pentium processing power.

Windows NT benefits in many ways from abandoning the segmented addressing system. First, the amount of available space for Windows NT applications is huge—

two gigabytes (GB)—and another 2 GB are reserved for the Windows NT operating system. Not many applications require even a significant fraction of that memory space. Second, Windows NT programmers do not have to battle with the 640 KB barrier. Making life easier for programmers means quicker software-development time.

Although Windows NT supports a linear address space of 4 GB, chances are your computer does not have 4 GB of RAM. So what is the advantage of having an address space greater than the amount of RAM in your computer?

Your computer can work only with data in RAM. When you initiate an action that requires more RAM than your computer has (such as starting a second application), Windows NT's virtual memory manager moves data out of real (RAM) memory into virtual memory (memory on the hard drive). Moving data between the hard drive and RAM is called swapping. The less RAM your computer has, the more swapping to disk your computer must perform, and the slower the performance of the application. That is because executing data already in RAM is dramatically faster than accessing data from a disk. (Virtual memory is discussed later in this chapter.)

Windows NT supports a 4 GB virtual address space. During setup, Windows NT suggests that you create a permanent area on your hard disk for a swap file that is at least the size of your RAM. So, if you have 8 MB of RAM, Windows NT wants at least an 8 MB swap file. (In practice, Windows NT prefers more space than that.)

The swap file in Windows 95 is limited to about 30 MB. Although most casual users find this adequate, it poses a significant barrier for larger applications and servers. Windows NT has no such barrier on the size of the swap file, enabling it to run applications that are too big for Windows 95.

The third benefit of using a linear address space is that programs run more quickly; the convolutions in memory management that programmers employ to overcome the 640 KB barrier are gone.

Finally, eliminating the 640 KB barrier means that memory managers are not needed. Memory managers, such as QEMM 386 and 386 MBAX, take device drivers, memory-resident applications, and operating systems out of conventional memory (the first 640 KB of RAM) and stuff them in upper memory (between 640 KB and 1024 KB). Memory managers are powerful and clever, but they often cause hardware conflicts, and they do not carry over from one version of DOS to another. To use a memory manager, you have to buy a new version of it with each new version of DOS. Windows NT eliminates the bother of memory management.

32-Bit Processing

The 80386 chip is a 32-bit processor, which means that the processor can move 32 bits (four bytes) of data at a time. Because DOS was designed for 16-bit operating systems,

Windows 3.1 is limited to this processing speed. Applications written for DOS and Windows 3.1 are thus called 16-bit applications.

In contrast, Windows NT is a 32-bit operating system. For that reason, it can use 32-bit processors to greater advantage. Application execution is a product of processor speed and the operating system; thus, if both can process data at 32-bits, the amount of time to perform a task is greatly diminished. In fact, 32-bit applications can run roughly twice as fast as their 16-bit counterparts.

With Windows NT, Microsoft wanted to escape the limitations of DOS—namely, segmented memory. Yet Microsoft wanted to remain backward compatible to DOS and Windows 3.*x* applications. To do this, Windows NT provides a DOS emulator, which is an environment that makes applications believe they are in a DOS operating system. This emulator is called the Virtual DOS Machine (VDM). 16-bit applications running on Windows NT, however, do not magically turn into 32-bit applications—they run at the slower 16-bit rate. They still run properly, but to take advantage of Windows NT, you need to purchase a 32-bit version of your application as it becomes available.

Understanding Multitasking

A second demonstration of Windows NT's power is its support for multitasking. A typical computer multitasks by switching between two (or more) active programs, running each for a short period of time before turning to another. If this switching is rapid and efficient enough, the programs appear to the human operator to be running simultaneously. Although multitasking is a nearly universal feature of larger computers such as Unix-based workstations, minicomputers, and mainframes, it only recently has become common on PC platforms.

For the end user, multitasking can mean the capability to print a document while still running a word processor, or to read one's electronic mail (e-mail) while a spreadsheet program does a recalculation. For a networked server machine, multitasking can mean the capability to support multiple user connections and services.

To fully understand multitasking, you should understand the concepts of tasks, memory management, privilege, and timeslicing. These features are discussed in the following sections.

Tasks

When a program is put into memory and run, it is known as a task, or process. The familiar DOS facility for accomplishing this is to type the name of the executable file, without the .EXE extension, at the command prompt. A sequence of instructions is read from disk (where it is stored as the EXE file), loaded into memory, and started at a predefined point.

The task consists of the sequence of machine instructions executed by the processor; the memory and any associated data occupied by those instructions; and other system resources such as stack space, opened files, or display windows. An operating system is said to support multitasking, then, when it can run more than one task at a time.

One of the basic jobs of a multitasking operating system is to ensure that tasks do not interfere with each other. Tasks must not overwrite each other's memory or data, or conflict with each other's use of the file system or peripherals. If a user is going to run his e-mail while a spreadsheet is active, it is unacceptable for the e-mail program to cause the spreadsheet to miscalculate or stop running. In addition, there is always the chance that some task will terminate abnormally, or crash. Even this should not affect the operating system or any of the other running tasks.

The operating system itself, when active, also is a task or collection of tasks. If a program were able to access and corrupt the operating system's resources, the computer's entire operation would be affected, and the machine might cease to operate at all until being reinitialized. Users of DOS and early generations of Windows are all too familiar with this situation of a "hung" computer requiring a reboot.

Memory Management

In a multitasking environment, it is critical that memory be closely managed by the operating system. The goal of memory management is to enable each task to run in its own section of memory, to which no other tasks have access. The capability to strongly enforce this separation determines to a large extent the fault tolerance of the operating system toward applications that misbehave and tie up the CPU.

Protected Mode

As stated earlier in the chapter, most modern microprocessors have a protected mode of operation, in which hardware features built into the processor itself enforce this separation. Attempts by a task to write to memory that it does not own—perhaps because of programming errors or invalid data—cause an exception or trap, and the offending task then can be terminated by the operating system without affecting other active tasks or the operating system itself.

Virtual Memory

A second aspect of memory management is virtual memory. The physical memory available to the system is utilized more efficiently by enabling idle sections of memory to be written, or paged, out to disk (so termed because a standard-sized piece of memory known as a *page* is the unit by which this process occurs, at a size characteristic to the processor type).

Programs running on older PC operating systems, such as MS-DOS, could use only the memory physically present in the PC. Often the hardware used two separate 16-bit numbers or addresses to refer to a particular location in memory, and the program had to be written in a special way to reflect this two-part, or segmented, physical address. Windows NT, on the other hand, enables all programs to use a single 32-bit address to refer to a memory location, whether or not the hardware actually has a physical memory address corresponding to the one the program uses.

Program-memory addresses are mapped into hardware-memory addresses automatically by the system. This is called virtual memory. A single physical memory address can be used for more than one virtual memory address. Data at virtual memory addresses currently not being used by a program can be saved temporarily on the disk, and another program or task can use the same physical memory for data at a different virtual address.

Privilege

Another memory-management tool is the capability to run tasks at higher or lower privilege levels. Tasks at higher privilege levels are capable of accessing the data and resources of tasks that run at lower privilege levels, but not vice versa.

This feature typically is used, along with memory protection, to run the operating system itself at a higher kernel privilege level, and all other tasks at a lower user privilege level. Thus, although the operating system can manipulate the execution of running user tasks, a user task cannot affect the operating system or other user tasks.

Kernel tasks have higher priority than user-mode tasks. User-mode tasks, for example, cannot infringe on kernel-mode memory. Kernel operations, on the other hand, can interrupt user tasks. User-mode tasks include all the applications that run on the computer, such as word processors and spreadsheet programs. These operations also include subsystems that enable those applications to run in Windows NT.

Kernel tasks include more elemental services. They communicate either directly or through the hardware abstraction layer (HAL) with the hardware of the computer. Some of those operations include the virtual memory manager, which controls how and when data in RAM is swapped to disk; and the input/output manager, which controls the operation of device drivers, network drivers, cache managers, and file systems. The kernel operations also are referred to as the Windows NT Executive. Except for a user interface, it is a complete operating system. In some cases, user tasks may want to legitimately access data owned by other user tasks. Various methods can enable such access of data, but it is always necessary that both tasks cooperate. A common example is shared memory, in which two or more programs attach to a section of memory and then can read from and write to it. The burden is on the cooperating programs to manage access to this memory because the operating system is no longer involved in its management.

Unix, OS/2, and Windows NT all use some variation of privilege. As with memory protection, support for privilege levels typically is built into the hardware of modern microprocessors.

Timeslice

A multitasking operating system needs some method for allocating processor time between the various tasks it is running. This can be done in a number of ways, most of which share the idea that tasks wait in a list, or queue, to get execution time. This time is allocated by a part of the operating system known as the scheduler.

The period of time during which a program runs is referred to as its timeslice. The process of switching from one program to another, saving information about the current state of the first, and loading saved state information about the second, is known as context switching.

In some operating systems, such as Windows 3.1 (real mode) and Novell NetWare 386, the tasks themselves must decide when to release the processor so that another task can be scheduled. This is known as cooperative, or nonpreemptive, multitasking.

Most such systems are programmed to cause a task to yield control of the processor on operations such as disk or console I/O, but an ill-behaved task can monopolize the processor and cause other tasks to wait interminably for processor time. Because such systems do not require the operating system to be capable of accessing user tasks directly, they can be implemented on processors that do not support privilege or memory protection. Cooperative multitasking implementations are inherently less stable, however; failure of a user program can more easily cause scheduling or memory-management problems.

In preemptive multitasking, the operating system is able to interrupt, or preempt, the execution of a user task without the cooperation of that task. This allows for a more stable system, but it is more difficult to implement, and it requires the processor to support privilege levels and protected memory.

Unix, OS/2, and Windows NT are examples of preemptive multitasking operating systems, as are nearly all operating systems used on larger computers. Under such a system, it is much more difficult for a user program to corrupt the operating system.

Although it is frequently said that "under normal circumstances this cannot happen," system corruption still occasionally does occur, usually when a user-installed device driver crashes, fatally affecting the system.

A device driver is a special process that runs in kernel mode and controls the operation of a physical device such as a disk, CD-ROM driver, network card, or parallel (printer) port. Because device drivers run at the same kernel-privilege level as the operating system and are closely linked with it, a malfunctioning device driver can corrupt the operating system and cause the computer to hang.

Device drivers are commonly packaged with hardware peripherals by the manufacturer and must be considered a likely suspect in system failures under OS/2 and Windows NT. For a comparison between OS/2 and Windows NT, see the section later in this chapter, "Comparing Windows NT with Other 32-Bit Operating Systems."

Most multitasking operating systems also support the concept of priority. Tasks can be assigned high or low priority, with higher-priority tasks scheduled ahead of lower-priority tasks. Task priority may be user controlled, dynamically controlled by the operating system, or both. An e-mail task, for example, might run at a lower priority than a spreadsheet task, checking for new mail only when the spreadsheet is idle and waiting for user input.

Windows NT supports three priority classes—High, Normal, and Idle—as well as five priority levels per class. These classes and levels are set by the program at process startup, but they may be adjusted dynamically by Windows NT during operation.

Understanding Multithreading

A third example of the power of Windows NT is its support of multithreading. If an operating system is able to execute more than one sequence of instructions within the same task, it is said to support multithreading.

Each thread is scheduled for execution (like the tasks in the preceding discussion), but threads within the same task are not separated from each other for purposes of resource ownership. They can access each other's data, and a file opened by one thread can be written to by another.

Threads are the unit of scheduler dispatch; processes are the unit of resource ownership, each of which consists in part of one or more threads. The threads must cooperate in their use of resources because the operating system enforces no separation or protection.

The programmer determines the number of threads in a process. Many processes contain only a single thread. A programmer may use multiple threads if a process initiates more than one action.

When a user schedules a meeting for a group of people in a scheduling program, for example, a number of things can happen (the personal schedule for each person is updated, an agenda is printed, and the person in charge of reserving rooms is notified). Each of these actions can be a thread in a process, or a programmer can make the entire process one thread. In this case, each action executes sequentially. (A multithreaded process, however, executes more quickly.)

Windows NT, OS/2, and NetWare 386 are examples of multithreading PC operating systems. Unix, in contrast, does not support multithreading, although this useful feature is now finding its way into some variants of Unix.

Multithreading enables the programmer to produce programs with interacting parts more easily. Threads can be started or stopped quickly because a new task and its attendant operating-system structures and protections do not have to be created or destroyed. For example, a common scheme for server-based processes is to create a new thread to service each new client connection; this is less practical if an entirely new process has to be created and shared memory areas set up.

Most multithreaded applications also can be written (albeit with somewhat more effort) under multitasking systems that do not support multithreading. For a server-based process, a pool of tasks might be created during initialization to service client requests. The capability to multithread is more a matter of increased efficiency and ease of programming than of extended functionality.

Microsoft is encouraging programmers to take advantage of multithreaded processing. In fact, Windows NT itself is multithreaded.

Understanding Multiprocessing

The two preceding sections discussed multitasking and multithreading on single-processor computers (that is, those with one central processing unit (CPU), such as a 486 or Pentium). If a computer has more than one processor, however, it truly can run more than one task at the same time without switching between them. By implementing multitasking (and perhaps multithreading) on such a computer, more timeslice is available for each task in the system. A system that is able to exploit more than one processor is said to support multiprocessing.

The creation of a newer, more powerful microprocessor is a huge undertaking, beyond the resources and expertise of all but a very few computer manufacturers. On the other hand, creating a computer with multiple processors, although certainly not a trivial task, is much simpler. Multiprocessing thus offers a means of producing higher-powered computers using existing processor technology—if an operating system is available to take advantage of its power.

Multiprocessing operating systems fall into two categories: asymmetric and symmetric. These systems are described in the following sections.

Asymmetric Multiprocessing

An asymmetric multiprocessing operating system has dedicated uses for some or all of its processors. For example, one processor might be dedicated to running the operating system itself, another to running a network operating system, and a third to running user programs.

Asymmetric multiprocessing is somewhat easier for the operating-system designer to implement because the operating system itself can be based on one processor, which controls the operations of the other processors in the system. The operating system need not even be designed explicitly for multiprocessing.

 Note An example of an asymmetric multiprocessing operating system is an adaptation of OS/2 that ran on a dual-processor Compaq SystemPro in the late 1980s.

There are certain drawbacks to this design, including the fact that the processing load is not evenly distributed among the processors. A bottleneck can occur when one processor is overloaded, causing all other processors to wait for tasks on that one processor to complete.

Symmetric Multiprocessing

A symmetric multiprocessing system can run any task or thread on any available processor. This sort of system is more difficult for the operating-system designer to produce because synchronization of operating-system tasks on different processors must be handled. The reward is the fuller utilization of the processor power available on the computer.

Symmetric multiprocessing makes you less vulnerable to problems associated with CPU failure. In asymmetric multiprocessing, if the CPU dedicated to the operating system fails, the system crashes. In symmetric multiprocessing, the operating system can use other CPUs. Symmetric multiprocessing also is more portable across platforms because the operating system is not dedicated to a specific CPU type.

Windows NT supports full symmetric multiprocessing. Although some adaptations of operating systems to multiprocessing systems have been produced, such as the OS/2 variant mentioned earlier, no other mainstream PC operating system has been designed from the beginning to support symmetric multiprocessing. This feature enables Windows NT to run on increasingly powerful computers without waiting for new generations of microprocessors to become available.

Understanding Windows NT Subsystems

You were introduced to kernel and user tasks earlier in the chapter. As you look further into the Windows NT architecture, you can see that there are protected subsystems within user-mode operations.

One subsystem controls system security, and most of the others relate to the diverse operating systems that Windows NT accommodates, such as OS/2, POSIX, and DOS; 16-bit Windows applications (the VDM); and 32-bit (Win32) Windows applications. All these subsystems, except for the security subsystem, work with the Win32 sub-system to translate their system requests into a language that Windows NT (the kernel) can understand.

Each subsystem acts like a server for client applications. In other words, OS/2 applications (clients) work with the OS/2 protected subsystem (server). The OS/2 subsystem, in turn, works with the Windows NT Executive to provide the services requested by the applications.

Microsoft chose this system architecture for several reasons. First, because each protected subsystem acts like a separate server, errors in one do not affect the others. Second, it is easy to add other subsystems to such an architecture. Third, each server can run on a separate processor, either locally or remotely. Finally, this architecture eliminates the duplication of kernel-mode operations.

Each subsystem makes similar requests of the Windows NT Executive. You can either create a system in which each subsystem has its own Executive functions, or share a single Executive among all the subsystems. Writing an operating system that provides a kernel for each subsystem is difficult and prone to errors. Microsoft chose instead to use the model of a network to share the Executive among subsystems.

The kernel mode is divided into discreet units, including the virtual memory man-ager, object manager, security-reference monitor, process manager, local procedure call facility, I/O manager, kernel, and hardware abstraction layer (see fig. 3.1).

The following list describes the function of each object in the Executive:

◆ **Virtual memory manager.** The virtual memory manager governs the movement of data in and out of virtual memory. When the user initiates an action that requires the computer to load data from disk into RAM, there sometimes is not enough RAM. The virtual memory manager selects the data to transfer from RAM to the TEMP file (called the paging or swap file) on the hard disk. The data that is stored in the TEMP file is known as virtual memory.

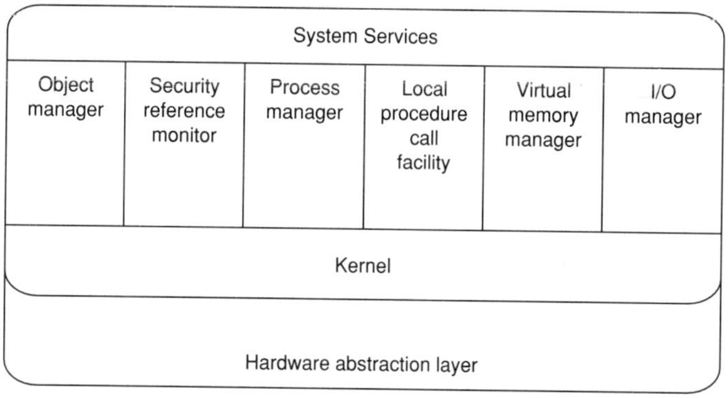

Figure 3.1

The kernel mode is comprised of many discrete units.

When the virtual memory manager loads the data, it makes sure that every running application has an exclusive subset of memory addresses so that the data from one application does not spill into the data of another.

◆ **Object manager.** Windows NT uses objects—abstract data types to represent system resources. The object manager creates, terminates, and manages these objects in the Executive.

◆ **Security reference monitor.** The security reference monitor implements Windows NT's security functions on the local computer.

◆ **Local procedure call facility.** Modeled on the remote procedure call (RPC) facility that acts between computers, the local procedure call (LPC) facility optimizes communications between protected subsystem APIs and their client applications.

Microsoft developers chose to create LPC because they feared that an application acting through a protected subsystem such as OS/2, which in turn acts through the Win32 protected subsystem to access the kernel, would be too slow.

◆ **Kernel.** The *kernel* gives all the other Executive managers elemental objects to implement higher-level requests. It schedules threads, coordinates the execution of multiple processes aimed at accomplishing a specific task, and responds to exceptions and interrupts.

◆ **I/O system.** The I/O system manages input/output devices, such as disk drives. A number of subprocessors comprise the I/O manager, including the following:

   ◆ **Network drivers.** Network drivers receive and transmit I/O requests to remote machines across a network.

   ◆ **Cache manager.** The cache manager is responsible for holding in RAM a certain amount of data that was the last data read from the disk drive.

Instead of reaccessing the disk drive to retrieve the same information, the data is read directly from the cache in RAM. This process is dramatically faster than accessing the hard drive.

◆ **Windows NT Executive device drivers.** Executive device drivers directly manipulate devices to receive or retrieve data.

◆ **File systems.** File systems translate file-oriented I/O requests into I/O commands for specific devices.

◆ **I/O manager.** The I/O manager manages device-independent I/O requests.

◆ **Hardware abstraction layer (HAL).** The hardware abstraction layer (HAL) translates Executive requests into actions in the computer's hardware. To move to a different processor, only this layer needs to be changed, because all hardware-dependent features, such as interrupt controllers and I/O interfaces, are hidden by HAL from the Executive. HAL makes Windows NT very portable across computer platforms.

Understanding Windows NT Networking

Windows NT provides support for two types of networking: peer-to-peer and client/server.

In peer-to-peer networks, every computer in the network can access every other. Computers can, for example, share files on their hard drives and share printers. Windows for Workgroups 3.1 offers peer-to-peer networking. Windows NT also includes this functionality.

One of the problems with peer-to-peer networks is that when several users access many computers, computer performance lessens. When someone else is accessing your hard drive, for example, it takes longer for you to open and save files on your system. In small office environments, peer-to-peer networking works fine; when there are more than 15 computers, another (more hardware-intensive) networking scheme is necessary.

 Note   For more information on networking with Windows NT, see Chapter 17.

In client/server networks, a dedicated computer with massive hard drives serves as the central repository for shared files. Instead of accessing files on other people's computers, the user looks for shared files on the dedicated computer, called the server. Windows NT supports client/server networking through the Windows NT Advanced Server edition (discussed in detail in Chapter 20).

 Note The term client/server derives from the idea that your computer, the client, makes requests of the server; the server (like a butler) carries out the request.

Understanding System Security

Windows NT is a secure system. The security system operates on the following three levels:

◆ Protects against people who are not authorized to log on to the system

◆ Protects against unauthorized access to files and system resources

◆ Protects the operating system and application processes from destructive applications and viruses

Windows NT also monitors attempts to breach the security system.

Windows NT, in its initial release, conforms to the U.S. government's Class C2 level of security. To qualify, it must contain the following features:

◆ A secure logon system, in which users identify themselves by a unique logon name and password

◆ Discretionary access control, in which the owner of a resource determines who has access to it

◆ Auditing, in which the system can detect and record events related to the security of the system and its components

◆ Memory protection, in which files are read- and write-protected from others in a network

 Note In future releases, Windows NT will satisfy the criteria for a Class B2 level of security (second to the top of seven levels).

The following sections discuss the security measures used by Windows NT.

Crash Prevention

System crashes on personal computers are frustrating. If more than one application is running during the crash, unsaved data may be lost. The magnitude of the consequences grows dramatically, however, if the computer is on a network. It is possible for one workstation to hang an entire system. A system crash in which dozens or even hundreds of accounts are open truly can be catastrophic. For this reason, the system must have adequate safeguards against such intentional or unintentional crashes.

Windows NT protects the system in four ways:

◆ Each application runs in a separate address space in virtual memory. One application cannot access another's virtual memory addresses.

◆ User mode is separated from kernel mode. If an application or a subgroup crashes in user mode, it cannot harm the operating system in kernel mode.

◆ Protected subgroups, such as OS/2 and POSIX, run separately from one another. Even if one protected subgroup crashes, the other subgroups are unaffected.

◆ Each page of virtual memory has indicators that indicate whether (and how) they can be accessed in user or kernel mode.

Logon and Access Security

One of the protected subsystems in Windows NT's user mode is the security subsystem—the gateway through which all users must travel. When you log on, the security subsystem looks at your user name and password to determine whether you have access to the computer system. If you do, it looks at your user profile, which specifies the files and system resources you can and cannot access, and what you can and cannot do with those files and resources. The system administrator may allow you to view a file but not change it, for example, or to print a document but not change the printer's setup.

With the user profile, the security subsystem creates an *access token*, which is the key that gets passed with whatever action you perform. It contains the specifics of what you can and cannot do on the system.

New Riders Publishing
INSIDE SERIES

The sophisticated security that Windows NT provides is overkill for users who work at home on their own computers. Security is absolutely necessary, however, when computers are linked to a network. Not only does a security system prevent criminals from stealing information and planting viruses, it also prevents inadvertent corruption of files by fellow workers.

Windows NT provides the following user groups:

◆ **Administrators.** Administrators have access to all system resources and rights and built-in capabilities in Windows NT. Administrators can create users and groups, shut down the system, force the shutdown of a remote system, and assign user rights.

   Administrators do not, however, have automatic access to all files on the system. The person who creates a file in the system is its owner, unless she declares otherwise. The owner of a file also determines its access rights. The administrator, however, can take ownership of the file.

◆ **Power users.** Power users have many administrative rights: managing printers, creating and modifying user accounts and groups, and creating common programming groups. Power users do not have the same number of rights as administrators; for example, they cannot take ownership of files, manage security logs, back up files and directories, or override the lock on a workstation.

◆ **Users.** Users are the most common type. Common group permissions include opening and closing files, and accessing system resources (such as printers). The administrator can select the permissions for each user, create subgroups of users (for example, secretary, accountant, and stockroom person), and assign permissions pertinent to the job description of each group.

◆ **Guests.** Guests use the system only occasionally. Often, their access to files and system resources is severely restricted. The administrator can choose, for example, to limit their access to only the files they create.

◆ **Backup operators.** Backup operators back up system files and directories to and restore them from a storage media, such as a tape drive.

These built-in groups have default rights and built-in capabilities. Permissions can be modified, but capabilities are an innate characteristic of the user type. To change capabilities, a user must change to a different user type. Tables 3.1 and 3.2 show the rights and capabilities of the various user groups.

TABLE 3.1
User-Group Rights

Rights	Administrators	Power Users	Guests	All	Users	Backup Operators
Log on	Yes	Yes	Yes	Yes	Yes	Yes
Access computer from network	Yes	Yes	No	No	Yes	No
Assume ownership of files	Yes	No	No	No	No	No
Manage security and audit log	Yes	No	No	No	No	No
Modify system time	Yes	Yes	No	No	No	No
Shut down system	Yes	Yes	Yes	No	Yes	Yes
Remotely shut down system	Yes	No	No	No	No	No
Back up directories and files	Yes	No	No	No	No	Yes
Restore directories and files	Yes	No	No	No	No	Yes

TABLE 3.2
User-Group Capabilities

Capabilities	Administrators	Power Users	Guests	All	Users	Backup Operators
Manage and create user accounts	Yes	Yes	No	No	No	No
Manage and create user groups	Yes	Yes	No	No	No	No
Define user rights	Yes	No	No	No	No	No
Lock workstation	Yes	Yes	Yes	No	No	No
Override workstation lock	Yes	No	No	No	No	No

Capabilities	Administrators	Power Users	Guests	All	Users	Backup Operators
Format hard disk of workstation	Yes	No	No	No	No	No
Keep local user profile	Yes	Yes	Yes	No	No	Yes
Share (or stop sharing) directories	Yes	Yes	No	No	No	No
Share (or stop sharing) printers	Yes	Yes	No	No	No	No

User Privileges

As described earlier, access tokens describe what a user can and cannot access. An *access token* is a small repository of information that accompanies a process, such as a request to open a file (see fig. 3.2).

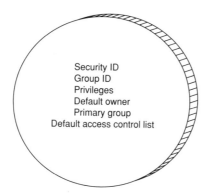

Security ID
Group ID
Privileges
Default owner
Primary group
Default access control list

Figure 3.2

An access token.

The access token contains the following information:

◆ **Security ID.** The user's logon name.

◆ **Group IDs.** The groups to which the user belongs.

◆ **Privileges.** The special services the user can use (usually none).

◆ **Default owner.** The default owner of the object the user creates (usually the user).

◆ **Primary group.** The group of security IDs that can use the object.

◆ **Default access control list (ACL).** The default list of groups and individual users and their read/write/execute privileges for user-owned objects.

The access token also includes the following services the user can perform: create token, open token, query token information, set token information, duplicate token, adjust token privileges, and adjust token groups.

Token is a term taken from networking jargon. Networking engineers borrowed the term from the public transit. Just as a bus or subway token buys you a bus or subway ride, an access token enables your process to travel in the system.

When a process tries to access an object, such as a file, Windows NT's Object Manager (in the Executive) examines the access token to determine whether the process can open a handle to the object.

Access Control Lists

Windows NT attaches security descriptors to all objects—including files, threads, events, and access tokens—when they are created. The security descriptor is an ACL that specifies who can use the objects created by the user and how they can use them. To assign security to an object, the creator of the object does one of three things:

◆ Explicitly states, in the ACL, which users and groups can use the object and which access rights (read/write/execute) they have.

◆ Names the object, but does not explicitly state the ACL. The security system looks in the object directory for the name of the object. In the directory, some elements of the ACL list might be marked "inherit." The security system applies those elements to the object.

◆ Does not name the object or explicitly state the ACL. In this case, the security system applies the default ACL listed in the creator's access token.

Security descriptors also contain an audit field, which enables the security system to set off alarms and send messages when it detects users trying to access objects restricted from them. For example, the security system records the security ID (the user's logon name) of a user who tries to modify a system-owned file in the security log.

ACLs actually are composed of a number of smaller lists, called *access control entries (ACEs)*. Each ACE contains the name of one user or group and their read/write/execute permissions (see fig. 3.3).

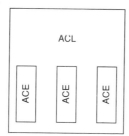

Figure 3.3

Every ACL contains a number of access-control entries (ACEs).

The security system reads through the ACEs sequentially, and stops reading at the first ACE that either grants or denies the process access to the object. If the security system reads all of the ACEs and does not find the security or group ID of the user, the security system denies access to the object.

The security system reads through the ACEs only when a handle to the object is first opened, not each time the handle is used. It is possible to change an object's ACL while it is in use. Even if the new setting disqualifies current users from accessing the object, after a handle is opened to an object, the object remains accessible until the process completes.

Some interesting inconsistencies can elude Windows NT's detection. Suppose, for example, that the security ID is JDoe, and he belongs to the Stockclerks group. If the first ACE grants permission to JDoe, the security system stops reading the ACEs and opens a handle to the object—even if the second ACE denies access to every one in the Stockclerks group.

Understanding How Windows NT Works with Your Existing Applications

One of the most appealing aspects of Windows NT is its capability to run applications written for a variety of operating systems, including OS/2, DOS, 16-bit Windows, and POSIX. The price Windows NT pays for this versatility is slower performance. Some of the applications in these operating systems are not compatible with Windows NT, and the ones that are compatible might run faster on systems that run only 16-bit Windows, OS/2, or Unix.

Win32 provides the graphical interface for Windows NT, and it handles inputs from other devices, such as your keyboard, scanner, mouse, and other pointing devices. Win32 also is the gateway into the Windows NT kernel for all operating systems that Windows NT supports.

When you double-click on an application, Win32 determines whether it is a Win32 application—that is, a 32-bit Windows application. If it is, Win32 controls the execution of the application. If not, Win32 passes control to the appropriate operating subsystem, called a *protected subsystem* (the VDM, for example).

DOS and 16-Bit Windows Compatibility

Using the Virtual DOS Machine, Windows NT is 100 percent compatible with DOS, Windows 3.1, and Windows 95 software, except for those programs that access the hardware directly or rely on their own device drivers—either for printers, disk drives, scanners, or video cards. Because, for security reasons, Windows NT permits access to the hardware only through the Win32 API or the Windows NT Executive, this type of software will fail.

There are a variety of applications that might be incompatible, including those that are display-intensive, such as paint programs; those that directly access fax, scanner, or terminal-emulation cards; those that access disk drives, such as disk-maintenance applications; and disk-doubling applications that have their own disk device drivers.

 Note You might be able to use some of these applications by upgrading their device drivers. Others need an application upgrade.

DOS applications appear in windows, just as they do in Windows 95. The only difference is that you can launch 32-bit Windows and 16-bit DOS programs from the DOS window. These programs are routed to the appropriate protected subsystem—Win32 or the VDM.

16-bit Windows applications open the VDM that, in turn, opens the Windows on Win32 (WOW) environment. WOW contains an emulation of Windows 95, DOS, and the Windows application. Each additional Windows application becomes another thread within WOW, not part of a new VDM.

In this way, WOW controls the multitasking of 16-bit Windows applications. This points out the only difference between the simulated (WOW) version of Windows 3.1 and Windows 3.1 itself: WOW controls multitasking, not the 16-bit Windows environment.

Most Windows 95 applications run in Windows NT. Although the 32- and 16-bit versions probably look identical, the 32-bit applications run directly through the Win32 API, and the 16-bit versions run in the VDM.

A number of applications written for Windows 3.0, particularly graphics-intensive applications such as paint programs, skipped the Windows API altogether and accessed the Window Manager directly for better display performance.

Windows NT uses its own window manager and graphical device interface (GDI), which controls display elements, in place of those in the 16-bit version of Windows. Applications that try to access the 16-bit version of the Window Manager or the GDI find them missing, with the Windows NT Window Manager and GDI in their place. For this reason, these applications do not run on Windows NT.

On the whole, you will find that 16-bit Windows applications run more slowly in Windows NT than in Windows 95. This is because of the massive overhead of Windows NT, the extra steps required to funnel system calls through the Win32 API, and the inability of 16-bit applications to take advantage of multitasking threads. As revisions of 16-bit software become available, the 32-bit applications will run faster on Windows NT.

OS/2 Compatibility

Current support for OS/2 applications is limited. Windows NT supports only 16-bit, character-based OS/2 applications (and only on *x*86 computers). As a result, most OS/2 2.*x* applications do not run under Windows NT.

In contrast to DOS and 16-bit Windows applications, OS/2 applications do not need an emulator because they were written for a multitasking, 32-bit environment. Instead, they work as clients to the OS/2 protected subsystem API.

POSIX Compatibility

Windows NT also provides support for POSIX applications. *POSIX* is a Unix variant, designed for the U.S. government, that supports application portability across computing platforms. Like OS/2, POSIX-compliant applications run as clients through the POSIX API protected subsystem. Also like OS/2, Windows NT's first version supports only character-based applications in POSIX. This is not a significant restriction for POSIX applications because, like Unix, its applications generally are character-based.

PowerPC Compatibility

Windows NT provides full support for PowerPC applications. PowerPC microprocessors are manufactured by Motorola and found most often in Apple computers.

Microsoft provides a full range of applications for PowerPCs, including development tools, Microsoft Excel, Word, Visual C++, Microsoft Test, and SNA Server. Third-party developers also offer business applications for Windows NT running on a PowerPC platform.

Comparing Windows NT with Other 32-Bit Operating Systems

Windows NT takes its place in the marketplace beside several other major operating systems, most notably OS/2 and Unix. This section compares and contrasts Windows NT with each of these competitors.

Windows NT and OS/2: A Comparison

Windows NT and OS/2 have common origins. The two operating systems, consequently, share many features. Microsoft and IBM worked together in the 1980s to produce OS/2 1.0. The relationship was rocky at times. When OS/2 commercially failed in 1987, Microsoft began to withdraw support from OS/2. When Windows 3.0 exceeded all sales expectations, Microsoft turned away from upgrading OS/2. Instead, Microsoft used its OS/2 research as the basis for Windows NT. To this day, IBM remains the sole supporter of OS/2. This section looks at the similarities and differences between OS/2 and Windows NT, including:

◆ Graphical user interface

◆ Operating-system architecture

◆ Virtual memory space

◆ Application compatibility

◆ Application-memory protection

◆ File systems

◆ Networks

◆ Script language

◆ Symmetric multiprocessing

◆ Cross-platform compatibility

◆ Security

Graphical User Interface

Both OS/2 and Windows NT use graphical user interfaces (GUIs). The center point for the OS/2 interface is called the Workplace Shell. The typical center point in previous versions of Windows NT is the Program Manager, although other third-party shells function as popular alternatives—for example, the Norton Desktop. In the latest version of Windows NT, the GUI is called Explorer.

In the Workplace Shell, all desktop objects, such as files, printers, and utilities, are treated the same. You can manipulate a file the same way you can a printer (within reason). You might, for example, copy a file from one directory to another as you copy the printer icon from one folder to another. This provides a uniform and easy-to-learn interface.

The Workplace Shell provides a desktop for direct access to all objects. OS/2 includes a folder icon for organizing desktop objects. Users can put anything on the desktop into a folder, such as a spreadsheet icon, a printer icon, and a fax icon. You easily can move icons from one group to another.

Windows NT's Program Manager shell is far less sophisticated than OS/2's Workplace Shell. Although the icon groupings provide structure, they require the user to traverse several layers of the interface before reaching the window in which the desired task appears. Microsoft recognized the inefficiency of the interface. For that reason, Microsoft developed Explorer, the GUI first seen in Windows 95, to create a more intuitive and powerful interface.

Operating-System Architecture

Both OS/2 and Windows NT are 32-bit operating systems. There are some differences between them, however. OS/2 2.1 completes many, but not all, of its tasks using 32-bit processing; Windows NT performs all tasks with 32-bit processing.

Both operating systems provide 16-bit processing in protected subsystem APIs for DOS and 16-bit Windows applications.

Both operating systems use message passing between applications and the operating system to facilitate multitasking. OS/2 implements message passing differently than Windows NT, however. In OS/2, messages and interrupts enter a single queue. Once there, they wait until the application they are bound for is ready to accept them. Each message is processed in the order in which it arrives. Problems occur when a message cannot be processed. It sits at the top of the queue, blocking all other messages from being processed thus hanging the entire system (see fig. 3.4).

Figure 3.4

OS/2's single message queue.

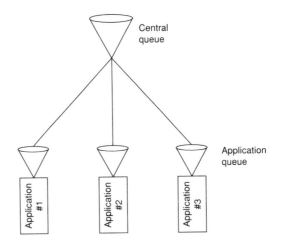

Windows NT also uses message passing to implement multitasking. Windows NT, however, does not use a central distributing queue as OS/2 does. Instead, messages are passed directly to the queue of each application (see fig. 3.5). If one of the messages cannot be processed, the operating system passes processing time to the next application. This feature makes Windows NT more difficult to crash.

Figure 3.5

Windows NT's decentralized messaging queues.

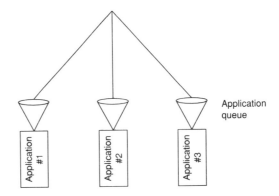

Virtual Memory Space

Both OS/2 and Windows NT use a 4 GB virtual-memory address space. Although Windows NT reserves 2 GB for the operating system and 2 GB for applications, OS/2 limits each application to 512 MB. For most users, these numbers far exceed even the smallest percentage of virtual memory that their applications will ever use.

A more realistic limit on virtual memory space for either Windows NT or OS/2 is the sum of RAM memory and free disk space. In other words, if you have 8 MB of RAM and 50 MB free on your hard disk, the maximum amount of virtual memory available

on your system is 58 MB, not 2 GB. In this respect, only users with very large disk drives can fully utilize the virtual memory potential of either operating system.

Application Memory Protection

Both OS/2 and Windows NT offer applications protection from other running applications by utilizing the built-in features of Intel microprocessors, called virtual 86 mode. Both OS/2 and Windows NT refer to this mode as the virtual DOS machine (VDM), as described earlier in the chapter.

Using VDM, if an application tries to use memory reserved for another application, OS/2 displays an error message, called the Hard Error Popup, and enables you to either terminate the errant application or display the contents of the debug registers.

These options leave the operating system and other running applications intact. DOS or Windows 3.1, in comparison, might display a system error message and the entire system might crash.

In addition to using the virtual 86 mode built into 80386, 80486, and Pentium processors, Windows NT provides a software version of the VDM. The simulated environment makes DOS run more slowly than it would on a PC running DOS. This is a result of the processing overhead of simulating the hardware VDM with a software program. The software VDM enables Windows NT to run DOS and 16-bit Windows applications on non-Intel processors.

OS/2 provides more flexibility than Windows NT when running Windows applications. In OS/2, you have the option of running all your Windows applications in the same VDM or in separate VDMs.

Running all Windows applications in the same VDM is faster than in separate VDMs because they share the same Windows operating system.

Because all the applications are running in the same VDM, there is the potential danger of one application crashing all the other running applications in that VDM. The damage is limited to that VDM; other VDMs, other running applications, and the operating system are impervious to the corruption in one errant VDM. As a user, you have to decide what best fits your needs: security or speed.

Application Hardware Protection

Hardware devices also are protected from errant applications in OS/2 and Windows NT. To enforce security (in Windows NT) and to exercise control over system resources, applications must access hardware devices, such as printers and disk drives, through a *virtual device driver (VDD)*. The VDD prevents more than one application at a time from accessing a hardware device.

Both Windows NT and OS/2 can tell when applications try to illegally access hardware devices. This situation is particularly important for Windows NT, whose security system must protect system resources, such as disk drives, from illegal access. You are given the option of terminating the offending application.

Some DOS and Windows applications were written to access hardware directly to speed program execution. These applications are incompatible with OS/2 and Windows NT.

File Systems

The file system that DOS uses is called the File Allocation Table (FAT). All DOS and Windows 95 applications use this format; Windows NT and OS/2 also support it. In addition to FAT, OS/2 also can use another file system, called the High Performance File System (HPFS). HPFS was designed to access files more quickly on large disk drives (over 200 MB). Access time is equal to that of using FAT for smaller disk drives.

HPFS uses multithreaded write-caching to disk, in which files are dumped into RAM and written to disk when there is time. This enables you to (almost) immediately proceed to another task without waiting for the file to save to disk.

HPFS also provides support for very large files and filenames, up to 255 characters long. It enables you to use a variety of characters such as spaces and multiple periods in filenames (unlike FAT filenames).

Windows NT does not, however, support partitioning HPFS drives using the format command. Partitioning a drive is the process of dividing a hard disk into sections. You can call each partition a different drive; for example, on one physical drive you might have drives E: and F:. Drive E: might be compressed and drive F: might not be, or drive E: might be NTFS and drive F: might use the FAT file system. Although Windows NT still supports HPFS, you cannot divide an HPFS hard drive into partitions.

Note   To create partitions on a disk, you use the MS-DOS fdisk command. When you type fdisk at the command line, fdisk takes you through three user interactive screens that allow you to specify the number and kind of partitions you want to create. If you want to use multiple partitions of a disk, you must use fdisk before installing Windows NT.

Although it is handy to have long, descriptive filenames, there is a limitation to their usefulness. Because DOS and Windows 3.1 can run in OS/2, OS/2 applications that are saved with filenames longer than eight characters are inaccessible by DOS and Windows 3.1. Windows NT, on the other hand, automatically reduces large filenames to the eight-character maximum allowed by DOS and Windows 3.1.

Although you might find it confusing to refer to the same file by using two different names, at least Windows NT enables you to take full advantage of longer names while maintaining compatibility with older operating systems.

HPFS offers another major advantage over FAT: extended attribute files, which describe the file to which they are attached. You can put almost any kind of information into the file, such as keywords you use to search for the file, the name of the owner of the file, or historical information about the file (such as who modified the file and when it was modified). You can use the Workplace Shell to record most information (by using the File section of the system-settings notebook). Applications are free to use the extended attributes file any way they please.

Extended attribute files can help you speed up tasks by searching for keywords in extended attribute files instead of in long data files; record information that cannot be part of a file, such as historical information; or perform tasks you otherwise might not be able to perform, such as when the file is write- or read-protected.

Windows NT can use three filing systems: FAT, HPFS, and its own file system, called New Technology File System (NTFS). Like HPFS, NTFS can access files on large disks more quickly than FAT. Unlike HPFS, however, NTFS can enforce the U.S. government's level C2 security; that is, system administrators can restrict users or user groups from accessing files, directories, and subdirectories.

Networking

Both OS/2 and Windows NT work with a variety of transport protocols, such as TCP/IP and IPX. OS/2 also uses IBM's protocol, SNA. Both operating systems can function as clients on Novell's NetWare systems. Only OS/2 can function as a server for NetWare, however.

Although both operating systems support client/server local area networks (LANs), only Windows NT supports peer-to-peer networking, which is less hardware-intensive and suited to small office installations. Instead of a dedicated computer (server) that serves as a storage facility, peer-to-peer networking enables users to access each other's hard disks.

Script Language

IBM created a new script language for OS/2, called REXX, to replace IBM's older, more difficult batch language. REXX is an easy-to-use, powerful language that you can use for a variety of tasks. For example, you can modify desktop objects, run automated tasks (such as downloading data about stocks at midnight every day), and run programs to change downloaded stock data into written and graphical reports.

You also can create macros for OS/2's Enhanced Editor with REXX. REXX runs on many platforms, from mainframe to microcomputer, from Unix to Macintosh. Many consider REXX to be one of OS/2's most valuable features.

Windows NT does not offer a script or macro language such as REXX. It does not even have the oft-maligned Windows Recorder applet found in Windows 95! In the future, however, Windows NT will be very strong in this area. Look for an object-oriented script language—often referred to as *Object Basic*—to be built into the next versions of Windows 95 and Windows NT.

Multiprocessing

As discussed earlier in the chapter, Windows NT fully supports symmetric multiprocessing. OS/2, in contrast, does not. Although multiprocessing computers are not on a typical desktop now, Intel has announced plans to sell multiprocessor chips within a matter of years. Multiprocessing provides orders-of-magnitude faster computing. When multiprocessors become common, the symmetric multiprocessing capability of Windows NT will be invaluable.

Cross-Platform Compatibility

Wouldn't it be great to take your favorite applications and run them on faster computers? For years, there have been CPUs that run faster than Intel processors—for example, DEC's Alpha series and MIPS processors. Although system administrators pine for faster processors because their favorite applications can't run on non-Intel processors, changing to a new platform is daunting.

Windows NT was designed to run on a variety of processors. The hardware abstraction layer (HAL) acts as the interface between function calls and the computer's hardware. When software developers want to port Windows NT to different processors, they need only to revise the HAL. Windows NT already is compatible with RISC processors.

In contrast, OS/2 2.*x* is tied to Intel-based processors. IBM promises that future versions will be portable.

Software developers have a vested interest in the portability of an operating system. If applications created for one platform can be ported easily to another, they save valuable developmental hours.

Application Compatibility

Both OS/2 and Windows NT can run DOS and 16-bit Windows applications. Windows NT, however, can run only character-mode OS/2 1.*x* applications. These applications, however, represent only a small minority of the OS/2 applications available.

OS/2 2.1 supports Windows 95 applications, in part, as a result of an agreement reached between IBM and Microsoft. In the process of disentangling who owned what of OS/2, Microsoft and IBM agreed to share with each other the source code of Windows 3.x and OS/2.

That agreement expired in September 1993. Without access to source code, it has become much more difficult to support new versions of operating systems. Because there are far more Windows than OS/2 applications in the marketplace, it is has been difficult for OS/2 to remain compatible with future versions of Windows NT.

The reverse is not true. Windows NT would not be crippled by deciding not to support OS/2 applications. It took IBM a year to support Windows 3.1 in OS/2, and that was with the benefit of seeing the Windows source code. OS/2 faces the real problem of losing compatibility with Windows applications.

In addition, Windows NT supports POSIX (character-based only) and 32-bit Windows NT applications; OS/2 does not. Because most POSIX (Unix) applications are character-based, this restriction does not significantly reduce the number of POSIX applications that can run in Windows NT.

Portability ensures an application's compatibility across processors; extensibility ensures an application's compatibility across operating systems.

Extensibility enables you to run a greater variety of software on your system. In that way, you can convert to an extensible system, such as Windows NT, more easily and cheaply because you do not need to give up your old applications. Also, because subsystems are relatively easy to add to Windows NT, it does not become outdated.

Each operating system in Windows NT is implemented in its own protected subsystem. This component architecture enables system administrators to update individual subsystems while Windows NT is running, without affecting the other subsystems. Adding new operating systems simply entails adding subsystems, not intertwining new code into current code. As a result, Windows NT is less vulnerable to bugs that come with operating-system updates (or additions).

Security

Windows NT's security system is much more comprehensive than that of OS/2. As described in this chapter, virtually every object in Windows NT—such as files, memory, threads, directories, and hardware—has security measures built in. Each process has a descriptor, defined by the capabilities of the user or user group, that system resources review before performing tasks.

Additionally, Windows NT monitors a series of security parameters, and it keeps a security log that notes events such as attempts to gain illegal access to the system or system resources, system shutdowns, and user logons.

OS/2 provides watered-down versions of some of Windows NT's security features, otherwise relying on other systems for security. For example, IBM's LAN Server records security-related events in a log, and provides some system-resource security. None of these security features, however, matches the sophistication of Windows NT.

Windows NT and Unix: A Comparison

Written in 1969, Unix is the benchmark against which all other powerful operating systems are measured. Just about every operating system, including DOS, borrows Unix concepts and terminology. (For example, the command to change directories is the same in DOS and Unix.) The enormous system requirements of Unix, however, both in memory and computational needs, and its arcane command language have largely prevented it from moving to the PC desktop.

Some companies have tried to bring Unix to the PC platform. Microsoft, for example, created Xenix, a variant of Unix, to run on a normal PC. Xenix was a commercial flop, causing Microsoft to license Xenix to Santa Cruz Operations (SCO) in return for a piece of the company.

In recent years, Unix variants have sprung up after Unix source code was released. Examples include: NeXTStep, SCO Unix, Solaris from SunSoft, and UnixWare from Univel/Novell. To include a discussion of each of these operating systems is beyond the scope of this book.

The Unix that is discussed in this section is generic, such as that supported by Unix System Laboratories (now owned by Novell). At its most basic level, Unix is a 32-bit, multiuser, multiprocessing, and multitasking operating system that supports linear memory addressing, virtual memory, networking, and sophisticated security.

The following section looks at the similarities and differences between Windows NT and Unix, focusing on the following areas:

◆ Process execution

◆ Multiprocessing

◆ Objects

◆ Interprocess communications

◆ Flat memory

◆ Modes

◆ Security

- Networks

- Cross-platform compatibility

- Multiusing

- Parallel processing

- Distributed file systems

- Applications

- Variants

- Size

- Market penetration

Process Execution

Both Windows NT and Unix have managers in the kernel that govern processes. In Unix, that manager is called the Process Scheduler. In Windows NT, the Process Manager and Object Manager in the NT Executive fulfill the same functions.

These managers determine which processes get executed, their priorities for execution, and when they get executed. They detect the length of time since the processes last received a CPU timeslice, and they monitor the access permissions of the process' owner. These managers also make sure that processes and subprocesses are executed in the correct order so that tasks are accomplished correctly.

Multiprocessing

Most variants of Unix support either symmetrical or asymmetrical multiprocessing; Windows NT supports symmetrical multiprocessing. Both operating systems also support remote procedure calls (RPCs), which enable one computer to spawn a process or thread, send it to another computer, communicate with it, and terminate it. In this way, one computer gets the benefit of two processors. To the user, however, everything appears to happen locally.

Objects

Windows NT treats everything—files, system resources, memory, and processes—as objects. Unix treats everything as if it were a file. For example, you generally find hardware device drivers in the /dev subdirectory. Windows NT's I/O Manager, likewise, makes device and network drivers appear as file systems to user-mode processes and higher-level executive processes.

The advantage of making everything look the same is that you then can manipulate everything in a similar way. Access to all objects (or files), for example, can be governed by the same security procedures. This makes adding and subtracting objects from the system easy because all objects respond to the same operations.

Device drivers used to be integrated into the operating code. Adding or revising a driver required the system administrator to shut down the entire computer system and then reinstall or rebuild the operating system. This process caused a variety of problems, especially the loss of computer time. By making device drivers independent entities—objects—they can be added while the computer is running without the threat of introducing bugs to other parts of the system.

Flat Memory

Both Unix and Windows NT use 32-bit addresses in flat (nonsegmented) virtual memory. Gone is the segmented memory of DOS and Windows 3.1, in which physical and virtual memory is broken into conventional, upper, expanded, high, and extended memory. Unix uses a 2 GB virtual-memory space; Windows NT uses a 4 GB virtual-memory space (2 GB for the application and 2 GB for the operating system). Both operating systems support 64 KB or more of physical memory.

Modes

Both Unix and Windows NT separate user and kernel modes (called *spaces* in Unix). Kernel processes have higher priority over user processes. Kernel processes, for example, can suspend user processes. Also, user processes are protected in memory from one another by kernel processes. Except for interprocess communications, user-mode processes do not interact with one another. Kernel processes, in contrast, interact both with other kernel and user processes.

In Unix, the system call interface (SCI) can change user processes into kernel processes to execute system-level functions, and then change them back to user processes. The SCI is the communication tool that goes between user and kernel mode. Because applications can cross the line between user and kernel modes, the operating system is vulnerable to errant applications.

In Windows NT, applications and protected subsystems (including different operating systems such as DOS and Windows 3.*x*) occupy user mode. Kernel processes execute user processes, but (unlike Unix) neither applications nor subsystems can penetrate kernel mode. When a user process wants the kernel to perform a task, it issues a system service call that starts one or more kernel-mode processes. Separating user and

kernel modes so completely makes Windows NT less vulnerable to errant applications that try to invade kernel-mode processes.

Security

Windows NT satisfies the government's C2 security requirements. Although Unix, by itself, satisfies C1 security requirements (which are slightly less stringent), many Unix variants satisfy C2 security requirements. For this reason, Unix and Windows NT provide similar security features, including object ownership, user and group access rights, and object-level security.

Both operating systems maintain detailed security logs that record security-related events, such as attempts to illegally access system resources. Both systems offer robust recovery systems after hardware, software, and power failures.

Networking

Both Windows NT and Unix offer powerful networking features that are based on the open systems interconnect (OSI) model. For example, both Unix and Windows NT support RPCs.

Unix can access a variety of Unix and non-Unix operating systems by using Sun's Network File System (NFS). Unix uses USL's remote file system (RFS) to share peripherals. Unlike NFS, however, RFS requires all computers to run Unix file systems.

NFS rides on top of the file system of the remote computer. For that reason, NFS supports a variety of file systems, including FAT (DOS), HPFS (OS/2), Unix, BSD, VMS (DEC), and—in the near future—NTFS (Windows NT).

Both Unix and Windows NT support client/server and peer-to-peer networking.

 Note   If you currently use third-party, NFS-client software with Windows NT version 3.1, you need to ask the third party for an upgrade for your NFS software so that it works with the current version of Windows NT.

Cross-Platform Compatibility

Unix runs on far more platforms than does Windows NT (from mainframes to microcomputers). Windows NT runs only on Intel, MIPS, PowerPC, and DEC Alpha processors. This list of platforms will grow as the product matures.

Multiusing

Unix was written specifically to enable more than one user to share a computer. Unix enables many users to use dumb terminals to access the same computer. Windows NT, on the other hand, is a single-user operating system. Although many computers can be networked together to a Windows NT server, the computers cannot be dumb terminals.

Parallel Processing

Unix offers full parallel-processing capabilities, including vectorized compilers. Windows NT offers a more limited form of parallel processing with synchronized multithreading.

Distributed File Systems

Unix fully supports distributed file systems. In Unix, files appear local, even though they can be anywhere in the network. Windows NT offers distributed file systems as well.

Applications

Unix applications already take full advantage of multitasking, multiprocessing, and multiuser functions. Windows NT applications also take advantage of 32-bit processing.

Variants

Because the source code of Unix was made available, many people hacked on Unix, creating many variants. Most of the variants now comply with set standards at the system level. There remains enough difference between the variants of Unix, however, that applications must be adjusted for each. Because there is no standard GUI for Unix, developers must write for Motif, Open Look, and others.

In contrast, do not expect Microsoft to release the source code of Windows NT. As a result, software developers do not need to worry about writing more than one version of their application for Windows NT.

Size

Unix is huge. It requires 60–95 MB of disk space and at least 8 MB of RAM for a single user. Although Windows NT is not small, a large part of the 75 MB that it requires is a swap file that you can adjust.

Market Penetration

There is no comparison between the number of Unix-versus-Windows operating systems, or the number of applications available for each. Unix has a great following in the scientific and engineering community. An entire generation of users and programmers has grown accustomed to the power of Unix.

The number of Unix users is small compared to the number of Windows 3.*x* users, however. If a significant number of those users decide to migrate to Windows NT, Microsoft could sell more NT operating systems in one year than Unix has sold in its 25-year history.

The number of applications that will run on Windows NT might even make Unix users envious and create converts. Third-party support might make the difference between the usability of Unix versus Windows NT and thus determine the predominant high-end operating system for the next 10 years. Although Unix applications have the advantage of being 32-bit applications, Windows NT applications will take only a short time to also become 32-bit applications.

Table 3.3 summarizes many of the functions of these systems that were discussed in this chapter.

Table 3.3
Functions of Windows NT, Unix, and OS/2

Function	Windows NT	Unix	OS/2 2.1
Multitasking	Yes	Yes	Yes
Multiuser	No	Yes	No
Multithreaded	Yes	Yes	Yes
Symmetric multiprocessing	Yes	Most variants	No
Virtual memory	Yes	Yes	Yes
Protected mode	Yes	Yes	Yes
C2-level security	Yes	Optional (some variants)	No
Object-oriented user interface	No	No	Yes
Portable	Yes	Yes	No
Networking	Yes	Yes	Yes

continues

TABLE 3.3, CONTINUED
Functions of Windows NT, Unix, and OS/2

Function	Windows NT	Unix	OS/2 2.1
Client or server	Both	Both (most variants)	Both
Runs DOS applications	Yes	Some variants	Yes
Runs 16-bit Windows applications	Yes	Some variants	Yes
Runs 32-bit Windows applications	Yes	No	No
Runs OS/2 16-bit applications	Character mode only	No	Yes
Runs OS/2 32-bit applications	No	No	Yes
Runs POSIX applications	Character mode only	Most variants	No

Summary

Although the long-term success of Windows NT certainly is open to question, the underlying technology behind the 32-bit operating system surely has few equals. This chapter examined the architecture of Windows NT and looked at its many strengths and occasional weaknesses.

The chapter covered such topics as Windows NT's 32-bit architecture, multitasking, multithreading, multiprocessing, networking, and security. It also chronicled the similarities and differences that exist between two alternative operating systems, Unix and OS/2.

The next chapter continues in this comparison mode, looking at the new features that a Windows 95 user will see when working with Windows NT.

Migrating from Windows 3.1 or Windows 95

If you are a Windows 95 user, one of the great benefits you will discover as you migrate to Windows NT is that Windows NT looks and feels almost exactly like the Windows you already know. With only a few additions, the Windows 95 interface is duplicated in Windows NT. This chapter introduces you to many of the non-Windows 95 features of Windows NT, including the following:

◆ Booting Windows NT

◆ Quitting Windows NT

◆ Using the Control Panel's non-Windows 95 features

◆ Using Print Manager's non-Windows 95 features

Most of the sections in this chapter do not provide detailed instructions about ways to complete tasks. Instead, they are meant to introduce you to many Windows NT functions. Later chapters in the book describe in more detail many of the features mentioned here.

Booting Windows NT

As you start your computer, you immediately notice the absence of the familiar DOS command line. Instead, you automatically boot up the graphical interface of Windows NT. Instead of seeing the traditional Program Manager used in Windows 3.1, an initial dialog box appears, as shown in figure 4.1.

Figure 4.1

Windows NT's secure attention sequence dialog box.

This securing dialog box forces you to press Ctrl+Alt+Del before proceeding into Windows NT. This key combination is normally used to reboot your computer or, in earlier versions of Windows as well as Windows 95, to close a "hung" application. Windows NT uses Ctrl+Alt+Del to ensure that no Trojan horse—a program loading before Windows NT—violates the security of your computer or network.

The Ctrl+Alt+Del procedure is but one example of why some people will migrate to Windows NT and some will not. Most of the security measures are entirely unnecessary for the individual user. For large companies managing confidential, mission-critical information, however, Windows NT can be the perfect secure fit.

After the Ctrl+Alt+Del key sequence, a second Welcome dialog box appears for logging on to the Windows NT system (see fig. 4.2).

Figure 4.2

Windows NT's logon window.

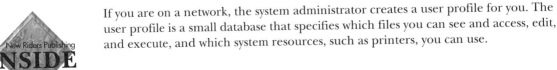

Windows NT is a secure system that can restrict your rights as a user. If you are not on a network, you are the superuser, which means that you can view and change all the files and use all the system resources. You enter your superuser password during Windows NT's Setup program.

If you are on a network, the system administrator creates a user profile for you. The user profile is a small database that specifies which files you can see and access, edit, and execute, and which system resources, such as printers, you can use.

Notice that Windows NT fills the Username field with the name of the previous user. If you logged on last, this feature saves you some typing.

After you supply your username, the name of your computer (or the server your computer belongs to), and your password, the security subsystem makes sure the entries are correct. If they are, the security subsystem creates an access token, which is your personalized key that enables you to view, edit, and execute files, or use system resources in Windows NT. The access token is derived from your user profile, which lists your privileges in the system.

The security subsystem sends the access token to the Win32 subsystem. Win32 displays Explorer.

Quitting Windows NT

To quit Windows NT, you need to take a few more steps than when you quit Windows 95. Choose **S**hutdown in the Start button menu, or press Ctrl+Alt+Del. Windows NT responds by displaying the Windows NT Security dialog box, as shown in figure 4.3.

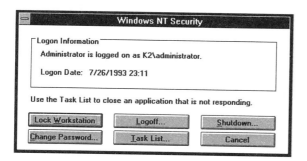

Figure 4.3

The Windows NT Security dialog box.

Stop   To end a Windows NT session, do not just turn off the computer! You might lose data.

To log off only, click on the **L**ogoff button in the Security window. To turn off the computer, click on the **S**hutdown button. Shutdown saves all changes in active files, then closes applications and services correctly.

Surveying Non-Windows 95 Windows NT Applets

Most of the familiar Windows 95 applets remain unchanged in Windows NT. A few non-Windows 95 applets also are included, as described in Table 4.1.

TABLE 4.1
Windows NT Applets

Application	Use
Mail	Sends and receives electronic mail. (This applet is included in Windows for Workgroups.)
Schedule+	Schedules meetings with fellow employees, creates a personal calendar, and sets alarms. (This applet is included in Windows for Workgroups.)
ClipBook Viewer	Shares excerpts of files across a network. (This applet is included in Windows for Workgroups.)
Introducing Windows NT	Shows a demonstration of the many features of Windows NT.
User Manager	Creates user profiles and user groups, and defines access rights.
Backup	Backs up the hard drive onto another storage medium, such as a tape drive. (This application is included in DOS 6.)
Event Viewer	Displays a list of events performed on a computer, such as warning messages, error messages, and information messages. Time, date, user, and source are included with the event description.
Disk Administrator	Partitions a disk, creates or deletes Administrator volume sets, extends volumes and volume sets, creates and deletes stripe sets, changes drive labels, and displays general information about a disk, such as partition information and free space.
Performance Monitor	Displays performance characteristics (by using Monitor charts and reports) of processors, memory, cache, threads, and processes—either on your computer or in the network.

Using the Control Panel's Non-Windows 95 Features

Most of the icons in the Control Panel are familiar, and the configuration utilities they start are identical to those found in Windows 95. Figure 4.4 shows the Control Panel icons.

Figure 4.4

The Control Panel.

There are, however, several non-Windows 95 ones, as shown in Table 4.2.

TABLE 4.2
Control Panel Icons

Application	Use
Cursors	Changes the appearance of the cursor.
Devices	Configures, starts, or stops device drivers.
Server	Starts and manages print, file, and communication services on the local computer.
Services	Starts, stops, pauses, or continues services (such as the printer) and defines setup options.
System	Specifies the default operating icon system. This is valuable only if you have more than one operating system installed on your computer.
UPS	Configures the uninterruptible power supply that saves open files during power failures.

Control Panel Features for the System Administrator

Windows NT provides the system administrator with the tools to assign users to groups, to define user access to files and system resources, and to field system errors. The following utilities detail how the system administrator can accomplish those tasks.

Server

When you click on the Server icon in the Control Panel, Windows NT displays the Properties window. This window shows you the number of users connected remotely (Sessions), the number of file locks (File Locks), the number of open resources (Open Files), and the number of open pipes (Open Named Pipes).

The following list describes some of the system administrator utilities accessed through the Server icon more completely.

◆ **Viewing sessions.** You can view the list of users working on the system and the resources they use by clicking on the Server icon and choosing the Users button in the Properties window. This dialog box shows the name of the user, the computer on which he or she is working, the number of resources being used, how long the present session has lasted, and how long the computer has been idle. When you select a user, the dialog box displays the resources used, how many times the user has used the resources, and times of use. From this dialog box, the system administrator can terminate one or all user sessions by clicking on the Disconnect or Disconnect All buttons, respectively.

◆ **Viewing resources.** You can view the list of resources in use on the system and the names of the users connected to them by clicking on the Server icon and choosing the Shares button in the Properties window. Windows NT displays the Shared Resources dialog box. From this window, the system administrator can eliminate from the system one or all resources by clicking on the Disconnect or Disconnect All buttons, respectively.

◆ **Replicating directories.** You can copy directories from a server to computers in the network by using the Directory Replication option. When you click on the Server icon and choose the Replication button in the Properties window, Windows NT displays the Directory Replication dialog box. In this dialog box, you specify the parameters, such as the computer and path, into which you are importing directories.

To prevent directories from being replicated, click on the Manage button in the Directory Replication window. Windows NT displays the Manage Imported Directories dialog box. This dialog box enables you to lock or unlock directories and view information pertinent to locking directories.

◆ **Alerting users.** Alert messages signal problems with resource use, such as a full disk. They also show problems with the server, such as printer errors, access problems, user-session problems, and power losses. The Alerts dialog box enables the system administrator to list users who should receive alert messages. Display the Alerts dialog box by clicking on the Server icon in the Control Panel and choosing Alerts from the Properties dialog box.

Services

When you click on the Services icon in the Control Panel, the Services dialog box appears (see fig. 4.5).

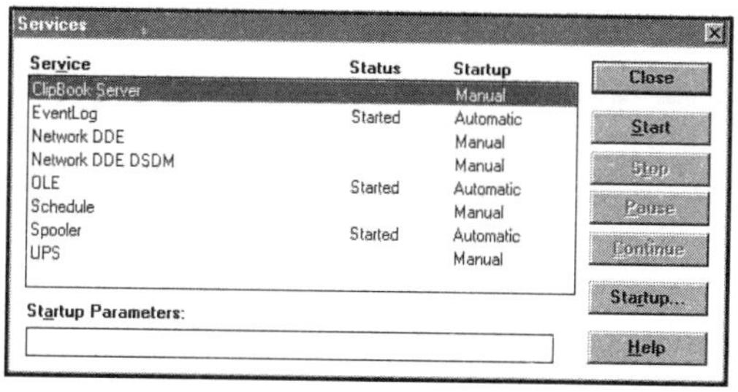

Figure 4.5

The Services dialog box.

The Services dialog box enables you to start, stop, pause, and continue system services. You also can specify parameters for services when Windows NT starts, including which services should start automatically. Services include servers, schedule, logon, and the uninterruptible power supply. The Services dialog box displays the status of each service on the computer. Many of these services, which are new to Windows 95 users, are listed in Table 4.3.

TABLE 4.3
Services Available in the Services Window

Service	Description
Alerter	Sends alert messages to selected users. This service enables users other than the system administrator to receive alert messages.
Computer Browser	Records and updates a list of all the computers in the network.
Directory Replicator	Copies directories from one computer to another.
Event Log	Maintains the event log that lists system, security, and application events.

continues

TABLE 4.3, CONTINUED
Services Available in the Services Window

Service	Description
Messenger	Sends and receives system administrator or Alerter messages.
Net Logon	Verifies user logon requests.
Schedule	Runs programs and commands at a defined time and date.
Server	Provides file, printer, and pipe sharing through remote procedure call (RPC) support.
UPS	Monitors the uninterruptible power supply.
Workstation	Establishes network communications and connections.

Devices

The Devices dialog box enables you to start and stop device drivers, and to specify which devices should begin automatically when the computer starts or when the system starts. Devices include network cards, disk drives, and printers.

Clicking on the Devices icon in the Control Panel displays the Devices dialog box, as shown in figure 4.6.

Figure 4.6

The Devices dialog box.

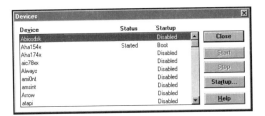

Control Panel Features

The Control Panel contains many applets that enable you to configure your system, set system variables, or install new devices. The following sections describe the function of the applets in the Control Panel.

Date/Time

The Date/Time dialog box enables you to specify your time zone and whether or not you switch to daylight savings time. Among other reasons, this feature eliminates the

need to reset your clock whenever you switch from daylight savings to standard time, and vice versa. The Date/Time dialog box is shown in figure 4.7.

Figure 4.7

The Date/Time dialog box.

Network

Clicking on the Network icon displays the Network Settings dialog box (see fig. 4.8).

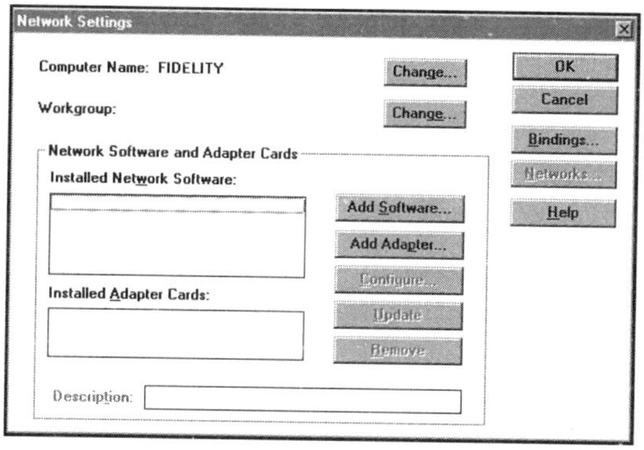

Figure 4.8

The Network Settings dialog box.

This new version of the Network utility bears little resemblance to that found in Windows 95. The Network Settings dialog box displays the software installed on the network and the network adapter cards installed in your computer. You can add, update, configure, and remove network software and adapter cards through this dialog box.

Joining Workgroups and Domains

You also use the Network Settings dialog box to join a workgroup or domain. By clicking on the Change button next to the Workgroup field, Windows NT displays the Domain/Workgroup Settings dialog box, as shown in figure 4.9.

A workgroup is a set of computers with names that appear together when you browse the network for resources. Anyone can join any workgroup.

Figure 4.9

*The Domain/
Workgroup
Settings dialog
box.*

Domain/Workgroup Settings dialog box:

Domain/Workgroup Settings	☒
Computer Name: FIDELITY	OK
Member of:	Cancel
⦿ **W**orkgroup: [ ]	**H**elp
○ **D**omain: [ ]	
☐ **C**reate Computer Account in Domain	
User Name: [ ]	
Password: [ ]	
This option will create a computer account on the domain for this computer. You must specify a user account with the ability to add workstations to the domain.	

A domain is a set of computers assembled by the network administrator. This set of computers also appears together when browsing the network for centralized user and group accounts. The network administrator assigns computers to domains, which provide you access to the network. If you change the name of the domain, you cannot log on to the network without asking for the network administrator's assistance. You can, however, still log on to your computer.

Windows NT server allows Windows for Workgroups computers connected in a subnet to browse the domain lists for the entire wide area network (WAN). This enables the Windows for Workgroups computer to be the browse master for a subnetwork. Other Windows for Workgroups and Windows 95 computers can query the browse master for domain information. The domain list is updated every fifteen minutes.

The following must be true for the browse master:

◆ It must be running Microsoft TCP/IP.

◆ The Windows Internet Name Service (WINS) must be running on one computer in the wide area network (WAN). The WINS is like a file system that spreads across computers. WINS keeps track of all of the names (and addresses) of the computers in the WAN. WINS enables one computer to find another in the network and one computer to find a file on another computer.

◆ The domain containing the browse master must have a Primary Domain Controller (PDC) and the PDC must be a WINS client. For more information about a PDC, see *Inside Windows NT Server,* published by New Riders.

◆ The browse master must be a WINS client and the workgroup name must be the same as the domain name.

The files that enable this functionality are located under \clients\wfw\update on the CD ROM software-distribution disk. Copy the files vserver.386 and vredir.386 to the \windows\system directory, and copy the net.exe file to the \windows directory on the browse master.

New Riders Publishing
INSIDE
SERIES

Renaming Your Computer

You also can rename a computer by clicking on the Change button next to the Computer Name field in the Network Settings dialog box. Windows NT displays the Computer Name dialog box (see fig. 4.10).

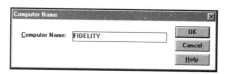

Figure 4.10

The Computer Name dialog box.

If you are connected to an NT Advanced Server domain, the new computer name must have an account on the active domain; otherwise, you cannot access files on the network.

Binding Network Cards

When you click on the **B**indings button in the Network Settings dialog box, Windows NT displays the Network Bindings dialog box. The Network Bindings dialog box enables you to unbind (disconnect) a network adapter card from all network components. You might do this if you rarely use one of the cards in your computer and want to eliminate from memory the software drivers associated with the card.

Changing the Default Network Order

If you click on the **N**etworks button in the Network Settings dialog box, Windows NT displays the Network Provider Search Order dialog box. If your computer is connected to more than one network, use this dialog box to set the order of networks through which your computer searches to complete various operations.

MIDI Mapper

The MIDI Mapper dialog box has a different look. In addition to choosing the driver to match your sound board, for example, the MIDI Mapper dialog box enables you to display the setup configuration, patch maps, and key maps.

System

You might have noticed the absence of the 386 Enhanced icon. In its place, the System dialog box (accessed by double-clicking on the System icon in the Control Panel) enables you to define, among other options, the size of the paging files to use for virtual memory. The System dialog box is shown in figure 4.11.

Figure 4.11

The System dialog box.

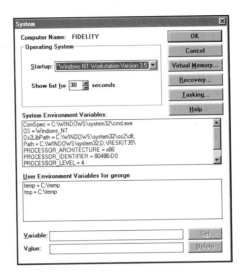

When an application requires more RAM than is available, Windows NT moves some memory from RAM into the paging file. As with Windows 95, Windows NT suggests an appropriate size for the paging files. Unlike Windows 95, however, you can spread the paging files across several drives.

The System dialog box also enables you to view (not edit) system environmental variables, such as those used with Path; and to view and change user environmental variables, such as the drive on which you want to put the paging file.

Using Print Manager's Features

The Print Manager in Windows NT is far more powerful than that of Windows 95. The Windows NT Print Manager is shown in figure 4.12.

Windows NT's Print Manager is actually three windows in one:

◆ **Print Manager window.** Provides the tools to work in the other two windows. It also displays the printers installed on your computer as icons, and displays the server to which your computer is connected.

◆ **Printer window.** Displays information about one of the printers to which your computer is connected on the network (the name of the printer appears in the title bar). It shows the printer queue with a variety of values associated with each print job, including the number of pages, the owner of the print job, and the name of the document printing.

◆ **Server dialog box.** (Accessed by choosing the Server Viewer option from the Printer menu.) Displays information about all the printers connected to your computer through the network.

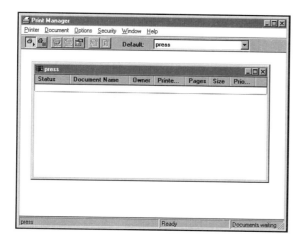

Figure 4.12

The Print Manager.

Summary

As you have seen in this chapter, Windows NT has a "look and feel" similar to Windows 95, but it also has capabilities far more extensive than its 16-bit cousin.

Because Windows NT is a secured operating system, not just an operating environment like Windows 95, its startup and shutdown procedures are much more structured and controlled. Consequently, you have to log on to Windows NT—even if you are running it on a standalone PC on which security is never an issue.

On the surface, Windows NT's Control Panel and other applets look identical to their Windows 95 counterparts. As you look more closely, however, you can see many key enhancements. The Control Panel, for example, has several revamped configuration utilities designed for the system administrator. Additionally, the Print Manager is completely overhauled and now provides extensive control over printers and print jobs.

As you work through the next chapter on installing Windows NT, and actually set up Windows NT on your machine or network, you have much to learn about the 32-bit operating system. Windows 95 users should take comfort in the similarity between the two interfaces. Thus, although you might not understand all the features on your Windows desktop, the resemblance of Windows NT to Windows 95 will make your transition to Windows NT much easier and smoother than you might have thought possible.

Comparing Windows NT and Windows 95

If you are in the position to decide which to purchase, Windows NT or Windows 95, you might legitimately ask why in the world Microsoft has two systems for the desktop. Complicating the issue even more is the fact that each product has a different production schedule, so that one has a better interface and more features than the other at one time, but then the other product catches up and surpasses the other. In this chapter we take a look at the similarities and differences of Windows NT and Windows 95. In truth, industry insiders believe that these two desktop systems will become unified in the not-too-distant future.

Origins of Windows NT and Windows 95

Before Windows 95 there was Windows 3.1. Windows 3.1 was intended for the personal user. This personal user worked on a non-networked computer of limited computing speed and limited memory capacity. Typically, personal computers had roughly 2 or 4 MB of RAM and, by today's standards, a small disk drive of between 100 and 250 MB. Windows 3.1's challenge was to run a graphical interface quickly in a limited computing environment.

Windows NT came onto the scene to answer the needs of business users and to compete with Unix. Unix had the overwhelming market share of client/server environments. In the early days, Unix was a command-line operating system requiring arcane knowledge of many commands that each took a wide assortment of parameters. Entire books were written about just Unix commands, such as sed and awk. The obscurity of the command set gave those who learned the commands the power to perform a wide range of tasks in a short amount of time, but it also ostracized those who did not have the time to learn the command set.

Graphical interfaces finally were developed for Unix. Some of the most common interfaces were Motif and Solaris, both based on the X Windows libraries. Many tasks in Unix, however, remain command-line operations in many Unix interfaces, such as copying and moving files. Some Unix front ends, such as Solaris, created applets that allowed the user to move files from one directory to another graphically. Other flavors of Unix, however, such as IRIX, still do not have a graphical interface for file manipulation.

Windows NT sought to make common system tasks, such as file manipulation, as graphical as they are in Windows 3.1. In theory, making the tasks more graphical would make them easier to perform by a larger number of people. Instead of learning a command set, users could learn how to interact with the graphical interface.

The other thrust of Windows NT was to provide a common operating environment in which a number of operating systems could perform. For example, when you install the Windows NT operating system, you can also run DOS, Windows 95, Windows 3.1, POSIX, and OS/2 applications.

Another goal of Windows NT was to make it portable across platforms. That portability now extends across four hardware platforms: Intel, Alpha AXP, MIPS, and PowerPC. That means that the applications you use on a MIPS platform can also run on an Alpha platform. Portability is of benefit to developers and users.

For developers, the benefit is that they have to make fewer ports of their programs. Previously, an application written for an Intel-based computer had to go through extensive changes so that it could run on a PowerPC-based computer.

Users benefit from increased portability because development costs are lower, which means that software prices can be lower.

Windows NT users were typically working in a networked environment with a series of servers and clients. For that reason, Windows NT included a variety of applications that benefited networked users only. For example, included in Windows NT is a scheduler that enables users to view one another's schedules and thereby schedule meetings. Windows NT also includes an e-mail application so that users can communicate using e-mail.

Blurring the Line Between Business and Personal Computers

Times have changed. The cycle in the computer hardware field is to make hardware faster, more powerful, and cheaper. The average user's system of one or two years ago is light years behind the capabilities of average users today. Compare, for example, the difference between the 386 machine with 2 MB of RAM and 140 MB hard disk with a Pentium computer with 16 MB of RAM and 1 gigabyte of hard disk space.

Because hardware has improved, the capabilities of the average user's machine have grown substantially. Today's personal PC matches the power of the business computer of just a few years ago. New applications now rely more and more on graphics and images that grind 386 performance into the ground. As the hardware has improved, the software manufacturers have pushed the envelope of what is possible on a personal computer. Whereas a few years ago, computer games consisted of a text-based interface, today's multimedia games integrate live actors in a navigable computer-generated background. CD-ROM drives were a novelty several years ago, now, for certain applications, they are a requirement. With the vast amount of information that can be stored on a CD-ROM disc, applications can use videos as part of their interface. Even an application as straight-laced as TurboTax, for example, uses movies to counsel users as they fill out their tax forms.

Only a few years ago, it was rare to find an application larger than 10 or 15 MB. On small disk drives, this amount of storage sometimes represented 10 percent of the available storage space. Now with 1 plus gigabyte drives selling for $300 or less, software developers feel they have the license to make applications very large. Windows 95 consumes roughly 80 MB of memory; Windows NT consumes 90 MB of disk space—and that is just the operating system! You cannot do anything with your computer with just an operating system. Put one of these operating systems on a 140 MB disk with one application and you have exhausted your drive. Now that you can purchase large disk drives so cheaply, developers are requiring you to purchase them—if you want to run the newest and best applications. Although the box for Windows NT Workstation states that you need 90 MB of disk space, Microsoft marketing materials encourage you to buy a drive 500 MB or greater.

And the poor 386 with 4 MB of RAM simply cannot adequately handle the computing requirements of today's operating systems and applications. RAM has not dropped much in price, but developers have asked you to buy it anyway. Windows NT, for example, requires 8 MB of RAM—but that is just for the operating system! Suppose you want to do something, like, run an application! You really have to jump on the 16 MB RAM bandwagon. In fact, although the Windows NT Workstation box says that 8 MB of RAM are required, Microsoft marketing materials suggest that you have a minimum of 16 MB.

As hardware manufacturers develop faster, cheaper, and more powerful devices, software manufacturers will continue to make more and more demands of the computer's resources. This trend will not end until it becomes impossible to make the hardware affordable to the average user: a point in time that is not yet in sight.

So, the great dividing line between the capabilities of home computers and business computers has become blurred. Consequently, the dividing line between the operating system designed for home personal computer users and business users is becoming more and more blurred.

Running Applications

Currently, a user can run just about every Windows 95 application on Windows NT. Windows NT requires slightly tighter guidelines on applications to ensure their reliability, but most major applications pass the test. In fact, all applications now marked with "Designed for Windows 95" must also work with Windows NT.

Starting with version 4.0 of Windows NT, Windows 95 and Windows NT have the same interface.

 Note   If you have Windows NT version 3.5 or 3.51, you can download the Windows 95 interface for Windows NT.

If you were to run down the time line about a year from now, you would see most of the differences disappearing between Windows 95 and Windows NT. The interface will be the same, and the operating systems will run the same applications. The only remaining differences between Windows 95 and Windows NT will be that Windows 95 does not offer a server whereas Windows NT does, and NT might support multiple operating systems, whereas Windows 95 will not.

Picking an Operating System Based on Your Needs

Today there remain some important differences between Windows 95 and Windows NT Workstation. The differences make one or the other operating system suitable to different computing environment. Use table 5.1 to quickly determine which operating system is more appropriate to your current needs and then use tables 5.2 and 5.3 to look more carefully at the similarities and differences between the operating systems.

Table 5.1 identifies three kinds of users:

- ◆ Those who use portable computers
- ◆ Those who work in engineering, scientific, or software development environments
- ◆ Those who work in various businesses who use a workstation or desktop computer.

Because business use covers such a wide range of application needs, the table breaks down the needs of business users into a variety of categories: compatible with existing software, security needs, the need for highly reliable software, and so on.

TABLE 5.1
Standard Uses of Windows 95 versus Windows NT Workstation

Application	Windows 95	Windows NT Workstation
Portable use	X	
Software Development		X
Widely compatible with existing software	X	
Need security features		X
Need a server in order to share assets		X
Need highly reliable applications		X

The next three sections explore the needs of each of these kinds of users so that you can understand in more detail why one operating system might be better than the other for these kinds of users.

Portable Computer Users

Portable computer users include all of those people who work with computers other than workstations and desktops. Portable computers include, for example, laptops, notebooks, Personal Information Managers (PIMS), and hand-held computers dedicated to specific tasks (computers that inventory personnel might carry while taking inventory of items in a warehouse). In a world where the computer is automating routine tasks to help reduce errors and speed up the time it takes to complete tasks, more and more dedicated, hand-held computers will arrive on the scene. The slightly larger computers, laptops and notebooks, are already a necessity for people who work away from the office. People who travel for a living, such as salespeople, trainers, and others use portable computers to accomplish tasks they would otherwise complete by hand.

All of these computers have a common set of operating system requirements:

◆ Integrated application environments that include e-mail, remote networking, and fax.

◆ Compatibility with current workstation or desktop operating system.

◆ Compatibility with applications and devices running on their workstation or desktop computer.

◆ Low RAM consumption.

◆ Low disk space requirements.

◆ Low battery consumption.

◆ Easy, plug-and-play configuration for attached devices.

◆ Simple file transfer between the portable computer and the workstation or desktop computer.

All of these requirements for the portable computer favor Windows 95 over Windows NT.

Engineering, Science, and Software Development

The needs of engineers, scientists, statisticians, software engineers, and other technical users most often includes the use of processing-intensive applications. These kinds

of applications run on the fastest platforms and require the most sophisticated operating systems. Often these applications have to run on multiple platforms, including *x*86, Alpha, PowerPC, or MIPS, that support symmetric multiprocessing (SMP).

Because the applications require high-performance computers and operating systems, Windows NT is the appropriate choice.

Business Uses

If you are buying an operating system for the business environment, either Windows 95, Windows NT, or a combination of the two might be appropriate. It all depends on your application needs, your budget, and your current computer hardware setup. The following three sections should help you decide between Windows NT and Windows 95, according to your business needs.

How Compatible Is Your Hardware and Software with Windows NT?

The cost of hardware and software can be a significant consideration when you not only factor in the cost of the hardware but also the cost of installing it. If you have had any system administration experience at all or have basic knowledge about IRQ, DMA, and memory address conflicts, you know that hardware and software installation can often be anything but trivial. In this section we look at some of the charges your company might incur by choosing one operating system over the other, for example:

◆ If you are not in a client/server environment, does your budget allow you to purchase the networking cards, cables, and the labor cost to install a network?

◆ Do you already have a server? If not, do you have funds to buy one?

◆ Do your workstations have 16 MB of RAM (12 MB is the minimum) and an extra 90 MB of disk space to hold Windows NT?

◆ Do you currently have a network administrator?

If you are not in a client/server environment already, how many people would be on your network? Client/server applications are more expensive than desktop applications when you have a small number of networked computers. The tables turn when the number of users you have is larger. System administration is also reduced when you have a large number of users in a client/server environment. One administrator can coordinate security, software upgrades, and general troubleshooting. Installing software and troubleshooting a large number of unnetworked desktop computers takes more time than in the networked environment. If the number of desktops is small, however, employing a system administrator might well be an unnecessary expense. The bottom line is, if you have many desktops and can afford it, networking is the way to go. In that case, Windows NT is the correct choice. If you do not have many desktops and security is not a major concern, you can remain unnetworked and install Windows 95.

If you are not in a client/server environment already, you can see that there are a number of hidden start up costs. If your budget does not allow you to create a network, or to upgrade the hardware on your network to handle Windows NT, Windows 95 is your best choice.

◆ Does your computer environment have peripherals and other devices that are supported by Windows NT drivers? For example, are your video cards, drive controllers, network interface cards, and proprietary 3270 devices compatible with Windows NT? You can find out easily enough by looking in the book that comes with Windows NT called, *Hardware Compatibility List.* It contains a list of all the devices that support Windows NT.

If your current peripherals and other devices do not support Windows NT, do you have the budget to replace them? If not, you might go with Windows 95. If your devices do support Windows NT or you do have the budget to buy new equipment, Windows NT is the better choice.

◆ Can the applications that you currently own run in Windows NT? Do they require Windows (or DOS) device drivers or TSRs? Have your applications been ported to Windows NT? Is there a client/server equivalent of your applications?

All future applications written for Windows 95 will also run in Windows NT. Older applications, however, might not. Windows NT places slightly higher restrictions on applications than Windows 95. Most Microsoft applications will run on both platforms, but you need to ask the manufacturer of other applications if they can operate in the Windows NT environment. If all of your current applications are compatible with the Windows NT environment, choosing Windows NT is a good idea. If, however, a lot of your software is not compatible, you have to consider whether or not you want to buy new software, train people how to use the software, take the time to port (if you can) old materials into the new software or keep the old software around so that you can access old materials.

Is Operational Reliability Crucial?

Windows 95 has actually turned out to be a very reliable system. Windows 3.1 was plagued with application crashes from memory and kernel errors.

Windows NT, however, was painstakingly created so that the operating system is completely isolated from running applications. What this means is that an application might fail because of its own errors, but the application crash cannot cause the

Windows NT operating system to crash. System crashes can cause real problems in some situations. Some of those situations include customer-oriented applications in which business is lost or a customer's patience is stretched because he or she has to wait for the system to reboot. Likewise, if your application is transferring information over a network on a regular basis, system crashes can cause the loss of data and real headaches in trying to recover.

 Note In the Windows NT environment, Win16 applications can still run. They are more crash resistant because Windows NT runs them in separate address spaces.

Win32 applications run more reliably in both Windows NT and Windows 95 because they also run applications in separate memory address areas, use multiple asynchronous message queues, and have structured exception handling. Even with Win32 applications, Windows NT provides a more reliable environment than Windows 95 because applications running in NT are isolated from the operating system and also because Windows NT can be configured to automatically restart applications that have crashed.

If the issue of application execution reliability is crucial to your business, Windows NT is the better choice.

How Important Is Security in Your Business?

Many kinds of data can be very important to your business. Human relations information is information, for example, that should not be shared. Company secrets, projects, or products might also warrant security measures.

While Windows 95 can be configured to help prevent naive users from corrupting their setup, Windows 95 does not have the security mechanism that can prevent malicious data stealing or corruption.

Windows NT, on the other hand, has significant security measures. The Windows NT system administrator can, for example, restrict a user's access to a file, a directory, a tree of directories, or to the entire system.

Users are identified by their logon ID and their password. Not knowing a password, or not having a logon ID in the system can prevent a user from even logging on to the system.

The system administrator can assign each user a set of permissions so that once users gain access to the system, they have a limited or unlimited use of the files, directories, and the execution of applications in the file system.

If system security is an issue for your business, Windows NT is the appropriate choice.

Similarities and Differences Between Windows 95 and Windows NT

When you look from the outside at Windows 95 and Windows NT, you notice that Windows 95 has caught up with many of the features of Windows NT. For that reason, it is sometimes hard to see how the operating systems are the same and how they are different.

In the next several sections we will look at the similarities and differences between the operating systems.

Similarities Between Windows 95 and Windows NT Workstation

Although Windows NT and Windows 95 were originally developed for different audiences, they share many features and technologies, including a common interface, support for 32-bit applications, OLE, and networking.

In the near future both platforms will share:

◆ Plug-and-Play capabilities

◆ 3D OpenGL APIs

◆ Multimedia APIs

Table 5.2 looks in more detail at the features of Windows NT and Windows 95 that are the same today or will be the same in the very near future.

TABLE 5.2
Windows NT and Windows 95 Similarities

Features	Windows 95	Windows NT Workstation
Application Support		
Win32 API support for 32 bit applications	Yes	Yes
OLE to associated data across applications	Yes	Yes
Preemptive multitasking of Win32 applications	Yes	Yes

Features	Windows 95	Windows NT Workstation
Runs all Win16 applications	Yes	No
Multimedia APIs, including dibEngine, directDraw, DirectSound, direct Input, Reality Lab 3D graphics libraries	Yes	Future
OpenGL graphics libraries used in 3D graphics	Future	Yes

Configuration and Interface

Features	Windows 95	Windows NT Workstation
Auto-detection of hardware during installation	Yes	Yes
Auto-configuration of hardware during installations	Yes	Yes
New Windows user interface	Yes	Yes
Plug-and-Play that helps you configure hardware as you add it to your system	Yes	Future

Networking

Features	Windows 95	Windows NT Workstation
LAN and peer-to-peer networking using the following protocols: TCP/IP, IPX/SPX, DDLSS, and NetBEUI	Yes	Yes
Open networking architecture which allows you to use a variety of transports, drivers, clients, and extensibility for including the use of third party networking applications	Yes	Yes
Remote Access Service (RAS) included	Yes	Yes
Universal inbox for e-mail and fax included	Yes	Future
Microsoft Network (MSN) client software included	Yes	Future

Administration

Features	Windows 95	Windows NT Workstation
Open administration architecture allows for third-party system administration applications	Yes	Yes

continues

TABLE 5.2, CONTINUED
Windows NT and Windows 95 Similarities

Features	Windows 95	Windows NT Workstation
Supports SNMP and DMI	Yes	Yes
Desktop configuration controlled by system policies	Yes	Future
User logons allow consistent computer configuration even when working on different workstations	Yes	Yes
Can monitor system performance remotely	Yes	Yes
Peripheral Support		
Fully compatible with 386DX, 486, and Pentium platforms	Yes	Yes
Includes disk compression	Yes (VFAT)	Yes (NTFS)
Support for PCMCIA (without rebooting system after adding a device)	Yes	Future
Technical Support		
Engineering team to solve problems at client's site	Yes	Yes
Service Pack includes updating for drivers, components, and problem fixes	Yes	Yes

As the table shows, NT Workstation and Windows 95 have a great many similarities. The next section, however, shows you their differences.

Differences Between Windows 95 and Windows NT

Originally, Windows NT and the rest of the Windows family were very different. Each were aimed at a different audience. The previous section shows how those differences have narrowed. There remain differences, however, between Windows 95 and Windows NT; differences that Microsoft expects to maintain.

Windows NT, for example, has a server part that Windows 95 does not. The Windows NT Server has extensive administration functions that allow system administrators to create permission sets for users that allow them, or do not allow them, to access the network and directories on servers. Performance monitors allow system administrators to monitor server usage. Windows 95 has none of these features, although you can use Windows 95 as a client for a Windows NT server.

Table 5.3 lists the differences between the two operating systems. Some differences are simply a matter of degree. Other differences show complete incompatibilities.

Before purchasing one of these operating systems, it is important to read through this table so that you can see at a glance whether or not the hardware and software you presently own will work in the Windows NT or Windows 95 environment.

TABLE 5.3
Differences Between Windows 95 and Windows NT

Features	Windows 95	Windows NT Workstation
Applications		
Runs MS-DOS applications	Yes	Many
Runs IBM Presentation Manager (through version 1.3)	No	Yes
Runs POSIX 1003.1 applications	No	Yes
System Resource Capacity	Large	Unlimited
Reliability		
Preemptive multitasking for Win16 applications	No	Yes
Operating system isolated from Win16 applications	No	Yes
Operating system isolated from Win32 applications	No	Yes
Automatic recovery from system failures	No	Yes
Files, directories, and applications can be hidden from specific users	No	Yes

continues

TABLE 5.3, CONTINUED
Differences Between Windows 95 and Windows NT

Features	Windows 95	Windows NT Workstation
Support for Peripherals		
Runs MS-DOS device drivers	Yes	No
Runs Win16 device drivers	Yes	No
Supports multi-processor configurations without changing applications or operating system	No	Yes
Minimum RAM required	8 MB	12 MB
Disk space required	40 MB	90 MB
Runs on a variety of platforms, including PowerPc, MIPS, and DEC Alpha AXF-based RISC systems	No	Yes

There are, in fact, many important differences between NT Workstation and Windows 95. You can use this list to help you decide which operating system is more appropriate to your needs.

Summary

This chapter looked at the history of Windows NT and the rest of the Windows family. You saw that although Windows NT was originally designed for a very different user than the user of Windows 3.1, Windows 95 and Windows NT share a great deal of features.

The chapter also took a look at many of the differences that still separate the two operating systems; differences that shall remain over time.

Several ways were suggested in which you could determine which operating system was more appropriate to your needs. You matched the type of user you are with an operating system, and you also looked in great detail at the requirements each operating system makes on your current hardware platform.

C H A P T E R

6

Installing Windows NT 3.51

The installation process for Window NT is simple, much like the installation of Windows 95. If you choose a custom installation, you need to know a number of things about your system.

This chapter tells you what you need to know to complete a Windows NT installation, including the following:

◆ Understanding hardware requirements

◆ Preparing to install Windows NT

◆ Understanding Windows NT setup

◆ Configuring Windows NT for users

◆ Solving installation problems

By preparing for the installation using the ideas in this chapter, you can make the installation run as smoothly as possible.

Understanding Hardware Requirements

The hardware requirements for Windows NT are more stringent than those to which the casual user is accustomed. The following list summarizes Microsoft's recommended minimum hardware configuration:

◆ A 32-bit processor, 386 (25 MHz) or higher. A Pentium is the preferred platform.

Note If your computer barely meets minimum hardware requirements, Windows NT runs like molasses. Instead of increasing your computer's performance, the 90 MB operating system drags out the simplest commands.

◆ Alternatively, Windows NT runs on RISC-based microprocessors, such as the MIPS R4000, PowerPC, and DEC Alpha.

  If you are a PC user, skip the discussions concerning RISC-based computers.

◆ A high-resolution video display, VGA or better.

◆ A minimum of 90 MB of free hard disk space (70 MB for the operating system; 20 MB minimum for the swap file).

◆ A high-density floppy drive for x86 processors. If you have only a low-density drive (one that holds only 1.2 MB of information), you need to buy a higher-density drive that holds either 1.44 MB or 2.88 MB of memory.

Make sure your computer's BIOS supports a 2.88 MB drive before you buy one.

Note Windows NT no longer supports 5.25 inch floppy drives.

◆ For RISC processors, a SCSI CD-ROM drive. Windows NT doesn't support all CD-ROM drives or SCSI controller cards. Check with manufacturers for Windows NT compatibility.

Note Access CompuServe (WINNT forum) to find out whether a drive or card is supported. Or, if you already own Windows NT, look in the Hardware Compatibility Guide that is included in the Windows NT product package.

◆ A minimum of 12 MB of RAM (16 MB is recommended).

Remember that minimum requirements mean minimum performance. You can put premium gas in a Model T, but it doesn't run any faster than on regular gas. Likewise, you can use Windows NT on a relatively slow computer, but program execution may be slower than with Windows 95. Exceed the minimum hardware requirements by as much as you can afford.

Optional hardware includes the following:

◆ A mouse or other pointing device.

◆ An SCSI CD-ROM drive for x86-based processors (required for RISC processors).

◆ A network card if you want to run Windows NT on a network.

The CD-ROM drive for x86-based computers is used simply to install Windows NT and future Windows NT applications. You can install Windows NT instead from 21 high-density floppies.

Windows NT can run on individual computers, but many of its features are geared for network environments such as sophisticated security, mail, and scheduling systems. Thus, if your computer is not on a network, you should consider whether Windows NT will benefit you.

Preparing to Install Windows NT

The Windows NT Setup program requires the following information:

◆ If your computer is on a network, you must know the computer's name and the name of the workgroup or domain to which your computer belongs.

   A workgroup is a group of servers and computers that can easily share information in a peer-to-peer manner (similar in functionality to Windows for Workgroups).

   A domain is a group of computers and servers, but a single security system governs access to the individual components of the group.

◆ If a printer is connected directly to your computer, you must know the port (LPT1, for example), and the brand and model number of the printer.

◆ If your computer is on a network, you must know the following features about the network adapter card in your computer:

The name of the adapter card

The Interrupt Request Number (IRQ)

The base I/O address

◆ You must know the partitions on your hard drive using disk-compression products. You cannot place Windows NT on a compressed partition.

◆ You must know the amount of free space on the hard drive. Eliminate files and applications from your hard disk until it has 90 MB or more of free memory. (You should know this information before you install Windows NT.)

◆ Decide whether you want to keep Windows NT as an upgrade to Windows 95 or as a separate operating system.

Consult your network card manual or your system administrator for information.

Understanding Setup

You can install Windows NT in the following three ways:

◆ From a CD-ROM or floppy disks

◆ Over a network

◆ By using the Computer Profile Setup

If your computer has a CD-ROM or floppy drive, install Windows NT directly from those drives. Windows NT takes more hard disk space when you install over a network.

The Computer Profile Setup enables system administrators in large corporations with many identical computer platforms to install Windows NT easily.

Installing Windows NT from a CD-ROM or Floppy Disks

Windows NT comes with a boot disk and a CD-ROM (or a set of 21 floppy disks). It has the information necessary to initiate Setup, including the Setup application, mechanisms to identify SCSI adapters on the computer, a list of the most popular SCSI device drivers (located in the *.SYS file), and the Setup instruction routine (called TXTSETUP.INF).

Windows NT does not support all CD-ROM drives and SCSI controllers. If you have problems, consult the manufacturer of your SCSI controller and ask if there is an updated device driver that is compatible with Windows NT. If there is not, consider buying a compatible controller card.

If your SCSI driver is Windows NT-compatible but is not contained on the boot disk, copy the driver to the boot disk. Then you should be able to proceed with the setup process by using your CD-ROM drive.

 Note   An SCSI connector is a 25- or 50-pin (SCSI-2) cable that enables fast throughput of data.

When you are ready to begin installation, put the boot disk in drive A (and the CD-ROM disk in its drive, if you have one) and reboot the computer. The Setup program begins in text mode. During the setup process, Setup reboots your PC again; at that time, the installation continues. Later, after you reboot the computer again, the program continues in graphical mode. The following discussions explain both of these modes.

A nice feature of the Setup program is that it creates an emergency disk. You use this disk to recover your system if you inadvertently erase a system file or the Boot Loader. To create the emergency disk, you need three blank 3.5-inch floppies.

Text-Mode Setup

The *text-mode* portion of Setup works like a traditional DOS display: no windows, few graphics, mostly text.

After you reboot the computer with the boot disk, the Setup Loader file (SETUPLDR) loads a file (Windows NTDETECT) that detects the hardware in your system. Setup then gives you the opportunity to choose Custom Setup or Express Setup.

Express Setup uses the hardware configuration detected with Windows NTDETECT, and assumes what you might like Windows NT to install.

Custom Setup enables you to control other important features, such as the size and location of the paging file. If you have more than one hard disk, or your hard disk has more than one partition, you might want Windows NT to put the paging file on the least-fragmented hard disk for optimum speed. Setup might otherwise automatically choose the drive with the most free space.

After you choose Express Setup or Custom Setup, Setup looks in your computer for one of the SCSI drivers listed on the boot disk. If it finds one of the drivers, it accesses the CD-ROM drive. If it doesn't, it continues to check hardware features such as the display adapter type, mouse, machine type, and keyboard.

Setup then asks you to confirm the disk drive, partition, and directory name where Windows NT is to be copied. Here, you can create or delete partitions on the disk. You might want to put Windows NT on its own partition if the rest of the disk is compressed. You also can change from the present disk file system, such as FAT (the file system used with DOS and Windows 3.*x*), to the Windows NTFS format.

If you change the format of a disk, you can reformat or convert from one disk filing system to another. Be careful! If you choose to reformat the partition, all files in the partition are destroyed. Converting the format, on the other hand, preserves the files on the partition.

The Windows NT File System (Windows NTFS) offers a number of advantages over FAT, including the following:

◆ Enables Windows NT's security system to enforce various access rights to files and directories

◆ Keeps an event log that you can use to restore the system if a power failure or other problem happens

◆ Accepts file names of up to 256 characters

◆ Enables DOS, Windows, OS/2, and POSIX programs, running through Windows NT, to access Windows NTFS files

Only Windows NT has access to partitions formatted in Windows NTFS. If you want to run DOS or OS/2 sometimes, instead of Windows NT, use the FAT format. DOS and OS/2 do not have access to files on Windows NTFS partitions.

If you format your entire hard disk with Windows NTFS, you can't even run DOS from your hard disk (although you can still run DOS-based applications through Windows NT).

You can change the file systems on any partition after you complete Setup. To change from Windows NTFS to FAT or HPFS (OS/2's high-performance file system), you must reformat the partition, which destroys the information on it. You need to back up all files on the partition before you reformat.

After you specify the destination for Windows NT, Setup uses CHKDSK to check the partition to confirm that it is in good shape. If so, Setup then looks on your hard disk to see whether Windows 3.*x* or Windows for Workgroups is installed.

If it is, Setup recommends that you upgrade to Windows NT, which means that Windows NT will go in the same directory as Windows 3.*x.* You can choose, instead, to create a new path for the installation (such as \WINNT), and leave Windows 3.*x* as is.

If you choose the default setting, it installs on top of Windows 95, and it is removed from your system.

At startup, you can run DOS, Windows 3.*x*, or Windows NT. If Windows NT is in a different directory from Windows 3.*x*, the two do not readily share information.

After you decide whether to upgrade Windows 3.*x* or provide a separate directory for Windows NT, Setup copies the core files of Windows NT to the hard disk, including the files that enable you to boot and operate in graphical mode. After you remove the boot disk in drive A, reboot your computer. The computer screen turns blue, which is your confirmation that Windows NT is loading. Windows NT then displays the device drivers it is loading into the system.

Graphical-Mode Setup

After rebooting, Setup continues in *graphical mode*, which looks like a traditional Windows display. It has windows, rich graphics, buttons, and task-completion indicators.

The first window that appears in graphical mode prompts you for your name and the name of your company. The second window asks for the name of your computer. Ask your system administrator if a name is already chosen for your computer or if the computer name is determined by applying a certain pattern or logic, such as DepartmentName02.

ote   Do not name your computer with the domain's name or workgroup's name. Windows NT will reject your choice.

If you chose Express Setup, Setup continues the installation process automatically. If you chose Custom Setup, however, you can install printer drivers, install network drivers, and create groups of applications already on your drive. If you install these features, Setup asks for the following information:

◆ **Virtual Memory.** Setup asks for the location and size of the paging file (PAGEFILE.SYS). The *paging file* is where Windows NT swaps data from RAM to disk when too much data must be loaded into RAM. Because the data is on disk, not RAM, it is called *virtual memory*.

Setup puts the paging file at the root directory of the hard disk because it operates faster that way. Setup displays the minimum size of the paging file (usually 20 MB) and a larger, recommended size.

If you chose Express Setup, Windows NT automatically makes your paging file the recommended size. In Custom Setup, however, you have the opportunity to change the size of the paging file, as long as it equals or exceeds minimum requirements.

◆ **Printer Setup.** You have full configuration control over your printers. You can specify a default printer, the port to connect it to, the size of its memory, the paper size and tray, and a variety of other variables.

Setup enables you to install printer drivers for printers shared by non-Windows NT computers. If, however, you need access to a printer shared by a Windows NT computer, you only need to put the printer drivers on the computer that is sharing the printer.

◆ **Network Setup.** Setup automatically detects and displays information about your network card, including the I/O port address, the memory address setting for the card, and the IRQ setting. You can check and correct these settings with Custom Setup.

After you approve the settings, Setup constructs the default client/server relationship and installs the appropriate network services and support files.

Setup displays the Network Control Panel so that you can confirm the software and hardware configuration of your network. After you approve the settings, Setup binds the network card to the system.

◆ **Workgroup and Domain Setup.** Setup enables you to join a workgroup, a domain, or both.

If you join a workgroup, Setup asks for your username and password. If you join a domain, Setup asks for the domain to which you want to belong. If the name of your computer is not listed in the domain, you must supply the name of an administrator and a password. Otherwise, you cannot join the domain.

 Note If you work on an isolated computer, it makes no sense to join a workgroup or a domain.

◆ **Application Setup.** Setup creates the application groups that are familiar to Windows 3.*x* users, including Main, Accessories, Startup, Games, and (not so familiar) Administrative Tools.

Note The Administrative Tools group in Windows NT is accessible only to members of the administrative group. Administrators use these tools to manage Windows NT. For example, administrators create users and user groups on the system, and define their access rights and permission sets (such as read-only permissions).

Setup detects all the applications on the hard disk and places them as icons into the submenu displayed by clicking on the Programs option in the Start button menu, as long as Windows NT and Windows 3.x are in the same directory. In Custom Setup, you can create the groups manually.

Now that you have completed the major installation steps, Setup is ready to make an emergency disk for you. Setup makes sure that the disk in drive A is not the boot disk before it copies the configuration information onto the disk.

Because you specified the name of the computer and the name of the workgroup and domain to which it belongs, the emergency disk applies only to your computer. You can't use someone else's emergency disk on your computer in the case of a disaster. Be sure to keep the emergency disk with the computer at all times.

To complete Setup, you are prompted to enter your time zone. Choose it from the drop-down list. Remove the emergency disk, reboot your computer, and begin to enjoy Windows NT.

When you reboot your computer, Windows NT starts. If you have other operating systems on the hard disk, the Windows NT Boot Loader asks you to choose the operating system you want to boot. (It starts Windows NT by default if you do not select another system within 25 seconds.)

Installing Windows NT over a Network

If a corporation has a large number of computers, the WINNT Setup utility makes it easier to install Windows NT on every computer. Windows NT Setup records all the Setup files found on the CD-ROM and floppy disks into a server directory, the *WINNT sharepoint*. (Setup /n, in Windows 95, performs a similar action.) All other computers on the network then install Windows NT from the sharepoint.

WINNT Setup is just like Windows NT Setup, except that it sits on a file server in its own directory, and it creates the boot disk on client computers.

The command to install the WINNT sharepoint is

```
SETUP -n -i initial.inf -s <source_path> -d <destination_path>
```

You can install a WINNT sharepoint on a non-Windows NT-supported network. The command that creates the WINNT sharepoint must run Windows NT, however. You must, therefore, install Windows NT on at least one computer in the network to perform this action.

Although you can install Windows NT over a non-Windows NT-supported network, your computer no longer sees that network after you install and run Windows NT.

If you use WINNT Setup to set up Windows NT on a computer, WINNT Setup first creates the boot disk that comes with the CD-ROM disk (and is the first disk in the set of installation floppy disks). WINNT Setup then downloads all files necessary to complete the installation into a directory called WIN_NT.~LS on the local computer.

WINNT Setup instructs you to reboot your computer with the boot disk in drive A. The rest of the setup procedure is identical to that described for the CD-ROM and floppy-disk installation.

 Note Starting with version 3.5, you cannot use 5.25-inch floppies during installation. For more information about installing Windows NT without the use of floppies, see "Installing Windows NT Without 5.25 Inch Floppies" later in this chapter.

Besides the obvious convenience of using WINNT Setup to install Windows NT on a large number of computers, WINNT Setup has some other advantages:

◆ Because the installation files reside on the local hard disk, the installation procedure goes more quickly because accessing a hard disk is faster than accessing a CD-ROM or floppy disk.

◆ More than one computer can use WINNT Setup simultaneously.

◆ If the system administrator customizes the Windows NT installation, that customization carries through to all computers on the network.

As you can see, there are many advantages to installing NT Workstation over a network.

Installing Windows NT by Using Computer Profile Setup

The Computer Profile Setup is appropriate for businesses in which all the computers on the network have identical configurations.

You complete the Computer Profile Setup in two steps. In the first step, Create Profile, you create an installation template. In the second step, Install Profile, you apply the template to all the computers.

You run the *Create Profile* utility on a computer that is configured exactly the same as all others in the network. This utility detects a wide variety of information about the computer's setup, including device drivers, program groups, and user databases. It then puts that information into a file (which has a CPS extension) with all other installation files.

The *Install Profile* utility takes the information in the CPS file and uses it as an installation template for all similar computers in the corporation. The user is prompted to supply only the name of the computer and the domain to which it belongs, if any.

Installing Windows NT on a RISC-Based Computer

Installing Windows NT on a RISC-based computer is the same as installing it on an *x*86 (Intel-based) computer. Only the task of starting the Setup program (from the CD-ROM disk) is different.

You can install Windows NT only from a CD-ROM disk on RISC-based computers. Consult the manufacturer of your system to find out the correct way to boot your system from a CD-ROM disk.

Although different computers start in different ways, once the Setup program starts, it is identical to the *x*86 installation described previously.

You must create a FAT partition, called the *system partition*, on your hard disk. The hard disk must contain at least 2 MB of memory to hold the files that load Windows NT, including OSLOADER.EXE and HAL.DLL (in the \OS\NT directory).

You can make the partition large enough to include all the Windows NT files. If your hard disk doesn't have a system partition, consult the manufacturer's instructions for creating one.

An installation procedure that works for some RISC-based computers is as follows:

1. After restarting your computer with the CD-ROM disk in its drive, select Run A Program from the menu on the ARC screen.

2. Type **cd:\mips\setupldr** at the prompt and press Enter.

   If Setup doesn't begin, try substituting the full device name in place of cd:.

If this procedure does not work for your system, consult your RISC manuals.

Installing Windows NT Without 5.25 Inch Floppies

When you install Windows NT, you are asked to supply three blank 3.5 inch floppies. Earlier versions of Windows NT allowed you to use 5.25 inch floppies; this version of Windows NT does not. If your computer has a 3.5-inch drive, you can consult your hardware documentation to find out how to boot off of the 3.5-inch floppy instead of the 5.25-inch floppy. If you do not own a 3.5-inch drive, you can either buy one for about $40, or install Windows NT without using floppies at all. To avoid using floppies, you must install Windows NT from a CD ROM or from a network distribution point.

Installing Windows NT Without Any Floppies

You can install Windows NT using the CD ROM even if you do not have floppy drives. To do so, you must use the /b switch with the winnt or winnt32 command. All of the files that are normally copied to 3.5-inch floppies are copied instead to temporary files on the first hard disk Windows NT finds that has enough room to hold the files. These files help you restore your system to its pre-NT state, should you ever decide to uninstall Windows NT. The only disadvantage to this method is the extra hard disk space required for the temporary files.

If you want to delete the temporary files from your hard disk where the boot information is stored, you need to store the boot information on disks. To do that, use the winnt command with the /o parameter. This command prompts you to put disks in the drive (when appropriate).

Installing Windows NT Automatically

You can use the unattended-setup mode to install or upgrade Windows NT. This setup method saves time when you are installing NT on five or more computers or when upgrading one or more computers.

Because setup is run unattended, you do not need to provide empty floppy disks. Setup records the pre-NT configuration data in temporary files on the hard disk. Make sure there is sufficient hard disk space on each computer to hold NT and the temporary files.

If you are upgrading to the latest version of Windows NT, use the winnt32 command along with the /u switch. The /u switch stands for "unattended."

If you are making a new installation of Windows NT, you must create an answer file.

The file contains the answers to the questions NT Setup asks during installation. Appendix B shows a sample answer file. You would not want to take the time to create an answer file for just one or two installations. It only makes sense to create an answer file if you are installing NT on five or more workstations.

When setup is run unattended, Setup does not check for floating-point division errors in Intel Pentium chips. To determine whether or not this is a problem in your system, run the utility pentnt. For more information about running pentnt, see the section, "Detecting Floating-Point Division Errors."

Configuring the Operating Systems

After Windows NT is installed, the system administrator has duties to perform for each of Windows NT's operating systems. The following sections discuss these responsibilities.

Detecting Floating-Point Division Errors

It was discovered that the Intel Pentium chip makes a floating-point division error in very rare cases. Most people do not have to worry about this shortcoming. If you run applications that perform extensive statistical number crunching, or if you want to correct the chip error for your peace of mind, you should disable the floating-point hardware on your processor.

 Note   You might also contact Intel to see if they will replace your defective chip.

If Setup detects the floating-point division error in your processor, it prompts you to disable the floating-point hardware on your processor. Windows NT then takes over floating-point processing by emulating the hardware.

If you choose not to disable the hardware during setup, you can use the pentnt utility on the command line at any time to disable the floating-point hardware.

The pentnt utility allows you to correct the floating-point error in two ways:

◆ Conditional emulation

◆ Forced emulation

The conditional-emulation option turns off only the floating-point hardware and enables floating-point emulation only if the pentnt utility detects the Pentium chip error. To correct the error in this manner, use the following command on the command line:

```
pentnt -c
```

The forced-emulation option turns off the floating-point hardware and enables floating-point emulation whether or not the pentnt utility detects the Pentium chip error. To correct the error in this manner, use the following command on the command line:

```
pentnt -f
```

Controlling Logon Scripts

Logon scripts automatically do such things as map network drives and copy files that the Program Manager or Explorer might refer to in the Startup group. You can specify that these scripts complete before any application in the Startup group starts. These scripts are user-specific.

To specify whether or not the scripts should complete before applications in the Startup group are run, use the User Profile Editor.

At the bottom of the window, click on the check box called Wait For Logon Script to Complete Before Starting Explorer if you want the scripts to complete.

Configuring the Uninterruptible Power Supply

An uninterruptible power supply (UPS) is a battery that feeds power to your computer in the event of an electrical outage. Despite its name, the UPS lasts for a finite amount of time. When the battery is about to be depleted, the UPS service in Windows NT warns users of the power failure and shuts down the system safely.

The UPS service by itself, of course, does nothing. You must purchase a UPS to work with the UPS service. Before purchasing a UPS, check the hardware-compatibility list that accompanies Windows NT to make sure the UPS and its serial cable are compatible with Windows NT.

You use the UPS window to set up a variety of options, including

◆ the port that is connected to the UPS device

◆ when the UPS sends a message to Windows NT that it should shut down

◆ the command file to execute when a power outage occurs

◆ the expected battery life

◆ the delay between the power outage and the warning message

To configure the UPS service, use the following procedure:

1. Double-click on the UPS icon in the Control Panel. Windows NT displays the UPS window.

2. Click on the Uninterruptible Power Supply is installed on check box.

3. Click on the down arrow to choose the port to which the UPS is attached.

4. Click on the Power Failure Signal check box if your UPS can send a signal that the power has failed.

5. Click on the Low battery signal at least 2 minutes before shutdown check box if your UPS can send a signal based on low power.

6. Click on the Remote UPS Shutdown check box if your UPS can receive a signal from the UPS service to shut down.

7. Click on the positive or negative radio button associated with each check box you checked in the UPS Configuration section. The polarities specify how your UPS communicates with the UPS service.

8. Click on the up or down arrows in the Expected Battery Life field to specify how long your UPS can power your computer.

9. Click on the up or down arrows in the Battery Recharge Time field to specify the number of minutes the UPS must charge for every minute it supplies power to the computer.

10. Click on the up and down arrows in the Time Between Power Failure field to specify the interval between the time a power outage is detected and the time a warning message is sent to the user.

11. Click on the up and down arrows in the Delay Between Warning Messages field to specify the interval between the initial warning message and the time the UPS service asks the users to stop using the computer.

12. If you have a command file that you would like run just before system shutdown, such as closing all remote connections, click on the Execute Command File check box and type the pathname and filename of the command file in the File Name: field.

Note Command files have one of the following extensions: .bat, .cmd, .exe, or .com, and they usually reside in the *systemRoot*\\system32 directory.

13. Click on the OK button.

After configuring the UPS service, it is important to test it. You do not want to wait for a real power outage to serve as the first test of your configuration. To simulate a power outage, pull the plug on the UPS device. Watch your computer for the notifications you specified in the UPS window.

You can take greatest advantage of the UPS service by coordinating its operation with other system services, including Windows NT Alerter, Messenger, and Event Log services. These services alert specified users that a power failure has occurred and that their remote connection to your computer must terminate immediately. The Event Log service records the event in the log file.

Coordinating all of these services requires that these services start automatically at bootup. You can specify that on the Services window, which you can display by clicking on the Services icon in the Control Panel.

You can specify which users and computers receive alerts in the Server window, which you can display by double-clicking on the Server icon in the Control Panel. For those computers to receive the alert messages, they each must run the Messenger service.

Configuring the Windows NT Environment

The system administrator can perform the following tasks to configure Windows NT for users:

◆ Set up accounts for users in workgroups and domains by using User Manager.

The User Manager, an application in the Administrative Tools group in The Start button menu, enables system administrators to create users and user groups.

◆ Set up access privileges for users by using the User Profile Editor. You can, for example, restrict the user from accessing games, specific directories, or the **F**ile **R**un menu.

◆ Define various user variables—for example, the local group to which the user belongs, the home directory, and the automatic expiration date of the account.

All of the administrative tasks help ensure the security of your system and its files.

Configuring the Windows 95 Environment

As in the past, all environment information for Windows 95 is in the WIN.INI and SYSTEM.INI files. If Windows 95 and Windows NT are in the same directory, Windows NT can use and update these files to configure the Windows environment. Windows NT, however, stores environmental information in a database called the Registry, not in these files.

If the operating systems are in the same directory, Windows NT can coordinate the two Windows environments in the following ways:

◆ Windows NT records the information in WIN.INI and SYSTEM.INI files into the Registry each time you start Windows NT. The changes you make to the Windows 95 environment transfer to the Windows NT environment.

◆ Changes made to the Windows NT environment also transfer to the Windows 95 environment. Windows NT updates the WIN.INI and SYSTEM.INI files when you shut down Windows NT.

If you erase Windows 95 from your disk, Windows NT provides empty WIN.INI and SYSTEM.INI files for Windows 95-based applications to record configuration data.

Configuring the DOS Environment

To create the DOS environment, Windows NT reads the AUTOEXEC.BAT file when you log on; it reads the AUTOEXEC.NT and CONFIG.NT files when you start DOS applications.

The AUTOEXEC.NT and CONFIG.NT files are the equivalents of Windows' AUTOEXEC.BAT and CONFIG.SYS files.

The AUTOEXEC.BAT and CONFIG.SYS files define a variety of variables that your operating system uses every time it runs. Some examples of these variables include the kind of keyboard you use, the mouse type, the applications you can start from any prompt, and the language (such as French) that your system uses to communicate with you.

The CONFIG.NT file supports, with few exceptions, the same configuration variables found in Windows 95, including country, device, dos, echoconfig, fcbs, files, install, loadhigh, rem, shell, and stacks. The variable echoconfig, if selected, displays messages from CONFIG.NT and AUTOEXEC.NT when you begin applications.

The AUTOEXEC.NT file supports, with few exceptions, the commands found in MS-DOS 5.0 and 6.2.

PIF Files

The AUTOEXEC.NT and CONFIG.NT files create the general environment for DOS applications. As in Windows 95, however, you can use *program information files (PIFs)* to customize the environment for individual applications.

In PIF files, you specify environmental variables for DOS applications running in Windows, such as the amount of expanded and extended memory to reserve for the application, the name of the file displayed in the application's icon, and the name of the file that initiates the application, such as maker.

The PIF files in Windows NT are somewhat different from those in Windows 95 because Windows NT is a preemptive multitasking operating system.

As in Windows 95, you can use the PIF editor (an application in the Main group) to create the PIF file, use the default PIF (DEFAULT.PIF), give the PIF file the same name as the DOS application to which it pertains, and create more than one PIF file for an application.

You can create more than one PIF file if you want Windows to reserve two different amounts of expanded memory for a DOS application, depending on the size of the data file processed by the application.

You can even continue to use old PIF files in Windows NT. However, Windows NT precludes the use of many PIF variables, and simply ignores them if they are set (for example, the priority settings or when the application runs exclusively in the foreground). Windows NT manages the timeslices that applications get, not the applications themselves.

Windows NT adds one new feature to PIF files. You can create start-up files to configure the environment for each application you run.

Configuring the OS/2 Environment

Launching an OS/2 application starts the OS/2-protected subsystem in Windows NT.

The OS/2-protected subsystem is the OS/2 operating system. You do not see OS/2's GUI (graphical user interface), however. Instead, you see Windows NT's GUI.

Remember that the OS/2 subsystem runs only character-based OS/2 applications.

The first time the subsystem starts, Windows NT uses the information in the Registry to configure the OS/2 environment. If no information is found, Windows NT uses the data in the original CONFIG.SYS file. If Windows NT doesn't find a CONFIG.SYS file, the following default information is added to the Registry:

```
PROTSHELL=c:\os2\pmshell.exe c:\os2\os2.ini c:\os2\os2sys.ini
    %SystemRoot%\system32\cmd.exe
SET COMSPEC=%SystemRoot%\system32\cmd.exe
```

Windows NT supports a subset of the configuration variables found in the OS/2 CONFIG.SYS files, including protshell, devicename, libpath, set, country, codepage, and devinfo=KBD.

The libpath variable adds path information in the Windows NT environment to the OS/2 library path. The devicename variable names device drivers for OS/2 applications that are compatible with Windows NT.

Some of the OS/2 commands that are not supported in Windows NT include set path, set compspec, set video_devices, set vio_ibmvga, set vio_vga, and set prompt.

Adding PCMCIA Cards

Windows NT supports certain modem cards, small computer system interface (SCSI) controller cards, network adapter cards, and hard disk PCMCIA cards. Check the book included with Windows NT entitled *Hardware Compatibility List* to make sure the card you buy is supported by Windows NT.

 Note   PCMCIA card and socket support is not included in Windows NT.

Make sure to shut down the workstation before installing your PCMCIA card. If you are installing an IDE (Integrated Device Electronics) or PCMCIA hard disk, you may need to reinstall Windows NT. If you have the choice, add the hard disk before installing Windows NT. When Windows NT is started, it should detect the newly installed device.

If you are adding a SCSI or network-adapter PCMCIA card, either make sure the Windows NT Workstation device driver is already installed, or reconfigure the network adapter card before shutting down Windows NT and inserting the card.

The following sections discuss detection of various cards.

Detecting Modem PCMCIA Cards

To install a PCMCIA modem card that is supported by Windows NT, shut down the Windows NT workstation and insert the card. Windows NT should automatically detect the presence of the new card. If you want to make sure, however, that Windows NT has detected the card, use the following procedure:

1. Determine the number of communication ports in use by double-clicking on the Ports icon in the Control Panel, as shown in figure 6.1.

Figure 6.1

The Ports icon in the Control panel.

Ports ——

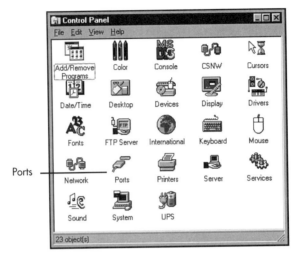

The Ports panel displays the number of ports in use along with a variety of other details, including the speed of communications operating through the port.

2. Alternately, type the mode command on the command line. Windows NT displays a message that describes the number of ports in use.

3. Shut down the Windows NT workstation.

4. Insert the modem PCMCIA card into its socket.

5. Restart Windows NT.

6. Repeat step 1 or 2.

Either of these steps should show that the additional communications port is open and listed in the Ports dialog box.

Installing SCSI PCMCIA Cards

SCSI PCMCIA cards can control a variety of hardware, including CD-ROMs and hard disks. Before you can use a SCSI card, you must first install the appropriate SCSI driver.

To install a SCSI PCMCIA card, use the following procedure:

1. Double-click on the Windows NT Setup icon. Windows NT displays the Setup dialog box.

2. Choose the ADD/Remove SCSI Adapters menu item on the Options menu. Windows NT displays the SCSI Adapter Setup dialog box, as shown in figure 6.2.

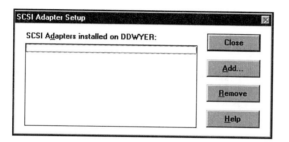

Figure 6.2

The SCSI Adapter Setup dialog box.

3. Click on the Add button. Windows NT displays a warning message saying that Windows NT might not start correctly.

4. Click on the OK button. Windows NT displays the Select SCSI Adapter Option dialog box, as shown in figure 6.3.

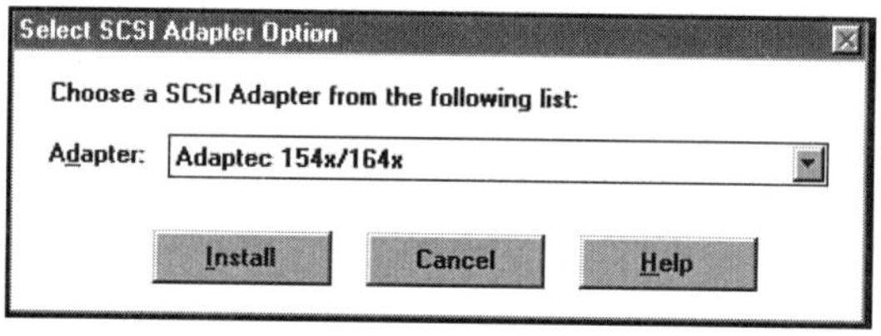

Figure 6.3

The Select SCSI Adapter Option dialog box.

5. Click on the down arrow and click on the name of the PCMCIA SCSI adapter card that you are using.

6. Click on the Install button.

7. In the Windows NT Setup dialog box, identify the source of the Windows NT Workstation distribution files.

8. Click on the Continue button.

   Windows NT installs the appropriate SCSI adapter files.

9. Click on the Close button on the Windows NT Setup dialog box.

10. Exit the Windows NT Setup dialog box by double-clicking on the dash box in the upper-left corner of the window.

Note If you want to determine whether or not Windows NT detects your SCSI card, check the registry at this point as described in the next section, "Detecting a SCSI PCMCIA Card."

11. Turn off the Windows NT workstation.

12. Insert the SCSI PCMCIA card.

13. Turn on the Windows NT workstation.

Once you install a SCSI PCMCIA card, you have to see if your system detects it. The following section explains how you can check to see if the card was detected.

Detecting a SCSI PCMCIA Card

If you want to verify that Windows NT has detected your SCSI PCMCIA card, use the following procedure:

1. After step 10 in the previous section, just prior to turning off your workstation, check the Registry of the following key:

   HKEY_LOCAL_MACHINE/HARDWARE/DEVICEMAP/SCSI

2. After completing the installation of the PCMCIA SCSI card as described in the previous section, check the Registry by double-clicking on the REGEDT32.EXE program in the File Manager. You can find this file in the \root\system32 directory. The File Manager displays the Registry Editor dialog box.

3. Find the following key in the Registry:

   HKEY_LOCAL_MACHINE/HARDWARE/DEVICEMAP/SCSI

   The Registry should contain a new key or the name of a new SCSI device. The Registry would contain the name of a new SCSI device if you had previously installed a SCSI device.

Stop Using the Registry editor can cause serious system errors. Make sure to take care when using it.

Configuring PCMCIA Network Adapter Cards

After inserting a PCMCIA network adapter card in your Windows NT workstation, use the following procedure to configure your system:

1. Double-click on the Network icon in the Control Panel window. Windows NT displays the Network Settings dialog box.

2. Click on the Add Adapter button. Windows NT displays the Add Network Adapter dialog box, as shown in figure 6.4.

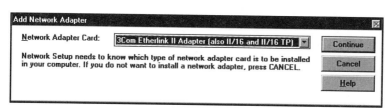

Figure 6.4

The Add Network Adapter dialog box.

3. Click on the down arrow and select your Network Adapter card from the list.

4. Click on the Continue button. Windows NT displays the Setup windows for your Network Adapter card.

5. Use the documentation accompanying your Network Adapter card to choose the settings in the Adapter Card Setup window.

6. Click on the OK button. Windows NT displays the Bus Location dialog box.

7. Click on the down arrow and then click on the PCMCIA selection.

8. Click on the OK button.

9. Identify the location of the Windows NT distribution files in the Windows NT Setup dialog box and then click on the Continue button.

10. Click on the OK button in the Network Settings dialog box. Make sure your network adapter card can be bound to your computer. For more information, see "Installing Network Adapter Cards" in the Control Panel chapter of the *Windows NT Workstation System Guide.*

11. Shut down the Windows NT workstation.

12. Insert the PCMCIA network adapter card into your computer.

13. Turn on your Windows NT workstation.

Now you should be connected to the network.

Solving Installation Problems

You can run up against a number of common installation problems. The following list describes some solutions to those problems.

Solving SCSI Problems

If Setup can't find your CD-ROM drive, try the following:

◆ Make sure that the last and first devices in a SCSI chain are terminated properly.

◆ Make sure that all terminations are removed from devices in the middle of a SCSI chain.

◆ Make sure that the last devices internally and externally are terminated properly if you have both internal and external devices in a SCSI chain.

◆ Make sure that your SCSI controller card is not terminated.

◆ Make sure that the drivers for your SCSI controller are compatible with Windows NT. If not, ask the manufacturer for an upgraded version of the driver.

◆ Make sure that the CD-ROM drive does not have 0 or 1 as an ID. 0 and 1 are often reserved for hard disk IDs.

Solving Boot Problems

If, after completing Setup, Windows NT doesn't start after rebooting the computer, check the following:

◆ Make sure that your hard disk has enough space for the paging file (20 MB minimum).

◆ Make sure that BOOT.INI values use the correct Windows NT path.

◆ If you see the message BOOT: Couldn't find NTLDR, insert another disk. (You have inadvertently erased the NTLDR file, and you need to copy it back to your systems file.)

◆ If you see a similar message about NTDETECT, copy NTDETECT.COM into your systems directory.

◆ You may see the following message:

```
Couldn't open boot sector file.
multi(0)disk(0)r disk(0)partitions(1)\bootsec.dos
```

This message means that the file BOOTSEC.DOS, which enables you to load alternate operating systems, is not at the root directory. This is trouble, and it is best to reinstall Windows NT.

If you have a second computer with the same disk tracks, heads, cylinders, and sections, you can copy its BOOTSEC.DOS file to your computer.

If this procedure fails, your entire hard drive may become unreadable. Try this rescue only if you are familiar with binary-editing tools and low-level disk structures.

If your boot problem is not listed above, try recopying BOOT.INI to your systems file and make sure that BOOT.INI and NTLDR are both in the system root directory.

Solving Networking Problems

If Setup cannot install on the network your computer is on, check the following:

◆ Make sure that the IRQ setting for the network card doesn't conflict with another device's IRQ setting.

◆ Make sure that the computer's name is unique and is not the same name as a domain or workgroup.

◆ Review Windows NT's error log by using the Windows NT's Event Viewer. It might identify the problem.

A variety of incompatibility problems can occur with specific pieces of hardware. If problems persist, call the dealer or manufacturer for technical help.

Summary

This chapter examined the four different ways of installing Windows NT, and explained Custom and Express setup procedures. You learned how to configure different operating systems in Windows NT. The chapter ended with suggestions for solutions to common installation problems.

After you get the Setup program running, installing Windows NT is no more difficult than installing Windows 95. As long as your computer equipment exceeds the minimum hardware requirement for Windows NT, and you are armed with the appropriate knowledge of your hardware before you begin the installation, Setup should proceed smoothly.

Configuring the operating system environments requires a bit more expertise, however. It is usually a good idea to let the system administrator set these.

C H A P T E R

7

Troubleshooting Installation Problems

Nothing is more frustrating than sitting down with a new piece of hardware or software and finding that it does not work right away. What you want is true plug and play: plug it in, install it, and watch it work.

While I sympathize with those feelings, the reality is that integrating enormously complex hardware and software created by thousands of different vendors is often a bumpy road. Although 1001 things can go wrong, there are many common errors you can detect and fix.

This chapter leads you through the maze of fixing your Windows NT installation. It is very likely that you will not have any problems, but if you do, try the suggestions in this chapter in the order they are presented. The most common errors are discussed first.

Using the Last Known Good Configuration Option

When you boot your system, before Windows NT Explorer displays, you see, for a brief amount of time, the following message:

```
Press Spacebar to use the Last Known Good Configuration.
```

If you are having trouble starting Windows NT Workstation, press the spacebar after seeing this display. When you do, Windows NT Workstation presents you with the following choices:

◆ Use Current Startup Configuration

◆ Use Last Known Good Configuration

◆ Restart Computer

If you cannot start Windows NT, select the second option. If Windows NT then starts up, you know that you changed the configuration of Windows NT such that it cannot start. Very likely the Registry has been changed in a harmful way. If Windows NT still does not start up, you know that the problem is probably not a configuration problem.

General Hardware Problems

Windows NT works with a wide variety of hardware. It does not, however, work with all hardware. Microsoft has gone to great pains to document all of the hardware Windows NT is compatible with. Before you even install Windows NT, look in the book included with Windows NT, called *Hardware Compatibility List*, to make sure your computer, SCSI card, and CD-ROM drive are listed. If they are not, you should immediately contact the manufacturer of the hardware to see whether there are new device drivers available that make your hardware compatible with Windows NT. If so, you can download these drivers over a modem and install the new drivers before installing Windows NT. If your hardware manufacturer simply chooses not to support Windows NT, your only choice is to replace the device.

System Error F002

System errors are never nice surprises. System Error F002 means that you have some faulty hardware, most likely a failure in your workstation's memory chips.

If you get this error, go ahead and take the cover off of your computer and make sure the SIMS (RAM memory) are seated correctly and make sure all of their pins are intact. If they are, run your computer's diagnostic program. In PCs, you generally interrupt boot up by pressing the Delete button. Workstations have their own diagnostic programs. In the diagnostic program, check to see whether all of the memory is being read, and also check to see whether or not the memory is the proper speed for your CPU.

Checking IRQ Conflicts

If a device is simply not responding, one possibility is that it is using the same interrupt request ID (IRQ) as another device on your system. IRQ IDs identify hardware to your computer so that your computer can work with the devices. Two devices cannot have the same IRQ ID and work.

On the PC, the easiest way to determine whether or not there is an IRQ conflict is to run the command msd at a DOS prompt. msd conducts a variety of tests on your system and then presents a simple interface in which you can click on the information you want to see. One of the options is the IRQ settings. When you click on it, msd displays the IRQ settings for your hardware.

Consult the documentation that accompanies the device in question to see whether its default IRQ ID conflicts with one of the IDs listed by msd. If so, change the IRQ setting on your device.

Changing an IRQ ID is often a hardware adjustment. The device might have a series of switches or jumpers that you need to set. Consult your device's documentation to learn how to set the IRQ ID for your device.

IDE and ESDI Hard Drive Support

With the price of hard disks plummeting and the size of applications growing, you might have added several hard drives to your system. Windows NT only supports up to two IDE or ESDI hard disk drives per controller card. There is no such limitation for SCSI drives.

If you have more than two IDE or ESDI hard disk drives in your machine, contact Microsoft technical support.

SCSI Device Problems

If you are adding SCSI devices to your system because you need a new hard disk to hold Windows NT or because you want to install Windows NT from a CD-ROM, you might innocently introduce some hardware problems into your system. The most common symptom of SCSI problems is that your system cannot "see" the SCSI device. For example, when you change directories to the SCSI drive, the drive is not found.

The following list gives you some SCSI installation tips and the means to problem solve SCSI errors.

◆ Make sure that the last and first devices in a SCSI chain are terminated properly.

A *terminator* is a resistor that terminates the SCSI line. On CD-ROM and hard disk drives, terminators look similar to integrated circuit (IC) chips: they have many legs and they stick into a socket. They are very often located near the SCSI connection for the device. Normally there are two or three terminators per device.

Terminating a device means that the terminators are plugged into their sockets. Unterminating the chain means that you pull the terminators out of their sockets.

◆ Make sure that all terminations are removed from devices in the middle of a SCSI chain.

Terminators found in the middle of a SCSI chain make any device on the chain after the terminated device invisible to the SCSI controller card.

If you only have external or only internal SCSI devices, most likely your SCSI controller card is at one end of the SCSI chain. It should therefore be terminated as should the last SCSI device in the chain.

If, however, you have both internal and external SCSI devices, most likely the SCSI controller card is in the middle of the chain and therefore should not be terminated.

◆ Make sure that the drivers for your SCSI controller are compatible with Windows NT. If not, ask the manufacturer of your SCSI device for an upgraded version of the driver.

◆ Your CD-ROM must provide SCSI parity to work. This is the case with the vast majority of CD-ROM drives, but not all drives, such as the NEC CDR-36 and CDR-37 drives.

◆ Check your SCSI cable and see how well it is seated. 50-pin SCSI connectors are easy to plug in wrong. Make sure the connector is seated completely in its receptacle.

Also check the condition of your SCSI cable. Cabling failure is one of the most common causes of SCSI device failures.

◆ Make sure that the CD-ROM drive does not have 0 or 1 as an ID. 0 and 1 are often reserved for hard disk IDs.

◆ Make sure that all of your SCSI devices have different IDs.

Because a SCSI card can control up to eight devices, each device must have a unique ID between 0 and 7. Generally, the way to set device IDs is using jumpers. Jumpers consist of three pairs of bare, stiff wires. You use small connectors to connect the pairs to create device IDs, as follows:

	Jumper Connectors		
ID #	1st Pair	2nd Pair	3rd Pair
0			
1	X		
2		X	
3	X	X	
4			X
5	X		X
6		X	X
7	X	X	X

For example, to make your CD-ROM SCSI ID 5, you put jumper connectors on the first and third pair of jumper wires. ID numbers 0 and 1 are often reserved for hard drives, but consult your SCSI card documentation for recommended hardware ID numbers.

ID 7 is often reserved for your SCSI controller card, so make sure not to use ID 7.

Floppy Drive Fails

On rare occasions you might find it impossible for your computer to read the original software distribution disks when you are trying to install an application. This happens because Windows NT checks disks more meticulously than does MS-DOS.

If you find that the floppy drive fails in this manner, switch to MS-DOS and install the application. If you are only running Windows NT, take your application to another computer that runs MS-DOS, format new disks, and use the xcopy command to copy the installation software to the new disks.

Updating Video Drivers

You can continue to use video drivers that worked with the first version of Windows NT; however, you will miss out on the benefits given by the newest drivers. The performance of the new video drivers is quite a bit better than the old drivers. In addition, the new drivers contain fixes for bugs that plagued the older drivers.

Even if you are using drivers that Microsoft did not provide, they should work. However, it is recommended that you contact your driver manufacturer to see if they have an update of their driver that works best with the newest version of Windows NT.

Should you have trouble with your video display, make sure the jumper connections on your video card do not enable IRQ2. Windows NT does not use interrupts with its video drivers.

Handling Startup Error Messages

There are three executables that take part in booting up your system: NTLDR, BOOT.INI, and NTDETECT.COM.

BOOT.INI has two parts:

◆ Part one defines which operating system on the hard disk is the default operating system. This part also defines the interval before which the default operating system starts. Users see this interval as a countdown in the opening screen of Windows NT. Before the countdown reaches zero, the user can choose to run any of the operating systems on the hard disk. When the countdown reaches zero, the default operating system starts.

Note   If you do not see a list of operating system choices, the length of the countdown was set to zero. You can edit that value in BOOT.INI.

◆ Part two contains the list of operating systems on the drives.

NTDETECT.COM generates a list of your system's hardware devices.

The third executable that plays a part in the boot up of your system is NTLDR (NT Loader). This program reads the BOOT.INI file and displays the operating systems listed in BOOT.INI along with the countdown.

NTLDR also executes NTDETECT.COM.

After all of these files execute, Windows NT finishes booting up by doing the following:

◆ Loading the low-level components of Windows NT

◆ Initializing the drivers

◆ Starting services (according to the Registry)

◆ Loading the high-level components of Windows NT

◆ Displaying the Welcome screen

Throughout the bootup sequence, a variety of error messages might display. The remainder of this section describes the most common error messages.

"Couldn't Find NTLDR" Error Message

The NTLDR program should be in the root directory of your startup hard disk. This error message means that the file is missing. You can correct the problem in the following ways:

1. In the File Manager, use the Search option in the File menu to find the NTLDR file.

2. You can copy the NTLDR file from either the CD-ROM or floppy software distribution disks. If you have the CD-ROM disc, you can use the following command to copy the NTLDR file to the root directory on the C drive:

```
D:> copy \i386\ntldr C:
```

To copy the file from floppy disks, use the following command:

```
A:> expand ntldr.$ c:\ntldr
```

Now NTLDR is placed correctly.

"Error 0000001E"

This error message signals a hardware or file system failure. To correct this problem, run the chkdsk (check disk) program on the hard disk drive in question.

Also make sure that all of your peripherals, including the CD-ROM drive, the SCSI hard drive, and the SCSI card, are on the list of supported hardware.

"Error 0x00000069 or 0x00000067" Error Message

This error indicates that Windows NT cannot communicate with the hard drive controller. If this occurs, try the following:

◆ Refer to the earlier section that discusses SCSI errors and verify that you do not have these kinds of problems.

◆ Make sure the hard disk controller does not have the same IRQ as any other device on your system. You can display the IRQ values by typing msd at a command prompt and clicking on IRQ.

◆ Confirm that the application that finds the operating systems on all disks, NTDETECT.COM, is in the root directory on the hard disk and the partition of the hard disk used to boot the system.

◆ Reduce the direct memory access (DMA) transfer rate on the hard disk controller.

◆ Confirm that you have not inadvertently erased any Windows NT system (.sys) files.

◆ Make sure your hardware and its device drivers are supported by Windows NT by looking in the *Hardware Compatibility List* book included in the software distribution.

Make sure that you have the latest BIOS for your system. If you have flash BIOS, you can upgrade to the latest version of it.

"NMI Hardware Error"

This is not a good error. As the message says, this is a hardware error. It might be connected with RAM memory or with the internal exchange of data. You might find that DOS or Windows 3.*x* runs perfectly well in this environment, but Windows NT cannot.

There are only so many diagnostics you can run, unless you are a technician, but here are some things you might do:

◆ Make sure all of the SIMM integrated circuits are seated properly in their receptacles. A SIMM is the chips that comprise your RAM. You likely have 8, 12, or 16 MB of SIMM memory.

◆ While your computer is booting up, you probably have the option to halt the boot-up process and run diagnostic tests. Choose this option and run as many diagnostic procedures as are available, including checking RAM memory.

◆ If your SIMMs run at different speeds, replace the slow ones so that all SIMMs run at the same speed.

◆ Clean up the motherboard of dust and grime. Check to see that foreign objects have not shorted out parts of the motherboard.

If these suggestions do not work, you need to take your computer into a service technician so that he can run more complete diagnostic tests on your computer.

Non-Windows NT Operating Systems Do Not Start

If you are trying to start some operating system other than Windows NT and cannot, read the BOOT.INI file to make sure the full pathname to the operating system is complete and accurate.

If the pathnames are correct, make sure that the file, BOOTSECT.DOC, is in the root directory of the system boot drive and partition. The BOOTSECT.DOC file records the boot history of the non-Windows NT operating systems on your computer.

Logon Problems

If Windows NT starts and gives you the opportunity to log on, 90% of your battle is won. Logon problems are most often resolved by you and your system administrator. Here is a list of common logon problems and their solutions:

◆ Wrong password. If you cannot remember your password, the only course of action you can take is to ask your system administrator to assign you a password. You can change the password later, once you gain access to Windows NT.

◆ Passwords are case sensitive. Make sure you accurately use the correct upper- and lowercase letters in your password. For example, the following words are unique passwords: PassWord, passWord, password, pAsSwOrD.

◆ Passwords have a minimum length. The system administrator can specify that your password must be eight characters long. When you start up on Windows NT, the system administrator usually gives you a generic password that you can then change. Make sure you know what your conventions for passwords are, according to your user account.

◆ Your account expired or was disabled by the system administrator. Each user has an account on the system consisting of, in part, a logon name and password and a set of permissions. These accounts routinely expire. Check with your system administrator to see if this is your problem. If so, ask the system administrator to extend the logon account for a more appropriate length of time.

◆ The system administrator can also specify times when you can and cannot log on to the system. If you cannot log on, ask your system administrator if you are locked out of the system during some parts of the day.

◆ There are network problems between your workstation and the Windows NT Server. Check your cabling to make sure there are no loose connections. Also, run any diagnostics you might have on your network adapter card.

Logon problems are frustrating. If you are in a standalone system, remember that you are the system administrator and can change the password using the Administration tools. If your computer is in a network, you can ask for the help of your system administrator.

Changing Your Password

One of the first tasks you perform when you start up the system for the first time is changing your password. To change your password, use the following procedure:

1. Log on to the system using the generic password given to you by your system administrator.

2. Press, at the same time, Ctrl+Alt+Del.

   Windows NT displays the Windows NT Security window.

3. Click on the Change Password button.

4. Type your old password, and your new password (twice—to confirm your spelling of it).

5. Click on the OK button.

When choosing your password, be aware that the system administrator may have stipulated a minimum password length. As for choosing a password, you should mix

numbers with letters, upper- and lowercase, and yet make it easy to remember. For example, you might choose 1Lk2sM (I like to swim). Combining cases and numbers and letters makes your password more difficult to guess.

Using Windows NT Diagnostic Tools to Correct Problems

Windows NT comes with a variety of diagnostic tools that you can use to solve some of your problems. This section lists the tools and gives you a brief introduction to their use.

Running System Diagnostics

Windows NT comes with the diagnostic program, WINMSD.EXE. This program is an upgrade of the familiar DOS program, MSD.EXE. WINMSD.EXE helps by displaying current configuration information. As a result, WINMSD.EXE can uncover configuration conflicts.

To run WINMSD.EXE, you can either type WINMSD at a command prompt, or double-click on the Windows NT Diagnostic icon in the Administrative Tools group.

Windows NT displays the WINMSD window.

You can click on any of the buttons in the display. The button names suggest the information they display, including the following:

♦ Information about Windows NT, including the version number, start up options, and environment variables.

♦ Information about the hardware on your workstation, including the CPU type, the BIOS version, video resolution, and CPU steppings.

♦ A mapping of physical memory use, such as the addresses where workstation devices reside, paging file information, and use of DMA.

♦ IRQ settings along with their associated devices.

♦ Information about the network your workstation is connected to, including configuration settings, transports, and statistics.

♦ Settings for printers, fonts, and system processes currently running.

All of these tools give you valuable insight into your system.

Recovering from System Errors

By default Windows NT takes no action when encountering a fatal system error (called a STOP error). You can, however, configure Windows NT to take the following actions:

◆ Enter a log entry in the system log.

◆ Notify an administrator.

◆ Create a core file that records the values of the computer's memory registers.

◆ Reboot the computer automatically.

You can use these actions together or individually. Most often you use them to keep the system running and to debug the problem that caused the system error. Microsoft support, for example, might ask for a core dump or a log file of the events that caused the system to crash.

Note The default name for the log file is memory.log. New system crashes overwrite the memory.log file. So, to retain logs of system crashes, copy the files to a new file name.

The only problem with using these actions is that they must remain active while the computer is on. That means that these drivers occupy roughly 60 to 70 KB of RAM. For some applications, that leaves too little conventional memory. Graphic-intensive applications, for example, often require large amounts of RAM.

To activate one or more of the actions previously listed, you must be logged on as a member of the Administrator group. Use the following procedure to configure system recovery.

1. Double-click on the System icon in the Control Panel.

   The System window opens.

2. Click on the Recovery button.

   Windows NT displays the Recovery dialog box.

3. Click on the Write an event to the system log checkbox if you want Windows NT to record a log event to the system log when a system error occurs.

4. Click on the Send an administrative alert checkbox if you want to notify the system administrator immediately that a system error occurred.

5. Click on the Write debugging information to: checkbox to save debugging information to a file. This information is similar to a core dump in the Unix world.

   If you check the Write debugging information to %SystemRoot% \MEMORY.LOG checkbox but leave the Overwrite any existing file checkbox unchecked, Windows NT will not record log information if a log file already exists.

 Note In order to use the Write Debugging Info option, the size of your paging file on the system drive (the system drive is specified by the SYSTEMROOT environment variable) must equal the amount of physical memory in your system plus 1 MB, for example, if you have 16 MB of RAM, your paging file must be at least 17 MB large. The other options, Write An Event, Send An Administrative Alert, and Automatically Reboot, require the paging file to be at least 2 MB in size.

6. Click on the Automatically reboot checkbox if you want your workstation to reboot automatically after a system error.

7. Click on the OK button.

These steps allow your computer to recover automatically.

Reusing Previous Configurations

When you install new software or hardware on your system, very often your configuration files are changed. You might find that when you try to start your computer to make the configuration changes take effect that your workstation does not work. If this should occur, one remedy is to use Windows NT's Last Known Good Configuration utility.

To use the Last Known Good Configuration utility, use the following procedure:

1. Power on your workstation.

2. When the words "OS Loader" appear, immediately press the spacebar on your workstation.

Windows NT displays the Configuration Recovery menu, which has the following options:

◆ Use Current Startup Configuration

◆ Use Last Known Good Configuration

◆ Restart Computer

Because the current configuration is causing your problems, forget option one. Instead, select the second option, Use Last Known Good Configuration.

Normally, when applications are installed, they automatically save the current version of the configuration in a file with the extension .old. The Use Last Known Good Configuration option moves the .old files to the currently active configuration file names. This action overwrites the configuration files that did not work.

Using the Information in the Repair File

Unfortunately, there are times when things are so bad that you cannot even get to the Use Last Known Good Configuration menu option. This happens, for example, when the boot file for your workstation gets corrupted.

Windows NT Setup can sometimes correct the corruption if you can supply it with the information contained in either the \systemRoot\REPAIR file, or on the disk created during the installation process which you were to label "Emergency Repair Disk."

If you cannot use the data in the \REPAIR file and you do not have an emergency Repair disk, you have to reinstall Windows NT.

To restore the system using the Emergency Repair disk, use the following procedure.

 Note This restore procedure pertains only to X86-based computers. If you are using a Risc-based computer, refer to the Troubleshooting chapter in the *Installation Guide*.

1. Place the Setup Boot disk in drive A, place the CD-ROM containing Windows NT in your CD-ROM drive, and start the computer.

   Windows NT displays a text-based screen that asks if you want to install Windows NT Workstation or repair corrupted files.

2. Type r to repair the corrupted files.

   Windows NT asks that you place the Emergency Repair disk in the floppy drive.

3. Place the Emergency Repair disk in the floppy drive.

   Windows NT Setup might ask for additional disks to configure the system.

   If you do not have an Emergency Repair disk, Windows NT Setup displays all of the installations it found on your system. Select one of the installations that you would like to repair.

4. After completing all of the tasks that Windows NT Setup requires, press Ctrl+Alt+Del to reboot the computer.

New Riders Publishing
INSIDE
SERIES

Rebooting the computer is necessary because it is only during bootup that most computers read their configuration information.

CONFIG.NT and AUTOEXEC.NT Errors

If you find that you cannot run MS-DOS applications or if you see error messages that involve CONFIG.NT or AUTOEXEC.NT, look in the \<systemRoot>\system32 directory to see that these files are present and that they are not corrupted. If you find that these files are corrupted or missing, you can copy new versions of them from the Emergency Repair disk.

Using Other Detection Tools

Windows NT provides some additional tools and log files to detect and correct system errors. If none of the previous sections corrected your problem, try each of the following suggestions:

◆ Run the Dr. Watson tool by typing, at the command prompt,

```
> drwtsn32
```

Dr. Watson can detect, define, and record application errors in a log file that can be of significant value when calling technical support.

◆ The Event Viewer can display log files that are records of error information produced by applications and system services. For more information about the Event Viewer, see Chapter 12, "Using Windows NT Applets."

◆ If you are using Windows NT default file system, NTFS, Windows NT repairs bad disk sectors automatically, records all file transactions, and logs important file information on the NTFS volume.

◆ The Messenger and Alerter system services send out messages warning of such things as power outages, security problems, and other user session problems.

◆ You can use the chkdsk utility to examine your hard drive, regardless of whether or not the hard disk uses NTFS, FAT, or HPFS as a file system. Chkdsk finds errors, such as lost clusters.

When you specify the /f parameter with chkdsk, chkdsk corrects the problems it finds.

◆ You can configure the Performance Monitor to broadcast alerts across the network and create an alert log. For more information about using the Performance Monitor, see Chapter 12, "Using Windows NT Applets."

◆ On the Windows NT CD-ROM software distribution disk is the Messages database. These descriptions can really help you troubleshoot your problems. This database provides extended descriptions of error messages.

To install the Messages database, click on the Run option in the File menu in the Program Manager window. In the text field, type the letter of your CD-ROM drive followed by WINNTMSG\SETUP, for example:

```
d:\WINNTMSG\SETUP
```

Setup installs the message database and displays a new program group with the Microsoft Windows NT Messages icon in it.

Dealing with Network Problems

Connecting your workstation to a network is wonderful because it extends your device resources; it also, however, extends the number of problems you might have when trying to run Windows NT. The next section takes a look at a number of common problems that can occur when connecting your workstation to a network.

Naming Computers

Each computer has a network address. It functions like the computer's phone number. Each network address, like each phone number, must be unique. Otherwise, specifying one workstation might put you in touch with two. When you dial a phone number, you want to connect to only one phone. The same is true for network addresses. If you join a network and the network address (called an IP (Internet Protocol) address) is already owned by another machine, your machine's IP address must be changed.

Because IP addresses are long numbers, it is often far easier to associate IP addresses with machine names. You might call your machine moon, for example. A machine's full name is also longer, it contains names that represent the net and subnet to which your machine is attached. Inside your own network, moon might be sufficient to find your machine. When a machine outside of the local network tries to find moon, however, it might need to specify the net and subnet as well, for example, moon.engr.sgi.com, where sgi is the net, engr is the subnet, and com specifies that sgi (Silicon Graphics) is a commercial entity. Other extensions are .edu, for educational institutions, and .net, for Internet providers.

Computer names, called domain names, must be unique on the local network. Just as it is okay for there to be two identical phone numbers in different area codes, the domain name of the computer only needs to be unique in its local network.

If you join a network and another workstation is already called moon, Windows NT will not provide a network connection.

Network Adapter Card Problems

Network adapter cards are the interface between your workstation and the network. If your card accepts more than one kind of cable, make sure you have configured the card for the correct cable type.

Network adapter cards must also have unique IRQ numbers, I/O port addresses, and memory buffer addresses. You can either set these numbers using jumper connections (on older cards) or through a software interface. If you do not know your workstation's setting, accept the default values provided by Windows NT Setup.

If you want to change the network settings for your network adapter card after Windows NT is already installed, you can click on the Network icon in the Control Panel. Windows NT displays the Network window.

If you have a RISC-based workstation made by Acer, MIPS, or Olivetti, it is not necessary for you to specify settings for built-in Ethernet capabilities.

Checking the IRQ Number

Just as IP addresses identify computers in a network, IRQ (interrupt request) numbers identify specific serial ports on your workstation. Windows NT supports up to 256 ports (COM1 to COM256). Serial ports are sockets where you plug in devices, such as a printer, mouse, modem, or network adapter card. Each device in your system must use a unique IRQ number, otherwise your CPU will not be able to communicate with the device.

On the PC, the MSD tool identifies all of the IRQ's used in your system. Before assigning a new IRQ number to your network adapter card, make sure that it is not already used by another device using MSD.

COM1 (IRQ 4) is usually connected to a mouse and COM2 (IRQ 3) is often attached to a modem. IRQ 5 is generally the second port for a parallel printer. Because this is rarely used in PCs, using IRQ 5 is a good setting for your network adapter card.

To set an IRQ number, use the following procedure.

1. Click on the Network icon in the Control Panel group.

   Windows NT displays the Network window.

2. Click on the device you are setting the IRQ value for in the Installed Adapter Cards list.

3. Specify an IRQ value in the Adapter Card Setup dialog box.

After making these changes, reboot the computer and see if your system works.

Checking I/O Port Base Addresses

The base addresses for I/O (input/output) ports are locations in memory where device drivers reside. The addresses are called base because the memory location is just the first memory location occupied by the device driver. Because there are so many locations in memory, Port Base Address conflicts are rare.

If, by chance, you do have a port base address conflict, use the Network window to change the memory address.

Checking Memory Buffer Addresses

A buffer is a defined amount of memory that a device can use as a temporary storage location. It is important that these buffers not overlap, otherwise you will get a memory fault error message.

You can use the Windows NT Diagnostics tool to see which buffer addresses are already used on your system. Setting the buffer addresses for peripherals often involves changing jumper connections.

Checking Services

Services should start automatically. If they do not, you can use the Services and Devices icons in the Control Panel group to check the status of the services.

You can also use the Event Viewer to see if there are any messages related to the shut down of services.

Fixing Printing Problems

If you find that you cannot print any documents, or the printing is garbled, check for the following conditions:

◆ Windows 3.1-based applications expect the printer driver to reside on the local computer even when a network printer is being used. An application might fail if the network printer is out of service. The best way to fix this problem is to get an updated printer driver that is supported by Windows NT.

◆ When you specify a printer using a Windows 3.*x* printer driver as the default printer, Windows 3.*x*-based applications might post error messages, indicating there are not enough system resources to run, or that the application has run out of memory. The problem is that Windows 3.*x* printer drivers are not compatible with Windows NT. The way to fix this problem is to use the Windows NT Printer Manager to specify the default printer.

◆ If you find that parts of one page are printed across many pages, Windows NT might begin printing before a complete page has been processed. This situation usually only arises if you are printing a complex document using a slow computer.

The best way to solve this problem is to make Windows NT wait so that pages can be completely processed before printing begins. To increase the delay time before printing begins, use the Registry Editor to go to the following Registry key:

```
HKEY_LOCAL_MACHINE\SYSTEM\CurrentControlSet\Control\WOW
```

and edit the following line:

```
LPT_timeout:REG_SZ:15
```

This line shows that Windows NT waits 15 seconds (the default) before printing. You can change the number at the end of the line to a larger number to increase the wait time.

Do not increase this number too much, however, because it delays the printing of all documents from MS-DOS and Windows 3.1 applications.

Summary

The challenge of making hardware and software made by many different manufacturers work together seamlessly can be overwhelming. Often, you need the expertise of technical support personnel because it is just too hard to be a master of all the components you own.

This chapter presented solutions to a host of troubles you might run into while installing, booting, and running Windows NT Workstation.

Optimizing Windows NT

Microsoft offers a variety of tools that you can use to optimize the performance of Windows NT. You can download these tools for free by reaching Microsoft at URL http://www.microsoft.com. At present, to reach the tools, you click on the following hyperlinks:

- ◆ Microsoft Products

- ◆ Microsoft Backoffice and Windows NT

- ◆ Microsoft Windows NT Workstation

On that page you will see the tools listed in the directories as follows:

- ◆ For tools that run on an x86 platform, download the i386 directory.

- ◆ For tools that run on a MIPS platform, download the MIPS directory.

- ◆ For the Win 32 API Profiler tool, download the WAP file.

- ◆ For the Win 32 API Logger tool, download the logger file.

- ◆ For the extensions to the Performance Monitor used with Pentium Counters, download the p5ctrs file.

◆ For the extensions to the Performance Monitor that enable it to measure total processor usage, download the totlproc file.

Note You can also obtain the performance tools discussed in this chapter and more by purchasing the Windows NT Resource Kit. The Resource Kit is a four book set with accompanying software.

This chapter describes the tools in the i386 and MIPS directories, WAP, logger, totlproc, and also the performance tools included in the software distribution of Windows NT. For more detailed information about any of these tools, consult the readme files that accompany each tool, or consult the *Windows NT Resource Kit.*

Improving Performance

Before you go through the trouble of learning a new tool, you might like to perform some simple tasks to see if your system performance improves significantly.

◆ PCs many times have a turbo function. Some games run so fast in turbo mode that PC makers allowed users to turn turbo off so that the games could proceed at a reasonable pace. When you run Windows NT, however, make sure the turbo mode is enabled.

◆ Decrease the video resolution. The higher the resolution, the more pixels your computer must display. For the vast majority of applications, high resolution does not add to the quality of the screen display. Word processors, for example, really do not need to be run in high resolution. Only when you want to deal with realistic images do you want to increase the resolution. Most games, for example, run with 256 colors at a resolution of 480 by 640. It is recommended that you decrease your resolution because higher resolutions are burdensome on the CPU.

To set the video resolution, click on the Display icon in the Control Panel program group.

◆ Check the maximum paging size. You set the paging size by clicking on the System icon in the Control Panel program group.

The paging file is space reserved on the hard disk where Windows NT puts a snapshot of a running application when a newly started application runs out of RAM. Instead of not allowing the new application to run, Windows NT swaps out an application to the paging (or swap) file, making enough room for the new application to run.

Windows NT Setup recommends the minimum size of the paging file. Make sure you do not go below that size. If your computer's performance is slow, try increasing the size of the paging file by 10 or 20 MB.

Microsoft Tools for Optimizing Windows NT

This section gives a brief description of the Microsoft tools you can use to optimize the performance of Windows NT. You can obtain these tools from the Microsoft Web site or from Microsoft's Windows NT Resource Kit.

Clearmem

The clearmem tool deallocates pages from RAM. The tool does not have parameters, so you invoke it only as follows:

```
> clearmem
```

Windows NT allows working sets to grow until memory limitations are reached, which forces the working sets to decline. If you run clearmem twice, most applications are forced out of RAM.

Clearmem determines the size of your computer's RAM and then allocates data to completely fill it. Clearmem then references this data very quickly, which eliminates most other pages from memory. In addition, it accesses files and, as a result, clears the cache.

Before running clearmem, make sure the paging size is at least as large as your computer's RAM. The paging size is the size of your swap file. The swap file is where Windows NT temporarily stores applications that are running but are not currently active. Windows NT is forced to store these inactive applications whenever the user invokes a new application and there is no room in RAM for it. When the user chooses to reactivate the inactive application, Windows NT swaps out another inactive application to the swap file and then moves the reactivated application into RAM.

If you run Windows NT as a server and you have configured Windows NT to maximize the throughput for network applications, you need to run clearmem more than twice to reduce the number of applications in RAM.

The Performance Monitor in Windows NT shows you whether or not clearmem has improved Windows NT performance.

Ctrlist

The ctrlist tool converts Performance Monitor counters, objects, and accompanying explanations into a text file. You might like to do this so that you can easily search the text file for information you might need.

The tool has no parameters, so you invoke it only in the following way:

```
> ctrlist > text.txt
```

Text.txt is the text file produced by ctrlist.

Datalog

Datalog provides unattended logging and alerting of system errors. It is a Performance Monitor service and is controlled by the Monitor utility. To invoke Datalog, you simply call it at the command line, as follows:

```
> datalog
```

The Datalog utility has no parameters.

Fastimer

Fastimer is the library that WAP uses. WAP is a tool that measures high precision timing. If you use the WAP tool, the Fastimer library has to be on your path.

Kill

The Kill utility derives its name from the Unix command that stops processes. The Kill utility also stops processes. You identify the process you want to stop by specifying the application name or the process ID, for example:

```
> kill myApp
```

or

```
> kill 1534
```

where myApp is the name of an application and 1534 is the process ID of a running application.

You can find out the processes running on your system by invoking the commands TLIST or PVIEW or by using the Performance Monitor.

If you use the name of the application to kill it, it terminates along with all other instances of the application, if there are any.

Lodctr

Lodctr is included with the software distribution of Windows NT 3.5 and later. You use it to load counters, new objects, and explanation text into the Registry. Performance monitors can use these additions to the Registry.

Stop If you run Lodctr twice without running Unlodctr in between, it becomes very difficult to remove monitoring objects and counters. Unused monitoring objects and counters take up unnecessary space in the Registry.

You should only change the Registry if you really know what you are doing.

NTimer

NTimer is a handy tool that enables you to tell how long a program runs. It gives you three measurements:

◆ total elapsed time (ETime)

◆ time in User Mode (Time)

◆ time in Privileged Mode (KTime)

The units of the time measurements are

```
hours:minutes:seconds.milliseconds
```

For example:

```
0:0:1.324
```

The accuracy of the measurements is relative to the resolution of the timer. In the x86 and MIPS architectures, the accuracy of the timer is within 10 milliseconds.

To use NTimer to measure the elapsed time, use the following syntax:

```
> ntimer programName.exe
```

where programName.exe is the name of the executable application you want to measure.

Perfmtr

Perfmtr (Performance Monitor) enables you to watch a variety of system performance numbers while the system is running. When Perfmtr starts, it presents you with a list of views from which you can choose. Choices include views of processors, memory, cache, threads, and processes either on your computer or on a remote computer in the network.

To invoke Perfmtr, use the following syntax:

```
> perfmtr
```

Perfmtr does not have any parameters.

Pmon

Pmon is a great tool to use while Windows NT is running when you want to look at a wide variety of memory statistics, including how much memory each running process is using and how much the cache is being used. The Performance Monitor can also display these statistics; however, Pmon displays the statistics in more detail.

For each running process, Pmon measures the following:

◆ Processor usage during the most recent update interval

◆ Total processor time

◆ The number of pages each process is using and the change since the last update interval

◆ The number of Page Faults that happened in the process

◆ Virtual memory use

◆ Pool usage estimates

◆ The priority of the process

◆ The number of threads in the process

To invoke Pmon, use the following syntax:

```
> pmon
```

Pmon does not have any parameters.

Profiler

Profiler samples the registers to determine which code blocks execute most frequently. Profiler changes the time clock interrupt rate so that interrupts occur every one millisecond.

Note Changing the interrupt rate does not change the rate at which Performance Monitor samples the system processor usage. Profiler also does not affect the rate at which the real time clock is updated by the system.

When the interrupt occurs every one millisecond, Profiler records where the instruction pointer is. It then increments a counter that keeps track of the number of times the pointer is found in that location, which corresponds to a public symbol.

Note Because static symbols are not public, Profiler records the number of times the pointer is found in the static symbol in the next lower public symbol.

The output of Profiler is stored in the current directory in a file named profile.out.

Stop Running Profiler repeatedly overwrites the profile.out file with new data each time. To save Profiler data, change the name of the file.

So that Profiler can see your symbols, use the switches -debug.full and -dubugtype:coff.

To invoke Profiler, use the following syntax:

```
> profiler
```

Profiler does not have any parameters.

Pview

Pview (process view) enables you to look at all of the processes running on a Windows NT system. Pview allows you to see how the running processes are using virtual memory. Pview also shows the priority of the processes and even the priority of their threads.

To invoke Profiler, use the following syntax:

```
> pview appName
```

Pview does not have any parameters.

Regini

Regini simplifies the installation of Extensible Counters for use by the Performance Monitor. Regini uses a specified text file to change the information in the Windows NT Registry.

To use Regini to install the Extensible Counters, put Regini on your path.

Setedit

The Setedit display looks very much like the Windows NT Performance Monitor. You can use Setedit, however, to change the chart setting files. For example, when you edit a legend line, you can enter instance names.

You can also use Setedit to find instances within Performance Monitor log files. Inactive instances are hard to find using Performance Monitor because it only recognizes instances that are alive at the start of a time window. You can, however, use Setedit to enter the name of an instance into a settings file. Then when the settings file is opened by the Performance Monitor the entered instance can be found easily.

To invoke Setedit, use the following syntax:

```
> setedit [setfile.pmc]
```

where setfile.pmc is an optional argument that specifies the name of the settings file to edit.

Tlist

Tlist is a simple utility that displays the names and process IDs (PIDs) of all running applications in a decimal format.

To invoke Tlist, use the following syntax:

```
> tlist
```

Tlist does not have any parameters.

Unlodctr

Unlodctr performs the opposite task of Lodctr: it unloads all objects used to monitor performance, such as counters, monitoring objects, and explanation text. Make sure to remove Performance Monitor support for monitoring objects that are being uninstalled.

Stop If you run Lodctr twice without running Unlodctr in between, it becomes very difficult to remove monitoring objects and counters. Unused monitoring objects and counters take up unnecessary space in the Registry.

Unlodctr is included with the software distribution of Windows NT 3.5 and later.

To invoke unlodctr, use the following syntax:

```
> unlodctr applicationName
```

Unlodctr looks in the application Name's Performance key for the First and Last counter values and removes the First counter, First help, Last counter, and Last help entries in applicationName's Performance key.

Vadump

Vadump (Virtual Address Dump) examines the address space used by a process. It shows the following:

◆ The state the process is in

◆ The size of each segment used in virtual address space

Some of this information also is included in Pview. You can, however, print the results of Vadump.

One application of Vadump is to see whether or not the virtual address space is over-allocated.

To invoke Vadump, use the following syntax:

```
> vadump -m -o -p PID
```

where PID is the process ID of an application. You can get the process ID of an application by using Tlist.

WAP

Windows API Profiler (WAP) is a tool that measures high precision timing. The tool is useful for determining which API calls take the longest to look up. WAP counts and times calls sent from applications to the system.

To invoke WAP, use the following syntax:

```
> apf32dmp appName
```

where appName is the name of the application whose calls you are measuring.

To end the WAP session, type the following command:

```
> apf32cvt undo appName
```

You can use the output of WAP to reduce or get rid of API calls that take a long time to process.

Wperf

Wperf is a performance monitor. It is simpler to use than the Performance Monitor and it has a different interface. After starting Wperf, you should enlarge the window and then click on the chart surface to reveal menus.

To invoke Wperf, use the following syntax:

```
> wperf
```

Wperf does not have any parameters.

wt

wt is a simple, symbolic debugger. When you execute wt, it displays the instructions executing in the running processes. You can use this information to trace calls in a program, and to measure the number of instructions between calls.

To invoke wt, type the following:

```
> wt
```

You can use the information provided by wt to reduce the number of instructions between calls.

Running Windows NT Diagnostics

The Windows NT Diagnostics application, WINMSD.EXE, enables you to print and view configuration information for a local or remote computer. Windows NT Diagnostics enables you to view the following:

◆ Information about the operating system, Windows NT, including its version number, system start options, and process, system, and user environment variables

◆ Information about your hardware setup, including BIOS information, CPU type, CPU steppings, and video resolution

◆ Information about DMA usage, physical memory, and the paging file

◆ A listing of drives and devices installed on the computer along with the drive's and device's port number and interrupt (IRQ) number

◆ A status report detailing the status of services and drivers in the system.

◆ Information about the network, including configuration settings, transports, and statistics

◆ Configuration information about printer and fonts settings

◆ A list of running system processes

You invoke Windows NT Diagnostics by double-clicking in the Administrative Tools group on the diagnostics icon.

Using the Performance Monitor

The Performance Monitor allows you to create charts, record log files, set alerts, and format reports so that you can better understand what is affecting the performance of your system. It uses counters in different objects, including the following:

◆ Cache

◆ Paging File

◆ Redirector

◆ LogicalDisk

◆ PhysicalDisk

◆ Server

◆ Memory

◆ Process

- ◆ System

- ◆ Objects

- ◆ Processor

- ◆ Thread

The counters increment whenever they are encountered in program execution. Not only can you count the number of times that the execution path has gone through a specific counter, you can also measure the time it takes to execute a certain branch of code by positioning counters at the beginning and ending of a branch. Using this information, you can detect such things as network bottlenecks, poor load balancing, resource usage, and unnecessary paging.

System performance is most commonly hindered when the demand for resources, such as CPU time, memory, hard disk, and networking hardware and software, exceeds the capabilities of the system. Applications make demands on most of these resources. Learning how applications interact with Windows NT Workstation can help you optimize the application's performance.

Summary

Microsoft provides many tools that can help you optimize the performance of Windows NT and its applications. The performance tools are included in the software distribution and through a WWW site.

Part II

Managing the Windows NT Desktop

Exploring Windows NT New Interface

S ince the inception of Windows NT, the NT interface has resembled the Windows 3.x interface. Windows NT always had more applets, such as Scheduler+, than Windows 3.x, but the look of the interfaces was the same. The similarity was intentional; users of one operating system found it easy to switch to the other.

The latest version of Windows, Windows 95, employs a dramatically different interface from Windows 3.1. Windows NT adopts the same interface in version 4.0. In Windows NT, the interface is called Windows NT Explorer.

The main difference between the Windows NT 3.x and Windows 4.0 interface is the use of the desktop metaphor. In version 3.x, applications and devices were grouped into application groups. You could move an application icon from one group to another, but you could not, for example, move an icon out of the Program Manager onto the wallpaper.

Windows NT Explorer dispenses with Program Manager. In Explorer, you can display files, applications, directories, and devices (such as printers) as icons on the root window, which is the wallpaper. Liberating application and device icons from application groups gives you more direct access to these objects; it also enables you to fill the desktop (the root window) with all of the tools you commonly need to accomplish your tasks.

Windows NT Explorer presents a radically new interface to the user. After you start an application, however, everything works just about the same as it did in version 3.x. So, although the new interface might at first be a shock, once you get familiar with finding application and device icons, and get familiar with placing them on the desktop, your biggest learning hurdle is over. Perhaps the only other novelty is getting used to using two mouse buttons on a regular basis rather than just one.

This chapter describes the Windows NT Explorer interface.

Getting Windows NT Explorer for Version 3.51

If you are running Windows NT version 3.51, you can download the Windows NT Explorer and duplicate most of what Windows NT version 4.0 has to offer. To download the Windows NT Explorer, use the anonymous FTP server at Microsoft and download one of the following files, according to the platform you are running:

For Intel platforms:

```
ftp://ftp.microsoft.com/bussys/winnt/winnt-unsup-ed/newshell/nt351nsi.exe
```

For Alpha platforms:

```
ftp://ftp.microsoft.com/bussys/winnt/winnt-unsup-ed/newshell/nt351nsa.exe
```

For PowerPC:

```
ftp://ftp.microsoft.com/bussys/winnt/winnt-unsup-ed/newshell/nt351nsp.exe
```

For MIPS:

```
ftp://ftp.microsoft.com/bussys/winnt/winnt-unsup-ed/newshell/nt351nsm.exe
```

Note If you are unfamiliar with FTP, you can use a World Wide Web (WWW) browser to open the following URL:

```
http://www.microsoft.com
```

From Microsoft's home page, click on the following hyperlinks:

```
Microsoft Products
Microcoft Backoffice and Windows NT
Microsoft Windows NT Workstation
Windows NT Shell Technology Preview
```

The final hyperlink presents you with a list of platforms, including PowerPC, Alpha, MIPS, and x86. When you click on the hyperlink corresponding to your platform, the hyperlink starts an ftp transfer of Explorer to your system.

Alternatively, you can use the following procedure to retrieve the file using FTP:

```
% ftp ftp.microsoft.com
Connected to ftp.microsoft.com
220 sizzle.asd.sgi.com FTP server (Version 4.2.321.2 Wed Feb 15
03:24:32 GMT 1995) ready.
Name (ftp.microsoft.com:clinton): anonymous
331 Guest login ok. Use email address as password
Password: clinton@washington.com
230 Guest login ok, access restrictions apply
ftp> cd /bussys/winnt/winnt-unsup-ed/newshell
250 CWD successful
ftp> get nt351nsi.exe
200 PORT command successful
150 Opening BINARY mode data connection for nt351nsi.exe
226 Transfer complete.
ftp> quit
221 Goodbye.
>
```

This procedure downloads Windows NT Explorer for the Intel platform.

The NT Shell that you download expands to a little over 20 MB. Make sure your hard disk has enough room to handle the uncompressed files.

To install the Windows NT Explorer, run the shupdate.cmd program residing under the directory corresponding to your computer's platform. If, for example, your machine uses a 486 or Pentium processor, use the shupdate.cmd file in the I386 directory. When you reboot your computer, shupdate.cmd converts a number of files to the new format and then displays Windows NT Explorer!

You should bear in mind, however, that shupdate.cmd is beta software. The purpose of publicizing the software is for developers to integrate Explorer into their Windows NT applications and report bugs to Microsoft. Windows NT Explorer at this point is very dependable. Do not be surprised, however, to happen upon some real problems. (My display, for example, occasionally flickers.) Being able to use the Explorer interface is probably worth the risk, however. To minimize your exposure to buggy code, make sure to get the latest version of shupdate.cmd at least once a month.

Using the Root Window

If you have run Windows 3.*x* or Windows NT 3.*x*, you have become very familiar with Program Manager. Program Manager is the window in which all of your application groups appear. Starting an application was as simple as double-clicking on one of the icons in an application group. Application icons could not exist outside application groups, and application icons could not be moved outside Program Manager.

Get ready for a shock. Program Manager is gone. Now, when you log on to Windows NT, you are greeted by the root window, as shown in figure 9.1.

Figure 9.1

The root window of Windows NT Explorer.

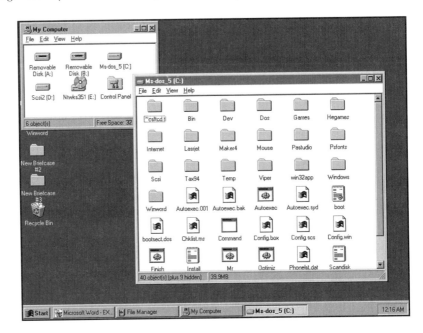

Once in the root window, you see the following three icons:

◆ My Computer

◆ Network Neighborhood

◆ Recycle Bin

Double-clicking on the My Computer icon opens an application group that includes an icon representing the familiar Control Panel application group, and an icon representing each storage medium on your computer. For example, if you have an IDE hard drive, a SCSI hard drive, and a CD-ROM, there would be an icon for each drive. If you double-click on any of the device icons, Explorer displays the files and folders on it.

Notice that Explorer dispenses with displaying the familiar hierarchical relationships between files and directories. Instead, Explorer displays files and folders on a desktop. Folders can contain files and other folders. Double-clicking on a folder opens it, and the contents of the folder are displayed in the window.

Double-clicking on the Network Neighborhood icon opens an application group whose applications facilitate using your computer on a network. If you did not install the networking software, the application group is empty.

The Recycle Bin is a '90s twist on the familiar trash can icon. To delete applications from the desktop, just pull them into the Recycle Bin.

Double-clicking on the Recycle Bin reveals the objects that have been deleted from the desktop. They appear in a window whose menus and menu choices are similar to those found in File Manager. You have the option of using a mouse to drag objects out of the Recycle Bin to replace them on the desktop, or you can delete them for good by using options in the File menu.

Using the Root Menu

When you clicked on the wallpaper in version 3.*x*, nothing happened. When you click on the wallpaper in Explorer with the secondary mouse button, the pop-up root menu displays, as shown in figure 9.2.

The options of the root menu have the following functions:

◆ **Arrange Icons.** Enables you to arrange the icons on the Root window by Name, Type, Size, or Date. You can also click on the last option, Auto Arrange, to rearrange the icons automatically. Clicking on this option toggles it on or off. Leaving it checked (on) places the icons on a grid; otherwise, icons can get placed on top of one another, and a great many jumbled icons can be difficult to read.

Figure 9.2

The Root menu.

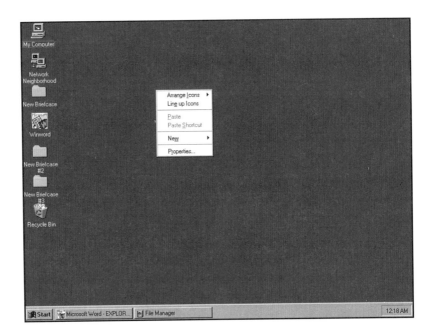

◆ **Line up Icons.** Positions the icons in the Root window in straight rows and columns. This is the manual equivalent to what Auto Arrange, under the Arrange Icons option, does automatically.

◆ **Paste.** Enables you to paste into the Root window an icon you previously cut from somewhere else. For example, if you double-click on the Recycle Bin icon, highlight one of the files in the Bin, then use the Cut option in the Edit menu to remove the highlighted file (and place it on the Clipboard), you can then use the Paste option, in the Root pop-up window, to paste the cut file into the Root window.

◆ **Paste Shortcut.** Enables you to paste a shortcut into the Root window. A shortcut is actually a link to an application. It appears as an icon in the Root window. Instead of using the Start button to execute applications, you can just as easily paste the icon of an application or device on the Root window so that you can double-click on it very easily to start the application.

◆ **Undo Delete.** Retrieves the last icon placed in the Recycle Bin and places it back on the Root window.

◆ **New.** Enables you to place new items in the Root window, including the following:

   ◆ **Folder.** Places a new, empty folder in the Root window.

   ◆ **Shortcut.** Enables you to define a Shortcut for the application in the active window. A Shortcut is a link to an application; it appears as an icon. When you double-click on it, the associated application starts. Creating a shortcut for an application is the only way to place the icon of an application on the Root window.

   ◆ **Briefcase.** Places a briefcase icon on the Root window.

   ◆ **Paintbrush Picture.** Displays the paint program familiar to Windows 3.*x* users.

   ◆ **Text Document.** Places a text icon in the Root window. When you double-click on the new icon, called New Text document, Windows NT displays a window of the Notebook application included in the Windows NT software distribution. In that window you can use the Open option under the File menu to link the New Text Document icon to the opened document.

   ◆ **Sound.** Places a sound icon in the Root window. The sound icon must represent a sound file. When you double-click on the new icon, called New Sound, Windows NT displays a window in which you can specify the pathname and filename of the sound file.

◆ **Properties.** Displays the Color window, which enables you to choose the colors used for the text, scroll bars, title bars, panes, and menus in all windows.

These tools enable you to create, delete, color, and name any icon that appears on the root window.

Using Shortcuts

When you click on New in the Root pop-up window and the Shortcut option in the sub pop-up window, Explorer displays the Create Shortcut window, as shown in figure 9.3.

In the text entry field, type the pathname and the name of the application or device you want direct access to. After you click on the **N**ext button, Explorer lets you confirm your selection by clicking on the Finish or **B**ack button to approve or disapprove the selection.

Figure 9.3

Creating a shortcut.

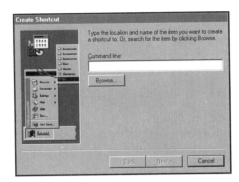

Using Briefcase

More and more people are using more than one computer to work on the same set of files. You might, for example, have a workstation and use a laptop computer for sales trips. Transferring files from one computer to another can lead to problems, such as overwriting the latest version of the file with an older version, or working on two instances of a file at the same time, which then requires that you somehow fit together the two differently revised files.

The Briefcase application takes the confusion out of this process. When you double-click on the briefcase icon for the first time, Windows NT Explorer displays the Welcome to the Windows Briefcase window, as shown in figure 9.4. This window explains how to use Briefcase.

Figure 9.4

Welcome to the Windows Briefcase window.

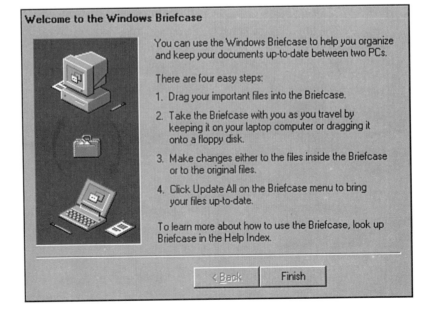

To use Briefcase, use the following procedure:

1. Drag (or Open) files that you want to work on with more than one computer into the Briefcase window, as shown in figure 9.5.

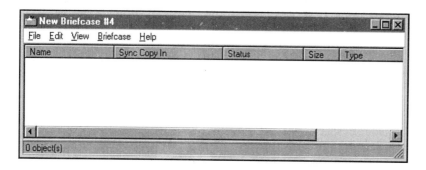

Figure 9.5

Manipulating Files in the Briefcase.

2. Keep a Briefcase on both your workstation and your other computer. To transfer all Briefcase files to a second computer by using a floppy disk, drag the Briefcase icon onto the floppy icon.

3. Work either on the files listed in the Briefcase or on the original files.

4. When you finish working on a file, use the secondary mouse button to click on the Briefcase icon. Explorer displays the icon window.

5. On the pop-up menu, click on Update All.

This option makes sure both computer systems have the latest versions of a file.

Using Icon Pop-Up Menus

When you click on an icon with the secondary mouse button, Windows NT Explorer displays an icon pop-up menu. The options on the menu vary according to the type of object the icon represents. The following list describes the common menu items:

◆ **Open.** Opens the window of the application that was minimized. This menu option is the equivalent of double-clicking on the icon with the primary mouse button.

◆ **Explore.** Used with document holders only, such as folders and briefcases, Explore shows the contents of the object in a display similar to the File Manager.

◆ **Cut.** Removes the icon from the Root window and places a copy of it on the Clipboard so that you can later paste it somewhere.

◆ **Copy.** Saves a copy of the icon to the Clipboard so that you can later paste it somewhere.

◆ **Create Shortcut.** Displays a new icon that is a shortcut to the icon you clicked on to display the icon pop-up menu.

◆ **Delete.** Removes the icon from the desktop and deposits it in the Recycle Bin.

◆ **Rename.** Enables you to rename the icon.

◆ **Properties.** Displays the Color window, which enables you to choose the colors used for the text, scroll bars, title bars, panes, and menus in all windows.

These tools make manipulating icons easy.

Recovering from Broken Applications

If you are coming from the Windows 3.x environment, you are already familiar with the problems of broken applications. You may have started an application and waited awhile until you realized the application was frozen. In Windows 3.x, the only way to recover was by pressing Ctrl+Alt+Del. Rebooting your computer meant that you had to reopen all of the applications you were running before the application crash.

Windows NT is wonderful in this regard. When an application crashes, you again press Ctrl+Alt+Del, but instead of rebooting, Windows NT returns you to the root window with the crashed application represented as an icon. The title to the icon says that the application is frozen.

When you click on the icon with the secondary mouse button, Windows NT displays the pop-up menu. You most commonly want to use the option that terminates the frozen application. (If you use the primary mouse button to click on the icon, you return to the frozen application.) When you terminate the application, the icon disappears—and that is all there is to it! No rebooting the system and reopening your applications.

Using the Taskbar

At the bottom of the root window is a bar called the Taskbar, as shown in figure 9.6.

There are four sections to the Taskbar:

◆ The middle part of the Taskbar, which is blank.

◆ On the far right side of the Taskbar, Explorer can display a digital clock.

◆ In the middle of the bar, buttons display for each running application. When you minimize an application, you can maximize it by clicking on its button in the Taskbar.

◆ On the very left of the Taskbar is the Start button, which enables you to start applications.

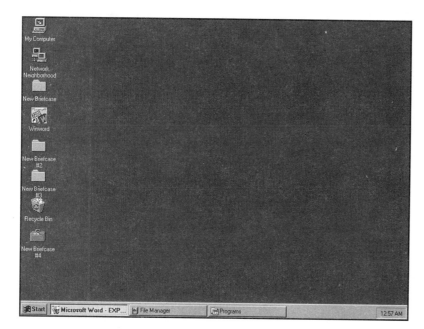

Figure 9.6

The Taskbar appears even when other applications are running.

This section describes the Taskbar in detail.

Setting the Display

Explorer enables you to arrange the windows in the Root window automatically. When you use the secondary mouse button to click on the part of the Taskbar that is blank, Explorer displays a pop-up menu, as shown in figure 9.7.

The options in the menu have the following definitions:

◆ **Cascade.** Arranges windows on top of one another, as shown in figure 9.8.

◆ **Tile Vertically.** Arranges windows next to one another without any overlap, as shown in figure 9.9.

Figure 9.7

The Taskbar pop-up menu.

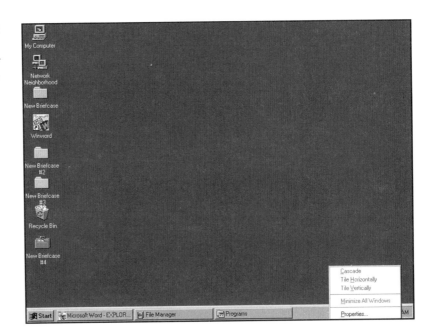

Figure 9.8

Cascading windows.

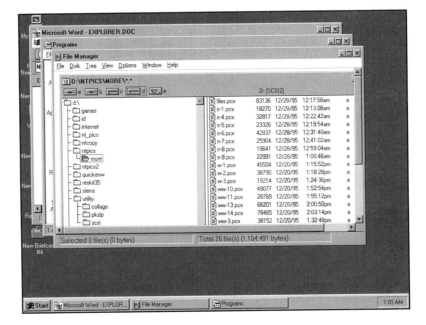

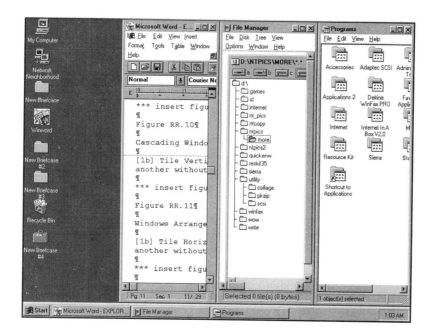

Figure 9.9

Windows arranged vertically.

◆ **Tile Horizontally.** Arranges windows on top of one another without any overlap, as shown in figure 9.10.

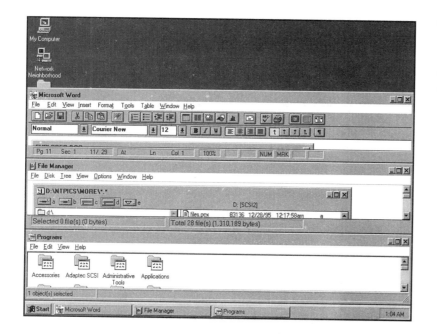

Figure 9.10

Windows arranged horizontally.

◆ **Minimize All Windows.** Makes all windows disappear from the Root window. This option does not appear when all windows are minimized.

◆ **Undo Minimize All.** Restores all windows minimized by the Minimize All Windows option. This option only appears after the user has clicked on Minimize All Windows.

◆ **Properties.** Displays the Taskbar Properties window.

These tools control the objects in the root window.

Using the Taskbar Properties Window

The Taskbar Properties window controls the display of the Taskbar. This window has two tabs: Taskbar Options and Start Menu Programs.

The Taskbar tab governs the display of the Taskbar. The window has four check boxes:

◆ If Always on top is checked, the Taskbar always displays on top of any other window. If this option is not checked, the Taskbar can sink under other windows.

◆ If Auto hide is checked, the Taskbar does not display; it does display if the box is unchecked.

◆ If Show small icons is checked, the size of the icons in the Start pop-up menu is reduced. If the box is unchecked, Explorer uses larger icons in the Start pop-up menu

◆ If Show clock is checked, Explorer displays a digital clock on the right side of the Taskbar.

Note If you hide the Taskbar, you might later decide to display it again. To display the Taskbar, use the following procedure:

1. Press Ctrl+Alt+Del.

   Explorer displays the Windows NT Security window.

2. Click on the Task List button.

   Explorer displays the Taskbar and the options in the Start pop-up menu.

3. Click on the Settings option in the Start pop-up menu.

   Explorer displays the Taskbar Properties window.

4. Click on the Taskbar icon.

   Explorer displays the Taskbar Properties window.

5. Uncheck the Auto hide check box by clicking on it.

6. Click on the OK button in the Taskbar Properties window.

The Start Menu Programs tab in the Taskbar Properties window enables you to modify the listings displayed by the Programs and Text Document options in the Start pop-up menu.

The top section of the Start Menu Program tab enables you to add or remove the applications and application groups listed by the Programs option in the Start pop-up menu. You can customize the listing most intuitively by using the Add and Remove buttons.

If you plan, however, to add and remove many applications from the Programs listing, it is easier to use the Advanced button. When you click on this button, Explorer displays the Exploring Start Menu window, which closely resembles the File Manager, as you can see in figure 9.11.

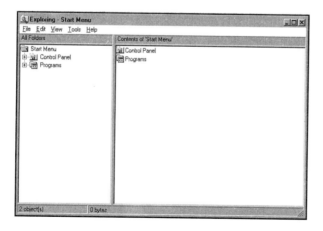

Figure 9.11

The Exploring Start Menu window.

You can use the Delete option in the File menu to remove applications from the Programs listing, or the Explore option in the File menu to add to the Programs listing.

In the bottom half of the Start Menu Programs tab is a section that enables you to remove all of the listings in the Documents option in the Start pop-up menu. All you have to do is click on the Clear button.

Reorienting the Taskbar

By default, the Taskbar appears across the bottom of the screen. If, however, you double-click on the digital clock, the Taskbar displays vertically on the right side of the screen, as shown in figure 9.12.

Figure 9.12

The Taskbar displayed vertically.

Try the Taskbar displayed each way. You might find that one orientation is better than another according to the layout of the applications you use most often. For example, if you mostly do word processing, a longer, narrower window more closely resembles an 8.5-by-11-inch sheet of paper than a wide, short window. In this example, displaying the Taskbar vertically is more appropriate to the word processor's display.

The only drawback to displaying the Taskbar vertically is that the application buttons are dramatically abbreviated. Because the application button includes the application's icon, it is still relatively easy to determine what application the application button represents.

Setting the Digital Clock

When you use the secondary mouse button to click on the digital clock, Explorer displays the Taskbar pop-up menu as shown in figure 9.7, with one exception, an additional menu item appears as the first option in the list: Adjust Date/Time.

When you click on the Adjust Date/Time option, Windows NT Explorer displays the Date/Time window (also accessible through the Control Panel), as shown in figure 9.13.

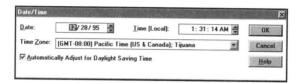

Figure 9.13

The Date/Time window.

You can use this window to set the computer's date and time.

Using the Start Button

On the very left of the Taskbar is the Start button. As its name suggests, Start is almost always the first button you click after you log on.

In case you are totally befuddled by the interface, Microsoft includes an animated message that slides the phrase "<- Start by clicking here" from right to left on the Taskbar if you either take too long to click on the Start button or are a first-time user of Windows NT Explorer.

When you use the primary mouse button to click on the Start button, Windows NT displays the pop-up menu shown in figure 9.14.

Figure 9.14

The Start pop-up menu.

The options of the Start menu are as follows:

◆ Programs

◆ Documents

◆ Settings

◆ Find

◆ Help

◆ Run

◆ Shut Down

An arrow to the right of a menu item means that a child menu will display if you choose the option with the arrow. Child menus can also have arrows beside menu options, in which case, more menus can be displayed at the same time.

The following sections explain each of these options.

Programs Option

Clicking on the Programs option lists all of the application groups that you used to see in Program Manager, as shown in figure 9.15.

Figure 9.15

The Programs option.

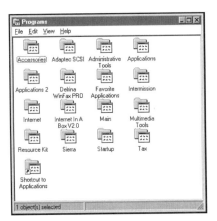

When you move the mouse cursor to one of the application groups, Explorer displays a child menu showing the applications in the application group, as shown in figure 9.22. Clicking on one of the applications in the child menu invokes that application.

Documents Option

Clicking on the Documents option lists documents that you have worked on recently in any application, such as Winword and Framemaker. Clicking on a document name opens the word-processing application and loads the document.

Settings Option

Clicking on the Settings option displays icons for the following:

◆ Executing the Taskbar application

◆ Displaying the Control Panel group

If you click on the Taskbar icon, Explorer displays the Taskbar Properties window.

For more information about this window, see the section, "Using the Taskbar Properties Window."

Find Option

Clicking on the Find option enables you to find files, folders, or computers in a network. When you click on Files and folders, Explorer displays the Find: All Files window, as shown in figure 9.16.

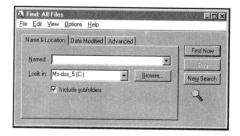

Figure 9.16

The Find: All Files window.

The Find: All Files window has the following three tabs:

◆ **Name & Location.** Finds files and folders by entering their names, pathnames, or both.

◆ **Date Modified.** Finds files modified on or between specified dates, as shown in figure 9.17.

Figure 9.17

The Date Modified tab.

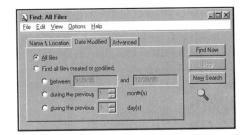

◆ **Advanced.** Finds files according to type or size, or files containing a specified word or phrase, as shown in figure 9.18.

Figure 9.18

The Advanced tab.

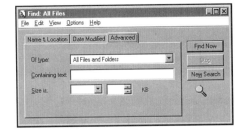

You can use the Find option on the Start pop-up menu to find a computer on a network. When you click on the Computer option in the sub menu, Explorer displays the Find: Computer window, as shown in figure 9.19.

Figure 9.19

Finding a computer.

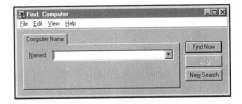

After typing in the name of a computer in the **N**amed: text field, you click on the F**i**nd Now button. Explorer reports any name matches of computers on the network.

Help Option

Clicking on the Help option in the Start pop-up menu starts the Help application.

Run Option

Clicking on the Run option in the Start pop-up menu displays the Run window, as shown in figure 9.20.

Figure 9.20

The Run window.

In the **O**pen: text field, type the pathname and the name of the application you want to run. This window is the equivalent of the Run option in the File menu of the Program Manager. You use it most often to install new applications on your computer.

Shut Down Option

Clicking on the Shut Down option in the Start pop-up menu displays the Shut Down Windows window.

After clicking on one of the three options, depending on whether you want to restart Windows NT, you click on the Yes button to shut down Windows NT, or the No button to return to Windows NT.

Alternative Uses of the Start Button

The preceding sections used the Start button by clicking it with the primary mouse button. When you click the Start button with the secondary mouse button, Explorer displays a different menu, as shown in figure 9.21.

The following sections explain the functionality of each of the menu options.

Open Option

Clicking on the **O**pen option in the secondary menu displays the Start Menu window with the application group called Programs, as shown in figure 9.22.

Figure 9.21

The secondary menu for the Start button.

Figure 9.22

The Programs application group.

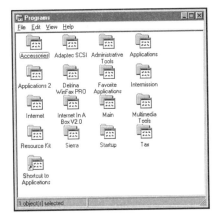

The programs listed under the secondary Start menu are the same programs that are listed when you click on the Programs option in the Start pop-up menu.

Using the **O**pen option in the secondary menu is the easiest to add or delete files or folders from the list of programs displayed by the Programs option. Deleting a file, for example, is as easy as highlighting it and clicking on the Delete option in the File menu.

Explore Option

Clicking on the **E**xplore option in the secondary menu displays the Exploring Start Menu, as shown in figure 9.23.

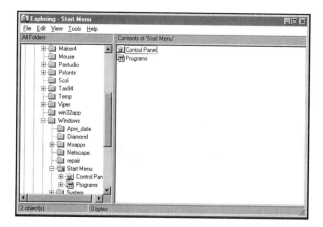

Figure 9.23

The Exploring Start Menu window.

You recognize this display as being similar to the File Manager display. The hierarchy of files and folders is made clear by lines and indentations. The files and folders listed are the same as those listed when you click on the Programs option in the Start pop-up menu.

By clicking on folders, you can reveal or hide their contents.

Find Option

Clicking on the **F**ind Option displays the Find window that enables you to search for files by specifying search criteria.

In the middle of the Taskbar you find buttons for each running application.

Application buttons are valuable because they do not get covered. They work like tabs: clicking on one restores the window or moves the window to the top of the displayed windows.

You might have had the frustrating experience of opening so many applications at the same time that weeding through the windows to find the application you wanted was laborious. It was so easy to lose windows in the heap of running applications.

By listing all running applications, you have instant access to their window by clicking on the button with the application's name. This functionality saves a lot of headaches.

When the running application's window is not minimized, the application button is black-and-white, and appears depressed. When the application's window is minimized, the application button is colored, and appears raised.

Using the Secondary Mouse Button with Application Buttons

When you click on an application button in the Taskbar with the secondary mouse button, Explorer displays a pop-up menu of actions you might want to perform on the application, as shown in figure 9.24.

Figure 9.24

The Application button pop-up menu.

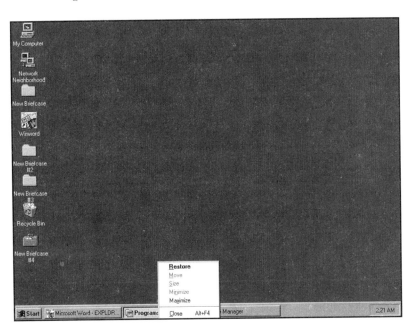

You recognize these options from the menu that would display in version 3.*x* if you single-clicked on an icon. The menu options in figure 9.24 have the following functions:

◆ **Restore.** Displays the window the same size as it was before it was minimized.

◆ **Move.** Enables you to move a displayed window.

◆ **Size.** Enables you to change the size of a displayed window.

◆ **Minimize.** Makes the window disappear.

◆ **Maximize.** Makes the window as large as the entire screen.

◆ **Close.** Terminates the application.

◆ **Run.** Displays the Run window, as shown in figure 9.25, which enables you to display the Clipboard or the Control Panel application group. The Clipboard is a buffer that contains information that you previously copied or cut.

Figure 9.25

The Run window.

Displaying a Minimized Window

You can minimize windows in a variety of ways, including the following:

◆ Click on the button with a dash in it on the top, right of the Title bar.

◆ Use the secondary mouse button to click on the application button in the Taskbar. This action displays the Taskbar pop-up menu from which you can click on Mi**n**imize.

◆ Use the secondary mouse button to click on a blank spot on the Taskbar. This action displays the Taskbar pop-up menu from which you can click on Minimize All Windows.

When you minimize a window, it disappears from the Root window. The application button, however, remains in the Taskbar. To reopen the application, you can perform one of the following tasks:

◆ Click on the application button in the Taskbar.

◆ Click on the application button in the Taskbar with the secondary mouse button. When Explorer displays the Application Button pop-up menu, click on the **R**estore option.

Getting rid of icons and replacing them with application buttons on the Taskbar eliminates the problem of trying to find icons burried under layers of windows.

The New Look, Feel, and Functionality of Explorer

If you have worked with Windows 3.x or Windows NT 3.x in the past, you see that the look, feel, and functionality of the windows in Explorer are different. For example, in the past, when you grabbed the corner of a window and pulled it, only an outline of the window expanded or shrunk. When you released the corner, the window would instantly resize to the shape of the outline. In Explorer, however, when you grab a corner and pull it, the entire window expands or shrinks in real time.

This section examines some of the new features in Windows NT that gives it such a different look and feel from Windows 3.x and Windows NT 3.x.

Using the Title Bar

The title bar in all Explorer windows is different from that in version 3.x. On the upper, left corner of the window in version 3.x, you used to see a box with a dash in it, as shown in figure 9.26.

Figure 9.26

The old title bar.

Double-clicking on the dash button terminated the window (and the application running in the window). Single-clicking on the dash button displayed the Control pop-up menu that enabled you to do such things as maximize, minimize, move, raise, lower, and close the window.

In Explorer, the dash button is replaced by a graphic, as shown in figure 9.27.

Figure 9.27

The new title bar.

The new icon performs the same function as the dash button—double-clicking on it terminates the window, single-clicking on it reveals the Control menu.

In version 3.x, on the right side of the title bar are the maximize and minimize buttons represented by buttons containing an up and down arrow, respectively (refer to fig. 9.26).

These buttons are replaced by three new buttons (refer to fig. 9.27). The functions of the buttons are as follows:

◆ The button with a dash minimizes the window.

◆ The button with a square maximizes the window, meaning that the window expands to the size of the screen.

◆ The button with an "X" terminates the window.

The "X" button provides a way to terminate a window using a single click. (The icon on the extreme left side of the Title bar requires that you double-click on it to terminate a window.)

Using the Help System

On some windows you see a button with a question mark in it on the right side of the Title bar. This button enables you to access pop-up help windows. If, for example, you click on the question mark with the primary mouse button, the mouse cursor changes to a question mark. If you then click on an object in the window, a brief description of the object you clicked on pops up, as shown in figure 9.28.

Figure 9.28

Using the question mark button.

If you click on a window object, such as a text entry field, with the secondary mouse button, the What's This? pop-up window displays, as shown in figure 9.29.

Figure 9.29

The What's This pop-up option.

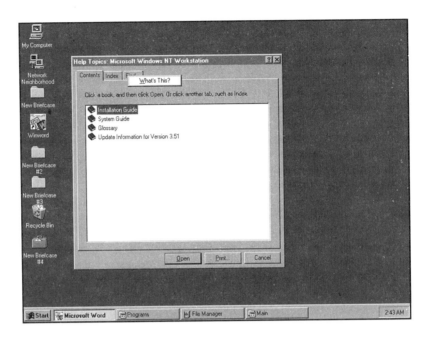

If you click on the **W**hat's This window with the primary mouse button, Windows NT displays brief, context-sensitive help.

 Note   You can only access help pop-up windows using either mouse button when the window has a question mark icon in the upper right corner.

Using Tabs in Windows

Windows NT Explorer uses a new windows library called Common Controls. One of the additions to windows that you will see as a result of the new library is the use of tabs.

Tabs function just like tabs on a manila folder: they stick out so you can find folders easily.

When you layer window upon window, it is easy to lose windows under the pile. The advantage of using tabs is that the tab for each pane on the window is always visible. Whenever you click on a tab, its pane moves to the top.

Note In the latest version of Windows NT Workstation, you can raise a window to the top of the stack of windows by clicking anywhere on the window that you want to raise. This feature alone is worth the cost of the upgrade!

Tabs can run across the top of a window as well as down the sides.

Using Folders

The visual metaphor of a folder suggests that the Explorer folder, just like a manila folder, can hold files and other folders. The use of folders is not entirely new to Windows. File Manager in version 3.*x* uses a folder icon as a symbol for a directory. When you click on a folder in File Manager, it actually appears to open and its contents are then displayed in the right side of File Manager. File Manager uses the visual metaphor of a hierarchy to suggest the relationship between directories and files.

Windows NT Explorer disassociates the folder icon with directories and hierarchies. Whenever you choose the **O**pen option in any of the Windows NT Explorer menus, the contents of folders, briefcases, and the Recycle Bin display, as shown in figure 9.30.

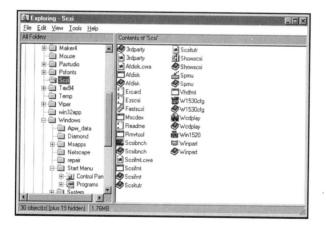

Figure 9.30

Using folders in Windows NT.

Note You can change the display in figure 9.30 to a hierarchically oriented display by choosing Details in the View menu. When Large Icon or Small Icon is selected, the display uses the icons of paper and folders.

Instead of seeing the folder in figure 9.30 as representing a directory, you just see the folder as something unto itself. For this reason, the use of the folder in Explorer is based more on what a folder in the real world is instead of a computer organizational concept: a directory. In this way, Windows NT Explorer provides a more intuitive interface made of images of commonplace things.

When you double-click on a folder, it opens to reveal its contents, which might be files or other folders.

Examining the New Look of Windows

Not only have the icons in windows changed, but the look of the windows has also changed. For example, when you pull down menus, you see a three-dimensional menu instead of the two-dimensional rendering found in version 3.x. Dividers that separate menu items in 3.x menus are simple lines, but in Explorer, dividers are carefully shadowed, three-dimensional crevices.

 Note   If you have worked on X systems with GUIs such as Motif or Solaris, you will notice similar images in Windows NT Explorer. The menus, for example, look the same. The use of horizontal scrolling in file listings and the use of folders to hold files is also reminiscent of Solaris.

Everything in Explorer is much more richly detailed in three dimensions.

Examining the Desktop

In version 3.x, the interface for starting applications was application groups filled with icons. All application groups appeared in the Program Manager. The interface was easy to use because it was graphical; starting an application was as easy as double-clicking on the icon for the application. This interface was much easier to use than entering commands at a system prompt. The interface, however, did not represent anything; it was simply a tool to start applications.

Windows NT Explorer succeeds in implementing the metaphor of a desktop. The desktop in Explorer is the Root window. On the desktop you can place many things, not just application groups. On the desktop you can place, for example, a file, an application group, a printer icon, an application icon, a folder; any icon that you find in any folder can be placed on the Root window for direct access, just as you might set out all of the items you need to do your work on a real desktop.

For people who have used GUIs such as Motif, Solaris, or System 7 by Apple, the desktop metaphor is not new. For those who have used only Windows 3.x or Windows

NT 3.*x*, the desktop metaphor is a welcome surprise. It frees applications from the confines of application groups and the trouble of memorizing what applications reside in which application groups.

Application Groups in Explorer

Application groups have not entirely disappeared. You can still create collections of applications because you tend to use them in conjunction with one another. If you bring forward the settings in your CONFIG.SYS and AUTOEXEC.BAT files when you install Windows NT, you can still access those application groups by choosing Programs in the Start pop-up menu.

Summary

The latest version of Windows NT not only offers added functionality, but a dramatically redesigned user interface. The interface resembles Unix interfaces, most notably Solaris and Motif. Users can use the Root window, called the desktop, to display icons for files, devices, folders, briefcases, and other programming objects. The freedom to place an icon representing hardware or software on the desktop enables easy access to all of these elements. Gone is the Program Manager that served as the root window for application groups. Application groups still exist, but they do not form the centerpiece for application activation.

Windows NT Explorer supports the new library, Common Controls. This library enables new window widgets, such as horizontal and vertical tabs within windows. Both tabs and the Taskbar help users locate specific windows when windows are piled upon windows.

The Explorer interface is so dramatically different from the 3.*x* interface that the new user might first experience shock. The success with which Microsoft engineers have designed a more intuitive interface using the desktop as the central metaphor enables even new users to quickly master the Explorer interface.

The Explorer interface made only the Program Manager obsolete. All of the other familiar applications and application groups, such as the Control Panel, found in version 3.*x* remain in Explorer. Because of the new freedom found in the desktop, however, the emphasis shifts away from application groups and toward a customized desktop.

Mastering the Windows NT Application Groups

In the earlier chapters, you learned the basics of the way Windows NT works. You also became familiar with the Windows Explorer and the basic skills you need to know to manipulate windows. This chapter introduces you to the members of Windows NT application groups and the following topics:

- ◆ Getting to know the desktop

- ◆ Introducing the application groups

- ◆ Running multiple applications

Getting to Know the Desktop

After you launch Windows NT and successfully log on, you are presented with the desktop. System commands are represented by pictures on the Windows NT desktop. These pictures take the form of icons, buttons, controls, and parts of application and document windows. You communicate by acting on one of these pictures, clicking a mouse button, or pressing a key.

Tip   In MS-DOS and Unix, you often use command-line switches to define the action the command is to take. Windows NT assigns the same information for a command by using option buttons, check boxes, list boxes, and combination boxes in a dialog box.

When Windows NT requires information about command options, a dialog box containing various controls appears. As discussed in Appendix B, dialog boxes are Windows NT's pictorial way of representing familiar command-line options. A key difference between working at a command prompt and working on the Windows NT desktop is that you do not have to remember the exact command switches—you just have to specify the options you want in the dialog box.

Tip   In Windows NT, you also can run a command-prompt session by double-clicking on the Command Prompt icon in the Main menu. The set of commands available is similar to that in MS-DOS.

If you are familiar with character-based environments, you might find working on the desktop awkward at first. After you understand the parts and get used to the rhythm, however, you probably will find the desktop more comfortable than the command lines of other operating systems.

Parts of the Desktop

The Windows NT desktop is organized into three layers: the Root window, the wallpaper layer, and the application layer. As figure 10.1 shows, each layer has particular functions attached to it.

New Riders Publishing
INSIDE
SERIES

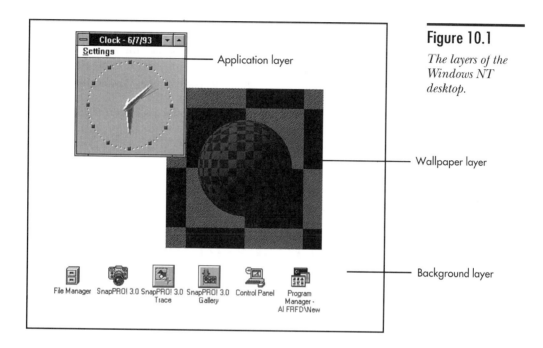

Figure 10.1

The layers of the Windows NT desktop.

The Root Window

The Root window is the background upon which everything else is laid. Uncovered, it appears as a blue background. You can place icons on the Root window that represent files, folders, applications, and devices. Windows NT 3.*x* did not have a Root window. You could only place icons within application group windows. (When you minimized applications in NT 3.*x*, an icon appeared on the Wallpaper, but its placement there was temporary: when you terminated the application, the icon disappeared.)

The Root window in Explorer also has functionality. When you right-click on it, a pop-up menu displays. The menu options are explained in Appendix B.

Wallpaper Layer

The *wallpaper layer*, also called the Root window, consists of a picture that fills the screen. Its purpose is to provide an individualized viewing screen so that you find working at your PC more comfortable.

Note Technically, wallpaper is a bit map that is displayed onscreen and stored in your Windows NT directory in a file with a BMP extension.

Application Layer

The *application layer* consists of any application programs you run. Application programs appear in a window. By clicking on these windows, you interact with the application and accomplish work, just as commands typed at an application command prompt enable you to accomplish the same work. A key difference between DOS and Windows NT is that in Windows NT, you can run multiple applications simultaneously (multitask), and these applications communicate directly with one another as you are working.

 Note   See Chapter 4 for more information on multitasking.

Introducing the Application Groups

An application group is a window that holds the icons of applications. You execute those applications by double-clicking on their icons.

There are no restrictions as to the type or number of icons that you can put in an application group. The concept of the application group, however, is one of grouping like applications.

When you work at your desk, you have certain tasks that you typically perform as part of your job. You also have tools with which you perform these tasks.

Windows NT application groups enable you to organize the applications you use into a window that represents that task. If you want to work on a sales report, for instance, double-click on the sales report group icon. The application group window that opens contains all the programs you need for that task. You might have your spreadsheet, calculator, word processor, notepad, and network mail programs grouped together, for example. To access the tool you need at the moment, double-click on the program-item icon.

When you install applications, they create their own application group. It might contain a game icon with icons for other games that you can preview (made by the same company).

Application Groups were the main organizational feature of Windows NT 3.*x*. In Explorer, however, they are buried. You can display application groups by right-clicking on the Start button and selecting Open. When you click on the Programs icon, all of the application groups you used in NT 3.*x* display, as long as you chose to carry the application groups over into NT when you installed it.

Vestiges of application groups are also apparent in the lists displayed with the Start button. Left-clicking on the Start button displays the names of the application groups you used in NT 3.*x*. When you highlight one of the list items, a child menu appears showing the applications in the application group.

Engineers chose to replace application groups with application lists in Explorer because the lists make the applications more accessible. Changing the content of the application groups and changing the properties of the list items, however, are more difficult when using the lists alone. To change the content of an application group or to change the property of an item on a list, it is easier to use the application groups themselves.

 Tip Use a reasonable number of application groups on your Windows NT desktop. Create groups that represent the major tasks you perform. Keep in mind that creating large numbers of application groups takes resources away from working applications. Later in this chapter you are shown the way to add items to application groups.

Several application groups can contain the same program-item icon, which enables you to create groups that represent the tasks you commonly perform at your PC (and have as many groups as you want). Your writing group, for example, might contain your word processor, style checker, dictionary, thesaurus, and encyclopedia programs. Your leisure group might contain various game programs, as well as the same word processor and encyclopedia. As you change tasks, you open the application group representing that task. All your tools are at hand and ready to go.

Windows NT creates six application groups when you install it: Main, Accessories, Games, StartUp, Administrative Tools, and Applications. These groups are explained in the following sections.

The Main Group

Just as you have tools you use to organize the way you work (such as a desktop calendar or a to-do list), Windows NT includes application tools you can use to organize its environment. These tools are in the *Main* application group, as shown in figure 10.2.

Figure 10.2

The Main group.

You find the following applications in the Main group:

♦ **File Manager.** Enables you to perform many file and disk operations, including running applications, formatting disks, managing file directories, and so on.

♦ **Mail.** Enables you to send and receive mail across your network.

♦ **Schedule+.** Enables you to maintain a calendar for yourself and to schedule meetings by accessing the calendars of other people on your network.

♦ **Control Panel.** Enables you to set up many Windows features by using various utilities provided by Windows NT.

♦ **Print Manager.** Enables you to manage Windows NT's print spooler. You can begin and stop print jobs, and change print job priorities here.

♦ **ClipBook Viewer.** Serves as a "transfer agent" to move data from one Windows NT application to another, including programs running on different networked computers.

♦ **Command Prompt.** Enables you to open a command-line window to perform operations.

The Control menu on the Command Prompt window has a new option, Properties. You display the Control menu by clicking on the dash button in the upper left corner of the window. The Properties option enables you to adjust the cursor size, command history size, fonts, screen size and position, and screen colors. The Command Prompt Properties window operates identically to the Console Windows Properties window. For more information about changing any of the window properties, refer to the discussion of the Command Prompt Properties window in Appendix B, "Learning How to Perform Basic Tasks with Windows NT."

◆ **Windows NT Setup.** Enables you to modify some of the basic Windows NT operational parameters. You can, for instance, change video-display resolutions by using the Setup program.

◆ **PIF Editor.** Enables you to establish special settings so that DOS applications run correctly under Windows NT. These settings are established in a program information file (PIF).

◆ **Windows NT Help.** Provides help on all aspects of using Windows NT.

◆ **Introducing Windows NT.** Presents a tutorial on using Windows NT and its features.

The Accessories Group

The *Accessories* application group is shown in figure 10.3.

Figure 10.3

The Accessories group.

You find the following accessory application programs in the Accessories group:

◆ **Calculator.** Provides an on-screen calculator for math operations.

◆ **Cardfile.** Provides the same functionality as a desktop card file.

◆ **Clock.** Displays the time in either analog or digital form.

◆ **Notepad.** Provides a quick, easy-to-use ASCII editor for composing short notes or editing small ASCII files.

◆ **Paintbrush.** Provides a basic drawing package that enables you to produce graphics suitable for inclusion in documents produced by Windows NT applications. Supports PCX, BMP, and MSP formats.

◆ **Chat.** Enables you to conduct a "live" conversation with another user of your network.

◆ **Terminal.** Provides basic terminal-emulation capabilities and enables you to access other computers by modem or serial-port connection.

◆ **3270 Emulator.** Emulates an IBM 3270 terminal for users who need to access data on mainframes that expect this type of terminal.

◆ **Character Map.** Enables you to insert characters not found on most keyboards, such as extended characters and special characters provided in symbol fonts.

◆ **Sound Recorder.** Enables you to record sounds that are input through a microphone attached to your sound board.

◆ **Volume Control.** Enables you to adjust the volume of the channels on your sound card.

◆ **Media Player.** Provides access to playback capabilities for any multimedia device or service, from sound files to Video for Windows files.

◆ **CD Player.** Enables you to play audio CDs by using the sound services of your computer. Of course, you must have a CD-ROM drive to use this applet.

◆ **Write.** Provides a basic word processor with selectable fonts, a search-and-replace function, and other basic features.

You can use the preceding accessories to perform standard work tasks as soon as you install Windows NT. You probably will find it necessary, however, to augment these basic applications with more powerful, off-the-shelf applications. If you plan on doing extensive word processing, for example, Write probably will not suit your needs. Instead, a word processor with more features than Write provides (such as Word for Windows, WordPerfect for Windows, or Ami Pro) is required.

Administrative Tools

The *Administrative Tools* group contains tools that enable you to perform system-level tasks on your computer, such as adding users, configuring hard drives, backing up the system, and monitoring security.

 Note As an individual user, you probably do not use these tools; Windows NT grants the privilege of using most of the features to the system administrator.

The Administrative Tools group is shown in figure 10.4.

Figure 10.4

*The Admin-
istrative Tools
group.*

You find the following programs in the Administrative Tools group:

◆ **User Manager.** Enables you to add user logon accounts to the system and to grant user privileges.

◆ **Disk Administrator.** Enables you to configure hard drives, set up partitions, assign drive letters, and create fault-tolerant disk mirroring.

◆ **Performance Monitor.** Enables you to represent the speed performance of each segment of the system and operating system graphically so that you can troubleshoot potential performance problems.

◆ **Backup.** Enables you to back up data to a tape drive.

◆ **Event Viewer.** Provides a view of the event log, which lists everything that happens on the system. This application enables you to review potential security problems or system problems by examining relevant actions taken by the operating system.

These options are explained in more detail in Chapter 11.

Games

The *Games* application group (as shown in figure 10.5) contains the following three games: Solitaire, Minesweeper, and Freecell.

Figure 10.5

*The Games
application
group.*

Note Microsoft notes that Solitaire is the most thoroughly tested program they ever produced!

Besides their recreational function, these games can help you practice basic Windows NT skills, such as using the mouse, and help you become familiar with Windows NT buttons, boxes, and scroll bars so that you can use other applications more effectively.

The Startup Group

The *Startup* application group is where Windows NT places applications that begin automatically. As figure 10.6 illustrates, Windows NT does not automatically install any programs in this group. Add to this group any applications that you want to run automatically whenever Windows NT starts up. The Startup group, therefore, serves much like the DOS AUTOEXEC.BAT file.

Figure 10.6

The Startup group.

File Manager is a good application to add to the Startup group, especially if you use it often. Loaded automatically, File Manager analyzes your hard drive's directory structure during startup. The next time you access File Manager after startup, File Manager does not have to repeat this analysis. If you start File Manager from its application group each time you need it, you have to wait while File Manager analyzes your drive's directory structure every time.

The Applications Group

The *Applications* group, as shown in figure 10.7, is where Windows NT places all of the application programs it finds already installed on your hard disk. Windows NT searches your drives and sets up the application files it finds in this group. If Windows NT misses one of your applications, you have to set it up on your own. You probably want to reorganize the applications you find here into other groups that more accurately reflect your working tasks.

Figure 10.7

The Applications group.

Modifying an Application Group

When you open an application group, the application group window appears in the same position it held the last time it was opened. If this position is not convenient, several methods for moving and resizing the window are available.

If you want to move the window, point to its title bar with the mouse pointer, press the mouse button, and drag the window anywhere in the Program Manager's workspace. After the window is in position, release the mouse button.

If you want to change the application group's window size, point at one of its borders with the mouse pointer. After the pointer changes to a double arrow, press the mouse button down, and drag the border to increase or decrease the window's size. You see an outline representation of the new size as you drag. After the window is the size you want, release the mouse button.

If you want to arrange several open application-group windows to get better access to the contents, use the Tile or Cascade options on the Window menu (see fig. 10.8).

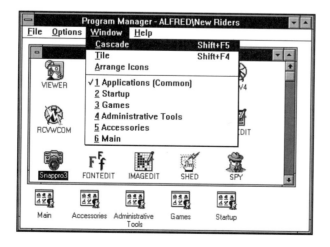

Figure 10.8

The Window menu.

The <u>T</u>ile option arranges the open windows edge to edge, like tiles on a wall. The <u>C</u>ascade option arranges the windows so that they fall from the upper left corner of the workspace toward the lower right corner. Each window's title bar and Control menu box are visible so that you easily can select a new application-group window.

Running Multiple Applications

One of the principal advantages of a windowed environment is its capability to run several applications at once. Windows NT makes it easy to switch between applications and also to find out which applications are running.

Tip

The method of multitasking used by Windows NT and Windows 95 provides an advantage over Windows 3.1. Windows NT and Windows 95 give each program its own slice of time, shifting the timeslice around all the programs so they all have a fair chance to execute. As a result, while one program works, so do all other programs.

In Windows 3.1, however, each program has to wait for the others to voluntarily yield the computer's resources before it can run. One busy application can prevent all applications from accomplishing work.

The easiest way to switch among applications is to click anywhere on the application window of the application you want to activate. The application's title bar is highlighted, and the application window moves to the top of the stack of running windows. The application is ready for input and commands.

You also can use the Alt+Tab key combination to switch between windows. While pressing this key combination, a box appears in the center of your screen (see fig. 10.9), listing the name of another opened application. Repeatedly pressing Tab while holding down Alt cycles you through the names of all running applications. When you reach the name of the application you want to switch to, release the Alt key. That application becomes the active application. If this application was running as an icon, it is restored to its original size and screen position.

Figure 10.9

Switching among applications by pressing Alt+Tab.

SnapPRO! 3.0 Trace

The second option is Alt+Esc. This option works like Alt+Tab, except that no dialog box appears. You move among the applications on the desktop. Each press of the key combination (Esc, while you hold down Alt) activates the next application on the list of running tasks. The application window or application icon is highlighted. Its open or minimized status does not change when the new task is made active, however. Icons become active, but they are not restored.

Summary

This chapter introduced you to the key parts of the Windows NT desktop, including the background, the wallpaper, and the application layer. The functions associated with each also were identified.

This chapter also explained the way Windows NT provides a powerful substitute for the command-line prompt. The concept of building application groups that represent your working style suggests that you can be more productive in Windows NT than at the operating-system prompt.

You learned that you can arrange the applications that help you accomplish your work the way you want on your desktop. Procedures for running and exiting applications also show that Windows NT can provide great flexibility as you work.

CHAPTER

11

Configuring and Customizing the Windows NT Desktop

T he Windows NT interface is very different from the DOS, OS/2, or Unix command line. Although you can change some of the characteristics of a character-mode operating system interface, the extent to which you can customize it is limited. With some difficulty, you can change the screen colors, system prompt, and a few other characteristics. Windows NT, on the other hand, offers a number of controls to enable you to fully customize both its appearance and performance.

The changes you make might be for aesthetic reasons, such as adding a wallpaper to your background or changing colors of some of your interface components. Other changes can improve productivity. If you prefer to use the mouse with your left hand, for example, you can swap mouse buttons. (See "Controlling the Mouse" later in this chapter for instructions about swapping mouse buttons.)

This chapter covers the following topics:

◆ Changing colors by using the Color icon

◆ Controlling fonts and ports

◆ Controlling the mouse

◆ Controlling the desktop

◆ Controlling printers by using the Printers icon

◆ Customizing the File Manager

In this chapter, you discover ways to make Windows NT look and perform the way you want. In typical Windows NT fashion, you can make the most of the changes with the click of a mouse button.

Introducing the Windows NT Control Panel

You can make nearly all changes to Windows NT by using the Control Panel, which is a typical Windows NT application (CONTROL.EXE) that has a number of tools for controlling and changing the Windows NT interface.

The Control Panel does more than help you put a pretty face on Windows NT, however. It includes tools for adding and customizing your printer, setting the system date and time, and controlling multitasking.

Figure 11.1 shows the Control Panel. Your Control Panel might appear slightly different, depending on your hardware configuration.

Figure 11.1

The Windows NT Control Panel.

New Riders Publishing
INSIDE
SERIES

Note You can change only those elements of the Windows NT operating system that your system administrator has given you the privileges to change.

Each icon in the Control Panel enables you to control or customize a particular aspect of Windows NT. The following list describes the controls available in the Control Panel:

- **Add/Remove Programs.** Provides an easy way to install and uninstall applications on your system.

- **Color.** Controls the colors of the Windows NT interface components, including the workspace, background, and borders.

- **Fonts.** Enables you to view installed fonts, install new fonts, and delete existing fonts.

- **Ports.** Provides controls for setting baud rate and other communication parameters for each of your system's COM ports.

- **Mouse.** Enables you to swap left and right mouse buttons and adjust mouse sensitivity.

- **Desktop.** Controls a number of desktop features: wallpaper, background pattern, icon spacing, window-border width, and cursor-blink rate.

- **Keyboard.** Controls the keyboard repeat rate or sensitivity.

- **Printers.** Provides a full range of tools for adding, configuring, and removing printers.

- **International.** Controls many features that vary by country, including the date and time, currency, and unit of measurement features.

- **System.** Provides control over your path, boot configuration, virtual memory, and multitasking options. This icon replaces the 386-Enhanced icon in other versions of Windows.

- **Date/Time.** Sets the system date and time.

- **Cursors.** Enables you to change the mouse cursors (or mouse pointers) used by Windows NT to display different systems' events relating to the mouse, including animated cursors.

- **Drivers.** Enables you to install, configure, and remove hardware drivers. Many users do not have the privileges to use this icon, and have to rely on their system administrator to perform these services.

◆ **MIDI Mapper.** Enables you to adjust the settings for the Musical Instrument Device Interface on your sound card.

◆ **Network.** Controls network features when Windows NT runs on a networked workstation. Many users do not have the privileges to use this icon, and must rely on their system administrator to perform these services.

◆ **Sound.** Assigns sounds to various events for systems with sound boards; provides warning beeps for those without sound boards.

◆ **Server.** Enables you to configure your computer as a network server. Many users do not have the privileges to use this icon, and have to rely on their system administrator to perform these services.

◆ **Services.** Enables you to start, stop, pause, and configure the elements of the Windows NT operating system known as services. Services are applications that run on a remote machine; they assist applications running on a local machine. Many users do not have the privileges to use this icon, and have to rely on their system administrator to perform these services.

◆ **Devices.** Enables you to start, stop, and configure the hardware and software devices that make up your system. Many users do not have the privileges to use this icon, and have to rely on their system administrator to perform these services.

◆ **UPS.** Controls the behavior of an uninterruptable power supply attached to your system. Many users do not have the privileges to use this icon, and must rely on their system administrator to perform these services.

The following sections explain these applets in more detail.

Adding or Removing Programs

When you click on the Add/Remove Programs icon in the Control Panel, Explorer displays the Add/Remove Programs Properties window. To install a new application on your system, click on the Install button. To uninstall an application, highlight the application you want to uninstall from the list of applications and then click on the Remove button.

When you click on the Install button, Explorer displays the Install Program From Floppy Disk or CD-ROM window. When you click on the Next button, Explorer looks through all of your drives to see if there are any executables called INSTALL.EXE or SETUP.EXE. It lists all such programs along with the disk they are on. If the installation program has a different name, you can click on the Browse button to locate it. To install the program, click on the Finish button.

Changing Colors by Using the Color Icon

After you double-click on the Color icon, the Color dialog box appears (see fig. 11.2). The basic Color dialog box includes controls for selecting a predefined color scheme for the Windows NT interface, adding a new color scheme, and removing a color scheme. A large display area shows an example of the interface as you change color schemes or individual interface components.

Figure 11.2

The Color dialog box.

Windows NT has 23 predefined color schemes to suit a wide range of preferences. To choose one of the schemes, select the drop-down list button in the Color **S**chemes list box. A list of available color schemes drops down. Pick a scheme; you can view it in the sample display. If you like the color scheme, select OK for your selection to take effect.

Some of the colors in the predefined schemes may not be exactly what you want. The Color dialog box includes a Color **P**alette button, which, when selected, expands the Color dialog box to include a list of screen elements you can selectively customize. Figure 11.3 shows the expanded Color dialog box.

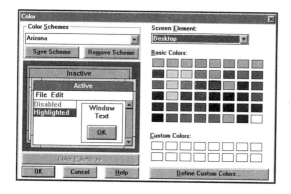

Figure 11.3

The expanded Color dialog box.

The following 21 Windows NT interface components can be customized by using the expanded Color dialog box:

- **Desktop.** Background that appears behind all Windows NT.

- **Application Workspace.** Area inside an application's window.

- **Window Background.** Background for each window.

- **Window Text.** Text inside a window.

- **Menu Bar.** Menu bar at the top of each window.

- **Menu Text.** Text in each menu bar.

- **Active Title Bar.** Active window's title bar.

- **Inactive Title Bar.** All inactive windows' title bars.

- **Active Title Bar Text.** Text in the active window's title bar.

- **Inactive Title Bar Text.** Text in the inactive window's title bar.

- **Active Border.** Active window's border.

- **Inactive Border.** All inactive windows' borders.

- **Window Frame.** All window frames.

- **Scroll Bars.** All horizontal and vertical scroll bars.

- **Button Face.** Face of control buttons.

- **Button Shadow.** Shadow around the bottom and right edge of control buttons.

- **Button Text.** Control button text.

- **Button Highlight.** Highlight at left and upper edge of control buttons.

- **Disabled Text.** Dimmed text in menus.

- **Highlight.** Highlight bar in a menu.

- **Highlighted Text.** Menu text when the item is highlighted.

To change the color of one of these items, select it from the drop-down list box. Then pick the color you want the selected interface component to be from the color-selection menu. After you finish changing colors, save the color scheme by name. If you do not want to save it, select OK for the new scheme to become active.

If you want to save the color scheme, select the S**a**ve Scheme button in the Color **S**chemes group box. You are prompted to enter a name for the new color scheme. Enter a name and choose OK. After you finish making changes, select OK again to exit the Color dialog box.

Using Custom Colors

The Color **P**alette in the expanded Color dialog box includes 16 spaces in which to store defined colors. To define a color, select the **D**efine Custom Colors button. The Custom Color Selector dialog box appears (see fig. 11.4).

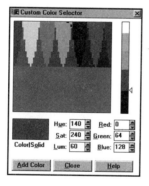

Figure 11.4

The Custom Color Selector dialog box.

The Custom Color Selector dialog box gives you a choice of controls to create custom colors. You can either click the mouse inside the Color display box to get a rough estimate of the color you want, or drag the cursor in the Color display box until you get the color you want. Then use the slider controls for hue, saturation, and luminosity to fine-tune the color.

To add the color to the Custom Colors menu, select the box in which you want to store the new color. Then click on the **A**dd Color button, and the color is applied to the selected box. To create a new color, return to the Color display box and use the same method to define your new color. After you have defined as many custom colors as you want, select the **C**lose button to close the Custom Color Selector dialog box. To close the Color dialog box, click on the OK button.

Controlling Fonts

The Fonts icon in the Control Panel enables you to view installed fonts, add new fonts, and remove fonts. After you select the Fonts icon, the Fonts dialog box appears (see fig. 11.5).

Figure 11.5

The Fonts dialog box.

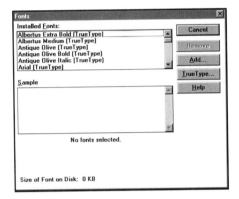

The list box in the Fonts dialog box displays all fonts currently installed for Windows NT applications in the *Registry*, which is the database that replaces the Windows 3.1 initialization files in Windows NT. To view a font, select it from the list box. A sample of the font appears in the **S**ample box. You can use this sample to identify fonts you no longer need or to identify a font you want to use in a document.

Some of the fonts listed in the Fonts dialog box have the description (TrueType) listed after their font name. TrueType fonts are scaleable fonts. Unlike raster fonts, such as the MS Serif font, TrueType fonts can be resized to any point size without a loss of print quality. You use TrueType fonts by selecting one when you need it.

In addition to TrueType scalability, other advantages of using TrueType fonts are the many available shareware and public-domain TrueType fonts. For little or no cost, you can add many new fonts. One source of TrueType fonts is the Windows NT forum on CompuServe. To access the Advanced Windows NT forum on CompuServe, type **GO WINNT** at any ! prompt.

To remove a font, highlight the font in the list box and then select the **R**emove button. The Control Panel prompts you to verify the deletion. Select **Y**es to delete the font or **N**o to cancel the command.

If you select **Y**es, the reference for the font is removed from the Registry and from memory. You can, however, add the font later without copying the definition file from the Windows NT distribution disks. If you prefer to delete the font file as well, check **D**elete Font File from the Disk check box when you confirm the deletion.

Use the **A**dd button to add a font. A file list box appears, which you can use to find the font-definition file (it usually has a FON or FOT file extension). After the file has been added, a sample appears in the Sample of Font box, and you can use it in your applications.

The **T**rueType button controls the way TrueType fonts are treated. Selecting the **T**rueType button brings up the TrueType dialog box. If you want to work only with TrueType fonts and exclude all others, select the **S**how Only TrueType Fonts in the Applications check box. Only TrueType fonts then appear in your application menus when you choose fonts.

Controlling Ports

The Ports icon displays a dialog box that you can use to set up the system's communication ports. Select the port to change from the Ports dialog box, and then click on the **S**ettings button. The Settings for COM*x* dialog box appears, which enables you to set the baud rate, data bits, parity, stop bits, and flow control used by the selected port. The Ports and Settings for COM*x* dialog boxes are shown in figure 11.6.

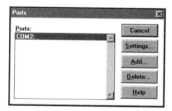

Figure 11.6

The Ports and Settings for COMx dialog box.

Setting Baud Rate

The *baud rate* controls the number of signals (per second) sent down the line. Because various devices use standard baud rates, you can make your selection from preset baud rates in the Settings for COM*x* dialog box. To choose a baud rate, select the drop-down list button beside the **B**aud Rate box. The Control Panel responds with a list of possible baud-rate values. Select the one you need from the list. If the baud rate you need is not displayed, enter the value directly into the **B**aud Rate box by typing from the keyboard.

Note Various devices require different baud rates. The sending and receiving devices must use the same baud rate. If you dial an information service that uses 2400 baud, for example, you cannot use 9600 baud on your system and increase performance. You must use whatever the device on the other end of the line is expecting.

Modems typically use baud rates between 1200 and 9600. Plotters and printers often run at 9600 baud. Computers connected by a null-modem cable can often use 19,200 baud, and some can go as high as 115,200 baud. Control Panel lists baud rates only to 19,200. To use 115,200 baud, you must enter it from the keyboard.

Setting Data Bits, Stop Bits, and Parity

Your system's serial ports (COM ports) are *asynchronous devices*. This means that the information flowing between the computer and the peripheral connected to the COM port is not synchronized. Some form of timing, therefore, must be implemented in order for the data transfer to take place properly.

The information is broken into packets of a specific number of bits. A *bit* is the smallest unit of information a computer understands. The data is transferred down the line as a word made up of four to eight bits. Most often, the word is made up of seven or eight bits.

To synchronize the data, the actual data (represented by data bits) is framed by a *start bit* and a *stop bit*, which enable the receiving device to know when it has received a word.

To specify the number of data bits, select the appropriate option from the **D**ata Bits drop-down list in the Settings for COM*x* dialog box. To set the number of stop bits, choose the appropriate number. Again, the values you select must match what the other device is expecting.

The **P**arity setting controls the way systems handle error checking. The available parity options are Even, Odd, None, Mark, and Space, as described in the following list:

◆ **Even parity.** A parity bit is added to the data stream and switched on or off to ensure that the total number of on (1) bits is always even. The receiving system checks the number of bits, and if it finds an even number, it assumes no transmissions were lost. If the receiving device finds an odd number, however, it assumes a transmission has been lost, and directs the sending device to resend the data.

◆ **Odd parity.** The parity bit is switched on or off to make sure that the total number of on bits is always odd. The receiving system checks the total number of bits to make sure that it is odd.

◆ **Mark parity.** The parity bit is always turned on. Mark parity provides only limited error checking because it does not check to see whether a bit was lost in transmission. Mark parity does, however, provide a pattern for the receiving system to look for.

◆ **Space parity.** The parity bit is always turned off. Again, this provides a pattern for the receiving system to recognize, but it does not provide for error checking.

◆ **None.** No parity checking is implemented.

Choose one of these options to define how you want to handle error checking.

Setting Flow Control

Flow control coordinates data transfer between two systems by providing a means for the receiving system to tell the sending system that it is ready to receive more information. Flow control also is called handshaking.

The three options for flow control in the Settings for COM*x* dialog box are Xon/Xoff, Hardware, and None, as follows:

◆ **Xon/Xoff.** A software method by which the Xon character (11 hex, DC3, or Ctrl-Q) is used to signal that the system is ready to receive. The Xoff character (13 hex, DC1, or Ctrl-S) is used to signal that the sending system must stop transmitting until it receives the Xon character again.

◆ **Hardware.** A dedicated line in the cable connecting the two devices is used to coordinate data transfer.

◆ **None.** No method of flow control is used.

After you determine the proper setting, select it in the **F**low Control drop-down list. When all settings are in place, click on the OK button to implement the changes. You then can set values for each of the other ports in your system.

Controlling the Mouse

The Mouse icon displays a dialog box that enables you to control mouse response with two variables: tracking speed and double-click speed. It also enables you to swap the function of the left and right mouse buttons.

Changing the tracking speed alters the response of mouse movement as you move it across the desktop. The mouse has two levels of acceleration that accelerate the cursor when the mouse moves more than a certain distance over a given period of time.

To reduce mouse acceleration, slide the button in the **M**ouse Tracking Speed slider bar to the left or use the left scroll button. To increase mouse acceleration, move the slider to the right or use the right scroll button.

The double-click speed defines the maximum time between clicks that the two clicks are recognized as a double-click. If the amount of time exceeds the double-click speed limit, the two clicks are recognized as individual clicks.

If you increase the setting by moving the slider to the left or by using the left scroll button, you increase the amount of time that can pass between the two clicks of a double-click. If you move the slider to the right or use the right scroll button, you decrease the time that can pass between the two clicks of a double-click.

The **S**wap Left/Right Buttons check box enables you to switch operation of the left and right mouse buttons. If you are left-handed and prefer to use the right mouse button as the select button, you can swap mouse buttons by checking this box.

 Tip   Another situation in which you might prefer to swap buttons is if you are using a spreadsheet such as Excel. You can select cells with your left hand while entering numbers on the numeric keypad with your right hand.

Controlling the Desktop

The Desktop icon gives you a number of controls to define the appearance of the Windows NT desktop. After you select this icon, the Desktop dialog box appears (see fig. 11.7).

Figure 11.7

The Desktop dialog box.

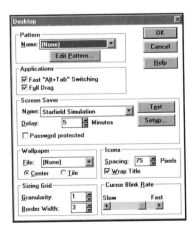

The Pattern group box sets the background pattern that appears over the desktop. You can select from 13 predefined patterns by using the drop-down list button. If you prefer, you can edit an existing pattern or create a new one.

If you select the Edit **P**attern button, the Desktop-Edit Pattern dialog box appears. You use this dialog box to create new patterns and add them to the list of available patterns. You also use it to remove a pattern from the list. (A pattern uses little additional memory.)

Using a Screen Saver

The next group in the Desktop dialog box is the Screen Saver box. A screen saver is a memory-resident program that monitors keyboard and mouse activity. When no activity occurs for a user-defined time span, the screen saver blanks the screen and, optionally, displays a dynamic pattern, such as a moving star field.

Note The VGA displays required by Windows NT do not generally need a screen-saver program to prevent burn-in. On VGA displays, a screen saver is more of a novelty than anything else.

One reason to use a screen saver, however, is to prevent the unauthorized use of your computer workstation. The Windows NT screen savers enable you to set a password that must be entered to regain access to the system after the screen saver has blanked the display. This serves two purposes: it prevents other users from seeing confidential data, and it prevents access to your system when you are away.

To choose a screen saver, select the N**a**me drop-down list button in the Screen Saver group box. Set the delay time by using the **D**elay scroll box. The delay time is the amount of time the system can be inactive before the screen saver blanks the display. To set a password, check the Passw**o**rd protected check box.

To set options for the screen saver, select the Set**u**p button. A configuration dialog box tailored to the saver you have selected appears (see fig. 11.8), enabling you to set parameters for the screen saver and to specify a password. If you want to test the screen saver, return to the Desktop dialog box and select the T**e**st button.

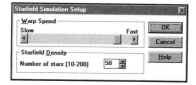

Figure 11.8

The Screen Saver Setup dialog box.

Using Wallpaper

The next group box in the Desktop dialog box is the Wallpaper group, which enables you to set up a wallpaper bitmap. Wallpaper appears over the desktop pattern, and the wallpaper image comes from a standard Windows NT bit-mapped (BMP) file.

 Note Although there are a number of standard bitmaps to choose from, you can create your own bitmaps in Paintbrush or another application that creates Windows NT bit-mapped files.

To use a new image as wallpaper, copy it to the Windows NT directory, and then select it by using the Desktop dialog box. Figure 11.9 shows one of Windows NT's standard wallpaper images.

Figure 11.9

A standard Windows NT wallpaper image.

You can convert graphics files, in various formats, to a Windows NT bit map and use it as wallpaper. The Windows NT forums on CompuServe and GEnie, in particular, have a number of wallpaper images in bit-mapped format that you can use. Many graphics forums on CompuServe offer images in GIF (pronounced "jif") format. Excellent shareware utilities, such as WinGIF, also are available on the Windows NT forums. These utilities enable you to view GIF files in Windows NT and convert them to other formats, including the Windows NT bit-mapped format. After converting a GIF file to bit-mapped format, you assign it as your wallpaper in the same manner as described previously.

 Note Windows 95 bitmaps can be used with Windows NT.

Remember that wallpaper uses more memory to display than a desktop pattern. If you find your system is running short of memory, consider removing your wallpaper to see whether it clears up the problem.

Controlling Printers by Using the Printers Icon and Print Manager

The Printers icon in the Windows NT Control Panel gives you the tools necessary for installing and configuring printers to use in Windows NT. When you select it, the Print Manager application begins (see fig. 11.10).

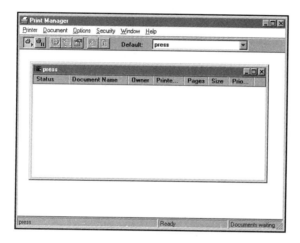

Figure 11.10

The Print Manager window.

The Print Manager window lists any currently installed printers, the default printer, and the status of the currently selected printer, and it includes buttons and menu commands for tasks such as adding and configuring a printer.

If you have not installed your printer yet, select the Create Printer option on the **P**rinter menu to choose from a list of supported printers. The **D**river drop-down list box lists all available printers (an extensive list). If your printer is listed, select it. If you have a third-party driver to install for your printer, select the last option, Other.

Print Manager then prompts you to identify the driver file for the printer. Specify the name of the file to install as a printer driver. (The file generally is provided on a disk that comes with the printer.)

After you install your printer, it must be configured. To configure a printer, select **P**roperties from the **P**rinter menu. The Printer Properties dialog box appears (see fig. 11.11).

Figure 11.11

The Printer Properties dialog box.

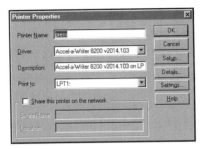

The controls and buttons in this dialog box enable you to set defaults for all the printer options. In general, you can use the default time-out values (usually accessed from the Setup button) unless you experience problems with the printer.

Note If you experience problems, try raising the time-out values.

Other options are available in the Printer Properties dialog box; they vary according to the type of port to which the printer is connected. If connected to an LPT port, the Settings button provides at least the time-out setting. If connected to a COM port, however, the Settings button is used to set communication parameters for the selected port.

If you select Settings, the Settings for COM*x* dialog box appears. Use the dialog box to set communication parameters for the port, including the baud rate, data bits, parity, stop bits, and flow control. You also can control the base I/O address for the port, and its interrupt.

If your printer is connected to a network, you can select the **C**onnect to Printer option from the **P**rinter menu. Choosing this option brings up the Connect to Printer dialog box (see fig. 11.12).

Any existing network queue connections are shown in the Shared Printers list box. To connect to an existing queue, select the queue, and choose the OK button. After you establish proper connections for the device, set options for your printer, as discussed for the Printer **P**roperties command. Set the options required for your printer, and then choose OK to activate the changes (see fig. 11.13).

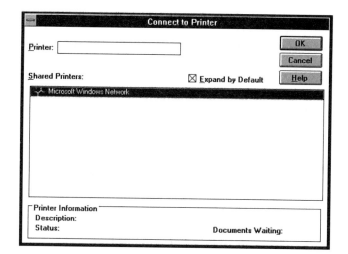

Figure 11.12

The Connect to Printer dialog box.

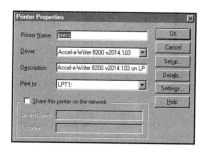

Figure 11.13

The options dialog boxes for the Accel-a-Writer 8200.

When you are satisfied with the setup for your printer, exit the Print Manager.

In Windows NT, all print jobs are scheduled through the Print Manager. The Print Manager enables you to reschedule print jobs that are pending in the print queue. You can move a print job in front of another if you decide it has a higher priority, for example. In addition, you can remove a pending print job from the queue if you decide you do not need to print it. Because Windows NT includes networking features, Print Manager enables complete, efficient control over network print queues.

Controlling System Options

The System icon in the Control Panel provides a dialog box that gives you control over system functions (see fig. 11.14). This dialog box enables you to set environment variables, manage virtual memory, and prioritize tasks when multitasking.

Figure 11.14

The System dialog box.

System	
Computer Name: FIDELITY	OK
┌Operating System──────────────────	Cancel
Startup: [Windows NT Workstation Version 3.5 ▼]	Virtual Memory...
Show list for [30 ⬦] seconds	Recovery...
	Tasking...
	Help

System Environment Variables:

```
ComSpec = C:\WINDOWS\system32\cmd.exe
OS = Windows_NT
Os2LibPath = C:\WINDOWS\system32\os2\dll;
Path = C:\WINDOWS\system32;D:\RESKIT35\
PROCESSOR_ARCHITECTURE = x86
PROCESSOR_IDENTIFIER = 80486-D0
PROCESSOR_LEVEL = 4
```

User Environment Variables for george

```
temp = C:\temp
tmp = C:\temp
```

Variable: [   ]   Set
Value: [   ]   Delete

Setting Environment Variables

Windows NT enables you to define environment variables that it uses to find directories with which it works. When Windows NT installs, it defaults to the settings in the System Environment Variables list box. You can add your own environment variables, displayed in the **U**ser Environment Variables list box. You might want to set a path variable so the system knows which directories to search for executable and data files. You also might want to include values for the commonly used temp and tmp variables.

To set an environment variable, enter the variable name in the **V**ariable text box. Enter the value in the V**a**lue text box. Use the S**e**t button to set the value of the variable, and the **D**elete button to delete unwanted variables. (You can modify only the **U**ser Environment Variables.) The values of the variables are stored as a part of your logon profile.

Controlling Virtual Memory

The Virtual **M**emory button in the System dialog box enables you to control the way Windows NT handles *disk paging*, which refers to Windows NT's capability to simulate memory by using a portion of your hard disk. This technique enables Windows NT to run very large applications or many applications concurrently. After you select the Virtual **M**emory button, the Virtual Memory dialog box appears, as shown in figure 11.15.

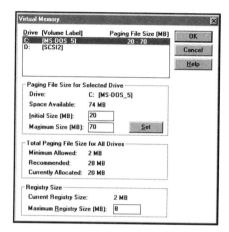

Figure 11.15

Virtual Memory dialog box.

To set up the paging file, select the drive that contains the file in the **D**rive [Volume Label] list box. Windows NT shows the amount of space available in the Space Available display in the Paging File Size group. It also places recommended file sizes (the defaults) in the **I**nitial Size and Ma**x**imum Size text boxes.

Note You can enter your own settings, but it is best to accept the defaults.

Current paging-file information is displayed in the Total Paging File Size for All Drives group of controls. To set up the paging file, click on the **S**et button, then click on the OK button.

Controlling Multitasking

Multitasking refers to the computer's capability to run more than one application (task) at a time. During multitasking, the computer services each task for a brief period of time, cycling through the tasks quickly, so it appears that the computer is doing more than one job at a time. It is not, however—it is just switching back and forth too quickly for you to notice.

You can prioritize various applications by using the three settings in the Tasking dialog box, which you access by clicking on the **T**asking button (see fig. 11.16).

Figure 11.16

The Tasking dialog box.

Select the **B**est Foreground Application Response Time option button to give the application currently in focus the most processing time. This eases your work with the current application, making it run as fast as possible.

Select the **F**oreground Application More Responsive than Background option button if you want to allocate more time to applications running in the background, but still want the primary application to run quickly.

Select Foreground and Background Applications **E**qually Responsive option button if you need to devote more time to background applications, and you do not mind slower performance in the current application. Windows NT provides these options to simplify prioritizing your applications. Experiment to see what best suits your working style.

Controlling Other Settings with the Control Panel

The Control Panel includes five other icons that control a range of options: International, Keyboard, Date/Time, Cursors, and Sound.

Using the International Icon

The International icon enables you to control many environmental settings that usually vary by country. These settings include the language used for case-sensitive tasks and sorting, the keyboard layout, unit of measurement (English or metric), date and time format, currency format, and number format. You select these settings using drop-down list boxes. Figure 11.17 shows the International dialog box.

Note   You can change many settings globally by selecting a different country setting. If you switch from United States to United Kingdom, for example, the Measurement, Date Format, Time Format, and Currency Format options change.

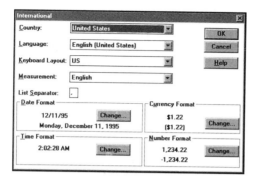

Figure 11.17

The International dialog box.

You can also adjust the **D**ate Format, C**u**rrency Format, **T**ime Format, and **N**umber format individually. To do so, click on the Change button next to the format you want to change. Adjust the controls in the dialog box that appears to suit your needs, then click on the OK button. By adjusting these formats individually, you can alter a particular country setting to suit specialized needs, such as a preference for Day-Month-Year date order in a U.S.-based business.

Using the Keyboard Icon

The Keyboard icon performs two tasks—it enables you to change the response rate of your keyboard and to control key response time. If you select the Keyboard icon, the Keyboard dialog box appears (see fig. 11.18), with a scroll bar to change the key **R**epeat Rate and **D**elay Before First Repeat.

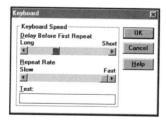

Figure 11.18

The Keyboard dialog box.

You decrease or increase the keyboard key repeat rate by moving the **R**epeat Rate slider to the left or right. Below the scroll bar is a text box in which you can test the change in repeat rate.

The **D**elay Before First Repeat slider controls the amount of time a key can be down before it begins to repeat. You can increase the time, for example, so that you can hold the key down longer without repeating characters.

Note If you are a "heavy-handed" typist, you might want to increase this setting. If you prefer a light touch on the keyboard, decrease this setting.

Using the Date/Time Icon

The Date/Time icon is very simple—all it does is set the system's date and time. In the dialog box (see fig. 11.19), you can use scroll arrows to change the date and time, or you can enter the new date and time directly. You also must set your Time **Z**one in the drop-down list box and decide whether to check the **A**utomatically Adjust for Daylight Savings Time check box.

Figure 11.19

The Date/Time dialog box.

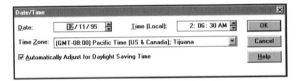

Using the Cursors Icon

The Cursors icon enables you to choose which mouse cursors appear in Windows NT. For instance, if you prefer to replace the hourglass as the wait icon, do the following:

1. Select the hourglass in the **S**ystem Cursors list box (see fig. 11.20).

Figure 11.20

The Cursors dialog box.

2. Click on the **B**rowse button to select an alternative cursor by filename.

3. Choose a filename in the list box. The cursor represented by that file appears in the preview box.

4. Click on the OK button to substitute the cursor you chose for the hourglass. (You always can reset to the system default cursors by clicking on the Set **D**efault button.)

Note In Windows NT, you can have animated mouse cursors. You can replace the hourglass, for example, with a self-peeling banana, or a barber pole that spins. These cursors are fun, but they might not be useful as substitutes for the cursors you use to take action. It is hard to see the hot spot for clicking and double-clicking with the peeling banana, because the shape of the cursor constantly changes.

Using the Sound Icon

The Sound icon enables you to assign sounds to various system events if your system includes a sound card. Windows NT includes four synthesized sounds, and you can add other sound files by copying the new WAV files to the Windows NT directory.

If your system lacks a sound card, the E**n**able System Sounds check box enables/disables a warning beep that sounds when you try an action that is not permitted (see fig. 11.21).

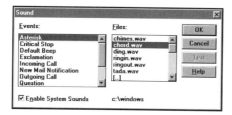

Figure 11.21

The Sound dialog box.

Working with the Application Group Window

If you prefer working with application groups than the application lists displayed with the Start button, you use the following procedure to display application groups:

1. Right-click on the Start button. A pop-up menu displays.

2. Left-click on the Open option. The Start window displays.

3. Click on the Programs icon. The Programs window opens and shows the application groups.

4. Click on the application group of your choice. The application group window opens.

You have four options for controlling the way the application group window functions. All four appear in the **O**ptions menu in application group window's menu bar.

The four options are as follows:

◆ **Auto Arrange.** Controls the way Windows NT handles icons in a group. If **A**uto Arrange is active, you see a check mark beside it. **A**uto Arrange causes the application group window to automatically rearrange item icons inside a group window when you open or resize the window. If **A**uto Arrange is disabled, icons remain stationary as you manipulate the window.

◆ **Minimize on Use.** Controls whether the application group window automatically reduces to an icon when you run an application. If enabled, the application group window shrinks to an icon when you select an application from a program group. If **M**inimize on Use is not enabled, the application group window remains on the screen.

◆ **Save Settings on Exit.** If enabled, this option saves changes to the desktop when you exit Windows NT. If, for example, you move groups or group icons around on the desktop and want to save your changes for the next session, check the **S**ave Settings on Exit option before you exit Windows NT.

◆ **Save Settings Now.** Saves the application group window's settings immediately without exiting the Windows session. This option prevents you from having to log off and then abort it in order to save settings for application group window.

These options are the only direct ways to customize the application group window. You can do a number of things indirectly, however, and many of them relate to the use of application group window.

Working with Program Groups and Program Items

A program group is a collection of program item icons that resides inside a group window. The group window can be resized, moved, minimized to an icon, or maximized to fill the display. Each of the program items inside the group window is represented by an icon.

Usually, the program item is an executable file, such as an EXE, COM, or BAT file. You also can use document files and macro files (really document files) as program items, as well as PIFs (program information files).

Some of the ways you can customize your application group window shell include creating groups, eliminating groups, and moving items from one group to another.

Creating a New Group

Many Windows NT applications create their own groups when you install the application, ensuring that all programs available with the new application are added to your Windows NT environment.

Note You also can create your own groups. You can, for example, place some of your existing applications in a common group for easier access. You can include the spreadsheet, the word processor, the Control Panel, the DOS icon, and a few other program items in the group. You can then keep only this group open on the desktop and still have access to all your main applications and tools.

Another reason to create a program group is to gather selected document files. You can associate a document file type with an application; open the application along with a document file simply by clicking on the document file's icon. You learn how to associate a file type with an application a little later. First, you need to learn how to create a program group.

To create a new group, select the **N**ew command from application group window's **F**ile menu. You see the New Program Object dialog box. Select the **P**ersonal Program Group option or the **C**ommon Program Group option and click on OK. (Personal groups appear only during Windows sessions during which you are logged on. Common groups appear for all users logged on to your system.) The application group window generates a new dialog box, called Program Group Properties, in which you supply the group description. The Personal Program Group Properties dialog box is shown in figure 11.22.

Personal Program Group Properties
Description:
Startup
OK
Cancel
Help

Figure 11.22

The Personal Program Group Properties dialog box.

The **D**escription field appears underneath the group's icon on the application group window desktop. After you supply a description and filename, choose OK. The application group window adds the group to the Registry and adds the new group window to the desktop. The new group is now ready to have program items added.

Creating a Program Item

As you read earlier, a program item can be an executable file—such as an EXE, COM, or BAT file—or it can be a document file or PIF. Regardless of the type of file it represents, a program item icon in a group only represents a file of some kind; it is not the file itself. If you delete an icon from a group, for example, only the reference to the file is deleted—the file itself is still intact.

To create a program item of any type, use the **N**ew command in the application group window's **F**ile menu. Click on the Program **I**tem option button, and click on OK. The application group window displays the Program Item Properties box, which you use to supply information about the new item. The Program Item Properties dialog box is shown in figure 11.23.

Figure 11.23

The Program Item Properties dialog box.

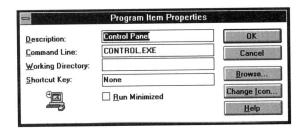

As you can see, the Program Item Properties dialog box is similar to the one you use to create a program group. The description in the **D**escription field is used as the description under the program item icon when it appears in a group window.

 Stop If your description is too long, it can overlap another item's description. A way to avoid overlapping is to turn on icon title wrap by using the Desktop icon in the Control Panel.

The **C**ommand Line field specifies the command to invoke when the program item is selected. If the item is an executable file, enter the name of the file, including the extension, in the **C**ommand Line field. If the directory containing the file is on the path, you can omit the drive and directory. It is a good idea, however, to always include the absolute path, including the drive, for the file. This eliminates potential problems.

You can enter any arguments required by the program on the command line as well. Arguments are characters following the filename that tell the program how to behave when it starts. The most common argument is the name of a file to load. Type arguments after the filename separated by blank spaces.

You also can enter the name of a PIF if the item is a DOS application that includes a PIF file or a DOS application for which you intend to create a PIF file. It is always a good idea to use a PIF for DOS applications you run under Windows NT and to specify the PIF for the program item, instead of the program's executable file. This ensures that the settings in the PIF are always used, which saves memory and avoids potential problems with video display and other characteristics.

In addition to executable files and PIFs, you can specify a document file in the **C**ommand Line field, even if you have not associated the file type with the application. (See "Associating Document Files with Applications" later in this chapter for more information.) This arrangement offers one of the easiest ways to launch an application and load a document file—click on the icon attached to the document, and the application loads automatically.

The **W**orking Directory setting specifies the directory that becomes active when the application is started. If you keep the application's document files in a specific directory, set **W**orking Directory to point to the document directory. If you leave the setting blank, the directory that has the program file becomes the working directory.

You also can assign a shortcut key to the application by using the **S**hortcut Key setting. A *shortcut key* is a combination of the Ctrl+Alt, Ctrl+Shift, or Ctrl+Shift+Alt keys with another key, such as A, B, C, or F6. If you have an application running in the background that has been assigned a shortcut key, press the shortcut-key sequence to bring the application to the front of the desktop (make it active).

Browsing for a File and Changing Icons

If you do not recall the location of a file you wish to enter into the Program Item Properties dialog box, use the **B**rowse button to find it. Select **B**rowse, and use the list box to find the file.

You also can use the Program Item Properties dialog box to change the icon associated with a program item. If you select the Change **I**con button, the Select Icon dialog box appears. Enter the name of the executable (EXE) file, Dynamic Link Library (DLL) file, or individual icon file (ICO) that contains the icon. The icons display in a scrollable viewing box. Select the icon you want, then choose OK for the change to take effect. The file PROGMAN.EXE contains several icons you can use for your new item.

Associating Document Files with Applications

For a document item icon association to work, the file extension must be associated with an executable file or a PIF. To associate a document file type with a program or PIF, open the File Manager and locate a document file of the type you want to associate with the application.

Select the file, and then select the **A**ssociate command in the File Manager's **F**ile menu. A dialog box appears, prompting you to enter the name of the application with which to associate the document type. Include the drive and path to the executable or PIF file, and then choose OK. File Manager adds an entry to the Registry for the new document association, which makes the association effective for future Windows NT sessions.

Replacing Application Group Window as the Windows NT Shell

Alternative shell programs have been very popular for Windows 3.1. As Windows NT launches, however, no third-party shells have been announced for Windows NT. Inevitably, replacements for application group window will appear. More than likely, they will install themselves into the Registry when you run the setup programs and provide a means of uninstalling themselves.

 Note   The shell for Windows NT is set by using a line in the Registry database. You can view the setting in the HKEY_LOCAL_MACHINE on Local Machine window. It is in the SOFTWARE\Microsoft\Windows NT\Current Version\Winlogon entry. You should not adjust this setting without expert help. A mistaken setting can leave your system without a shell, and you with no way to access commands and programs in Windows NT.

At present, trying to change your shell gives you no advantage. It is very unlikely that you have this privilege. When third-party shells become available, use the facilities they provide for changing shells.

Customizing the File Manager

Just as you can customize the application group window the File Manager includes a few parameters you can customize. For example, you can have the File Manager minimize automatically whenever you invoke an application by clicking on its file in the File Manager. To set this option in the File Manager, select the **O**ptions menu and check the **M**inimize on Use command. The next time you execute a file by clicking on it in the File Manager, the File Manager minimizes to an icon after it executes the application.

Other Settings in the Options Menu

Other settings in the **O**ptions menu are **C**onfirmation, **F**ont, Customize Tool**b**ar, **T**oolbar, **D**rive Bar, **S**tatus Bar, **O**pen New Window on Connect, and Save Settings on **E**xit.

◆ The **F**ont option enables you to specify the font to be used to display directory and file listings. Select the font name, style, and size from the list boxes. The Display **L**owercase for FAT Drives check box controls whether the entries in a directory window are displayed with upper- or lowercase letters for drives using the FAT file system. If it is not checked, files and directories are listed in capitals. If you want to display lowercase on NTFS and HPFS drives as well, check the Display Lowercase for All **D**rives box as well.

◆ The Customize Tool**b**ar option opens a dialog box that enables you to select which File Manager commands appear as buttons on the toolbar. Highlight the predefined buttons in the list boxes, and use the **A**dd and **R**emove buttons to change which items are on the toolbar. If you need to reset to the factory default, click on the R**e**set button. Clicking on the C**l**ose button activates your changes. For example, you can add Compress and Uncompress buttons to the toolbar to compress or uncompress files and directories. The Customize Toolbar window shows you all the buttons you can add to (or subtract from) the toolbar.

◆ The **S**tatus Bar option controls whether File Manager displays a status bar at the bottom of the parent window. Depending on the type of information you display in File Manager, the status bar lists the current drive letter, available disk space, number of files selected, and number of bytes used by the selected files. Although this information is helpful, it takes a little additional time for the File Manager to calculate and display. If speed is an important consideration and you do not need to see the information in the status bar, you can turn the **S**tatus Bar option off (see fig. 11.24).

◆ The **T**oolbar and **D**rivebar options control whether these items are displayed (a matter of preference). No performance advantages are associated with displaying or not displaying these items.

◆ The **C**onfirmation option controls the way File Manager handles file and directory deletions, among other tasks. The Confirmation dialog box has six check boxes you can use to control whether File Manager requires confirmation of certain actions before they are carried out. Unless you are an experienced user, consider leaving all of the options checked for safety. They make it more difficult for you to lose data.

Figure 11.24

File Manager's options.

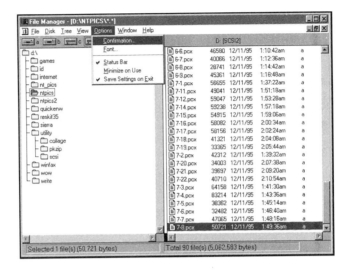

◆ The **O**pen New Window on Connect option controls whether a shared directory is displayed in a new document window when you connect to it. Leaving this setting checked is a convenience. When you connect to a shared directory over the network, you have visual confirmation that the connect has taken place.

◆ The Save Settings on **E**xit option controls whether File Manager saves the settings in the current session. After you go to the trouble of setting your preferences for the File Manager, save them so they take effect every time you use File Manager. When you select E**x**it from the **F**ile menu, File Manager saves your preferences in its initialization file (WINFILE.INI). The next time you launch File Manager, the same settings are in place.

Use these options to control the appearance and behavior of the File Manager.

Controlling File Display Information

You also can control the type of information that File Manager displays about the files in each directory. The **V**iew menu includes three options: **N**ame, **A**ll File Details, and **P**artial Details. These options control the type of information displayed about each file:

◆ The **N**ame option displays only the name of each file in the directory—nothing else—enabling you to fit more files into the display window.

◆ The **A**ll File Details option displays the filename, size, modification data, modification time, and file flags (such as archive, hidden, and so on).

◆ The **P**artial File Details option enables you to select any combination of size, last modification data, last modification time, and file flags.

The **V**iew menu includes parameters you can use to sort the file listing. You can choose to sort by name, file type, size, or last modification data.

The By File **T**ype option in the **V**iew menu enables you to set the types of files to be displayed in a directory window. You can choose any combination of directories, programs, documents, or other files, as well as hidden/system files.

Compressing and Uncompressing Files

Files often contain much unused space. This unused space, however, takes up room on your disk drive. A compression utility can reduce the size of a file by a factor of one to 10 times.

The compact command compresses files on NTFS partitions and displays the compression state of directories. Compression states of directories can either be compressed or decompressed.

 Note New Technology File System (NTFS) was developed for NT to provide file and system security.

If you compress a directory, the current files in the directory remain unchanged. When new files are saved to the directory, however, they are compressed. Defining the compression state of a directory to be compressed is a way of automatically compressing everything in the directory.

If you uncompress a directory, you simply deactivate the automatic compression. The files in the directory are not automatically uncompressed. This state is equivalent to choosing not to compress a directory.

 Note The compact utility is not compatible with volumes compressed with the DriveSpace or DoubleSpace utilities available with the MS-DOS operating system. To use the files on these volumes with the compact utility, first decompress them.

Table 11.1 shows you the switches that you can use with the compact utility.

TABLE 11.1
Switches Used with the Compact Utility

Switch	Description
/c	Compresses all of the files in the current directory. The current directory is also marked as being a compressed directory so that any file later saved to the directory is automatically compressed.
/c/s	Compresses all of the files in the current directory as well as all of its subdirectories. The current directory and its subdirectories are marked as being a compressed directory so that any file later saved to the directory is automatically compressed.
/c/s C:*.tmp	Compresses all files that have the extension .tmp in the root (\) directory and all of its subdirectories. Neither the root directory nor any of its subdirectories are marked as compressed directories unless the directory name ends with the extension .tmp.
/c/f C:\filename	The \f switch forces recompression of the specified filename. If the system crashes during compression, a file might be in a partially compressed state. The \f switch forces the entire file to be recompressed.
/u C:\tmp	The \u switch removes the compression designation of a directory, the tmp directory in this example. The compression of the files in the specified directory is not affected. All files saved to the specified directory in the future, however, are not automatically compressed.

Moving and Copying Compressed Files

When you copy a file, you retain the original file, make a copy of it, and place the copy anywhere in the hierarchy of directories and files.

When you move a file, you change the location of the file from its origin to anywhere in the hierarchy of directories and files. A copy of the file does not remain in the original location.

When you move a file, it retains its state of compression. For example, if you move an uncompressed file to a compressed partition of an NTFS disk, the file remain uncompressed. When you move a compressed file to a noncompressed disk, it remains compressed.

When you copy a file, the copy takes on the characteristics of the disk partition it is copied to. For example, if an uncompressed file is copied to a compressed partition, the file is automatically compressed as it is saved. Likewise, if you copy a compressed file to an uncompressed disk partition, it is automatically uncompressed as it is saved.

Any file moved or copied from a non-NTFS partition to an NTFS partition takes on the compression state of the NTFS partition.

Summary

Although this chapter does not cover all the facets of customizing the Windows NT interface, you now have an overview of the types of preferences you can change and a good understanding of the methods you can use. You have seen how to change the color scheme, control fonts and ports, customize the mouse, change the desktop settings, control your printer, and customize the application group window File Manager.

Many of the changes you make to the Windows NT interface are purely aesthetic— they do not affect performance. These changes still can increase your overall productivity by giving you a more useful and comfortable tool.

Take a half hour to go through the Windows NT interface and set it up as you prefer. Even if your only gain is comfort, the time is well spent.

C H A P T E R

12

Using Windows NT Applets

The usefulness of Windows NT lies in its 32-bit architecture and 32-bit commercial applications that are designed to run on the Windows NT platform. There are also some useful, albeit relatively simple, applications that come with Windows NT. These applications—which typically are scaled-down versions of more sophisticated, off-the-shelf applications—are commonly referred to as applets.

This chapter looks at Windows NT applets, and discusses the following:

◆ Surveying single-user applets

◆ Exploring multiuser applets

◆ Using administrative tools

Once you master Windows NT applets, you will have mastered much of the functionality the operating system has to offer.

Surveying Single-User Applets

There are several single-user applets included with Windows NT. Most of these are identical to their Windows 95 counterparts; some are enhanced versions of the Windows 95 applets; some are different. These Windows applets are described in the following sections.

◆ **3270 Emulator.** The 3270 Emulator is a basic terminal-emulation program that enables connection to an IBM 3270 mainframe. Emulating an IBM 3178/79 terminal, this applet enables you to connect to the host computer in one of the following three environments: Virtual Machine/Conversation Monitor System (VM/CMS), Time Sharing Options (TSO), and Customer Information Control Systems (CICS). The 3270 Emulator is shown in figure 12.1.

Figure 12.1

The 3270 Emulator adds built-in communications power to Windows NT.

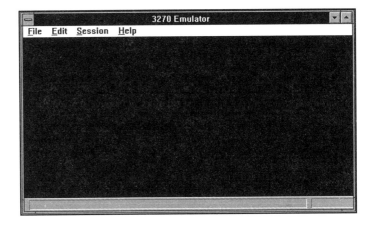

◆ **Calculator.** Calculator provides the basic functions of a normal hand-held calculator. You can optionally change its display to that of a scientific calculator to provide additional capabilities.

◆ **Cardfile.** Cardfile features a simple flat-file database that stores addresses and other commonly accessed information. Because it has no querying capability, its usefulness is primarily for small amounts of data.

◆ **CD Player.** The Windows NT CD Player enables you to play audio CDs on your CD-ROM drive. CD Player is shown in figure 12.2.

◆ **Character Map.** Character Map contains a grid that displays the entire character set for a specific font. This applet is useful when you need to use a special "high-ANSI" character, and do not know the Alt+num keyboard equivalent. Use Character Map to copy special characters to the Clipboard and paste them into other Windows applications.

Figure 12.2

The CD Player.

◆ **Clock.** Displays an on-screen digital or analog clock showing your PC's system time.

◆ **File Manager.** Enhanced in Windows NT, File Manager is used to perform file-management tasks within Windows NT. File Manager eliminates the need to perform command-line operations on such activities as creating and deleting directories, moving and copying files, and running EXE files. File Manager is shown in figure 12.3.

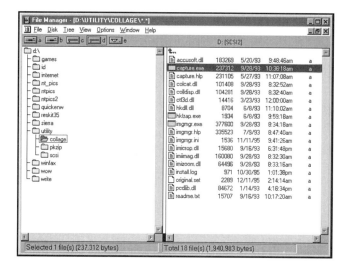

Figure 12.3

The File Manager.

◆ **Media Player.** Media Player is used to play multimedia files, such as WAV and MIDI sound files, and AVI (Video for Windows) video clips. It also can be used with any Media Control Interface (MCI) connected to your PC.

◆ **Notepad.** Notepad is a basic text editor for working with ANSI text files. It provides limited editing features, similar to DOS's EDIT utility.

◆ **Paintbrush.** Paintbrush is a useful paint program for working with BMP or PCX graphics. Although its tool palette and features are much more limited than commercial paint applications, Paintbrush is very useful for basic bit-map manipulation.

◆ **PIF Editor.** PIF Editor is a special utility that creates and edits program information files (PIFs).

Note   Program information files (PIFs) are used by Windows NT to run character-based DOS applications.

◆ **Sound Recorder.** Sound Recorder is like an on-screen audio tape recorder. It enables you to record, play, and even edit WAV sound files. You can also use the Sound Recorder to change the format of saved sound files. To change the format of a sound file, see the section "Converting Sound Formats in Sound Recorder" later in this chapter.

◆ **Terminal.** Terminal is a basic communications program that enables you to connect to remote computers, online services (such as CompuServe), bulletin-board services, and mainframes. This applet provides TTY, DEC VT-100, and DEC VT-52 terminal-emulation support.

◆ **Write.** Write is a basic word-processing program you can use to write letters and view WRI documents.

The following sections explain these applets in greater detail.

Using CD Player

This applet enables you to create a CD database to define CD and track titles, define the order of play, and set a variety of related options. After you have defined the title and/or tracks of a CD, CD Player automatically recognizes the CD when you place it in the CD-ROM drive. (CD Player is shown in figure 12.2.) The controls of CD Player mimic those of a real CD player.

You can also start CD Player from the command line by using the cdplayer parameters, /play and /track. For example:

```
> cdplayer /play [drive][trackName]
> cdplayer /play [/track | trackList]
```

Here, drive is the name of the CD-ROM drive—for example, d:. trackName must include the drive name with the name of the track—for example, e:\track04.cda (the .cda extension is required). If you want to play the playlist on drive d:, use the backslash, as follows:

```
> cd player /play d:\
```

The /track parameter plays the tracks in the specified track list. The track list is a list of tracks to play. The track list overrides any track list embedded in the CD. The /play parameter must precede the /track parameter.

The trackList parameter can be used with the /track parameter to specify the track list. The track list is the list of tracknames to play. Tracknames are preceded by the CD-ROM drive letter.

To play track04, for example, you would type the following command:

```
> cdplayer /play d:\track04.cda
```

To play three different tracks, you would type the following command:

```
> cdplayer /play /track d:\track06.cda d:\track02.cda d:\track04.cda
```

Now that you know how to play sound media, the next applet explains how to play other kinds of media.

Using the Media Player

The interface for the Media Player resembles a tape recorder, as shown in figure 12.4.

Figure 12.4

The Media Player.

The Device menu enables you to specify the kind of media to play. The media can be any of the following:

◆ Video for Windows

◆ Sound files

◆ MIDI sequencer files

◆ CD audio

The buttons on Media Player enable you to play, stop, fast forward, rewind, and pause the playing media.

To run Media Player from the command line, use the following command:

```
> mplay32 [parameter] [fileName]
```

fileName is the name of the file or device Media Player plays. Table 12.1 lists the parameters you can use with the mplay32 command.

TABLE 12.1
mplay32 Parameters

Parameter	Description
/close	Closes a file after it has been played. You can use this parameter only after using the /play parameter.
/embedding	Runs an OLE server.
/midi [fileName]	Opens a MIDI file. If the filename is not specified, Media Player opens a dialog box that asks the user to specify a file.
/open [fileName]	Opens the specified file. If the filename is not specified, Media Player opens a dialog box that asks the user to specify a file.
/play [fileName]	Plays the specified file. If the filename is not specified, Media Player opens a dialog box that asks the user to specify a file.
/vfw [fileName]	Opens a Video for Windows (.VFW) file. If the filename is not specified, Media Player opens a dialog box that asks the user to specify a file.
/wave [fileName]	Opens a wave (.WAV) file. If the filename is not specified, Media Player opens a dialog box that asks the user to specify a file.

Use these parameters to affect the playing of the media.

Converting Sound Formats in Sound Recorder

You can use the Sound Recorder to change the format of saved sound files. To convert a sound file, use the following procedure:

1. In the Sound Recorder window, click on the Properties option in the File menu.

    Windows NT displays the Properties For Sound window.

2. Click on the down arrow in the Choose from box and click on All formats, Playback formats, or Recording formats.

3. Click on the Convert Now button.

   Windows NT displays the Sound Selection window.

4. Use the down arrows in the Name, Format, and Attributes boxes to specify the attributes of the sound format you want to save the sound file as.

5. Click on the OK button. This action confirms the format selection.

6. Click on the OK button in the Properties for Sound window. The Properties for Sound window disappears.

Once you change the sound format, it is just as easy to change it back to its original format using the same procedure.

Exploring Multiuser Applets

Windows NT also includes four multiuser applets. They are called multiuser because they can be used by a workgroup as well as by a single individual.

For example, although the Windows 95 Clipboard enables you to exchange data between applications on a single desktop, the Windows NT ClipBook Viewer enables you to exchange data between desktops as well. The following sections look at the four Windows NT multiuser applets: ClipBook Viewer, Mail, Chat, and Schedule+.

ClipBook Viewer

Windows NT users probably work daily with more applications on their desktop than do users of most other operating systems (especially those that do not support multitasking).

A key factor is the ease at which data exchange can be carried out in the Windows NT environment. Windows NT uses a storage area known as the *Clipboard*, which enables you to send data from one application and insert a copy of that data into other applications.

Windows NT 3.*x* has a utility, called the Clipboard Viewer, to view the contents of the Clipboard. Windows NT provides a much more powerful tool: the *ClipBook Viewer*, which is an expanded workgroup version of the Windows 95 Clipboard Viewer.

Although you can use the ClipBook Viewer to view, save, and delete data contained in the Clipboard, you also can use it to exchange data between desktops within your workgroup.

Note The actual storage area for your data is not the ClipBook Viewer. The Clipboard is a much more ethereal entity: a class of Application Programming Interface (API) functions located in the USER library that manage the exchange of data between applications. The ClipBook Viewer is simply a window to that data.

Using the Clipboard

Nearly all Windows applications use the Clipboard. To use it, you need to choose one of three commands found under the **E**dit menu. These commands are described as follows:

◆ Cu**t** removes the selection from the active window and places it in the Clipboard.

◆ **C**opy duplicates the selection from the active window and places it in the Clipboard.

◆ **P**aste inserts the contents of the Clipboard into the active window at the position of the cursor.

 Tip If you are cutting and pasting using options in the Edit menu, you are wasting time. The much easier way is to use the following key combinations:

◆ Ctrl+C to copy the highlighted text

◆ Ctrl+X to cut the highlighted text

◆ Ctrl+V to paste the copied or cut text at the current location of the cursor.

Although these keystrokes are far more efficient, not all applications support them. For those applications that do not support these keystrokes, see if you can configure the keyboard entries so you can implement these keystrokes.

The capability to exchange data between Windows NT applications is not as simple as it may appear. To understand this complexity, think about the unique data types of the applications you use (see table 12.2).

TABLE 12.2
Variety of Available Data Types

Application	Works Primarily With
Word for Windows	Formatted text or Ami Pro
Notepad	Unformatted text
WordPerfect for DOS	OEM text
Excel or Quattro	Spreadsheet data (including Pro for Windows numbers and formulas)
Paintbrush	Bit-mapped graphics
Micrografx Draw	Vector graphics or Aldus Freehand
Microsoft Sound System	Sound

The variety of data types that exists between applications can lead to some potential problems. For instance, how can you transfer formatted text from WordPerfect for Windows to Notepad (which accepts only unformatted text)? If you have ever tried to open up a WordPerfect file (or another word processing file) with Notepad (or another text editor), you know that the result is garbled: text is sandwiched between formatting specifications.

Does this same logic carry over to Clipboard data exchange between WordPerfect and Notepad? No. WordPerfect data is not pasted as unintelligible text into Notepad because of the way in which the source application (WordPerfect), the Clipboard, and the receiving application (Notepad) work together.

Note The contents of the Clipboard are always treated as a single unit. You can never paste part of the Clipboard contents into a document.

When you copy data to the Clipboard, the source application sends data in as many formats as it is able to send. For example, among the formats WordPerfect transfers to the Clipboard is text (consisting of unformatted characters). Notepad is able to accept the WordPerfect data because it also supports text format, and is thus able to paste it correctly into a document.

The source application ultimately is in control of the way the data is formatted. The source application determines the type of format to support; the receiving application makes a determination about which format to accept when it pastes the data. As a result, some of the formatting or information on the data may be lost if the same data formats are not supported in the receiving application.

There is no ceiling on the amount of data you can store in the Clipboard. In fact, you are limited only by the amount of memory your computer has. As a result, imagine the lag on system resources that would result if the source application had to supply the Clipboard with multiple formats of the same data. To get around this problem, most applications tell the Clipboard which types of formats they support, and furnish data in that format when a receiving application requests it from the Clipboard.

 Note You have no control over the formats being copied and pasted. The source application determines which formats to send to the Clipboard; the receiving application looks at the available formats and accepts the highest available format. In other words, you cannot force Notepad to accept RTF—Notepad alone makes that determination.

Using the Clipboard Window

When you start the ClipBook Viewer by double-clicking on its icon in the Main group, the ClipBook Viewer appears with two child windows: Local ClipBook and Clipboard.

Use the Clipboard window to work with data on your desktop. Remember that the Clipboard window is not the Clipboard—it is only a window showing the contents of the Clipboard. As a result, the ClipBook Viewer does not need to be running to be able to use the Clipboard.

You can perform the following tasks by using the Clipboard window:

◆ **Clearing the contents of the Clipboard.** To delete the contents of the Clipboard, activate the Clipboard window and choose the **D**elete option from the **E**dit menu or press the Del key. You are asked to confirm this deletion by clicking on the Yes button in a message box.

An alternative method of clearing the contents of the Clipboard does not require you to open the ClipBook Viewer at all. Instead, it can be done within the application in which you are working.

For example, if you are in a word-processing application, select a space, and then choose the **C**opy command from the **E**dit menu. The space is inserted into the Clipboard, overwriting its previous contents.

◆ **Viewing data in different formats.** The **V**iew menu for the Clipboard window lists the data formats sent by the source application to the Clipboard. To change the display of the data, select one of the formats from the list. You will notice that Default Format is initially checked. This setting signifies that the Clipboard window has automatically selected the format being displayed from

the list of available formats. If the source application is running, Default Format displays the contents of the Clipboard window in the format preferred by the source application. If it is not running, the ClipBook Viewer selects the best format left available.

◆ **Saving the contents of the Clipboard.** You may need to save data in the Clipboard for a later time. There are two ways to save Clipboard data.

You can save the contents of the Clipboard as a page to the Local ClipBook, which is a permanent storage area for data that you can recall later or share with other workgroup members. To save to the Local ClipBook, select the Local ClipBook window and choose the **P**aste option from the **E**dit menu. In a dialog box, you are asked to name the page you are creating, and you have the option to declare it as a shared item (available for use by others). Click on the OK button.

You cannot save formatted text in the Local ClipBook or as a CLP file. When you paste the formatted text into a Local ClipBook page or save it as a CLP file, it immediately is converted to text format (even if the source application is still running).

You also can save the contents of the Clipboard to a Clipboard file (as in Windows 95). To do so, choose the Save **A**s option from the **F**ile menu. Enter a filename in the Save As dialog box, and click on OK. Clipboard files have a default extension of CLP.

Under most circumstances, you will want to use the Local ClipBook to store contents of the Clipboard. The Local ClipBook enables you to view and share such data much more easily than by working with CLP files.

When you shut down a Windows NT session, Windows NT saves any contents remaining in the Clipboard as a CLP file. You can access that data during a later session.

Using the Local ClipBook

The Local ClipBook is a centralized storage location of Clipboard items. Each separate entry in the Local ClipBook is called a *page*. Pages can be viewed in a list (by choosing the Table of **C**ontents option from the **V**iew menu), in Thumbnail view (by choosing the Thumb**n**ails option), or as a display of their actual contents (by choosing the Full Page option).

Figure 12.5 shows the Local ClipBook, displaying its pages in Thumbnail view.

Figure 12.5

*The Local
ClipBook.*

Sharing Data by Using ClipBook

Although the ClipBook Viewer is a useful and powerful tool for an individual desktop, it also can be used to exchange data between desktops. Because all members of your workgroup that run Windows NT have their own ClipBooks, you can access remote data from their ClipBooks, and others can access your Local ClipBook.

Sharing Data from Your Local ClipBook

To enable other users to share your local data, check the Share Item Now box as you paste a new page into your Local ClipBook. If you check the share box, a second dialog appears for you to set specific options.

◆ **Start Application on Connect.** Checking the Start Application on Connect box causes the source application to start whenever another user accesses this data. This option is useful when creating dynamic links between applications.

   Dynamic data exchange is discussed in Chapter 15.

◆ **Run Minimized.** Checking the Run Minimized box forces it to run in a minimized state.

◆ **Permissions.** Clicking on the Permissions button displays the ClipBook Page Permissions dialog box. In this dialog box, you can set the type of access you want other users to have to the ClipBook page. You can designate the following levels of access: Full Control, Change, Read and Link, Read, and No Access.

After setting these options, other users can connect to, and work with data in, your ClipBook.

Accessing Remote ClipBook Data

You can access shared data on other users' computers and copy it to your Clipboard. To do so, you need to connect to the remote computer's ClipBook by choosing the **C**onnect option from the **F**ile menu.

In the Select Computer dialog box, specify the computer you want to connect to by entering the name or selecting a name from the Computers list. After clicking on the OK button, a new window opens in your ClipBook Viewer window, displaying the remote ClipBook.

 Note   You work with the shared pages of the remote ClipBook in the same way that you work with your Local ClipBook.

To disconnect from another computer, choose the Disconnect option from the **F**ile menu.

Mail

One of the best business tools of the information age is electronic mail (e-mail). The use of e-mail within offices can make business communication much more efficient and useful than past forms of written communication.

An e-mail package is a standard element of a typical local area network. Windows NT includes Mail, which is a simplified version of Microsoft Mail. Mail enables you to send and receive electronic mail (both text messages and files) across your workgroup.

Setting Up Mail

To run Mail, use the following procedure.

1. Double-click on its icon in the Main group.

   As Mail loads up for the first time, it prompts you to designate a post office.

 Note   A post office contains information about user accounts for a workgroup and also functions as a depository for the workgroup's messages.

You can create a new post office or connect to an existing one. If the administrator has not already established an account for you in the post office, you need to create the account.

Note A post office is used by the workgroup, not by a single individual. Thus, all workgroup members have mailboxes within a central postoffice.

2. Typically, a post office has already been set up for your use by the administrator. If so, choose the **C**onnect to an Existing Postoffice in the Welcome to Mail dialog box.

   The Network Disk Resources dialog box appears.

3. Select the desired post office by typing its path in the Network Path text box.

   Alternatively, you can locate the appropriate path by selecting a computer from the top box and the desired path in the lower box.

4. After clicking on the OK button, Mail asks if you currently have an account in the postoffice. If so, click on the **Y**es button and you are prompted for your password. If you do not have an existing account, click on the **N**o button.

   A dialog box appears, asking for the following information about you:

   ◆ **Name.** Enter your full name (up to 30 characters in length). [Required]

   ◆ **Mailbox.** Enter a name (up to 10 characters) that you will use as a logon name to Mail. It is recommended that you use your Windows NT user name to avoid the necessity of remembering several user names. [Required]

   ◆ **Password.** Enter a password (up to 8 characters) for use as you start Mail. Be sure to choose a password that you can remember. [Required]

   ◆ **Phone #1.** Enter your primary phone number.

   ◆ **Phone #2.** Enter a secondary phone number.

   ◆ **Office.** Enter your office number or location identifier (up to 32 characters).

   ◆ **Department.** Enter your department name (up to 32 characters).

   ◆ **Notes.** Enter any additional information in this field (up to 128 characters).

5. After entering this information, click on the OK button.

   Mail displays the Inbox window. You are now ready to begin using Mail.

ote If you do not connect to an existing post office, you can create a new post office by choosing the Create a new Workgroup Post office option from the Welcome to Mail dialog box. You are required to administer the post office if you create it, however.

Sending a Message

To send a message to one or more users on your network, click on the Compose button from the Mail window, or choose the Compose Note option from the Mail menu. The Send Note window appears, as shown in figure 12.6.

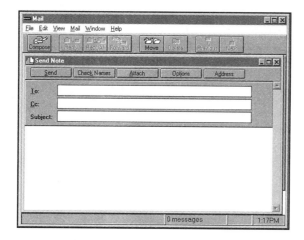

Figure 12.6

The Send Note window.

When you send a message, you have to define the following three elements:

◆ **Recipient.** Declare the users to which you want to address the message. You can send a message directly to other workgroup members or send it as a carbon copy (cc:).

ote A carbon copy (cc:) is a carryover from traditional written business communications, in which a copy of a letter is sent to all interested parties.

Enter the user name(s) of the person(s) in the **T**o text box. If you want to view an address list of users in the workgroup, click on the A**d**dress button. The Address dialog box appears.

Select the name of one or more persons from the list, and click on the **T**o button. (Alternatively, you can double-click on a name in the Directory box.) After you have selected the appropriate names, click on the OK button to return to the Send Note window.

If you want to send a carbon copy of the message to another user, enter the user name in the **C**c text box. You can click on the A**d**dress button to add user names to the cc: list as well.

Tip Move between fields in the Send Note window by pressing the Tab key or by using your mouse to click on a new field. The Enter key is not used for this purpose.

◆ **Subject.** Declare a subject of the message so that the recipient understands the message's basic purpose and content before she reads it. Enter the subject for the message in the Subject text box.

Tip Keep in mind that e-mail tends to be less structured or formal than standard paper letters. Because you typically are sending text, formatting and page layout is immaterial.

◆ **Message.** Enter the actual text of the message. Use the large box at the bottom of the window as your area for writing the message. The actual text-editing capabilities in the message area are meager (roughly parallel to Notepad), but you can use the standard cut, copy, and paste commands.

Tip You can view the message area in a proportional or fixed font. Use the Change Font option on the **V**iew menu to switch between them.

Before sending the message, you may want to set options for the message. Click on the Opt**i**ons button to display the Options dialog box. Set the desired options, as follows:

◆ **Return receipt.** If this box is checked, you will be notified when the message recipient(s) reads the message.

◆ **Save sent messages.** If this box is checked, Mail saves a copy of your message for you. This option enables you to keep a log of your correspondence.

◆ **Priority.** Electronic messages can have priority levels. Set your message to the appropriate level by choosing the High, Normal, or Low options. The recipient of the message sees the priority of the message in his Inbox.

When you have completed the message and set the desired options, click on the **S**end button to send the message over the network to the mailbox of the addressee.

Reading a Message

When you receive an e-mail message from another workgroup member, it is placed in your Inbox, as shown in figure 12.7.

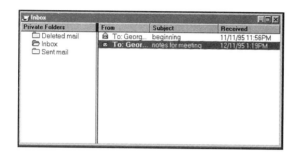

Figure 12.7

An Inbox with incoming mail.

Notice that an unread message has a closed envelope icon beside it. To read the message, double-click on the message entry from the Inbox, or select the entry and press Enter. Your message appears in a message window.

Note
The left side of the Inbox displays a list of available folders. You can store your e-mail in a variety of folders, just as you store written correspondence in a filing cabinet.

To view the contents of a folder, click on the appropriate folder icon. Also, by double-clicking on the button at the top of the window, you can switch between private and shared (public) folders.

Responding to a Message

After you read an e-mail message, you might want to respond to that message. Instead of having to create a new message and then reenter the recipient name and subject, you can reply to the existing message.

To reply, click on the Reply button from the toolbar, or choose **R**eply from the **M**ail menu. The message window appears (see fig. 12.8).

Mail automatically addresses the letter, adds "RE: " to the subject of the message, and provides the original text of the message in the message area below a line.

When you choose the **R**eply command, your response is sent only to the person who sent you the message. If other users are receiving carbon copies of the message, you probably want to send your reply to them as well. To do this, click on the Reply All button, or choose Reply to All from the **M**ail menu.

Figure 12.8

Replying to a message.

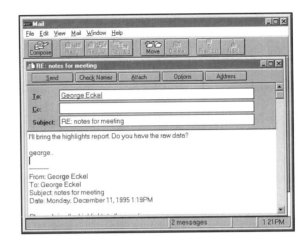

Removing Messages

To delete messages from your mailbox, select the desired message from the Inbox list, and click the Delete button on the toolbar. Mail moves the message to the Deleted mail folder (see fig. 12.9), where it is deleted as you exit Mail.

Figure 12.9

Deleted messages are placed in the Deleted mail folder.

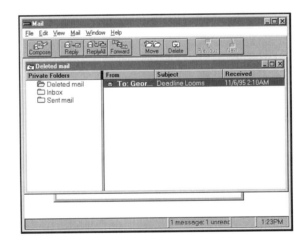

If you decide to undelete the message before you exit Mail, click on the Move button to move the message to a different folder.

Chat

Chat is a tool you can use to have a "live" conversation with another workgroup member over the network. To run Chat, double-click on the Chat icon in the Accessories group. The Chat window appears, as shown in figure 12.10.

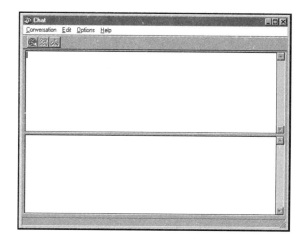

Figure 12.10

The Chat window.

Think of Chat as a different type of phone, and a Chat conversation as a different kind of phone call. To conduct a Chat conversation, do the following:

◆ **Call another user.** Call another workgroup member by clicking on the Dial button on the toolbar or by choosing the **D**ial option from the **C**onversation menu. Choose the computer name of the person you are trying to call, and click on OK.

Chat then calls the computer you choose, and waits for the person whom you are calling to answer. The status bar at the bottom of the Chat window notifies you of the call's status.

Tip   Think of the computer name as a phone number, because each phone number has a physical location to which it is associated.

◆ **Conduct a conversation.** If a user answers the Chat request, the caller can begin typing in the top window while the receiver types in the bottom window. A conversation need not be unidirectional; you both can type information simultaneously if needed.

◆ **Hang up.** When you are finished with the conversation, you or the other workgroup member are free to hang up and terminate the conversation. To do so, click on the Hangup button from the toolbar, or choose the **H**angup option from the **C**onversation menu. When the person with whom you are conversing hangs up, you are notified by Mail in the status bar.

If another workgroup member calls you and requests an online Chat conversation, you can answer the call by clicking on the Answer button from the toolbar or by choosing the **A**nswer option from the **C**onversation menu. If Chat is not open, Windows NT automatically starts it for you.

Schedule

Schedule+ is a miniature personal scheduling manager for use in scheduling appointments and tasks, jotting notes, and maintaining a calendar book.

Schedule+ also can be used as a workgroup scheduler. Using Schedule+, workgroup members can have a public schedule to help with setting meetings and viewing others' schedules. To run Schedule+, double-click on its icon in the Main group.

Note   Schedule+ is much more advanced than the limited Calendar applet provided in Windows NT 3.x.

Schedule+ uses the same user name and password as Mail. If you already have established these in Mail, you do not have to do so again in Schedule+. Instead, enter your user name and password in the Password dialog box. The Schedule+ Appointment List window appears (see fig. 12.11).

Figure 12.11

The Schedule+ window.

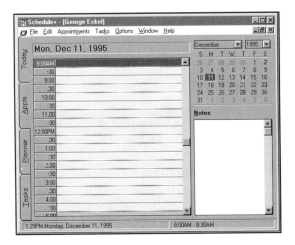

The Schedule+ window can be divided up into the following four areas:

◆ **Tabs.** The tabs on the left of the window enable you to view different pages of Schedule+. Click on one of the four tabs to switch between page views.

◆ **Calendar.** The monthly calendar shows the current month by default. To view a different date, select the appropriate month and year from the list boxes above the calendar, and click on the date in the calendar.

◆ **Daily schedule.** The main part of the window is a daily schedule for the date specified above it (and in the calendar beside it). Enter appointments and block out activities in this box.

◆ **Notes.** Enter any miscellaneous comments related to the current day in this box.

The following tasks explain how to accomplish primary tasks using the four areas in Schedule+.

Scheduling an Appointment

To schedule an appointment in Schedule+, designate the block of time for the activity by selecting an initial time (12:00 p.m., for example), then drag the mouse to the end time (2:00 p.m.).

From the Appointments menu, choose the New Appointments option. The Appointment dialog box appears (see fig. 12.12).

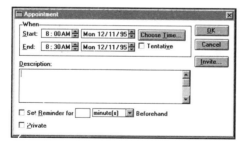

Figure 12.12

The Appointment dialog box.

Set the following appointment details in this dialog box:

◆ **When.** In the When box, your **S**tart and **E**nd times for the appointment already have been set. Modify them if necessary. You can declare the appointment as tentative by checking the Tentati**v**e box.

◆ **Description.** Enter text in the **D**escription box to describe the appointment. Use as much space as necessary. Schedule+ places this text in the time block that you specify in your daily schedule of the main Schedule+ window.

◆ **Reminder.** Check the Set **R**eminder for check box if you want Schedule+ to issue a reminder before the time of an appointment. Enter the amount of time before you want the reminder issued in the space provided.

◆ **Private.** If you want to keep the description of your appointment private from other workgroup members, check the **P**rivate box.

◆ **Invite.** Click on the **I**nvite button to invite other workgroup members to attend the appointment. In the Select Attendees dialog box, choose the persons you want to invite from the post office list.

You do not need to enter information in each field.

Using the Planner

The Planner window (see fig. 12.13) displays the times you and other workgroup members have set appointments.

Figure 12.13

The Planner window.

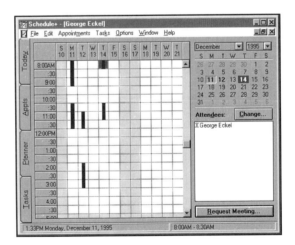

The Planner window can be divided into the following four areas:

◆ **Tabs.** The tabs on the left of the window enable you to view different pages of Schedule+. Click on one of the four tabs to switch between page views.

◆ **Time slots.** The main part of the window is an appointment grid, displaying the time slots of set appointments. To view an appointment, double-click on its time slot in the Planner window. Schedule+ displays the Appointment Book window of the person who scheduled the appointment.

◆ **Calendar.** The monthly calendar shows the current month by default. To view a different date, select the appropriate month and year from the list boxes above the calendar, and click on the date in the calendar with your mouse.

◆ **Attendees.** The Attendees box displays the names of the workgroup members whose appointments are shown in Schedule+. To change the list, click on the Change button, and choose the desired workgroup members from the Select Attendees dialog box. In addition, if you want to send a meeting request to each of the attendees, click on the Request Meeting button.

Using the Task List

You can use the Task List to list and prioritize activities you need to perform. Access the Task List by clicking on the Tasks tab of the Schedule+ window (see fig. 12.14).

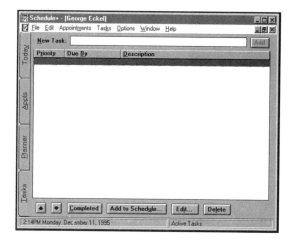

Figure 12.14

The Tasks window.

The Task List has the following options:

◆ **Add task.** To add a new task, enter its description in the New Task text box and click on the Add button (or press Enter). The new task is added to the Task List.

◆ **Edit task.** You can edit a task after it has been placed on the Task List by double-clicking on the list item (or by selecting the item and clicking on the Edit button). The Task dialog box appears, enabling you to change the task's description, project, due date, and priority.

◆ **Add project.** Schedule+ enables you to group tasks by project. To add a project, choose the New Project option from the **T**asks menu. In the Project dialog box, enter a project name in the Name text box. Check the Private box to prevent other workgroup members from seeing the contents of this list.

◆ **Completed task.** When a task is completed, remove it from the list by selecting it and clicking on the **C**ompleted button.

You can master these tasks easily and thereby gain some control over projects you embark on.

Scheduling a Recurring Appointment

Schedule+ can automatically schedule a recurring appointment (a board meeting every Friday at 10:00 a.m., for example) for you. Click on the Appts tab, and set the desired date by using the calendar. Next, select the desired time block by dragging your mouse from the starting time to the ending time.

Choose the New Recurring Appt option from the Appoint**m**ents menu to display the Recurring Appointment dialog box (see fig. 12.15).

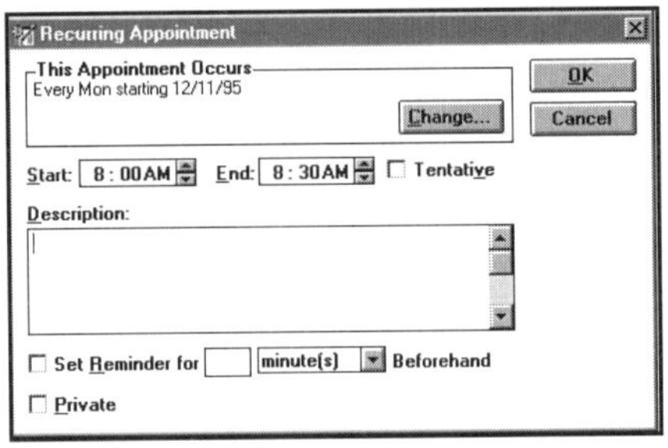

Figure 12.15

The Recurring Appointment dialog box.

Click on the **C**hange button to display the Change Recurrence dialog box. Select the desired pattern by setting its occurrence (daily, weekly, biweekly, monthly, yearly), day of week, and duration.

Using Administrator Tools

A new set of applets, called Administrator Tools, is provided in Windows NT to help administrators configure and monitor their Windows NT networks. These tools, discussed in the following sections, include the Disk Administrator, User Manager, Performance Monitor, Event Viewer, and Backup.

Note These utilities are not for everyone's use—they are available only to users with administrator-level rights on the network.

Disk Administrator

The Disk Administrator is a powerful tool that is used to configure local and networked hard drives. It enables you to work with any physical or logical FAT (File Allocation Table, used by DOS), HPFS (High Performance File System, used by OS/2), and NTFS (NT File System) drives. It does not, however, currently support drives compressed using MS-DOS 6.0's DoubleSpace.

To run Disk Administrator, double-click on the Disk Administrator icon in the Administrative Tools group. The Disk Administrator window appears, as shown in figure 12.16.

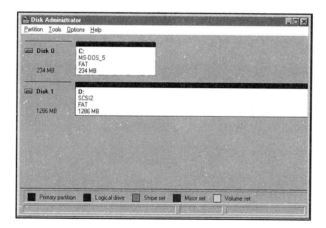

Figure 12.16

The Disk Administrator.

Disk Administrator enables you to perform many of the same tasks as DOS's FDISK utility. Although it may seem strange to perform such low-level functions on your disk in a graphical environment, Disk Administrator is much more powerful than its DOS counterpart.

 Note Disk Administrator does not provide the capability to convert FAT drives to NTFS. This command must be performed by using the command-line utility CONVERT. Formatting a drive must also be performed by entering **FORMAT** at the command prompt.

Compressing Files

The compress utility can compress and uncompress files residing in NTFS partitions. Compression ratios vary according to the type of file. Text files, for example, often do not compress much—perhaps 1.5 to 1. Graphics files, however, can often compress a great deal—perhaps 9 to 1.

To compress files on your NTFS partitions, use one of the following procedures:

1. In the File Manager, hold down the Ctrl key and use the mouse to highlight all of the files you want to compress.

2. Click on the Compress option in the File menu.

Or

1. In the File Manager, hold down the Ctrl key and use the mouse to highlight all of the files you want to compress.

2. Click on the Properties option in the File menu. Windows NT displays the Properties dialog box, as shown in figure 12.17.

Figure 12.17

The Properties window.

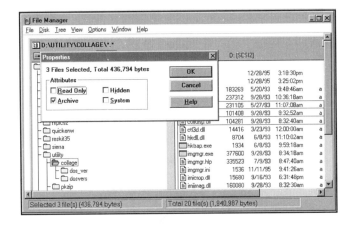

3. Click on the Compressed check box.

User Manager

User Manager is used by the administrator to manage user accounts on the Windows NT network. To run User Manager, double-click on the User Manager icon in the Administrative Tools group. The User Manager window appears, as shown in figure 12.18.

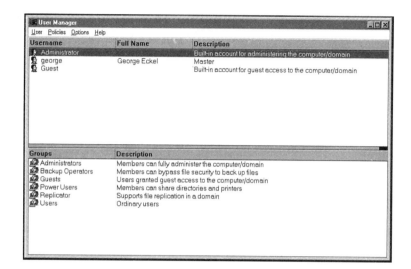

Figure 12.18

The User Manager.

The top portion of the window displays a list of user names for the entire system. Data tracked includes the following:

◆ **Username.** Refers to the logon name that you enter as you log on to the system.

◆ **Full Name.** Used to enter the complete name of the user. Although this data is not used by Windows NT, it is helpful for the administrator to work with full names rather than cryptic user names.

◆ **Description.** Used to enter optional comments about a particular user (such as title or position in the company). This is another field not required by Windows NT.

You can view or modify additional information on a specific user by double-clicking on the entry in the Username list. The User Properties dialog box appears, as shown in figure 12.19.

Although the administrator can modify some of the settings, such as Full **N**ame and **D**escription, she cannot change or view the password. A password is proprietary to each individual user.

When a new account has no password, or an existing account's password has expired, the administrator can add a password to the account. The administrator can view or modify additional information about the user by clicking on the **G**roups or P**r**ofile button. As you finish working with a user account, click on the OK button to return to the User Manager window.

The lower portion of the User Manager window lists the user groups that are defined for the system. You can double-click on each of these entries to display additional information about each group. When you double-click on an entry, the Local Group Properties dialog box appears (see fig. 12.20), in which you can enter a description of the group as well as view all of the members of the group in the Members list.

Figure 12.19

The User Properties dialog box.

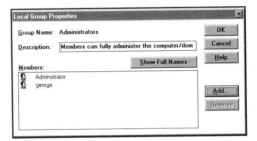

Figure 12.20

The Local Group Properties dialog box.

Add additional users to the group by clicking on the **A**dd button. Delete a user from the group by selecting a user name from the Members list and clicking on the **R**emove button.

Performance Monitor

Performance Monitor enables the administrator to track the performance of the system. To run Performance Monitor, double-click on the Performance Monitor icon in the Administrative Tools group. The Performance Monitor window appears, as shown in figure 12.21.

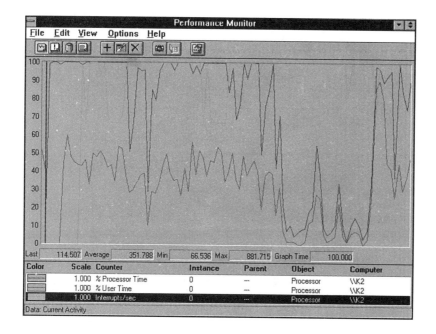

Figure 12.21

The Performance Monitor.

Event Viewer

Event Viewer is another tool that can be used by the administrator to track system-operation logs kept by Windows NT. The system logs document-system events (for example, errors and warnings encountered), application events (such as crashes), and security events (such as invalid password entries).

To run Event Viewer, double-click on the Event Viewer icon in the Administrative Tools group. The Event Viewer window appears, as shown in figure 12.22.

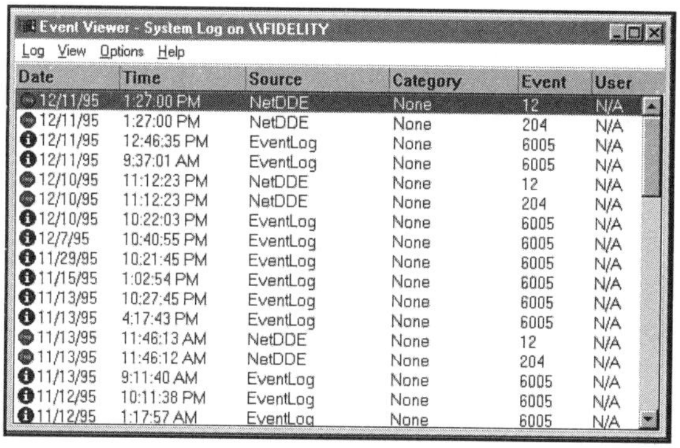

Figure 12.22

The Event Viewer.

Backup

The final tool is Backup, which, as its name implies, is used to back up and restore volumes, directories, and individual files. To run Backup, double-click on the Backup icon in the Administrative Tools group. The Backup window appears, as shown in figure 12.23.

Figure 12.23

The Backup window.

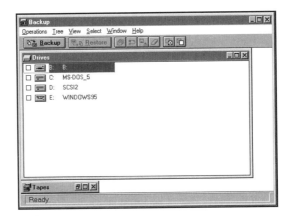

Summary

Although the acceptance of the Windows NT operating system is not based on the applets that are included with it, these mini-applications do play an important role for users of the environment. This chapter looked at the applets that come with Windows NT, and divided them into three groups: single user, multiuser, and administrative.

The single-user applets make up the largest group of NT applets. Most in this group are identical to those included with Windows NT 3.*x*. Some, such as File Manager, have been enhanced; a few, such as 3270 Emulator and CD Player, are new applets designed for Windows NT.

Multiuser applets are workgroup-based. They include ClipBook Viewer, Mail, Chat, and Schedule+. These applets facilitate workgroup data exchange, communication, and schedule coordination.

The final group is a set of Administrative Tools, including Disk Administrator, User Manager, Performance Monitor, Event Viewer, and Backup. These tools can be used only by users with administrator-level rights.

Printing and Managing Fonts

Managing fonts on your desktop has never been easier than in Windows NT. You can create and print professional-looking documents on virtually any output device by using the fonts included with Windows NT.

If you think back to earlier versions of Windows, recall that they always have been much friendlier environments in which to manage fonts than DOS. Fonts are dealt with at the operating-environment level rather than at the application level. With third-party font managers, users worked with text that would look the same on-screen as the printed out copy. Windows NT, however, has become much more sophisticated than earlier Windows versions by seamlessly integrating a scaleable font technology into its environment.

Additionally, Windows NT makes printing easier, more seamless, and more painless than previous 16-bit versions of Windows or DOS. In fact, once you get your printer configured the way you want it, Windows NT frees you from worrying about the printing process. Instead, you can think about the quality of your printer's output.

As this chapter looks at the world of fonts and printing in Windows NT, it focuses on the following topics:

◆ Introducing fonts in Windows NT

◆ Using TrueType Fonts

◆ Embedding fonts

◆ Substituting fonts

◆ Comparing TrueType fonts with PostScript Type 1 fonts

◆ Installing and removing fonts

◆ Using other screen fonts

◆ Installing and configuring printers

◆ Managing print jobs with Print Manager

 Note   Although typeface and font are used interchangeably in PC circles, a distinct difference exists between the two. A typeface is the basic design of characters; a font is the complete set of characters for a given typeface at a particular point size and style.

Introducing Fonts in Windows NT

As you work in Windows NT, you'll become acquainted with the following four distinct groups of fonts:

◆ **Bitmap or raster fonts.** These fonts are created by arranging pixels in a particular pattern to appear and print in a fixed point size. A unique bitmap must be created for each character, point size, and type style.

Windows 3.0 fonts, such as Helvetica or Times Roman, are bitmap fonts that come in 8-, 10-, 12-, 14-, 18-, and 24-point sizes. A separate file is needed for each point size and style (normal, bold, italic, and bold italic). These screen fonts cannot be downloaded to printers; as a result, these screen fonts usually are different from what actually is printed by the printer.

◆ **TrueType fonts.** These fonts, known as *outline fonts*, are generated by using mathematical calculations. An outline font is a set of mathematical instructions

for each character that contains a series of points to form an outline. An outline font is scaleable because you can increase or decrease the point size of a font by multiplying or dividing by the desired factor.

An outline font can be scaled in a wide range of sizes, from 2 to nearly 700 points (although many Windows NT applications might limit this actual range). All mathematical instructions for a font can be stored in a single file rather than in multiple bitmap files. TrueType fonts are compatible with all devices except plotters.

With TrueType support, font management in Windows NT is very similar to Windows 95.

◆ **Device-specific fonts.** Device-specific fonts are either installed on the printer or downloaded, and are controlled more by the device than by Windows NT. Windows NT does not map device-specific fonts; instead, it relays the logical font request to the device—printer or software—whose job it is to map the fonts properly. PostScript fonts are considered device-specific fonts.

◆ **Vector fonts.** Vector fonts are scaleable fonts, consisting of tiny dots and line segments. Vector fonts typically are used only when outputting to a plotter, although a few dot-matrix printers support vector fonts. Windows NT comes with three vector fonts: Modern, Roman, and Script. Because of their makeup, vector fonts do not have the same quality as the other types of fonts. Thus, most Windows NT applications do not even display vector fonts in their font lists.

Using TrueType Fonts

Windows 3.1 introduced a breakthrough in font technology on the PC platform. Before Windows 3.1, you had to purchase a third-party font manager, such as Adobe Type Manager (ATM), to achieve identical screen and printer output. Without ATM, you probably worked with Helvetica and Times Roman on-screen, and found your documents looking quite different when you printed them out. Not so in Windows 3.1, which integrated the scaleable font technology known as TrueType into the operating environment. Windows NT incorporates this same TrueType font technology into its operating environment.

TrueType was developed jointly by Apple and Microsoft. The TrueType fonts included with Windows NT match those of Apple System 6.0.5, and can be used on the Macintosh without conversion. The basic TrueType fonts included with Windows NT (see fig. 13.1) are designed to match the core PostScript fonts.

Figure 13.1

TrueType fonts included with Windows NT.

Arial
Arial Italic
Arial Bold
Arial Bold Italic

Courier New
Courier New Italic
Courier Bold
Courier Bold Italic

Times New Roman
Times New Roman Italic
Times New Roman Bold
Times New Roman Bold Italic

αβχδεφγηιφκλιμνοππλωψαψ (Symbol)
☞♌♓☎♏↗♋≈✝♐☒◆✳○♋ (WingDings)

Note   The 14 standard TrueType fonts in Windows NT were made by Monotype, one of the major font foundries. These fonts have been widely praised for their outstanding quality; in fact, many consider them superior to their PostScript Type 1 counterparts.

Although TrueType is the new kid on a block traditionally dominated by PostScript, its acceptability has been widespread. This acceptability centers on four factors, which can be summarized as follows:

◆ **Ease of use.** One of the greatest strengths of TrueType is that it is closely integrated in the Windows NT environment. In fact, the Windows NT Graphical Device Interface (GDI) was designed specifically for this purpose. No other font manager is as easy to use. Installing, removing, and working with TrueType fonts is effortless. Even applications designed for Windows 3.0 can use TrueType fonts because of the way Microsoft integrated TrueType into the GDI. Moreover, new TrueType Application Programming Interface (API) functions give applications greater control over the placement and manipulation of characters.

Note   TrueType can be used in Windows 3.0 applications, but the printed document might not be exactly WYSIWYG in the same way that Windows 3.1 and Windows NT documents are.

◆ **Identical screen and printer output.** TrueType enables you to work with fonts that appear the same on the screen as they will on the printer.

Note TrueType is almost WYSIWYG. Because of the differences in dots-per-inch between your monitor (usually around 96,120 dpi) and printer (usually 300,600 dpi), no font technology is absolutely identical.

◆ **Scaleable.** No longer do you need to design your document around the sizes of the Windows NT bitmap fonts (8, 10, 12, or 14). If you use bitmap fonts with point sizes other than the built-in ones, they look jagged as they are resized. TrueType fonts are scaleable fonts that can be displayed and printed in virtually any size above two points. Figure 13.2 shows the letter "Q" in Arial typeface at 12 and 62 points. As you can see, the two are directly proportional.

Figure 13.2

TrueType fonts are scaleable.

◆ **Portable.** TrueType fonts are printer portable, meaning that a TrueType document prints identically on any output device, regardless of the printer's page description language (PDL), such as PostScript or Hewlett-Packard's PCL. TrueType also is portable across platforms so that a document created in Windows NT can be seamlessly moved to a Macintosh.

How Windows NT Handles TrueType Fonts

Although TrueType looks identical on the screen and printer, the process that Windows NT goes through to display TrueType on these various devices is different.

Suppose you start Word for Windows and begin typing an office memo. Based on the character specifications—such as font, point size, and style—Word asks Windows NT for the appropriate bitmap to represent each character in the document.

Windows NT finds the appropriate TrueType font file, based on the information provided by Word, and sends it to the TrueType rasterizer. The TrueType rasterizer converts the outline instructions into a bitmap, and returns the bitmap to the GDI to display. This bitmap then is sent to the device driver for displaying on-screen. This process is shown in figure 13.3.

Figure 13.3

The process of displaying a TrueType font.

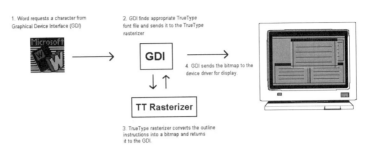

1. Word requests a character from Graphical Device Interface (GDI)

2. GDI finds appropriate TrueType font file and sends it to the TrueType rasterizer

GDI

4. GDI sends the bitmap to the device driver for display.

TT Rasterizer

3. TrueType rasterizer converts the outline instructions into a bitmap and returns it to the GDI.

As shown in figure 13.3, TrueType font outlines are converted to a bitmap to appear on-screen (as well as to print), based on the result of mathematical instructions for a particular point size. TrueType outlines are device-independent, and thus are an ideal representation of the font. However, 96-dpi screens and even 300-dpi laser printers do not have enough resolution to display or print the character properly because the size of a pixel is too large.

If nothing is done to correct this, diagonal lines and curves within a font outline look jagged because the optimum outline of a character is in units smaller than a pixel. A diagonal line might need only part of a pixel to represent it, for example, but because the pixel is the smallest unit of measure, the pixel needs to be either on or off. If the pixel is on, the line looks too wide; if the pixel is off, the line is too narrow.

To prevent this from happening, before TrueType creates the bitmap, it first optimizes the bitmap by using *hints* (instructions that optimize the look of the scaled outline character by changing its outline to produce a better-looking character).

Without hints, a lowercase "m" or "n" might have different widths for each of its legs. Hinting distorts the original outline characters so that the "m" and "n" bitmaps displayed have identical legs, regardless of the number of pixels available.

Hints are less important when the font is larger and the resolution is greater on the output device. Although hints are needed when printing or displaying on devices below 800 dpi, new 600-dpi laser printers, such as the HP LaserJet IV, can produce the desired results with fewer hints.

Note   Both TrueType and PostScript support hinting, but they use different techniques. PostScript Type 1 hints are a set of instructions given to the rasterizer, telling it how the character can be modified. The PostScript rasterizer then is responsible for carrying out these instructions. In contrast, TrueType hints are carried out by the font itself rather than the TrueType rasterizer.

The significance of this difference might not be obvious, but it can affect the performance and quality of the hint. First, TrueType hints are faster because they

New Riders Publishing
INSIDE
SERIES

are performed by the font producer during the development of the font instead of at run time by the rasterizer. Second, built-in hints can improve the quality of the generated TrueType font because the font designer, not the rasterizer, is in control of the final appearance of the font. Third, potential hinting problems can be resolved during the development process instead of at run time. As a result, the TrueType font rasterizer is quicker and more efficient at executing the font code.

A PostScript rasterizer interprets PostScript hints; a TrueType rasterizer simply processes the TrueType font's hints. PostScript can be thought of as a high-level interpreted language; TrueType can be considered a low-level assembler-like language.

When you print your TrueType document, the way the fonts are dealt with is based on the type of printer being used. On LaserJet and compatible printers, TrueType generates LaserJet soft fonts and downloads only the characters needed by the printer to print the text, instead of entire font files being sent. (Typical soft fonts require downloading entire character sets.) Characters are printed as text, not as graphics.

On PostScript printers, TrueType downloads smaller characters (14-point characters and below) as Type 3 fonts (bitmap), which is faster than downloading an outline font. For larger fonts, TrueType sends a Type 1 outline for each size that needs to be rasterized by the PostScript printer.

On dot-matrix printers, TrueType sends text as graphics for each pass of the printhead. Although printing TrueType on a dot-matrix printer is slow, the quality is remarkably good.

TrueType Font Embedding

TrueType solves the problem of transferring Windows 95 and Windows NT documents between computers. Before TrueType, a document created on a computer with a specific set of fonts could not be properly displayed or printed on a second computer without the same set of fonts being installed. As a result, document sharing within an office environment was limited to those workstations that were equipped with identical fonts and font managers. When sending a document to a typesetter, you also had the legal dilemma of whether to include copyrighted font files on the disk to ensure that their output was identical to that of the service bureau.

TrueType eliminates these problems through a technology called *font embedding*, which embeds the fonts in the document so that they still can be displayed and/or printed when opened on a computer without those fonts installed. A font is specifically coded by the developer to have one of the following three embedding qualities:

◆ **No embedding.** If a font allows no embedding capabilities, the source application does not embed the font in a document when it is saved. The receiving computer is forced to make a font substitution when the document is opened on the computer. PostScript and most other current non-TrueType fonts are in this class.

◆ **Read-only.** If a document contains one or more read-only fonts, you can read and print the document, but the receiving application does not allow you to edit it until every read-only embedded font has been removed.

◆ **Read/Write.** The read/write option enables you to read, modify, and print the document with the embedded TrueType fonts. Moreover, the application in which you open the embedded document asks you whether you want the font installed permanently. The standard TrueType fonts that come with Windows NT are all read/write fonts (as are the fonts that come in the TrueType Font Pack). If a font is read/write enabled, you can distribute an embedded document to whomever you choose; there are no copyright restrictions placed on you.

Note   The actual significance of font embedding will be felt in forthcoming versions of major Windows 95 and Windows NT applications. Currently, the 16-bit version of Microsoft PowerPoint is the only Windows application that supports font embedding.

Windows NT Font Mapping

If you have worked with fonts for any length of time, you know a vast number of fonts are available that are virtually identical in appearance, but have copyrighted face names. Font mapping eliminates any possible confusion by Windows when it searches for exact face names.

Windows NT enables you to substitute fonts that are not found on your system with installed fonts. This process is known as *font mapping*. When you open an existing document or create a new one, an application requests a font from Windows NT by listing its face name and other characteristics. If there is no exact match with a physical font (a font that can be transferred to the printer and screen), Windows NT must try to map that request to the closest possible physical font.

Note Windows NT advanced font-mapping capabilities are available in Windows 3.0. Both Windows 3.0 and 3.1 have a core-mapping facility, which selects the physical font that most closely matches the requested font. Windows 3.0 requires that all font requests go to the core mapper—even when a font request has a match. Windows NT speeds up the process considerably by making an "end-around" the core mapper when an exact match is found (that is, the core mapper is not even accessed).

When an application requests a font from Windows NT, Windows NT has to decide which font to use based on the following conditions:

◆ **Font does not exist.** If the name of the font does not exist, Windows NT always selects the appropriate TrueType font by matching the font characteristics (point size, serif/sans serif, monospaced/proportional).

◆ **Font matches a bitmap font.** To ensure compatibility with Windows 3.0, a bitmap font is used and stretched when needed for displaying at all point sizes if the name of a font matches only a bitmap font.

◆ **Font matches a bitmap and TrueType font.** If the name of a font matches a bitmap and TrueType font, the bitmap font is used at the point sizes for which there is a bitmap; the TrueType font is used at the remaining point sizes.

◆ **Font has a duplicate face name.** If two or more fonts have the same name, most applications list only the font name once. TrueType fonts are always listed first.

◆ **Font does exist.** If the name of the font exists, Windows NT ignores the substitution table and uses the specified font. This action might seem obvious, but it is very useful.

Comparing TrueType with PostScript

Before Windows 3.1 and Windows NT, PostScript was the unquestioned leader of scaleable font technology. With TrueType's introduction into Windows 3.1 and Windows NT, however, the landscape has changed considerably. PostScript still dominates the high-end desktop publishing, graphics design, and typesetting markets, but TrueType is making inroads into these territories. No longer does a business have to look to a PostScript printer to print professional-looking documents.

PostScript is a page description language (PDL) developed by Adobe and Apple in the mid-1980s that quickly became the standard PDL used by serious typographers. Type 1 fonts are the industry standard and are used by every service bureau.

PostScript printers have a set of Type 1 fonts built into them: often Helvetica, Times Roman, Palatino, and Avant Garde. There are two major kind of PostScript fonts: Type 1 is a set of scaleable typefaces; Type 3 fonts typically are bitmap fonts used primarily for printing text at small sizes.

Note   A page description language (PDL), such as PostScript or Hewlett-Packard's PCL, is a set of instructions used to manipulate fonts, graphics, and color, and to set printer options. PDLs are resident in a printer or printer cartridge.

Although TrueType font technology is built into Windows NT, PostScript (through Adobe Type Manager) is integrated into OS/2 2.1.

The debate now rages over which scaleable font technology you should use: TrueType or PostScript. Table 13.1 lists the major differences between the two font technologies. PostScript is still the best choice for desktop publishing and graphics design because of its universal support by service bureaus. TrueType is the best choice for normal use and in standard business communications. Thus, if your chief concern is to produce professional-quality documents, you cannot go wrong with TrueType.

TABLE 13.1
TrueType vs. PostScript Type 1

Category	TrueType	PostScript
Operating System	Windows NT	OS/2 2.x (Adobe Integration Type Manager)
Scaleable font technology	Yes	Yes
Universally available	Yes	No for all Windows NT users
Hinting instructions	Font	Font carried out by Rasterizer
Industry standard	No	Yes for typesetters/service bureaus
Estimated number	2,500	Over 20,000 fonts available
Overall level of sophistication	Mixed	High typeface
Printer portability	Virtually any printer	With ATM, virtually any printer
Platform portability	PC, Mac	All major platforms

Note The fast rise of TrueType and the affordable quality fonts in the TrueType Font Pack have created a price war between the major font foundries. The result is that never before have there been as many quality TrueType and Type 1 fonts available at such reasonable prices.

Although PostScript has a much richer library of available fonts, the number of quality TrueType fonts grew rapidly with the success of Windows 3.1 and Windows NT. Microsoft introduced the TrueType Font Pack for Windows, which contained 44 typefaces. These fonts are designed to be combined with the standard TrueType typefaces to make an equivalent to the standard set of PostScript fonts. Many new CD-ROMs also are available that contain TrueType fonts.

Note One of the best sources for free or shareware fonts is the DTPFORUM on CompuServe. You can find hundreds of TrueType (and PostScript Type 1) fonts in Library 9. Although some are of dubious quality, there are many decorative fonts that can enrich your font library.

Working with Fonts

Windows NT provides the Font section of the Control Panel to enable you to install and remove TrueType, bitmap, and vector fonts. It also allows you to set TrueType options. The Fonts dialog box is shown in figure 13.4.

Fonts dialog box screenshot: Installed Fonts: Albertus Extra Bold (TrueType), Albertus Medium (TrueType), Antique Olive (TrueType), Antique Olive Bold (TrueType), Antique Olive Italic (TrueType), Arial (TrueType). Buttons: Cancel, Remove, Add..., TrueType..., Help. Sample. No fonts selected. Size of Font on Disk: 0 KB	**Figure 13.4** *The Fonts dialog box.*

Installing Fonts

The process of installing fonts in Windows NT is straightforward. To install TrueType, bitmap, or vector fonts, click on the Fonts icon in the Control Panel to display the Fonts dialog box (see fig. 13.4). Click on the **A**dd button to display the Add Fonts dialog box, as shown in figure 13.5.

Figure 13.5

The Add Fonts dialog box.

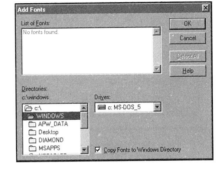

Use the Dri**v**es and **D**irectories controls to select the path that contains the font files you want to install. When you change directories, Windows NT looks for font files located in the path and lists the font names in the List of **F**onts box. You have a choice of the following fonts to install:

◆ **Single font.** Select a single font from the fonts list by clicking on it with your mouse.

◆ **Group of fonts.** Select a group of fonts by clicking on each font while holding down the Ctrl key. You also can select a range of fonts by dragging your mouse down the list.

◆ **All fonts.** Select all fonts by clicking on the **S**elect All button.

By default, the **C**opy Fonts to Windows Directory box is checked. With this option checked, Windows NT copies each font to the WINNT\SYSTEM32 directory.

It usually is best, from a font management point of view, to centralize all your fonts into a single location. If you have large numbers of fonts located on a CD-ROM or network drive, however, you can save space on your hard drive by keeping the fonts at the other location. Remember, though, if you do not copy the file to the WINNT\SYSTEM32 directory, Windows NT needs to access the CD-ROM or network to use it. Windows NT prompts you to insert the disk containing the fonts when required.

Note Avoid using fonts stored on a network disk because you add to the network traffic each time Windows NT accesses that font.

When you are ready to add the selected fonts, click on the OK button.

Although you might want to have as many fonts as possible available to you when you are working, installed fonts slow the time it takes to load Windows NT and most applications, and they drain memory. You probably do not notice much of a difference unless you have at least 100 fonts installed.

Note The general rule of thumb is to install only the fonts you use regularly. You can always remove a font from Windows NT without deleting the font file, and add the font later if you need it.

Removing Fonts

To remove a TrueType, bitmap, or vector font from Windows NT, click on the Fonts icon in the Control Panel to display the Fonts dialog box. Select the font(s) from the Installed **F**onts list and click on the **R**emove button. The Remove Font dialog box appears (see fig. 13.6), asking you to confirm your action.

Figure 13.6

The Remove Font dialog box.

In the dialog box, you also have the option of deleting the font file from your hard drive by checking the **D**elete Font File From Disk box. Click on the **Y**es button to remove the specified font. (If you are deleting a group of fonts, click on the Yes to **A**ll button to avoid confirming the removal of each font.)

Setting TrueType Options

The Font section of the Control Panel also enables you to specify that you want to use TrueType exclusively on your machine. To set this option, click on the **T**rueType button in the Fonts dialog box.

The TrueType dialog box appears (see fig. 13.7), and displays the **S**how Only TrueType Fonts in Applications check box. If you work with TrueType exclusively, you can restrict applications from listing all other available fonts.

Figure 13.7

The TrueType dialog box.

Note This option applies only to Windows applications that support TrueType. You cannot use TrueType fonts in a DOS or POSIX application, for example.

Understanding Bitmap Fonts

Windows NT includes five bitmap fonts that are available for screen use, as described in table 13.2.

TABLE 13.2
Windows NT Screen Fonts

Font	Point Sizes Supported	Font File Name (? = A-F)
Courier	10, 12, 15	COUR?.FON
MS Sans Serif	8, 10, 12, 14, 18, 24	SSERIF?.FON
MS Serif	8, 10, 12, 14, 18, 24	SERIF?.FON
Small	2, 4, 6	SMALL?.FON
Symbol	8, 10, 12, 14, 18, 24	SYMBOL?.FON

These fonts are essentially the same set of bitmap fonts from Windows 3.0 (although Windows NT changed the names of two of them: Helv instead of MS Sans Serif; Tms Rmn instead of MS Serif). They are exactly the same as the fonts in Windows 95.

These fonts are not listed in all your applications (Word for Windows, for example). Many applications list only those fonts that can be printed to the default printer. Consequently, they are listed if you have a dot-matrix printer as the default, but not if a laser printer is set as the default printer. Some applications, such as ObjectVision or Paradox for Windows, enable you to design a document for either the screen or printer; their font lists can vary.

Understanding System Fonts

System fonts are used in various parts of the Windows NT interface, such as dialog boxes and menus. Each of the following three fonts are required by Windows NT:

◆ **System font.** The *system font* is the default font used by Windows NT in menus, dialog boxes, window titles, and caption bars. The system font is proportional, and it is based on the type of display you are running. The system font varies, depending on the display on which you run Windows NT.

◆ **Fixed font.** The *fixed font* is a monospaced font, and it was the former default font for 16-bit Windows versions (prior to 3.0). Some applets (Notepad, for example) and applications that require a monospaced font use the fixed font.

◆ **OEM font.** The *OEM font* is a monospaced font based on the code page by the system. The OEM font plays several roles—it determines the height of dialog boxes, and is used by the ClipBook Viewer to display OEM Text.

Understanding DOS Session Fonts

Windows NT enables you to change the fonts of your DOS applications that run in a windowed DOS session. Variable-sized fonts enable you to customize the size of the text and window to a size that is suitable for you. *DOS session fonts* are based on the code page of the computer.

To change the font in your DOS-based application, open the program in a window, and choose the **F**onts command from the window's control menu. In the Font Selection dialog box, select the appropriate font size from the **F**ont list: 4×6, 5×12, 6×8, 7×12, 8×8, 8×12, 10×18, 12×16, or 16×8.

Use the Window Preview and Selected Font to see what the window and font will look like. If you want every windowed DOS session to have the same configuration, check the **S**ave Settings on Exit box, and click on OK.

Using the Windows NT Print Manager to Configure Printers

Windows NT print-management capabilities are more extensive than previous 16-bit versions of Windows. The Print Manager utility in Windows 3.1 and earlier was a basic manager of print jobs and did little else. In fact, some 16-bit Windows applications bypassed the Print Manager altogether and managed printing by themselves.

In contrast, Windows NT controls printing much more tightly so that all printing must be done through its Print Manager. Windows NT also integrates the printer-setup commands into Print Manager so that all printer controls are accessible through the Print Manager window.

Installing and Configuring Printers

When you are ready to install or configure a printer, open Print Manager—from either the Control Panel (double-click on the Printers icon) or the Main group (double-click on the Print Manager icon). The Print Manager window appears, as shown in figure 13.8.

Figure 13.8

Windows NT Print Manager.

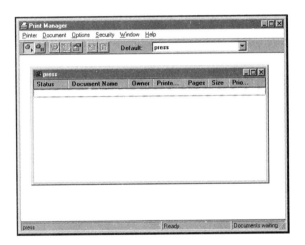

Print Manager displays a child window for each of the installed printers, and shows the name of the default printer at the top of its window in the Default list box. In addition to displaying printers, the Printers dialog box enables you to perform a number of operations, including configuring your printer connection, setting up your printer options, and installing and removing a printer.

If you want to install a new printer, choose the Create Printer option from the **P**rinter menu. The Create Printer dialog box opens, as shown in figure 13.9.

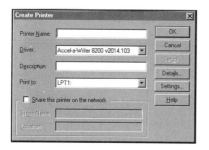

Figure 13.9

The Create Printer dialog box.

The Create Printer dialog box offers several options:

◆ **Printer Name.** Enter a name (fewer than 32 characters) to be used to identify the printer in Print Manager and Windows NT dialog boxes.

◆ **Driver.** Select the desired printer from this list.

◆ **Description.** Enter a description to inform users about the printer.

◆ **Print to.** Select a destination for your print job. You can choose one of the following options:

LPT1–LPT3. These names identify your computer's parallel ports. Most printers use LPT1. If you select an LPT port, you can click on the Settings button to specify how long the Print Manager waits for a printer to come back on-line and accept information. (A printer might not accept transmissions following an error condition or during a large print job.)

COM1–COM4. These names identify your computer's serial ports. If you select a COM port, you can click on the Settings button to specify additional information. The Ports dialog box appears (see fig. 13.10), displaying a list of valid ports you can configure. Choose one and click on the **S**ettings button.

Figure 13.10

The Ports dialog box.

Note Most printers support the default COM port settings; if yours does not, refer to your printer manual to determine the correct configuration for the COM port.

The Settings for COM2 dialog box is shown in figure 13.11.

Figure 13.11

The Settings for COM2 dialog box.

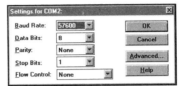

In the Settings for COM2 dialog box, you can configure the following five settings:

◆ **Baud Rate.** Determines the speed at which characters are sent through the port.

◆ **Data Bits.** Determines the number of data bits used to represent each character.

◆ **Parity.** Determines the method used for error checking. This setting checks to ensure that the correct number of bits has been received.

◆ **Stop Bits.** Determines the amount of time between transmitted characters.

◆ **Flow Control.** Determines the handshaking method used by the receiving device to control the flow of data.

If you need to configure advanced port settings, click on the **A**dvanced button. In the Advanced Settings dialog box, two additional settings appear:

◆ **Base I/O Port Address.** Determines the address used by the port in your computer's I/O address space.

◆ **Interrupt Request Line (IRQ).** Determines the interrupt used by the COM port.

Note There may be no user-configurable advanced settings for your COM port. If not, Windows NT notifies you, and returns you to the Settings for COMx dialog box.

Under most circumstances, do not make any changes to the default settings configured by Windows NT. If you have problems, first try to change your hardware configuration to match the defaults used by Windows NT.

◆ **FILE.** Tells Windows NT that print jobs will be sent to a file rather than a printer.

◆ **Network Printer.** Enables you to specify a route that is not listed. When you select this option, the Print Destinations dialog box appears, as shown in figure 13.12.

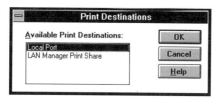

Figure 13.12

The Print Destinations dialog box.

The list of available options depends on the network to which you are attached. By default, there are two options: Local Port (adds the name of a port); and LAN Manager Print Share (adds a LAN Manager print share—versions 2.*x* of LAN Manager).

◆ **Share This Printer On The Network.** Click on this box to make the printer available to others on the network. Windows NT automatically creates a DOS-compatible share name, and places it into the Share Name text box (refer to fig. 13.10). Edit as needed. In addition, you can edit a description of the location of the printer in the Location text box.

Another option available in the Create Printer dialog box is the Details button, which, when clicked on, will display the Printer Details dialog box (see fig. 13.13).

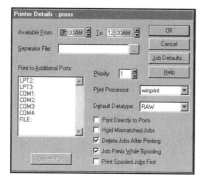

Figure 13.13

Printer Details dialog box.

In the Printer Details dialog box, there are several options you can specify for the printer:

◆ **Available From.** Specifies the hours you want the printer to be available for printing.

◆ **Separator File.** If you want to send a file to be printed before each new print job, enter the file in this text box. Clicking on the ellipsis button enables you to browse through the directory tree for a specific file.

Note Separator files enable you to print a page at the beginning of each document so that you easily can separate printed documents. These files also enable the printer to switch between PCL and PostScript printing.

To specify either of these options, enter the name of one of the separator files (DEFAULT.SEP, PSLANMAN.SEP, PCL.SEP, or PSCRIPT.SEP) that are included with Windows NT in this text box.

Windows NT's default separator file is DEFAULT.SEP. Use this file to print a blank page before each new print job.

◆ **Print to Additional Ports.** If you want to pool one or more printers together with your current printer, select the port(s) to which the other printer(s) is attached. The printer then sends the job on to all other selected printers each time a print job prints on the current printer.

◆ **Priority.** Specifies the priority of print jobs sent to the printer. Enter a number between 1–99 (the higher the number, the higher the priority).

Note Suppose you would like to use different priority levels for your printer, depending on the specific document you are printing. Instead of manually adjusting this setting each time in Print Manager, you can create two or more instances of the same printer (using different printer names), and set each printer to a different priority level.

When you need to print a document quickly, you print to the "Extraordinarily Urgent" printer. For normal use, you can use the "Just Plain Average" printer, tagged with a lesser priority. Finally, if you have a document with no priority for printing, you can choose the "Maybe Next Year" printer, tagged with the lowest priority setting.

◆ **Print Processor.** Provides the capability to change the print processor if a specific application requires this option. Most applications use the WinPrint processor.

◆ **Default Datatype.** Enables you to specify a different default datatype. This is another option you normally do not need to change from the default setting. Options include RAW, NT JNL 1.00, and TEXT.

◆ **Print Directly to Ports.** Check this box to eliminate print spooling and transfer data directly to the printer.

◆ **Job Defaults.** Clicking on this button displays a dialog box that enables you to set default settings for printed documents. The actual dialog box depends on the printer you are configuring.

◆ **Tray/Form Assignments.** In the Print Manager window for a PostScript printer, you can specify the type of paper or form that is in the tray.

PostScript printers have the added benefit of enabling you to specify the type of paper or form that is in the tray. Here is how you do it.

1. In the Main Program group, click on the Print Manager icon.

   Windows NT displays the Print Manager.

2. Click on the Properties option in the Printer menu.

   Windows NT displays the Printer Properties dialog box

3. Click on the Setup button and Windows NT displays the PostScript Printer Setup dialog box.

4. Click on the tray that you want to edit.

5. Click on the Change button.

   The Change Form Assignment window displays.

6. Click on the type of form you want in the selected tray.

7. Click on the OK button.

In the PostScript Printer Setup window, the selected form type with an asterisk displays beside the tray.

Installing a Printer

After you have defined all options for your printer, click on the OK button. When you add a new printer, Windows NT copies the driver file from your driver disk into the Windows NT SYSTEM directory. The driver is then used to communicate between Windows NT and your printer.

If the printer driver is not already on your system, Windows NT prompts you to insert the appropriate CD-ROM or floppy disk (one of the Windows NT distribution disks or an updated driver on a separate disk) into a CD-ROM or floppy drive. When you insert the disk and click on OK, the driver file is copied onto your system.

Windows NT enables you to install the same printer several times. Multiple configurations of the same printer are helpful if you frequently change the port to which your printer is attached, or if you frequently need to print to both a printer and a file by using the same printer.

Suppose, for example, that you frequently do desktop publishing work, and that you use a PostScript printer in your office. You also need to print to a file when you take a job to your typesetter.

Note You might call a printer "Legal" if you want it to use legal-size paper. You might call the same printer "Envelope" when printing envelopes. You can change the settings for each print job, or name the printer differently to retain all the settings. If you change printer setups often, giving the printer different names saves you a lot of time.

Although you can use a single installed PostScript printer and change port settings between printer and file output, a much easier solution is to install two instances of the same printer driver. Configure one (such as LPT1) to your printer port, and configure the second to FILE. You then can switch between the two printers.

Note If you install a printer more than once, Windows NT does not need to reinstall the printer driver. Instead, Windows NT uses the printer driver installed the first time.

Setting a Default Printer

You easily can set the default printer in Print Manager by selecting one of the installed printers from the Default list box at the top of the Print Manager window (refer to fig. 13.8).

Removing a Printer

If you are no longer using a printer and want to remove it from your printer list, select the printer window or icon in Print Manager, and choose the **R**emove Printer option from the **P**rinter menu. Print Manager asks you to confirm that you want to delete the printer before doing so.

When you remove a local printer, Windows NT does not actually delete the printer driver file on your hard disk. Instead, it only removes the printer's name from the list of available printers.

If you want to add the printer again to the list, you can use the Create Printer option to re-create your printer setup. Because the driver you intend to use still resides on your hard disk, you do not have to use the Windows NT distribution disk (CD-ROM or floppy) to copy the driver file onto your computer.

Setting Up a Printer

After you install and connect a printer, you still might need to set up some settings specific to your particular printer. You have two ways to set up a printer, depending on where you are working within Windows NT:

◆ **Print Manager.** Click on the Setup button in the Create Printer dialog box (accessed by choosing the Create Printer option from the Printer menu).

◆ **Windows NT Applications.** Virtually all Windows applications enable you to print text or graphic data. If so, then they also should have a Print Setup command on their File menu that displays installed printers. Click on the Setup button in that application's dialog box.

The exact setup options depend on the type of printer you are using. The most popular printer options include LaserJet and PostScript laser printers, and dot-matrix printers.

Configuring a LaserJet Printer

The most popular laser printers available today are HP LaserJet or compatible printers. If you have a LaserJet, configuring it is a relatively straightforward process. Click on the Setup button in the Printers dialog box, or choose Print Setup from the File menu of most Windows applications to display the dialog box shown in figure 13.14.

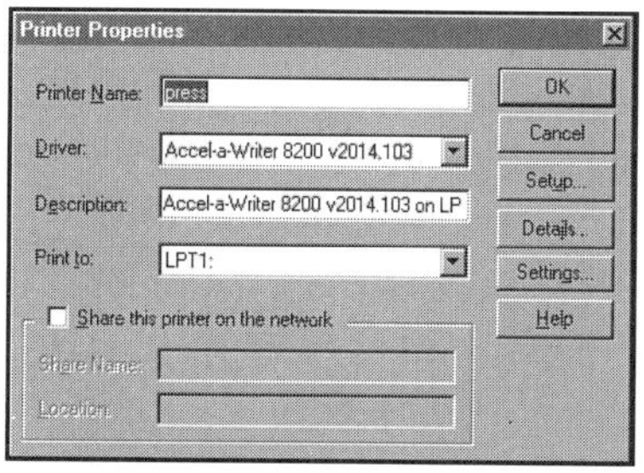

Figure 13.14

The HP LaserJet dialog box.

Note Even though most laser printers print at 300 dpi, more advanced printers, such as the LaserJet series, have resolution-enhancement capabilities. With special software, LaserJet printers can vary the size of the ink dots printed on a page. (The LaserJet IV uses Resolution Enhancement Technology and prints at 600 dpi.) These features improve dramatically the grayscale output and sharpness of photos and art.

Configuring a PostScript Printer

To print PostScript fonts, you need a PostScript-compatible printer, which involves more options than any other type of printer. To set these options, your PostScript driver dialog boxes can lead you through as many as four levels of nested dialog boxes. To display the initial setup dialog box, click on the **S**etup button in the Printers dialog box after you select your PostScript printer, or choose P**r**int Setup from the **F**ile menu of your Windows application.

The initial dialog box, shown in figure 13.15, provides the basic paper source, size, and orientation, as well as the number of copies.

Figure 13.15

The PostScript Printer Properties dialog box.

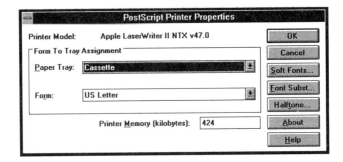

Note You do not need to have a PostScript printer to use the PostScript printer driver. You can set up the PostScript settings as usual, and print the job to a file. This can be useful if you want to print a PostScript file on a printer that is not attached to your system, or if you need to submit a PostScript file to a service bureau for typesetting.

If you want to print a PostScript document to a file, choose FILE as your destination when you connect your printer.

Configuring a Dot-Matrix Printer

A dot-matrix printer has fewer available options to configure. If you have a dot-matrix printer, click on the **S**etup button in the Printers dialog box after you select the dot-matrix printer in Print Manager. Figure 3.16 shows a dialog box for an Epson 24-pin dot-matrix printer.

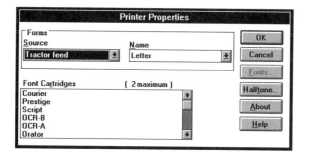

Figure 13.16

The Epson LQ-850 dialog box.

Setting Printer Security

You can restrict the access that users and groups of users have to a printer. Such restrictions include the permission to print documents, control printer settings, change printing orders, and pause the printer. To do so, choose the **P**ermissions option from the **S**ecurity menu in the Print Manager window. Windows NT displays the Printer Permissions dialog box.

You can specify access restrictions for each user or group by making selections from the **T**ype of Access list box. Possible options include Full Control, Manage Documents, Print, and No Access. In addition, you can add to the list of users or groups by clicking on the **A**dd button.

Owning a Printer

Owners can change access permissions for a printer. You can take ownership of a printer if you have Full Control access or are a member of the Administrators group. To own a printer, choose the Owner option from the **S**ecurity menu in Print Manager. The Owner dialog box is displayed, as shown in figure 13.17. Click on the **T**ake Ownership button.

Figure 13.17

The Owner dialog box.

Connecting to Remote Network Printers

To access a remote network printer, your computer must be connected to it. You can do this by clicking on **C**onnect To Printer in the **P**rinter menu in Print Manager. Windows NT displays the Connect to Printer dialog box, which lists the remote printers available to you in the **S**hared Printers box.

To select a shared printer, enter its name in the **P**rinter text box. If the **E**xpand by Default box is checked, you can select a remote printer from the **S**hared Printers list.

If the **E**xpand by Default box is not checked, double-click on a network in the **S**hared Printers list; it expands to show the domains or workgroups on that network. Double-click on the domain or workgroup name to display the names of its remote printers. When you are ready to connect, click on the OK button.

Managing Print Jobs with the Print Manager

In addition to installing and configuring printers, the actual management of Windows NT print jobs also is done through the Print Manager. Print Manager acts as a print-spooling utility that, when activated, receives print jobs from all Windows NT applications, logs them into a queue, and sends the jobs to one or more printers at the appropriate time.

The Print Manager icon is located in the Main group, but you do not have to run it to be able to use it. When you print a document from an application, Print Manager opens automatically until the print job is over; then it closes automatically. Print Manager stays open only if a printer needs your attention.

You can, however, use the Print Manager to view the print queue and perform other print management tasks.

Changing the Print-Queue Order

You can change the order of files in the print queue. This capability is helpful if you are printing a number of documents and you want to print a lower-priority document first.

To move a print job, select the desired job from a printer window with your mouse, then drag and drop it into a new position. Figure 13.18 shows the print queue.

There are two limitations to changing the queue order. First, you cannot move a job that is currently being printed. Second, you cannot move a print job from one printer to another.

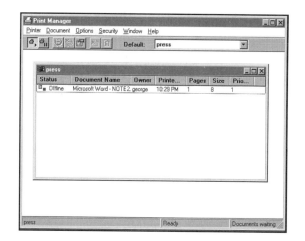

Figure 13.18

The Print Manager queue.

Deleting a Print Job

If you want to cancel a pending or current print job, select the job from the print queue and choose **R**emove Document from the **D**ocument menu. A message box confirms your action.

Setting Document Details

By double-clicking a document in a print queue or selecting a document and choosing **D**etails from the Document menu, you can view the Document Details dialog box.

This dialog box enables you to view specific details about the print job, such as its title, status, number of pages, and size (in bytes). It also enables you to set various options for the document, including:

◆ **Notify.** Specifies the user name notified when a document has printed. The default name is the document owner.

◆ **Priority.** Determines the priority the document is given in the print queue. Highest numbered priorities are printed before lower numbers. Values range from 1–99.

◆ **Start Time.** Specifies the time at which to start the print job. Note that because there are no date settings, a print job must print within 24 hours.

◆ **Until Time.** Specifies the time at which you would like a document to cease printing.

Troubleshooting TrueType Printing

Although TrueType is an innovative font technology, there always are compatibility problems with the scores of printers and printer drivers available today. In time, these problems will be solved by Microsoft and the printer manufacturers.

Note   Overall, the single best thing you can do with a printer problem under Windows NT is to get the latest driver available. The best resources for this are the printer manufacturer's forum, the Microsoft Software Library on CompuServe, or the Microsoft Download Service (MSDL): (206) 936-6735.

Summary

With the integration of TrueType technology into Windows NT, printing is easier and more seamless than ever before. The type quality of TrueType is matched only by PostScript and other advanced font technologies.

This chapter discussed TrueType fonts and how they can be used in Windows NT. It also described other fonts used by Windows NT for on-screen use.

You learned about the Windows NT Print Manager, which is a powerful, integrated print-management facility. (Print Manager is a far cry from its weak Windows 3.1 counterpart.)

Using Print Manager, you can install, configure, and remove printers; connect to network printers; and set levels of authorization for users on your network. You also can use it to control document queues, including prioritizing print jobs, setting document details, and removing documents from the queue.

Windows NT brings a whole new level of sophistication to printing on the PC platform. With TrueType and the new Print Manager, printing can be as simple or detailed as you require.

Part III

Creating Solutions through Integration

C H A P T E R

14

Running DOS, OS/2, and POSIX Applications

hen you move to Windows NT from DOS, character-mode OS/2, or Unix, you need not abandon your existing applications. You can run DOS, OS/2, and POSIX-compliant applications from within Windows NT, sometimes with better performance. You even can access a command prompt from within Windows NT. If you have previous Windows experience, this information is nothing new. Windows users always shell out of Windows to DOS.

Note POSIX is a standard developed by a consortium of Unix vendors designed to bring order to the various Unix environments available, each of which is slightly incompatible with the others. POSIX-compliant Unix applications can run on Windows NT.

In Windows NT, you can operate more than one DOS, OS/2, or POSIX session simultaneously, and each session is an emulation of a *x*86 microprocessor with its own memory, devices, and environment variables. Because each session is an emulation of a different *x*86 machine, the term *virtual* is used. These multiple virtual machines are all preemptively multitasked, just as is any other program running under Windows NT.

This chapter provides more hands-on instruction for using Windows NT with DOS, OS/2, and POSIX applications. In particular, this chapter covers the following topics:

◆ Setting up a DOS, OS/2, or POSIX application by using Setup.

◆ Setting up terminate-and-stay-resident (TSR) programs.

◆ Using the Program Information File (PIF) Editor to create PIFs that customize your DOS applications.

◆ Starting DOS, OS/2, and POSIX applications under Windows NT.

◆ Switching among non-Windows NT applications.

◆ Cutting-and-pasting data among non-Windows NT applications.

This chapter shows you the way to set up and run your DOS, OS/2, and POSIX applications with Windows NT. You learn to manage character-mode windows, switch between character-mode tasks, and cut-and-paste among applications. In the last part of this chapter, you explore the customization options available for configuring the Windows NT multitasking environment for use with DOS programs.

Setting Up a Non-Windows NT Application

Sometimes you want to run a non-Windows NT application under Windows NT. What is a non-Windows NT application? The five categories of non-Windows NT applications are as follows:

◆ Windows applications written for Windows versions 3.1 and older

◆ Character-mode OS/2 applications

◆ POSIX-compliant Unix applications

◆ DOS applications

◆ Memory-resident DOS programs (TSRs)

If you have an older Windows application (written for Windows 3.1 or 3.0), contact the manufacturer to obtain an updated version. Because Windows NT and Windows 95 are 32-bit operating systems, and Windows 3.1 is a 16-bit operating system, you will obtain great performance benefits if you update your applications to 32-bit.

Windows NT runs almost all Windows 3.1 and 3.0 applications, but it must emulate Windows 3.1's 16-bit operating system by using software. This additional software layer between the program and the operating system might slow performance.

 Note   Windows NT should run all of the software for the operating systems with which it is compatible. Because Windows NT is a secure operating system, however, it does not allow any program to have direct access to the hardware. Some programs may seek direct access to the hardware, attempting to bypass the operating system to gain speed advantages. Programs that are created by using these techniques may not be fully compatible with Windows NT.

The rest of this chapter discusses running the other five types of non-Windows NT applications: OS/2 applications, POSIX applications, DOS applications, PowerPC applications, and TSRs. From the first, you have read that DOS, OS/2, and POSIX applications run under Windows NT. This is worth repeating: you need not do anything out of the ordinary to run such applications under Windows NT. In fact, most of the techniques described in this chapter pertain to both non-Windows NT and Windows NT applications. Only certain techniques (editing PIFs or loading TSRs, for example) are specific to DOS applications, and even these processes are for special cases.

For the purposes of this chapter, assume that your DOS, OS/2, and POSIX applications are already installed on your hard disk, but have not been set up to run under Windows NT. If you have never installed such an application, it is not particularly difficult, but it is time-consuming.

Almost every application comes with an installation guide that leads you through the installation process. One installation disk usually is labeled the *setup* or *install* disk; start with that disk. The setup program almost always is called SETUP.EXE or INSTALL.EXE (the file might have a .BAT file extension). To install the application, type the name of the setup program, press Enter, and off you go. The program prompts you to answer a list of fairly easy questions; usually, the default responses to these questions work fine.

After the application is on your hard disk, you must set it up to run under Windows NT. Again, this is a straightforward process: you can use the Windows NT Setup program.

The following sections describe ways to set up your DOS, OS/2, and POSIX applications to run under Windows NT by using each of these two options.

Setting Up Memory Resident Programs under Windows NT

The last category of non-Windows NT applications is that of DOS memory-resident programs (TSRs). These programs do not run like regular DOS applications, so they are categorized separately. Memory-resident programs expect a single-task environment; they also expect to address memory directly. Unlike most DOS applications, however, they expect to be loaded when the PC boots. These programs run only while other applications are running. When you close them, memory-resident programs are not unloaded from memory (thus, they are called terminate-and-stay-resident programs). TSRs are used for the following two functions:

◆ **Utilities.** TSRs function as utilities, such as device drivers, that run only when certain pieces of hardware are accessed. Two common examples of this type of TSR utility are network software (protocols) and mouse drivers.

◆ **Pop-ups.** TSRs function also as pop-ups, whose menus become visible only when a special key combination is issued. This type of TSR is used as communication programs or personal-information managers. When you access them, they momentarily suspend the operation of any other DOS application being used.

Note In one sense, the pop-up TSR was a multitasking pioneer. Before the wide availability of the graphical user interface, it was the best way to interrupt activities in one application to take care of other business.

TSRs often create unusual side effects when they run in an environment, such as Windows NT, that is already set up for multitasking. Some applications, however, require a TSR, for example, a mail program. For that reason, this section shows you how to set up a TSR. Pop-up TSRs that emulate multitasking are of less value because their functions are duplicated in Windows NT.

Note Although Windows NT enables you to use your favorite TSR, you should avoid using TSRs, if possible, because they often conflict or duplicate the functionality of Windows NT.

Under Windows NT, you should not load TSRs from AUTOEXEC.BAT or CONFIG.SYS. Although Windows NT maintains two files with these names so that you can configure your DOS environment, you should include only the commands necessary to make the DOS environment functional for you, such as essential device drivers.

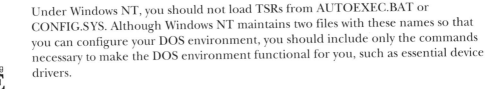

If you load additional programs in AUTOEXEC.BAT and CONFIG.SYS, Windows NT makes a copy of them to serve each DOS session you start. This reduces the total amount of memory available for running applications. Instead, start TSRs from a batch file that contains the commands for all the TSR programs you plan to use with the application you are starting. After placing all the TSR commands in the batch file, follow them with the command to start the application. Then save the batch file. You should make a PIF for this batch file, and install the PIF. (See "Understanding Program Information Files for DOS Applications" later in this chapter for more information on PIFs.)

The TSR probably requires a special key combination to start it. If this combination is reserved by Windows NT (for example, Windows NT reserves Ctrl+Esc to open the task switcher), you must edit the TSR's PIF to enable the key combination to be used to start the TSR. After you edit the TSR's PIF, Windows NT can no longer use that reserved key combination. You cannot access a TSR from either the Windows NT desktop or a Windows NT application; you can access it only from a DOS application.

Now you know the way to set up non-Windows NT applications. Most of the time, setup is totally automatic. In every case, Windows NT detects that you are setting up a DOS application and takes the appropriate steps.

By now, you probably have some sense of what a PIF is; the following section gives you a closer look, in case you ever have to change one.

Understanding Program Information Files for DOS Applications

Windows NT requires a program information file (PIF) to optimize the DOS environment for each DOS program you run. Many common DOS applications come with customized PIFs to optimize their performances under Windows NT. Under Windows NT, each DOS application inherits the DOS environment you define when you configure Windows NT. PIF parameters customize the DOS application's environment and issue a command to execute the DOS application itself. In that respect, PIFs are like DOS batch files.

The difference between batch files and PIFs is that you have to create the batch file to customize a DOS environment and run a program. On the other hand, Windows NT can install the DOS application's own PIF, create a custom PIF for you, or use the Windows NT default PIF, _DEFAULT.PIF.

Note If you are familiar with Windows 3.1, you know that you can run a DOS program without creating a PIF. If you do so in Windows NT, the DOS environment set up for the program will be based on default values that might not suit the program. Under Windows NT, it is best to create a PIF for each DOS application.

The following three ways enable you to install a PIF for a DOS application that you want to run under Windows NT:

◆ Let Windows NT Setup provide the PIF automatically when you install an application. This normally is done when you first install Windows NT, but it can be done anytime you want to add a DOS application to a Windows NT program group.

◆ Create a custom PIF manually by using the PIF Editor.

◆ Use the default PIF, _DEFAULT.PIF, and use the PIF Editor to modify it to suit the DOS application.

Editing a PIF is not usually a daily occurrence. After a PIF is established, there are few reasons to change it. Because you might encounter a situation where you want to edit one, however, a little how-to advice is in order. The following sections explain how to use the PIF Editor, how to edit both a standard and an imported PIF, how to provide multiple PIFs for the same application, and how to provide lists of the PIF options for standard and 386-Enhanced modes.

Starting the PIF Editor

The PIF Editor looks like (and works like) all other Windows NT applications. You can find it in the Main program group. Start the PIF Editor in the usual manner—by double-clicking on its icon. Alternatively, run it from the Start button menu by choosing **R**un and supplying the following command-line parameters:

C:\WINNT\SYSTEM32\PIFEDIT.EXE

After you start the PIF Editor, the PIF Editor screen for 386-Enhanced mode appears because Windows NT runs DOS applications in this mode. Figure 14.1 shows the 386-Enhanced mode PIF Editor dialog box. (The PIF Editor dialog box for Standard mode is shown in figure 14.2, later in this chapter.) You learn about each of the dialog-box options later in this chapter.

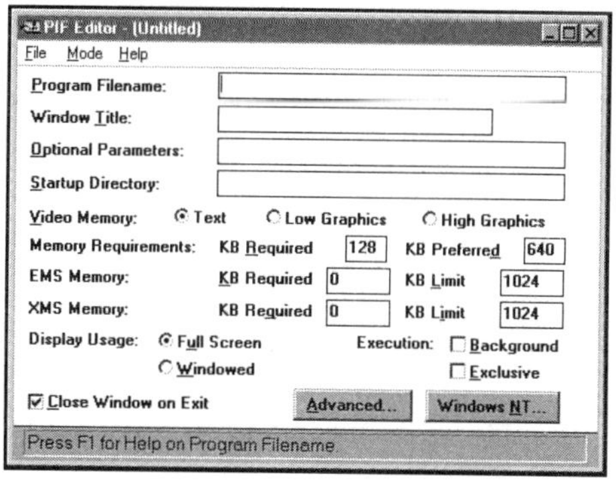

Figure 14.1

The PIF Editor for 386-Enhanced mode.

Note You can create PIFs for both standard and 386-Enhanced modes. The PIF Editor Mode menu contains the items **S**tandard and **E**nhanced; the current operating mode is checked. You can edit a PIF for either mode, regardless of the fact that Windows NT is running in 386-Enhanced mode. If you select Standard mode, a warning appears—saying that the PIF you are about to create has the wrong type of parameters for the current mode. You can, however, proceed with your PIF editing session.

Editing a Standard Windows PIF

Windows NT contains several DOS applications, and each has its own PIF. One of these applications is QBasic. This section uses this PIF to show the way to edit an existing program information file.

Suppose that you like to work with QBasic when you make the transition to Windows NT. If you work with such a DOS application often, perhaps to maintain simple programs that you use exclusively in your office, you can optimize this PIF for your purposes. You might, for instance, want to change QBasic's working directory to a directory that holds only your QBasic programs.

You are ready to edit the PIF file associated with the DOS application. Follow these instructions to edit the DOS Prompt PIF:

1. Start the PIF Editor.

2. Select **O**pen from the **F**ile menu.

3. From the list box that contains several PIFs, select a file with the extension .PIF. A dialog box appears.

4. Enter a name in the **S**tartup Directory text box.

5. Save the PIF by selecting **F**ile and then choosing **S**ave.

Note Many DOS applications have their own PIFs that enable them to run under Windows NT. You can import an application's PIF and edit it with the PIF Editor. The PIF Editor can edit old PIFs.

Using PIF files gives you great flexibility in the execution of their corresponding application.

Using Multiple PIFs for the Same Application

Suppose that you frequently multitask with a project-management application that runs under DOS. You want to minimize its use of resources under Windows NT most of the time you use it, but you have one special project data file that requires all available memory. Whenever you use this special project data file, you need at least 512 KB of memory. The PIF you use specifies only 256 KB of memory, which is usually enough, but not when using the large project data file. You can create a customized PIF specifically for your project.

Follow these instructions to create a second PIF for this DOS application:

1. Start the PIF Editor and open PROJ.PIF.

2. Under the **F**ile menu in the PIF Editor, use the Save **A**s option instead of **S**ave. This option enables you to assign a new name to the PIF you are editing. Name the special PIF **SPECPROJ.PIF**. You now can make editing changes to SPECPROJ.PIF, instead of to the original PIF.

3. For the Memory Requirements parameter, set both the KB **R**equired and KB **D**esired options to **512**.

4. Add the filename of your special project to the **O**ptional Parameters edit field so that the project file is opened automatically.

   Anything you enter in the **O**ptional Parameters field is passed to the DOS project manager, as if you entered the text on the DOS command line. If you start the project management application by entering PROJECT SPECPROJ.DAT, for example, enter **specproj.dat** in the **O**ptional Parameters field.

5. Change the Window **T**itle field so that you can distinguish between the special project icon and the normal one. For example, enter **Special Project**.

6. Save the new PIF by selecting **S**ave under the PIF Editor's **F**ile menu. Windows NT adds the new PIF in the Windows NT directory on the hard disk.

Note   A PIF usually is located in your default user directory. Unless you created the PIF in another directory, you don't have to specify a path in the **C**ommand Line field.

The preceding exercises introduced you to some typical PIF-editing sessions. The PIF Editor dialog box also has a number of other variables that you can manipulate. These variables change, depending on whether you are targeting the PIF for Standard or 386-Enhanced mode.

Note   Unless you do a lot of work with DOS applications, you might never have to modify a PIF beyond what you've done so far. If you use DOS applications under Windows NT frequently, however, you will appreciate the complete lists of PIF parameters provided in the following sections.

Examining PIF Options for Standard Mode

Figure 14.2 shows the PIF Editor dialog box for Windows NT Standard mode.

```
PIF Editor - [Untitled]
File   Mode   Help

Program Filename:      C:\DOS\QBASIC.EXE
Window Title:          Microsoft QBASIC
Optional Parameters:
Startup Directory:     C:\DOS
Video Mode:            ● Text   ○ Graphics/Multiple Text
Memory Requirements:   KB Required  128
XMS Memory:            KB Required  0        KB Limit  0
Directly Modifies:     □ COM1    □ COM3    □ Keyboard
                       □ COM2    □ COM4
□ No Screen Exchange          □ Prevent Program Switch
☑ Close Window on Exit        □ No Save Screen
Reserve Shortcut Keys:  □ Alt+Tab   □ Alt+Esc   □ Ctrl+Esc
                        □ PrtSc     □ Alt+PrtSc

Press F1 for Help on Program Filename.
```

Figure 14.2

The PIF Editor dialog box for Standard mode.

Table 14.1 presents the PIF options available in Standard mode, with a description of each option.

TABLE 14.1
Basic PIF Options in Standard Mode

Option	Description of Function
Program Filename	The name and path of the file that starts the DOS application, including the file extension. An example is C:\WORD\WORD.EXE. You can specify an environmental variable by using the SET command and % parameters.
Window **T**itle	Appears below the icon and in the title bar at the top of the window (if the application runs in a window instead of full-screen). It is optional—if you leave it blank, the application's name is used.
Optional Parameters	Accepts the same information you enter on the DOS command line to pass to the DOS application when it starts. This optional field has 62 characters, and typically is used to specify a file to be opened at start-up.
Startup Directory	Becomes current on start-up; it is where the application looks for data files.
Video Mode	Selects how much memory is needed to save and restore your DOS application's screen contents. The options are Text and Graphics/Multiple Text. (The Text option uses less memory and should be checked if your DOS application normally runs in Text mode.)
Memory Requirements	The number in the KB **R**equired option specifies the minimum amount of conventional memory that must be available to start the DOS application (128 KB is recommended). If less than this amount is available, Windows NT displays a message recommending that you try to free some memory. Regardless of the amount of memory you specify here, Windows NT gives the DOS application as much memory as it has available.
XMS Memory	Allocates extended memory to a DOS application. The KB Required option specifies the minimum amount of XMS needed. The KB L**i**mit option specifies the maximum amount of memory to be allocated—an important option if you are multitasking with DOS applications in a memory-limited environment. Refer to the manufacturer's specifications for the application's memory-usage requirements.
Directly Modifies	Excludes other applications from accessing certain system resources while the DOS application is active, thus giving the DOS application exclusive use of the PC hardware while it is running.

Option	Description of Function
No Screen **E**xchange	Saves memory in a memory-limited situation. It disables the capability to save screen contents with the Alt+PrtSc or PrtSc keys.
Prevent Program S**w**itch	Saves memory in a memory-limited situation. It disables Windows NT's task-switching capability. This option requires you to exit the DOS application in order to switch back to Windows NT or a Windows NT application. Normally, you can use Alt+Esc to switch back to Windows NT or a Windows NT application that is running at the same time. Because this option makes operating inconvenient, do not use it unless you have severe memory limitations.
Close Window on Exit	Closes the application's window when it finishes. If left unchecked, Windows NT maintains an inactive window with the last screen full of information from the application. In this situation, you have to manually close the window.
No Save Screen	Frees more memory for the DOS application by disabling screen saving. There is some risk, however, of introducing unwanted side effects if the DOS application does not maintain its own screen contents.
Reserve Shortc**u**t Keys	Warns Windows NT that Windows NT cannot use the selected key combination during the operation of this DOS application. The selected key combinations are reserved for use with the DOS application for the duration of the DOS session.

If you are running in 386-Enhanced mode, and chances are that you are, read the next section to understand the options you can set.

Examining PIF Options for 386-Enhanced Mode

Unless you are supporting users on a network who need Standard-mode PIFs, you need to create PIFs for 386-Enhanced mode. In this mode, you have two types of PIF options: basic options, similar to the Standard-mode options listed in the preceding table, and advanced options.

From the PIF Editor dialog box for 386-Enhanced mode, click on the **A**dvanced button; the Advanced Options dialog box shown in figure 14.3 appears.

The Windows **N**T button next to the **A**dvanced button opens a dialog box containing two text boxes that enable you to enter the name of the CONFIG.SYS and

AUTOEXEC.BAT files to use with this program. You can use these options to specify custom configuration files to use with the program you are running. You should base these files on the AUTOEXEC.NT and CONFIG.NT files that Windows NT uses to establish the basic DOS environment for all DOS programs. To do so, edit these files and save them using a new name.

Figure 14.3

The PIF Editor Advanced Options dialog box for 386-Enhanced mode.

The advanced parameters affect special features, such as preemptive multitasking, use of the HMA, and virtual memory. Table 14.2 lists the basic 386-Enhanced PIF parameters; table 14.3 lists the advanced 386-Enhanced parameters.

TABLE 14.2
Basic PIF Options in 386-Enhanced Mode

Basic Option	Description of Function
Program Filename	The name and path of the file that starts the DOS application, including the file extension. An example is C:\WORD\WORD.EXE. You also can specify an environmental variable by using the SET command and % parameters.
Window **T**itle	Appears below the icon and in the window title bar (if you elect to run the application in a window). It is optional—if you leave it blank, the application's name is used.
Optional Parameters	Accepts the same information you enter on the DOS command line to pass to the DOS application when it starts. This optional field has 62 characters, and typically is used to specify a file to be opened at start-up.
Startup Directory	Becomes current on start-up; it is where the application looks for data files.

Basic Option	Description of Function
Video Memory	Selects the amount of memory needed to save and restore your DOS application's screen contents. The options are Text, Low Graphics, and High Graphics. The Text option uses the least memory (less than 16 KB). Low Graphics corresponds with CGA resolution and consumes about 32 KB; High Graphics is suitable for EGA and VGA, but it requires about 128 KB of memory.
Memory Requirements	The number in the KB **R**equired option specifies the minimum amount of conventional memory that must be available to start the DOS application (128 KB is recommended). If less than this amount is available, Windows NT displays a message, recommending that you free some memory. KB Preferre**d** enables you to set the limits for the amount of memory that the application can use (up to a maximum of 640 KB; specify less memory if you want other applications to have more memory available to them). Regardless of the amount of memory you specify here, Windows NT gives the DOS application the memory it has available.
EMS Memory	Emulates expanded memory for those DOS applications that require it (few do). Some older applications run better if they have access to EMS. You can set the **K**B Required and KB **L**imit values as specified in the preceding entry.
XMS Memory	Allocates extended memory to a DOS application. The KB Required option specifies the minimum amount of memory needed (usually 0, because most applications do not require XMS to run). The KB L**i**mit option specifies the maximum amount of memory to be allocated. In limited-memory situations, prevent Windows NT from using XMS by setting both options to 0. Refer to the manufacturer's specifications for the application's memory-usage requirements.
Display Usage	Specifies whether you want the application to start the session in a full screen (F**u**ll Screen) or a window (**W**indowed).
Execution	**B**ackground specifies that execution of this application can take place concurrently while other applications maintain the foreground focus. **E**xclusive suspends the execution of all other DOS applications while this session has foreground focus.
Close Window on Exit	Leaves the window up after the DOS application terminates (useful if the DOS application displays output before terminating—the output remains so that you can read it).

Note   Windows NT does not use the Close Window on Exit PIF option. If you need the DOS window to stay on-screen after a program exits, start the DOS window and run the program from the DOS command prompt in the DOS window.

TABLE 14.3
Advanced PIF Options in 386-Enhanced Mode

Advanced Option	Description of Function
Multitasking Options	
Background Priority	Determines what portion of the processor's attention this application receives when it operates in the background. Enter a value from 1 to 10,000; the value is compared to the values given to all other DOS applications' foreground and background processing values, and represents a proportion of the sum of all the values.
Foreground Priority	Determines what portion of the processor's attention this application receives when it operates in the foreground. Enter a value from 1 to 10,000.
Detect Idle Time	Gives up resources during idle time. Turn this option off for communication programs that need to remain active in order to detect activity on the communication line.
Memory Options	
EMS Memory Loc**k**ed	Expanded memory is not swapped to the hard disk.
XMS Memory L**o**cked	Extended memory is not swapped to the hard disk.
Uses **H**igh Memory Area	Windows NT loads the application in HMA whenever HMA is available, freeing memory for other DOS applications. If the application cannot be loaded in HMA, you have no adverse effects.
Lock Application Memory	Disables memory swapping to the hard disk. Although this option may speed up some applications, it consumes memory and slows down the multitasking environment in memory-limited situations.
Display Options	
Monitor Por**t**s	Experiment with this option if your display shows irregularities when you switch tasks to and from the session.
Emulate Text Mode	Speeds up the display of text; particularly useful with word processing applications.

Advanced Option	Description of Function
Retain Video **M**emory	If your application switches display modes (from text to graphics, for example), select this option. It ensures that Windows NT holds enough memory in reserve to accommodate your application's video requirements as you switch between applications. Otherwise, Windows NT gives the application's allocated memory to the application that needs it most. The memory given to another application may not be available when you return to graphics mode.

Other Options

Allow Fast **P**aste	Disable this option if you paste from the Clipboard into the application and nothing happens.
Allow **C**lose When Active	Choose this option if you want Windows NT to automatically close the application when you exit Windows NT. Normally, Windows NT does not close any active DOS application when you exit Windows NT. By selecting this option, you incur the potential for loss of data.
Reserve **S**hortcut Keys	This option warns Windows NT that, during the operation of this DOS application, Windows NT cannot use the selected key combination; the selected key combinations are reserved for use with the DOS application for the duration of the DOS session.
Application Shortcut Key	Enter the key combination that causes this application to become the active application when pressed.

Note Windows NT does not actually use many of the PIF settings available in the PIF Editor. Check the Help file, included with the PIF Editor, for the latest information about which settings Windows NT uses. All these settings are included for compatibility with other versions of Windows.

After you have made your selections, close the PIF editor and run the application.

Operating DOS, OS/2, and POSIX Applications

The following sections describe how to start, switch, and cut-and-paste among DOS, OS/2, and POSIX applications running under Windows NT. Some of the details described might seem complicated, but they are things you need to know to begin a deeper exploration of Windows NT. Remember that the normal operation of non-Windows applications under Windows NT is not complicated; with minor exceptions, these applications intermingle seamlessly with Windows NT applications and with other non-Windows applications.

Starting DOS, OS/2, and POSIX Applications

After you set up non-Windows applications under Windows NT, you start them like any other Windows NT application—by double-clicking on the icons. The following list describes the options for running DOS, OS/2, and POSIX applications under Windows NT:

◆ Double-clicking on the icon to run the application as it was set up automatically by the Windows NT Setup program. For DOS applications, this method runs the PIF that was created by Windows NT when you set up the application.

◆ Selecting **R**un from the Start button menu. Generally, this is the method you use to run the application's EXE file directly, but you can call the PIF for DOS applications in this way, too.

◆ Double-clicking on the application's EXE filename from the File Manager. You also can execute a PIF in this way.

◆ Starting the Command Prompt application and running the application from the command line.

◆ Running the application automatically when Windows NT starts up. You can do this by moving the application's icon into the StartUp program group.

Windows NT has two other important features that involve loading a data file when you start a non-Windows application. In command-line interfaces, you can call an application and pass the application a data filename by including the filename on the command line (for instance, PROJECT SPECPROJ.DAT). This loads the data file as you start the application. Windows NT enables you to do this in the following ways:

◆ Open File Manager, and locate the data file. Click on the data file's entry in File Manager, drag the data file over its parent EXE or PIF file, and drop it.

◆ If you have associated the data file's extension with the application by using File Manager's **F**ile, **A**ssociate command, you can double-click on the data filename in File Manager. File Manager automatically starts the appropriate application, and loads the data file (this procedure also works for Windows NT applications and data files).

The following sections describe how to switch among applications running under different operating systems.

Switching among DOS, OS/2, and POSIX Applications

Being able to run more than one DOS, OS/2, or POSIX application concurrently brings a new dimension of productivity to Windows NT. You probably are familiar with formatting a floppy disk while running another application. It is just as simple to use a communications program that sends and receives data over a modem, or a terminal-emulation program with an active session to a mainframe or Unix server. Running two non-Windows applications concurrently is as easy as clicking four times. As always, however, there are some finer points to discuss.

Start your applications, as described in the preceding section. You can start as many applications as you have available memory. After you start a DOS, OS/2, or POSIX session, it becomes the active one until you switch from it. Windows NT provides the following options to switch among non-Windows applications:

◆ If the active application is running in a windowed session, click on another window or icon to change the focus. If your DOS, OS/2, or POSIX session is in a full screen, make the session windowed by pressing Alt+Enter.

◆ Press Alt+Tab to switch to the most recently active application, regardless of whether it is a Windows NT application or a non-Windows application. Hold the Alt key and press the Tab key multiple times to cycle through your running applications.

◆ Start the Task List, and select the task you want to switch to from the list box.

◆ Minimize all running applications into icons, and select the one you want from these icons. Although this is not the best way to switch tasks, it works, and it can come in handy.

◆ Use a shortcut key combination to start another application. Remember that you can specify shortcut keys in the Program Item Properties dialog box.

Because it is so easy to run DOS, OS/2, and POSIX applications, you might start several that you are planning to use sometime during your day when you start your computer. Besides cluttering up your display, they all cut into system resources, which can be a serious problem. (System resources include devices as well as memory.)

Do not start applications of any type that you do not use right away. Although Windows NT is a multitasking environment, and you are encouraged to run more than one application, the more applications, the less memory and resources available to a single application.

Adjusting Run-Time Characteristics by Using the Control Menu

Several characteristics of the way in which a DOS, OS/2, or POSIX application runs can be controlled from the Control menu. For example, to start a windowed DOS session, select the Control menu's **S**ettings option, and examine the parameters as they are reviewed in the following list. The changes you make from the Control menu are in effect only during the application's session; they do not change the settings in the DOS application's PIF. The parameters are as follows:

◆ **Display Options.** This parameter controls whether the DOS session runs in a window on the Windows NT desktop or in full-screen DOS mode.

◆ **QuickEdit Mode.** Enables you to select and edit information displayed in a DOS window using the mouse.

◆ **Save Configuration.** Causes the configuration information for the DOS session to be saved on exit.

In addition to these PIF Editor parameters, the Control **S**ettings menu offers a **T**erminate option. This option terminates the DOS session that has crashed (does not respond to commands typed from the command prompt), and enables you to abandon an unresponsive session and return to Windows NT.

Stop Use the **T**erminate option only as a last resort. It causes the loss of unsaved information.

Each of these options works for OS/2 and POSIX sessions as well. The DOS session was used as an example.

Note A difference between Windows NT and Windows 3.1 is that Windows NT can survive a **T**erminate operation much more successfully. Although it is unlikely that you will destabilize the operating system by using **T**erminate under Windows NT, do not use it frequently.

Freeing Up System Memory

Do you see an Out of Memory error message when you run DOS applications? Everybody can use more memory, and, as you learned earlier in this chapter, memory is one of the cheaper PC hardware resources these days. If your DOS applications operate slowly on your PC, try to get more memory for your system.

As the number of applications that open under Windows NT grows, you can get an Out of Memory error message when you try to start another application, regardless of

the number of memory chips you have. When this happens, close any applications—Windows NT or DOS—that you are not using. If you still continue to see the message, try the following maneuvers:

◆ Minimize any Windows NT applications that you are not directly working with but need to keep running.

◆ Cancel any background processing that is not needed (for instance, a background print job).

◆ If your DOS, OS/2, or POSIX application is running in a window, try running it full-screen.

◆ Clear the Clipboard.

◆ Set the Desktop's Wallpaper option to None (some wallpaper bit-map images are large files and require CPU cycles to display properly).

A number of memory-management techniques have been presented for DOS, OS/2, and POSIX applications, but hardly anything has been said about memory management for Windows NT applications. Windows NT applications are very cooperative about their use of memory. They ask for it when they need it, use it, and give it back when they are done; the memory management is handled by Windows NT. Non-Windows applications, on the other hand, do not expect to run with any other applications, so they require a certain amount of memory when they start up, and they keep it while they are running.

Pasting Data among Non-Windows Applications

DOS, OS/2, and POSIX applications operate slightly differently than Windows NT applications in their use of the Clipboard. There are several methods for moving data from the application to the Clipboard, depending on the mode in which the application is running. These methods, illustrated in the remainder of this section, work for DOS, OS/2, and POSIX applications. (For purposes of illustration, these examples use a DOS application.)

If the DOS application is running in a full screen, you can move the entire screen contents only to the Clipboard—the normal Windows NT cut/copy/paste editing tools are not available. For a DOS application running in a window, you have the following options for moving information to the Clipboard:

◆ Move selected material only

◆ Move the contents of the DOS-session window

◆ Move the entire desktop

The following example shows ways to exchange data from a full-screen DOS session to the Clipboard. If you do not have a standard DOS application, such as Word or Lotus 1-2-3, on your computer, don't worry. The following example works from the DOS command prompt:

1. Start a DOS command-prompt session, and make sure that it occupies a full screen.

2. Issue the DOS directory command by typing **DIR** and pressing Enter. The directory list for the current directory appears. Remember that, in a full-screen DOS session, your only option is to copy the entire contents of the screen to the Clipboard.

3. Copy the contents of the screen to the Clipboard. To do this, press PrScr. Your display may flicker for a moment.

4. Switch back to Windows NT and view the Clipboard (select ClipBook in the Main program group and examine the Local Clipboard document window). You should be satisfied that PrScr really does copy the full screen to the Clipboard.

In the next exercise, you exchange data from a windowed DOS session to the Clipboard. If you viewed the contents of the Clipboard in the preceding exercise, your session is probably running in a window at this point. If it is not, press Alt+Tab to switch to the full-screen DOS application, and then switch it into window mode by pressing Alt+Enter.

1. Select **E**dit from the session's Control menu. Use the mouse or press Alt+spacebar to open the Control menu.

2. Select Mar**k**. Notice that the cursor appears in the upper left corner of the window. Find the text you want to select by moving the cursor with the mouse or the arrow keys.

3. Select the text by holding Shift and moving the arrow keys, or by holding the left mouse button and dragging. If you are used to the way a word processor marks text with the arrow keys—in consecutive characters, words, or lines—the behavior of the Control menu's marking mechanism might be a little foreign. Text is marked in rectangular columns, with no regard for verbal content. You mark a block of characters from a matrix of characters.

4. Complete the copy operation by pressing Enter or by choosing **C**opy from the **E**dit menu.

The other two ways to copy text from a windowed DOS session are as straightforward as full-screen mode. To copy the entire contents of the windowed DOS session, press Alt+PrScr. To copy the entire desktop, press PrScr.

After you have some data cut to the Clipboard, you paste it into a DOS session by selecting **P**aste from the **E**dit menu. This command works a little differently, depending on whether the target session is windowed or full-screen.

To copy from the Clipboard into a windowed DOS session, make sure that you have something in the Clipboard, and that your DOS session is in a window. If you still have the DOS Prompt session in a window on the screen, move the cursor to a point in that session where you want the text in the Clipboard to be inserted. Select **P**aste from the Control **E**dit menu. The new text appears, beginning at the cursor. You cannot cut and paste formatted text among DOS applications; the formatting is lost when you move it into a DOS session.

To copy from the Clipboard into a full-screen DOS session, make sure that what you want to paste is already in the Clipboard. The Clipboard is harder to view when an active full-screen DOS session is in progress. Switch the DOS prompt session into a full screen, and place the cursor where you want the insertion to go. Now, minimize the full-screen session by pressing Alt+Esc. Click once to open the Control **E**dit menu, and choose **P**aste. Double-click on the session's icon to restore it. The text is inserted at the point at which the cursor was located before the paste.

Summary

The complexity of computers always expands to meet your ability to understand them. Working with DOS, OS/2, and POSIX applications under Windows NT, however, is the exception. It is no more difficult to set up, start, or switch tasks with one of these applications than it is to do the same things with a Windows NT application.

As you conclude this chapter, take a moment to reflect on what you have learned about Windows NT so far. If you have been following the examples, you should be getting used to the logic as well as the rhythm and pace of the graphical user interface. By now, you've used the basic application templates: the **F**ile and **E**dit menus, the list boxes, and the dialog boxes that focus your attention and make it easy to do complicated tasks. In the next few chapters, you greatly increase your knowledge of Windows NT applications.

Exchanging Data between Windows Applications

T here are many ways in which the Windows NT environment makes it easier and faster to do common (and uncommon) tasks. The most important of these are integration and interoperability. Windows NT's Dynamic Data Exchange (DDE) is a powerful tool that enables the user to dynamically exchange information between applications.

Note Object Linking and Embedding (OLE), another feature of Windows NT, enables the user to create compound documents that contain information (objects) from a number of sources and seamlessly integrate the information into a single document. By using OLE, the compound document can contain objects from any source, including nontraditional document sources.

By using DDE, graphs that are produced in a Windows NT application can be truly data-driven; when the data changes at the source, the graphic changes at the destination. Documents can be kept up-to-date automatically, thus reducing errors and downtime for maintenance. The best feature of DDE is its inherent ease of use; most DDE links are no more complicated to create than pasting data from the Clipboard.

This chapter covers the following topics:

◆ Cutting-and-pasting

◆ Linking and embedding

◆ Understanding end-user DDE

◆ Understanding programmable DDE

Examining Traditional Cutting-and-Pasting

Under Windows NT, users no longer have a "glass cage" (a web of proprietary data formats) around each individual application, as they did under character-based operating systems. In a character-based system, each program maintains its data in a proprietary format. Given the proper conversion program, the information from one program can be translated into a format that can be used by another program. Alternatively, because most programs can read and write ASCII files, users can convert one application's information to plain text and import it into another application. When this is done, however, all original formatting is lost.

With most character-based applications, inserting graphics into a document is, at best, a cumbersome and time-consuming enterprise. The graphic is often represented by a reference to the image file and can be seen pictorially (if it can be seen pictorially at all) only in a preview mode.

Even under the most favorable circumstances, transferring data from one application to another is a chore. Although your character-mode application might enhance the operating system by compensating for these difficulties, each of your applications

must use the same conventions for extending the operating system; otherwise, they cannot communicate or share data. With rare exceptions, you cannot maintain an open channel of communication through which data can regularly pass from one program to another.

To prepare a document that requires information developed in several different programs—for example, a proposal that calls for narrative text written in a word processor, financial data created in a spreadsheet, and illustrations from a drawing or paint program—you must get a hard copy of each of the elements and then sit down with scissors and a paste pot to create a composite. You then photocopy or print the composite by using offset techniques.

Some character-mode programs incorporate the scissors-and-paste-pot metaphor into their feature set. Earlier programs had a text buffer that enabled the transfer of text from one application to another. Other programs use the metaphor of the Clipboard.

Whatever name is used for that holding area, users can mark a piece of text for copying or cutting to the buffer or Clipboard, perform the copy or cut, and then paste that text back into the document at another place. The text buffer (or Clipboard) serves much like a temporary scratch pad to hold text data during a transfer operation.

This Clipboard is merely used to move text from one part of the same document to another, however; when the document is closed, whatever data is on the Clipboard or in the buffer is lost. You cannot carry over the data from one program to another.

Note WordPerfect for DOS, by using its Library and Office DOS shell applications, moves the user a bit further in a more advanced direction. The shell's Clipboard holds the cut or copied information, enabling the user to paste it into another program's document—but only if that program has a cut-and-paste feature that the WordPerfect shell recognizes.

Impatience with the impenetrable glass cages that surround individual applications has grown, thus creating innovation. Software developers came up with the idea of the integrated program, which gives the user a word processor, database, spreadsheet, and communications module in one package. Each module can function independently, but the true strength of integrated applications lies in the capability of the application modules to work together and exchange information. An integrated program gives a consistent interface across several modules in the package. Data created in one module in the integrated program usually can be used in another module.

With the advent of Windows 3.0 (and especially with Windows 3.1 and Windows NT), problems with proprietary data formats are ending. As you learn in this chapter, applications under Windows NT can be integrated tightly. Perhaps even more significant, applications can be interoperable: they are capable of exchanging information and running simultaneously in the same computer. You benefit from access to multiple applications that are available with one keystroke—each application exchanges data with the others.

The day is approaching when computing no longer will be program-centric. Traditional character-based applications are characterized by the many arcane keystroke commands that are required to perform various functions. Many word processors, for instance, require a complex series of keystrokes to mark a block of text and to change the blocked text's typeface to bold. There is no way to represent all the commands and command sequences on the screen; the user requires help from keyboard templates, users' guides, and other printed materials.

The model that integration and interoperability give is document-centric, in which the document is the center of attention and the applications that create the documents are only tools. Document-centric applications are inherently more intuitive and require less time to learn, leaving more time for using the application.

 Note In Windows NT, a document can be a text document, a spreadsheet, a database, a drawing or picture, or the output from different Windows NT applications.

Even within the Windows NT environment, degrees of integration and interoperability exist. You can achieve the most seamless flow of information at the highest end by using stand-alone programs such as Microsoft Word, Lotus Ami Pro, Microsoft Excel, and Polaris PackRat. These programs have or support Windows macro languages and incorporate OLE and DDE.

An integrated program, such as Microsoft Works for Windows, gives you flexibility to share data among its modules and with other programs that are running under Windows NT. Integrated programs also offer a convenient way to gain access to tools when disk space is at a premium, as it can be on a laptop or small computer.

At the lower end, the desktop accessories that come with Windows NT—Write, Schedule+, and Cardfile—enable you to perform limited data sharing. To take advantage of integration and interoperability in the Windows NT environment, however, you need more robust tools.

Examining Linking and Embedding

For the DOS or Unix user who is just getting started with Windows NT, the appeal of the graphical environment lies in its attractiveness as a shell and in its capability to multitask DOS and POSIX applications. Windows NT, however, offers much more than task switching and cutting-and-pasting between DOS and POSIX applications and among DOS, POSIX, and Windows NT applications.

You cannot fully realize the enormous power of Windows NT until your core applications are Windows-specific applications, especially those that support the Windows functions known as linking and embedding.

 Note Linking and embedding is an umbrella term for the methods that enable users to share functionality and integrate data across diverse applications.

The technical specifications for both DDE and OLE protocols are still evolving, and so is the jargon. Early on, the industry used DDE and OLE as separate terms.

Both DDE and OLE enable you to share data among Windows NT applications. They are extensions of the data sharing discussed in the sections on the Clipboard.

 Note This chapter and the next help you become familiar with the differences and similarities between static data exchange with the Clipboard and dynamic exchange of data using DDE and OLE. These chapters also show you ways to take advantage of these Windows NT features.

Windows NT offers two different ways to implement Dynamic Data Exchange. The first, interactive DDE, uses the regular interface of the application you use to manually create a link. The commands you need to create links between one application and another are accessible directly from the applications' menus.

The second method, scripted DDE, requires writing code in the application's macro language to establish a link. Each method is discussed in this chapter.

 Note A macro is a set of instructions that can be invoked with a single keystroke. Macros are used to automate a series of frequently performed repetitive tasks.

A macro can be nothing more than a collection of simple commands, such as applying a particular style to a paragraph in a document; or it can provide an entirely new function in the application, such as retrieving data from a database and inserting it into a spreadsheet.

A macro also can be a "program" to perform a specific task, such as a link with an application to retrieve data.

DDE enables you to share information and also to send commands from one application to another to control the behavior of the receiving application.

OLE currently is available only through the Clipboard's copy-and-paste metaphor. Everything you require to accomplish an OLE task is part of the application's standard menu interface. The commands are on the menus; you do not need to do any macro programming.

Dynamic Data Exchange

Dynamic Data Exchange (DDE) is an internal communications protocol that Windows NT uses to enable one application to talk to or exchange data with another application. Although DDE normally is used to transfer information between applications, it also can be used within an application. DDE is a powerful tool for the user who needs to exchange information between applications.

DDE creates a communication channel through which data is sent from one application to another. This channel is known as a *link*. DDE links normally are live; when there are changes in data within the originating application, the other application is updated through the link—automatically or on demand, depending on whether you have created an automatic or a manual link.

DDE and OLE Terminology

Table 15.1 defines some standard DDE and OLE terms that are used throughout this chapter and the next, as well as related terms that you may encounter in other discussions.

TABLE 15.1
Standard DDE and OLE Terms

Term	Related terms	Meaning
Object	Data, information	Any piece of data that can be manipulated as a single unit, such as a picture, chart, spreadsheet range, or section of text.
Source	Server application	The application in which a linked or embedded object is created, such as Microsoft Excel or WordPerfect for Windows. Also, the application that sends data requested by another application via DDE.
Source document		The document in the source application in which the data (object) was created. Also, the sending end of a data transfer through a DDE link.
Destination application	Client application	The application whose document will receive an object. Also, the application that requests data from another application by DDE.
Destination document	Target, client, or host document	A document that contains embedded or linked data (see also Container document). Also, the receiving end of a data transfer through a DDE link.
Compound document		A single document made up of parts created in more than one application.

Term	Related terms	Meaning
Container document	Target, client, or host document	A document that contains either embedded or linked data (objects). (See also Destination document.)
Automatic link	Hot link	A link that automatically updates the destination document when the source document is changed.
Manual link	Warm link	A link that requires user intervention to update the destination document when the source document is changed.
Cold link		Data that is transferred once (by a straight cut or copy and paste, or by a one-time DDE request) and cannot be updated dynamically. The term cold link is a misnomer—the described function is not really a link at all.

By using the terminology in table 15.1, linking (DDE) refers to creating data in one application (the source application), such as a spreadsheet, and linking it to the destination document created in another application, such as a word processor. When you change or update the information in the source document, the change is reflected at the same time in the destination document. The item is stored in the source document, and can be linked to several different destination documents.

Links can be established in several different ways. Later in this chapter, you are shown various methods for linking applications.

As you work in an application, you might need to gather data from another source; you can include a table of spreadsheet data in your word processing document, for example. To do this, you can use a DDE link to the other application. Typically, you choose a DDE link between applications when one or more of the following situations occurs:

◆ You want to access data that resides in another application on your system.

◆ You want to have access to the information in its native, stand-alone application.

◆ You want to share the information in more than one instance within a document or use it as an element in more than one document.

◆ You want DDE to take over a server application by remote control to perform a task.

Suppose, for example, that you regularly prepare a summary sales report that you send, at specific intervals, to managers in your company—once a week to sales managers, twice a month to department heads, and once a month to the chief financial officer. These reports are based on sales figures you track and total every day in Microsoft Excel. You can create a boilerplate report in Microsoft Word and include in it a link to the range of your Excel worksheet that shows the running sales total.

As you update the figures in Excel every day, the updated total automatically is piped to the report document through the DDE link. Every time you open the Word document to print it out and send it to the managers, it reflects the latest data from your Excel worksheet.

Object Linking and Embedding (OLE)

Object Linking and Embedding does not create a simple link, as does DDE. A DDE link always is connected to the source document; the information never really is contained in the destination document. OLE, on the other hand, embeds information that you generate in another application into your current document, and that data becomes a part of the current document. The current document "owns" the embedded data, which then cannot be shared directly with other documents or applications.

 Note OLE objects can be linked or embedded, depending on the capabilities of the OLE server.

The real power of OLE is that it not only embeds the data in your document, but it also identifies to Windows NT the application in which the data was created. When you want to edit the embedded information (see object in table 15.1), you double-click on it; the source application, with all its tools and attributes, appears on top of the current document. When you exit from the source application, you are returned to the current document, and the embedded object is updated to reflect your changes.

 Note In OLE 2.0, the source application will substitute its menu for the menu of the container application. A second window does not open.

Updating an OLE object does not occur automatically. Because the data is contained within the destination document, you must explicitly send updated data from the source document after you have made changes to it.

By using the terms in table 15.1, you can further define embedding (OLE) as creating an object in the source application, which you then can access directly from the container document. The object created is said to be embedded in the container document. When the object requires editing, Windows NT immediately returns you to the source application, in which you make the necessary changes. (You do not have to open or switch to the source application; Windows NT takes care of that for you.)

Windows NT then updates the container document to reflect those changes, and the object is stored in the container document.

Applications That Support DDE

Almost 2,000 Windows applications are on the market, but not all of them support DDE (some do not need to support it). A screen saver or font manager, for example, does not need DDE capability.

An application can support DDE as a client, server, or both. DDE support can be found in the high-end word processors, spreadsheet programs, database applications, fax-generating applications, desktop publishing programs, communications programs, and electronic mail packages. Consult an application's documentation or on-line help to determine if it supports DDE.

 Note You should consider updating your DOS or POSIX applications to Windows NT applications. Updating enables you to take greater advantage of multitasking in the Windows NT environment, as well as DDE and OLE. The time you save sharing data and switching between applications is worth the upgrade cost.

To find out if the Windows NT application you are using (such as Word, Excel, PageMaker, or Works) has interactive DDE capabilities, pull down the menus and look for commands such as Paste **L**ink or Paste **S**pecial. Usually, these commands are on the **F**ile or **E**dit menus (see fig. 15.1).

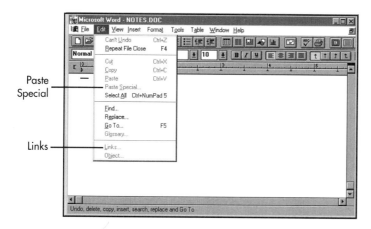

Paste Special

Links

Figure 15.1

The Paste Special and Links commands in Word's Edit menu.

Note The Paste **S**pecial command in Microsoft Excel and the spreadsheet module of Works do not refer to DDE. The Paste **L**ink command does. When you select the Paste **S**pecial command in Word and the word processing module of Works, you are offered the further option of Paste **L**ink when appropriate.

In addition, a command called **L**inks might appear on the menu (refer to figure 15.1). This command enables you to edit or update the links. If you see these commands, you can be sure your application supports at least one form of DDE.

Note that the **L**inks command on Word's **E**dit menu in figure 15.1 is dimmed when no links are in the document. The **L**inks command also might appear on the **F**ile menu, as it does in PageMaker.

 Note Do not be intimidated by the prospect of setting up a DDE function. After you know how to use the Clipboard—in other words, after you can cut, copy, and paste—you have what you need to create DDE links.

A second application of DDE is through the use of macros. You must consult the application's documentation to see if your application supports DDE macros, which are available only in applications that have (or understand) a macro language.

You can, for example, create a macro in Word's macro language (sometimes called WordBasic) that requests data from or passes data to Polaris PackRat. Even though PackRat itself does not have a macro language, it understands the DDE commands that it receives by macros from Word, Excel, Ami Pro, and other applications.

Although this chapter includes discussions and examples of DDE macros, a full discussion of programmable DDE is beyond the scope of this book. Each application that supports programmable DDE has its own variations of syntax, and you must turn to the vendors of the respective applications for documentation on their specific DDE code.

Applications That Support OLE

OLE is a newer technology than DDE, and fewer applications support it. Because of its power and ease of use, however, it has been an instant hit with end users. Full support for OLE is an intrinsic part of Windows NT, making OLE a standard that developers are likely to support. Many high-end applications include OLE support now.

Note In most applications, the menu options Paste **L**ink and Paste **S**pecial are found under **E**dit. Some applications, however, do not follow this convention. In Microsoft PowerPoint, for instance, the **I**nsert command is under the **F**ile menu. When you choose it, you see a list of all types of objects available on your system that can be embedded. If you are learning a new application and you want to use DDE or OLE, look first under **E**dit for Paste **L**ink or Paste **S**pecial, then check under **F**ile or **I**nsert for other options that indicate link operations.

You can recognize OLE-compliant applications by looking for another set of commands on the menus. These commands, usually found on the **I**nsert or **E**dit menu, refer to inserting objects, as shown in figure 15.2.

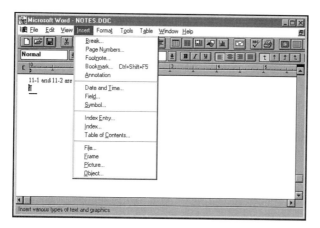

Figure 15.2

The Object command on the Insert menu in Word.

Note Microsoft now is shipping several applications that are designed specifically to create or edit embedded objects. These so-called embedding applications include the Equation Editor, which creates the notation of scientific and mathematical formulas; MS Draw, for pictures created in or convertible to the Windows NT Metafile Format (WMF); MS Graph, which produces sophisticated graphs from tabular figures without requiring a separate spreadsheet program; Note-It, which inserts pop-up notes anywhere in your document; and WordArt, which enables you to create special text effects for formats, such as logos and headlines.

Some of these embedding applications are bundled with Windows NT, including those applications that comprise the Multimedia Extensions. Others are bundled with individual Microsoft applications. No single application comes with all of them. After you install an embedding application on your system, however, its parameters are written into the appropriate section of the Registry database (see fig. 15.3). This enables any application that supports OLE to recognize and use the embedding application.

Figure 15.3

Listing the objects that are available for embedding.

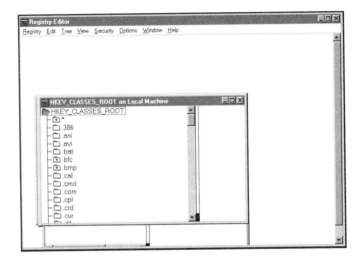

Tip

You can embed worksheet ranges and charts created in Excel; entire documents created in Word or other word processors, such as Ami Pro for Windows NT; and bitmaps created in Paintbrush.

Cardfile and Write, two of the desktop accessories that come with Windows NT, both support OLE. By choosing the **O**bject command, you can see a list of the objects available. (In Cardfile, you must choose **P**icture on the **E**dit menu to have this option.) For example, text that was created in PowerPoint is embedded in a Cardfile card.

Understanding Interactive Dynamic Data Exchange

You learned that DDE links are easy to set up by using commands on your applications' menus, with no macro programming required. If you have Word for Windows and Excel for Windows, open them now so you can work through the following examples on your computer. If you do not have these programs, you still can follow

the examples to learn ways to use DDE links and what to expect from other applications that support DDE links.

Note A hot link automatically updates the receiving document when the data in the source changes.

A warm link notifies the user that a change has been made, but the user must specifically make a request to the server to update the data.

When a DDE link is created in a document, it needs to know the following things about the source to which it is going to be linked:

◆ The name of the source application

◆ The name of the source document (file name)

Note A document can be a text document, a graphic, a portion of a graphic, or a spreadsheet range.

◆ Specific reference to the data to be linked, such as a spreadsheet range or text in a word processor

Note You do not need to name the range in Excel. If you have several links in one document and want to examine or edit them, however, it is easier to know which one is which if the links refer to named ranges rather than to row-and-column designations.

The following example shows you the way to link a named range in Excel to a document in Word.

First, create a range in Excel, name it, and save the Excel worksheet. In the following steps, you can substitute other names and numbers for the names and numbers provided. Remember, however, that a DDE link must include the name of the source document. If you do not name and save the worksheet now, later you will need to edit the links to show the worksheet's name. Of course, you are required to assign the spreadsheet a name the first time you save it.

1. Create a six-cell matrix in Excel. In cells from A1 to C1, label the columns **First**, **Second**, and **Third**. In the row beneath the labels, in cells A2 to C2, enter the numbers **1000**, **1500**, and **1750**.

2. Highlight the range, and define its name as **Range1**. Define the range name by choosing the **D**efine Name option under the Fo**r**mula menu.

3. Save the worksheet as **EXAMPLE1.XLS**. Until you save the worksheet, it has no name. (You will use this worksheet in the following chapter.)

4. Highlight the range, select the Excel **E**dit menu, and choose **C**opy.

5. Open a new document in Word. Select Word's **E**dit menu (refer to fig. 15.1), and choose the Paste **S**pecial command. The Paste Special dialog box appears (see fig. 15.4). The name of the source document is automatically included in the link field that is inserted into the Word document.

Figure 15.4

*Word's Paste
Special dialog
box.*

Word automatically identifies the source application (Microsoft Excel Worksheet), the source document (EXAMPLE1.XLS), and the name of the range (Range1).

Tip

Remember that the Clipboard maintains the data that you place there in several different formats, which are supported by the source application, the destination application, or both.

In figure 15.5, for example, the **V**iew menu in the ClipBook Viewer displays the available formats, with those that the running applications support activated. (Those not supported are grayed out.) ClipBook Viewer displays the formats currently available for the item on the local Clipboard.

You now need to create a connection between the worksheet and the document. You do this by highlighting any choice in the **D**ata Type list box except Microsoft Excel Worksheet Object. This activates the Paste **L**ink button. By clicking on the Paste **L**ink button, Windows NT establishes a DDE connection between the Word document and the named range in the Excel worksheet, and places the data from Excel into your Word document, as displayed in figure 15.6.

Figure 15.5

The ClipBook Viewer View menu.

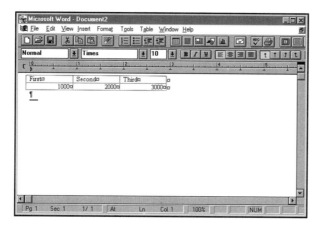

Figure 15.6

The Excel range, after being placed in Word.

 Tip   If you choose the Microsoft Excel Worksheet Object in the Paste Special dialog box, Windows NT embeds the range in your document as an OLE object, instead of creating a DDE link from your document to the range in the worksheet.

You now have a link field in Word, pointing to the range in the Excel worksheet. You can examine the syntax of the link by placing the cursor in the table, selecting the View menu, and then choosing Field Codes. You also can press Shift+F9.

You can switch back to the contents of the link—the table—by pressing Shift+F9 again. The switches indicate the formatting that you chose in the dialog box, in this case, \r and \a. The \r switch denotes a Rich Text Format switch; the \a switch denotes an automatic switch.

Tip

Word automatically puts the switch *mergeformat into the field, which tells Word to format the results of the field. For more information on this switch, consult your Word documentation.

Make sure that the pointer still is somewhere in the table, and then select the Edit menu. A new option is on the menu—the Microsoft Excel Worksheet Link option (see fig. 15.7). Choose this option to make Excel the foreground application and to see the worksheet to which the Word document is linked. The linked range is highlighted.

Figure 15.7

The Word Edit menu, showing the Microsoft Excel Worksheet Link option.

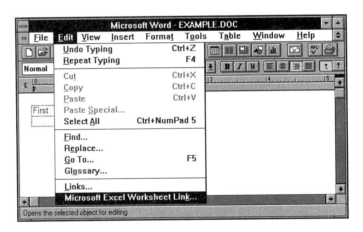

To further demonstrate the linking feature, create two more ranges—one on the same worksheet and the other on a new worksheet. On the EXAMPLE1.XLS worksheet, create a two-cell matrix, and insert the numbers **12345** and **67890**. Name the matrix **Range2**. Follow the previous steps to create a link to your Word document.

Next, create a new Excel worksheet, save it as **EXAMPLE2.XLS**, and create a six-cell matrix on it. Label three columns **AAA**, **BBB**, and **CCC**; in the row beneath the labels, insert the numbers **111**, **222**, and **333**. Name it **Range3**. Again, follow the preceding steps to create a link to your Word document.

Stop   Be sure to save your Excel worksheets.

You now should have three Excel ranges in your Word document, as shown in figure 15.8.

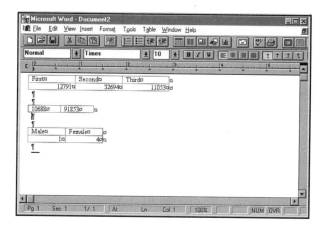

Figure 15.8

Three live links to Excel.

Switching between Applications

As you learned in earlier chapters, Windows NT enables you to move back and forth between applications in various ways. In the preceding examples, you did the following to switch between Word and Excel:

◆ Selecting the Control menu (or using Ctrl+Esc to start the Task List dialog box), highlighting the desired application, and choosing the Switch To command. You can click on the Control menu icon (directly to the left of the title bar), or use Alt+space bar to activate the Control menu.

◆ Minimizing the current application and maximizing the other.

◆ Pressing Alt+Esc to cycle through the applications on your desktop.

◆ Pressing Alt+Tab to cycle through the open applications.

You also can move between applications by taking advantage of the link between the two applications. Place the pointer in any of the three Word tables that are linked to the Excel worksheets, and then choose Excel Worksheet Lin**k** from the **E**dit menu. This moves you instantly to the linked range on the Excel worksheet and highlights the range.

The name of the Excel worksheet appears in the document's title bar, as shown in figure 15.9. Later, you see how this compares to what appears on an Excel document's title bar when you use embedded objects.

Figure 15.9

Excel worksheet names EXAMPLE2.XLS and EXAMPLE1.XLS in the title bars.

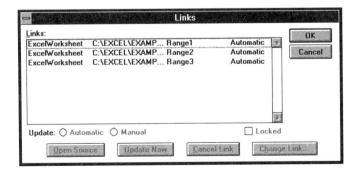

You also can examine and edit the links. You need to edit the links if you rename your Excel worksheets or move them to another directory, for example.

You can edit a link by choosing the Field **C**odes option in the **V**iew menu and making the changes in your document. You also can use the Links dialog box, which you access by choosing the **L**inks option under the **E**dit menu (see fig. 15.10).

Figure 15.10

The Links dialog box.

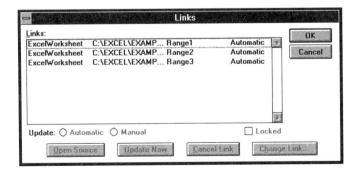

Tip   If you move or rename a source document, you must edit the link to reflect the change, or Word does not know where to find the linked data.

To edit a link, select it in the list and click on the C**h**ange Link button. The Change Link dialog box appears (see fig. 15.11).

```
┌─────────────────────────────────────┐
│ ⊟            Change Link             │
├─────────────────────────────────────┤
│ Application:                 ┌──────┐│
│ ┌─────────────────────────┐  │  OK  ││
│ │ExcelWorksheet           │  └──────┘│
│ └─────────────────────────┘  ┌──────┐│
│ File Name:                   │Cancel││
│ ┌─────────────────────────┐  └──────┘│
│ │C:\EXCEL\EXAMPLE1.XLS     │          │
│ └─────────────────────────┘          │
│ Item:                                │
│ ┌─────────────────────────┐          │
│ │Range1                   │          │
│ └─────────────────────────┘          │
└─────────────────────────────────────┘
```

Figure 15.11

The Change Link dialog box.

In the Change Link dialog box, you can edit the three elements that DDE needs to know to maintain the link: the application name (Excel Worksheet, in this example), the path and file name (of the source document), and the data item (the unit of information—a named range in this example).

Understanding Advanced DDE

You probably repeat tasks when you use an application such as Excel or Word. For instance, you might frequently mark a block of text in Word and apply a style to it. Such frequently repeated tasks can be automated by using macros. Most advanced applications, such as Word for Windows, Lotus 1-2-3 for Windows, and Excel, feature facilities for creating and maintaining macros.

When you use an application's macro language to manage DDE communication with another program, you enable transfer of data and also send commands that make the other program do something. From within a Word macro, for example, you can send a series of commands that start Excel, ask it to open a particular worksheet, enter data in the worksheet, make Excel create a chart from that data, and finally copy the chart and paste it into the Word document. You can program all types of tasks in other applications without ever leaving the word processor.

In the following example, Word and Excel act as the front end to a database program. DDE commands issued by Word or Excel cause the database program to perform some of its native functions—such as a search by remote control.

Using Macros to Access Information

Polaris PackRat is a Windows personal information manager (PIM) that is used as a contact database, an appointment calendar, and a project manager. It is an example of a program that, although it has no accessible DDE functions on its menus, understands and can respond to DDE commands from other applications. PackRat is shipped with a number of macros that are written in the macro languages of Word, Excel, Ami Pro, and others.

These macros enable programs to engage in a two-way conversation with PackRat. Through the mechanism of these macros, PackRat can receive commands and data from applications and send data to other applications when requested to do so. It cannot, however, initiate the DDE communication with another program because it has no macro language of its own.

Other programs can be accessed through DDE, but PackRat is used in these examples because it represents a new generation of Windows add-ins.

 Note An add-in is a program that adds specific functions or capabilities to an existing application. Add-ins for DOS programs have existed for some time and have become available for Windows NT applications. In addition to behaving as an add-in to applications such as Word and Lotus 1-2-3, PackRat also operates as an independent Windows NT application.

The prerequisites for a DDE link include the name of the source document and a reference to the data within the source document. In general, Windows NT recognizes the source application of DDE data when the DDE link is created. When manipulating DDE links through a macro language, however, you have to explicitly provide Windows NT with the source application's name.

As explained earlier in this chapter, a DDE link represents a channel for the exchange of data between applications. These channels are managed by Windows NT and normally are invisible to the user. When you created the Excel-to-Word DDE links in the previous example, Windows NT established the DDE channel, through which Excel and Word can exchange data. When you work with DDE through macros, you deal directly with DDE channels and messages.

Each macro language has its own DDE syntax. Because the details of application macro languages differ, not everything discussed in this section may make sense if you have not worked with the macro language. Thus, the following examples are intended only to give you an overview of different macros. Although a complete discussion of macro languages is beyond the scope of this book, the brief discussion given here may point the way to further work.

A Sample Macro

The DDE commands most often found in macro languages include the following:

◆ **Initiate.** The Initiate command—in WordBasic, DDEInitiate()begins a DDE communication with another application. This command opens a channel to the external application and passes the application information required to begin a DDE dialog.

◆ **Poke.** The Poke command is used by the client application to send a value to a data item in the server application.

◆ **Request.** The Request command is used by the client application to retrieve the value of a data item in the server application.

◆ **Terminate.** The Terminate command is sent by the client application to the server application to immediately end the conversation.

The arguments to the command are the other application's name (usually its commercial name, such as "PackRat") and a word indicating the source of the data Word wants to access (in the case of PackRat, the source is "System"). The command returns a numeric value—the number of the communication channel—that DDEInitiate opens. The following example demonstrates the DDEInitiate macro command:

```
ChanNumFN = DDEInitiate("PackRat", "System")
```

In the preceding syntax, the user assigns a variable name—ChanNumFN—to the channel number that is returned by the DDEIntiate call.

The following lines are from a WordBasic macro that enables the user to search PackRat's Phone Book facility for a name and address. If the search is successful, the name and address then are imported into the Word document at the current location of the cursor.

```
DDEPoke(ChanNumFN, "STARTSEARCH", "P")
DDEPoke(ChanNumFN, "FULLNAME", dlg.Nam$)
DDEPoke(ChanNumFN, "COMPANY", dlg.Comp$)
DDEPoke(ChanNumFN, "ENDSEARCH", "")
```

In the preceding syntax, DDEPoke sends PackRat the search criteria that the user has entered in the dialog box. The "STARTSEARCH" entry in the first DDEPoke command puts PackRat in search mode; the next two DDEPoke commands tell PackRat the data to retrieve (dlg.Nam and dlg.Comp). The last DDEPoke turns off PackRat's search mode.

Tip   Because these examples are very application-specific, do not worry about what dlg.Nam$ or "ENDSEARCH" means. Look at the overview of data-exchange possibilities with DDE.

In the following lines, DDERequest is the command that tells PackRat to retrieve the data and send it back to the user:

```
LName$ = DDERequest$(ChanNumFN, "LASTNAME")

FName$ = DDERequest$(ChanNumFN, "FIRSTNAME")
```

The first data retrieved from PackRat is LASTNAME; it is assigned to the WordBasic variable LName. The second bit of information returned from PackRat is FIRSTNAME; it is assigned to the variable FName. These values then can be inserted by Word into the active document, for instance. The WordBasic variables can be used later in the macro as needed.

Getting Used to DDE

Some users do not like DDE because the commands that invoke DDE are not uniform across all the applications that support it. You have seen this in the Word and Excel menus. In Excel, the **E**dit menu has the Paste **S**pecial option, which has nothing to do with DDE, and the Paste **L**ink option, which does invoke DDE. In Word, on the other hand, you must select the **E**dit menu and choose Paste **S**pecial to get to the Paste **L**ink option.

This inconsistency between applications makes users think that DDE is too complicated or too obscure to use. You will be comfortable using DDE links if you remember the following points:

- ◆ Pasting a DDE link is really a Clipboard function.

- ◆ If interactive DDE is available in an application, a reference to links appears on a menu—usually under **E**dit, **F**ile, or **I**nsert.

The difficulties in using DDE are disappearing as applications evolve. Many users, for instance, would feel overwhelmed writing macros in WordBasic because they are not programmers. WordBasic, as is obvious from the preceding example, is very much like a programming language. Developers, however, are now finding very clever ways to make users feel more comfortable with tasks once thought to be reserved for programmers.

Note   MicroPhone II is an example of a communications program that has a very powerful macro language included with it. You can write macros to automate any MicroPhone II function, including DDE transactions with other programs.

You do not have to master programming, however, to use the macro language. Any command in the language can be created from the Script Manager dialog box, which you access by using the **E**dit Scripts command on the S**c**ripts menu (see fig. 15.12)

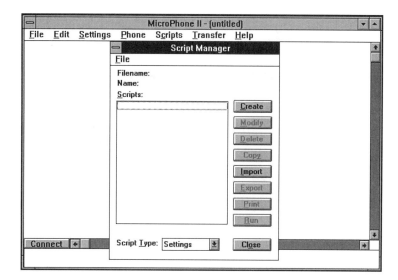

Figure 15.12

MicroPhone II's Script Manager dialog box.

To create a DDE transaction, click on the **C**reate button to start writing a script in the macro language. This action causes the Create Settings Script dialog box to appear, as shown in figure 15.15. Each command in the macro language is described by an English term in the list box that appears in the lower left corner of the dialog box. To initiate a DDE transaction, scroll through the list box until you find the DDE command and select it by clicking on it, as shown in figure 15.13.

After you have selected the DDE command, the second list box immediately to the right becomes active (also shown in figure 15.13). This list box shows you the possible DDE actions you can take.

When you select Initiate to start a conversation, a text box appears directly below this list box. You enter the application and the data source for the DDE conversation in this text box (see fig. 15.14).

Figure 15.13

Selecting the DDE command in the list box.

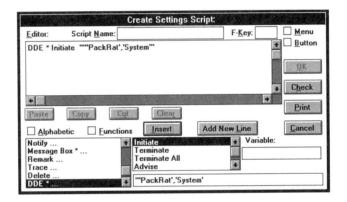

Figure 15.14

Entering the application and data source for a conversation.

Tip

Enclose these items in single quotes, as shown. MicroPhone II supplies all other necessary elements of the syntax. The only parts of the command you need to type are the arguments for the Initiate command, enclosed in single quotes and separated by a comma. To insert the comma in the script, click on the Insert button just above the second list box.

The other DDE commands illustrated in the previous WordBasic script can be created in the same way. You need to know only that you want to create a DDE command and express that in the left list box. You need to choose a DDE action in the right list box, and you need to be able to fill in the arguments for the command, if any. To build a DDE macro correctly, you need a working knowledge of the seven DDE actions and what arguments they take.

Each of the actions and the necessary arguments are explained in detail in the Help file that accompanies MicroPhone II. (Figure 15.15 shows the screen that explains the Initiate command.) You access this Help file by selecting the **D**DE option on the **H**elp menu.

New Riders Publishing
INSIDE
SERIES

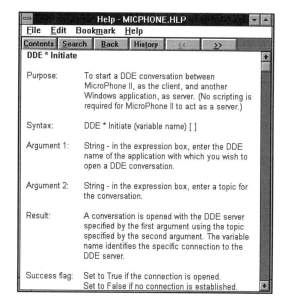

Figure 15.15

The Help screen for the DDE Initiate command.

Using DDE is becoming easier and easier. By the time you update to the next version of your applications, the menu items that enable you to work with DDE will have become fairly standardized. You also will find that developers have created automated ways to script macros for working with DDE. Getting used to DDE is something that all users should do, because it makes you work much more productively.

Summary

Windows NT has eliminated the glass cage that has surrounded character-mode applications for many years. It now has the capability to share data between applications without losing vital formatting and time. Dynamic Data Exchange enables you to create a live link between one application and another. When you change the data in the original application, the DDE link updates the data in the linked application.

By using DDE links, you can link data in spreadsheets, documents in word processing programs, and pictures in graphics programs. You have seen the way an Excel worksheet is linked to a Word document and to a PowerPoint file.

Through the use of an application's macro language, you can automate many time-consuming tasks. Although it is outside the scope of this book, the reader is encouraged to investigate DDE macro programming further.

C H A P T E R

16

Using Object Linking and Embedding

You saw in the last chapter that Windows NT enables you to share data between applications by using Dynamic Data Exchange (DDE). This chapter explains Object Linking and Embedding (OLE), which is a mechanism for inserting a vast amount of information and data into a document. The information and data are treated as objects—that is, collections of information that you can treat as a single unit and manipulate as a single unit.

Most of the examples in this chapter discuss fairly straightforward cases—the way to insert Excel spreadsheet fragments into a Word document, for instance. Windows NT also enables you to include multimedia in your compound document. Multimedia includes voice annotation, full-motion video, music, and other information. (To take advantage of Windows NT's multimedia capabilities, you must have the appropriate hardware for sound generation and video display installed on your computer.)

This chapter covers the following topics:

◆ Examining OLE

◆ Embedding non-OLE objects

◆ Understanding the Object Packager

◆ Introducing OLE client and server relationships

Examining OLE

Windows NT offers an extended feature of Dynamic Data Exchange (DDE). Object Linking and Embedding (OLE) is a Windows feature that extends the Clipboard and DDE methods of data exchange to a new level. It enables the user to combine the services of various applications by placing information from the source application(s) into the receiving application's document. Although OLE's technical underpinnings are complex, you do not need to know what goes on under the surface of the interface.

 Note   A compound document is a document that contains data elements created in more than one application. A classic example is a document that you create and manage with your word processor. The document becomes a compound document when you add a table you created by using your spreadsheet, a graphic you created by using your presentation's graphic program, and a voice annotation you created by using the Windows Sound Recorder.

After you create a DDE link, the container document must keep track of the name of the source application, the name of the source document, and the identifier for the data to which the link points. Most applications enable you to examine and modify the links, so you also must be aware of the name of the source application, the source document, and so on. You also must have some idea of the way the linking mechanism functions.

OLE packages the data into an object that contains much more information than a DDE link. If you examine the syntax for an embedded object in applications that enable you to, such as Word and Excel, you see an indication of the kind of object. This indication of object type tells Windows NT what the source application is. The object (with information about its formatting, the way it is drawn, what colors it uses, and so on) is stored in the container document.

In DDE, the container document maintains information that points to data stored elsewhere. In OLE, the container document maintains the object. You do not need to know the source application's name; all you need to know is what kind of object you want to embed.

 Note A linked object is independent of the compound document; an embedded object exists only within the confines of the compound document.

To demonstrate essential differences between DDE and OLE, the following exercise uses the EXAMPLE1.XLS Excel worksheet that you created in Chapter 15. In the following example, you embed DDE rather than use it to link the range named Range1. For this exercise, open both Word and Excel.

1. Begin with a new document in Word, switch to Excel, and open EXAMPLE1.XLS.

2. Select the Formula menu, and choose the **G**o To command.

3. From the list of named ranges, select Range1. This takes you to the range and highlights it for you.

4. Select the **E**dit menu, and choose **C**opy.

5. Switch back to Word, select Word's **E**dit menu, and choose the Paste **S**pecial option. The Paste Special dialog box appears (see fig. 16.1).

Figure 16.1

Choosing the Microsoft Excel Worksheet Object option in the Paste Special dialog box.

 Note In Chapter 15, you were instructed not to choose the Microsoft Excel Worksheet Object item when the Paste Special dialog box appears. This item enables you to activate OLE embedding, not DDE linking. Now, however, choose Microsoft Excel Worksheet Object to continue this example.

6. Choose the Microsoft Excel Worksheet Object item in the Paste Special dialog box. Note that the Paste **L**ink button becomes grayed out, meaning that you cannot activate DDE linking.

7. Click on the **P**aste button. An OLE object is created and embedded in your document because you selected the Microsoft Excel Worksheet Object item.

You now see an embedded object in your Word document, as shown in figure 16.2.

Figure 16.2

The Excel range, embedded in the Word document.

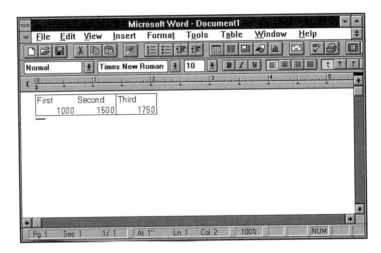

If you click anywhere on an embedded object, sizing handles appear around the object. The following message appears in the status line at the bottom of the screen: `Double click to Edit Excel Worksheet`.

Note Sizing handles are little squares around the perimeter of the object that enable you to change its dimensions.

To examine the syntax of the embedded object, select the **V**iew menu, and choose the Field **C**odes option. You see the EMBED code appear; it references an Excel worksheet (see fig. 16.3).

Note To continue with this exercise, select Field **C**odes from the **V**iew menu again, which returns you to a normal view of your document.

Select Word's **E**dit menu. Note that, as illustrated in figure 16.4, a command is added: Microsoft Excel Worksheet O**bj**ect. When you created a DDE link, this command was called Excel Worksheet Lin**k**.

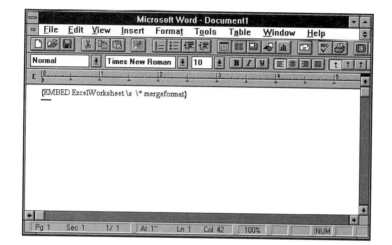

Figure 16.3

The EMBED field tells you what kind of object is embedded.

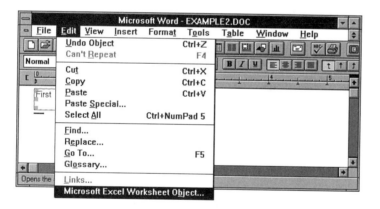

Figure 16.4

Word's Edit menu, showing the Microsoft Excel Worksheet Object option.

You can make Excel the foreground application by choosing the Microsoft Excel Worksheet Object command or by double-clicking on the object. Windows NT launches Excel (if it is not already launched) and passes it the embedded spreadsheet data. After Excel is active, your embedded spreadsheet data is already in the open spreadsheet. Notice that the text in the title bar of the spreadsheet is different (see fig. 16.5). The title bar informs you that you are working with an Excel object that is part of your Word document.

Figure 16.5

The Excel worksheet title bar shows that it is an object embedded in the Word document.

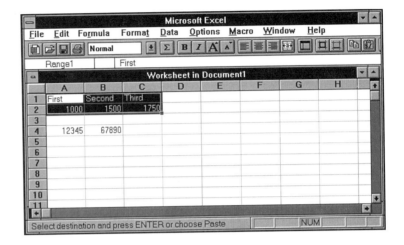

Note   In OLE 2.0, double-clicking on an embedded object does not open a new window for the source application. Instead, the source application's menu bar replaces the container application's menu bar, enabling you to edit the object by using the services of the source application while still in the container application's window. This is called *in-place* or *in-situ editing*.

You cannot name this worksheet—the system automatically does it for you. The file also does not show up anywhere in your list of files. This worksheet does not exist as an independent entity; it exists only as an object in the Word document. You can still edit the worksheet as if it were a normal Excel worksheet.

If you are following along with this example, select **W**indow in the Excel menu bar, and choose EXAMPLE1.XLS. Compare the title bars of your embedded spreadsheet data and EXAMPLE1.XLS (see fig. 16.6).

With the XLS worksheet as the active window, select the **F**ile menu (see fig. 16.7). Note the **S**ave command. Make the worksheet object the active window, and again select the **F**ile menu.

Notice in figure 16.8 that the **U**pdate command has replaced the **S**ave command on the menu.

You can experiment with updating the embedded data. From within Excel, make sure that the worksheet object is the active window. Experiment by changing one of the numbers in the six-cell matrix, and choose **U**pdate from the **F**ile menu. You then return to the Word document, the embedded worksheet object is updated, and Excel closes (if no other spreadsheets are open in Excel).

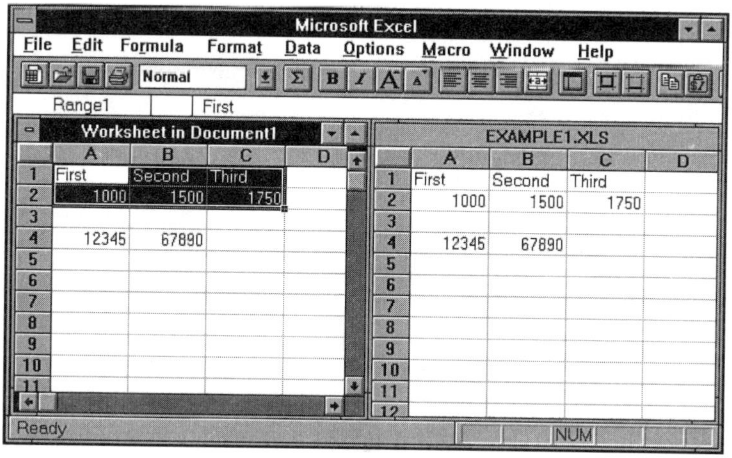

Figure 16.6

The Excel workspace, showing the XLS worksheet and the Word worksheet object.

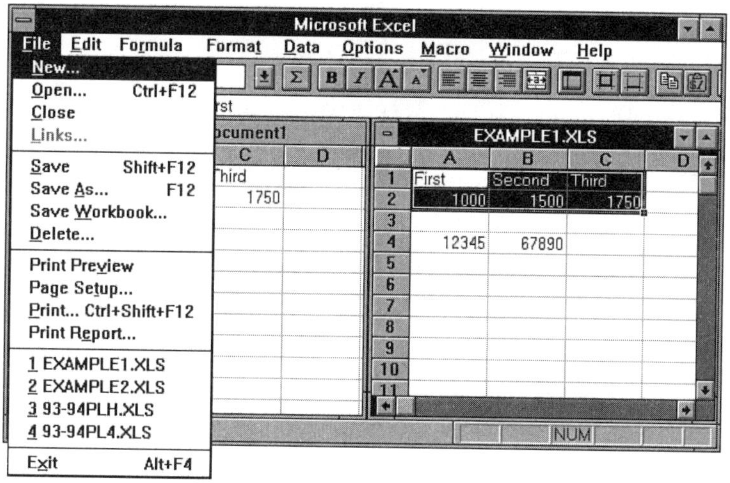

Figure 16.7

The Excel File menu.

Suppose, for example, that you change the amount in the third column of the worksheet from 1750 to 2000. The Word document automatically updates with the new number (see fig. 16.9) when you choose **U**pdate in the Excel **F**ile menu.

The Microsoft Excel Worksheet Object embedded in Word can be changed only by Excel. You can change the text face used for the numbers or the border around the numbers only by using Excel. Follow these steps:

1. Double-click on the embedded object. This opens Excel and loads the embedded worksheet object.

2. Highlight the six-cell matrix.

3. Access the Format menu, then select a border from the **B**order menu and a pattern from the **P**atterns menu.

4. Select **U**pdate from Excel's **F**ile menu.

Figure 16.8

Excel's File menu and Update command when the worksheet object has the focus.

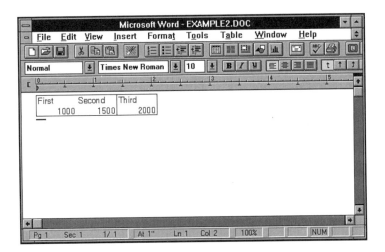

Figure 16.9

The Word document, after the spreadsheet data is updated.

The changes you just made—by using Excel's tools—are reflected in the Word container document (see fig. 16.10). You have just edited a Word document in Excel!

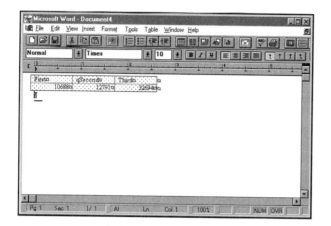

Figure 16.10

The embedded object now has a border and a pattern.

In the preceding exercise, you began with information that already existed in an Excel worksheet. You can, however, create an Excel Worksheet object from scratch, directly from Word, by following these steps:

1. Make sure that you have Word running, then create a new document by selecting **F**ile and choosing the **N**ew command.

2. Select the **I**nsert menu, and choose **O**bject (see fig. 16.11).

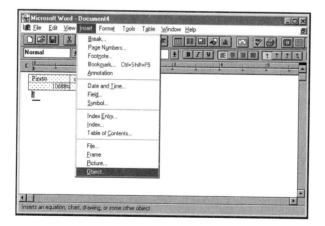

Figure 16.11

*Word's **I**nsert menu, showing the **O**bject command.*

3. Select Microsoft Excel Worksheet from the Object list box (see fig. 16.12).

Figure 16.12

Choosing Microsoft Excel Worksheet from the Object list box.

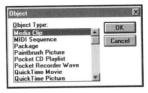

Excel opens. Instead of Sheet1 appearing, however, a screen appears that has all the basic attributes of a normal Excel worksheet except for a different title bar. This title bar tells you that the worksheet is an object to be embedded in Word (see fig. 16.13).

Figure 16.13

*The worksheet that appears after choosing Microsoft Excel Worksheet from the **O**bject command.*

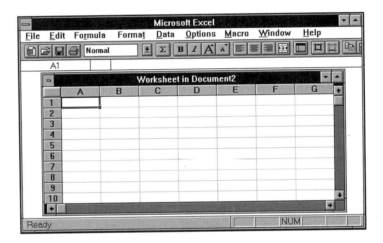

Add some data to this worksheet. As before, enter **First**, **Second**, and **Third** in cells A1, B1, and C1, respectively. Enter **1000**, **1500**, and **2000** in cells A2, B2, and C2. When you select **U**pdate from Excel's **F**ile menu, you return to Word with new data embedded as an OLE object.

Embedding a Microsoft Draw Object

Embedded objects often are created by applications that cannot be used as independent programs. You can call these applications (sometimes called *applets*) only from within a program that supports OLE; their sole purpose is to produce objects to embed in other applications.

Note Some of these embedding applications are Microsoft's Note-It, WordArt, Microsoft Graph, and Microsoft Draw. These applications are classic add-ins, as described in Chapter 10.

If you try to run an embedding application, such as a stand-alone program like Microsoft Word (by clicking on the name of the EXE file in File Manager, for example), you receive a message such as the one shown in figure 16.14.

Figure 16.14

The Windows NT error box appears when attempting to run an OLE server applet by itself.

If you want to embed a Microsoft Draw object in your Word document, for example, you must do it in the Word document. Select Word's **I**nsert menu, and choose the **O**bject command. Choose Microsoft Drawing from the list box; Windows NT brings up the Microsoft Draw screen (see fig. 16.15).

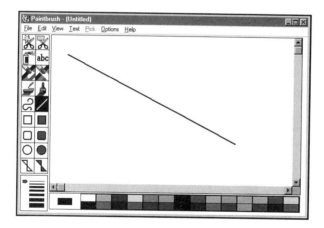

Figure 16.15

The Microsoft Draw screen.

The title bar tells you that the object you create here is part of your Word document. You can use the functionality of the drawing program to create your object. You even can import a clip-art picture (or another graphic file into Draw, and use it as an OLE object), which you can modify. That piece of clip art becomes an embedded object after it passes through Microsoft Draw.

The Microsoft Draw **F**ile menu (see fig. 16.16) offers several options. You can import clip art by using the **I**mport Picture command. You also can update the current object, stay in Microsoft Draw, and continue to edit the object by using the **U**pdate command. You can return to your Word document by using the E**x**it and Return to Document1 command. If you choose the last option, you are asked if you want to update the object in your Word document.

Figure 16.16

The Microsoft Draw File menu.

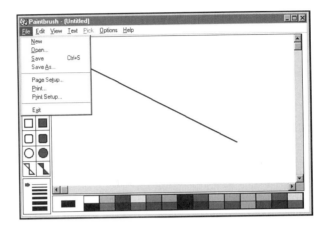

Notice that the Microsoft Draw **F**ile menu has no **S**ave option. Remember, an embedding application can only produce objects for embedding in destination documents—you cannot save a graphic produced in Microsoft Draw as a file. The graphic becomes part of the destination document when you select **U**pdate or E**x**it and Return to Document in the Microsoft Draw **F**ile menu.

When you return to Word, select the **V**iew menu, and choose Field **C**odes; or click on the drawing object, and press Shift+F9 to see Word's field description of the object, as shown in figure 16.17.

Figure 16.17

Word's EMBED field identifies the Microsoft Draw object.

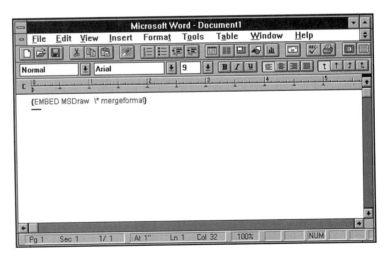

Follow these steps to edit an OLE object in Word's compound document in Microsoft Draw:

1. With the drawing object still highlighted, the following text appears on the status line at the bottom of the screen: `Double-click to Edit Microsoft Drawing`.

2. Double-click on the object, or select the Edit Microsoft **D**rawing command on Word's **E**dit menu to bring up the Microsoft Draw screen, with the object loaded.

3. Make any modifications by using Microsoft Draw's tools.

You can also embed a sound recorder object. The next section shows you how.

Embedding a Microsoft Sound Recorder Object

Microsoft Sound Recorder enables you to put a microphone graphic anywhere in your document and include a voice message with it. It differs from Draw in that it is a separate application. (For example, you can save WAV files by using SoundRec.)

 Note   Sound Recorder also can act as an OLE server.

To embed an object, follow these steps:

1. Select **O**bject from the Word **I**nsert menu, and choose Sound Recorder from the Object list box.

2. Click on the microphone button, speak your message into the microphone, and then click on the stop button.

3. To embed the voice note in your document, open the **F**ile menu and select the **U**pdate option (see fig. 16.18).

Figure 16.18

Creating and editing Sound Recorder objects.

Note To use the Sound Recorder application, you need to have a sound board and microphone installed on your computer.

If you double-click on the Sound Recorder object in Word, you do not return to Sound Recorder. Instead, Sound Recorder plays back the voice message you created.

To return to the Sound Recorder, you must select Sound Object from Word's Edit menu, as shown in figure 16.19.

Figure 16.19

Opening a Sound Recorder object embedded in a Word document.

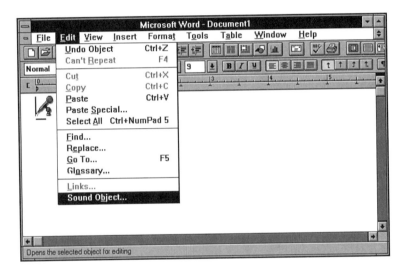

Embedding Non-OLE Objects

You might need to embed objects from applications that are not OLE-compliant. You may have a table derived from a non-Windows NT database, for instance, that you want to include in a report. Although you can export the database data in an ASCII-file format and import the ASCII file into your Word document, you lose the benefits of DDE and OLE.

Specifically, you have no way to return to the source application to view or edit the data. For Windows NT to apply OLE actions on the data, you must be able to somehow create an object from the data.

Windows NT has a way to create an OLE package data from non-OLE applications to make the data OLE-compliant. Normally, you can embed data from OLE-compliant

applications only in a Windows NT document. Packaging data from non-Windows NT applications wraps the data so that Windows NT can perform OLE actions on it. The package contains the data and enough information about the source application. Windows NT can launch the source application to enable you to view or edit the data in its source application.

Object Packager

Windows NT provides a utility, called the *Object Packager*, that enables you to wrap non-OLE data in an object package and embed the package in your document. The package is represented by an icon that stands for the contents of the package. Object Packager gives you complete freedom to change the package's contents and appearance (the icon) in your document. To access the package, click on the icon with the mouse; Windows NT invokes the source application, which then displays the data.

Note Under Windows NT, you no longer have to be content simply reading a document. With the capability of OLE to embed information and data from a wide variety of sources, you can read some portions of a document, view full-motion video, and listen to voice or music recordings. Windows NT always gives you new ways to access information.

In addition to some rather obvious sources of data, you can package operating system commands, batch files, and data files. (Windows NT usually recognizes the source application by the file extension of the data file.)

Using the Object Packager

To package a non-OLE object, double-click on the Object Packager icon, which normally is found in the Accessories program group.

Note Windows NT may not install the Object Packager in a program group on installation. You can find its executable file, PACKAGER.EXE, in the \WINNT\SYSTEM32 directory if Windows NT does not undertake the installation.

The Object Packager is divided into two windows that are placed side by side. You specify the content of the package in the right window and the appearance of the package in the left window. The content window of the package normally displays a brief description of the package contents. The appearance window displays the icon that is used to represent the package when it is embedded in a document (see fig. 16.20).

Figure 16.20

*The Object
Packager.*

The process of creating a package with Object Packager is as follows:

1. Locate the data and add it to the content window.

2. Determine the package appearance.

3. Copy the package to the Clipboard.

4. Embed the package in the destination document by pasting it from the Clipboard into the destination document.

Except for assembling the package in the first two steps, no difference exists between working with OLE packages and working with static data transfers by using the Clipboard.

In the following example, you see how easy it is to embed a DOS command in a document:

1. Double-click on the Object Packager.

2. Select the **F**ile menu, and choose the **I**mport command.

3. Use the file-selection list to choose an executable file, such as the TREE.COM in the \WINNT\SYSTEM32 directory.

4. Select the filename by double-clicking on it. The Object Packager closes the file-selection list and puts a description of the package contents in the Contents window (see fig. 16.21).

Figure 16.21

*The Object
Packager with
TREE.COM in
the Contents
window.*

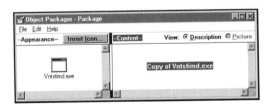

The Object Packager selects an icon to represent the package and inserts the icon in the Appearance window. The selected icon in this example is the Windows NT icon for Object Packager. To change the icon, select the Insert **I**con button at the top of the Appearance window.

Note   Most Windows NT applications have icons bound into them. The bound icons are available to use for other applications.

Object Packager displays a dialog box with the name of the executable file providing the icon—in this case, PACKAGER.EXE. You can use the **B**rowse button to select another executable file to provide an icon. PROGMAN.EXE has many icons available. Figure 16.22 shows the selection of a knife icon to represent the package.

Figure 16.22

The Object Packager with the knife icon in the Appearance window.

5. Select the **E**dit menu, and choose the Copy Pac**k**age command to copy the OLE package to the Clipboard (see fig. 16.23).

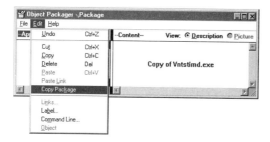

Figure 16.23

The Object Packager Edit menu, showing the Copy Package command.

6. Switch to the document in which you want to embed the package. Move the pointer where you want to embed the package.

7. Select Write's **E**dit menu, and choose **P**aste.

   Windows NT inserts the package and its icon in the document at the selected spot (see fig. 16.24).

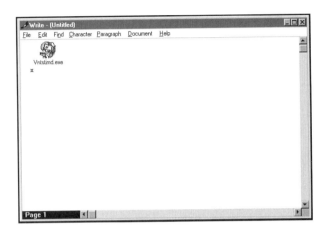

Figure 16.24

*The OLE package
embedded in a
Write document.*

Note   Windows NT offers many ways to specify the content of the data you want to
package. An in-depth discussion of OLE packaging and the many variations
possible is beyond the scope of this book.

Introducing OLE Client and Server Relationships

OLE follows a client/server model in the relationship between source applications
and destination applications. In OLE, source applications act as the server that
provides services to the client application that uses the services. When you use OLE to
embed an Excel spreadsheet range in a Word document, for example, Excel (the
server) provides spreadsheet services to Word (the client). When you want to view or
change the spreadsheet data, that data is copied into Excel, in which you can work
with the data.

Similarly, data packaged by using the Object Packager initially is obtained from a
multitude of server applications. To use the preceding voice-recording example, for
instance, the server application is the DOS or Windows NT program that digitizes the
sound and saves it on disk. When you play back the recording, a program provides
playback services. (Of course, the same DOS or Windows NT application can provide
playback services.)

Windows NT maintains a database of known servers and clients that they service.
The server-application information is stored in a file (REG.DAT) in the Windows
NT directory. Windows NT also provides a registration information editor
(REGEDIT32.EXE) that enables you to add new server applications to the database
or to modify the characteristics of existing server applications.

Editing the Registry Database

In Windows NT, unlike other versions of Windows, editing the Registry database is a dangerous operation. All configuration information for Windows NT is contained in the database, not in the files SYS.INI and WIN.INI. Accidental changes to the Registry can render Windows NT inoperable. As Microsoft's own product support staff is fond of saying, you can really "hose your system."

Make certain that you know what you are doing before you open the Registry Editor. Use Windows NT Setup, Control Panel, and application setup programs to make the changes you need to make to your system before you use the Registry Editor.

Summary

The technologies of linking and embedding have propelled users toward the fulfill-ment of an old promise: the capability to manage many different kinds of information in a seamless flow.

In this chapter and Chapter 11, you learned that you can create links that enable data to be shared across applications with just a few keystrokes or clicks of the mouse. You have seen the way to use two powerful tools, DDE and OLE, merely by employing simple Windows NT techniques that you already know. You also learned ways to link a spreadsheet range with a word-processing document and ways to embed several kinds of objects, text, and graphics in a document.

This chapter took you on a brief tour of Object Linking and Embedding, which promises to bring even greater interoperability to many functions that previously were unreachable by users. OLE is a powerful tool for the informed user, and it will play a greater role in future Windows NT developments. This chapter has only touched upon the ultimate potential of Object Linking and Embedding.

So far, you have been exposed to a variety of ways that Windows NT can increase your productivity. But keep in mind that the concepts and ideas presented in a book cannot substitute for hands-on experience. Continue to work on as many examples as necessary to gain experience and become comfortable with your new Windows NT skills.

Part IV

Managing the Windows NT Network

Exploring Networking with Windows NT

The vast majority of PCs used in business today are connected to a network. PC network packages, such as Novell NetWare and Microsoft LAN Manager, are sold as add-on products, with versions available for specific systems such as DOS and OS/2.

Since Windows 3.1, Microsoft has tried to integrate networking more closely into the operating system, presenting a standard interface for network management through a Network utility under the Control Panel. Just as Windows 95 depends on DOS for its underlying operating system functionality, it depends on an underlying DOS network package for its networking capabilities.

In this chapter, you will examine Windows NT networking, including

◆ Understanding Windows NT and Microsoft LAN Manager

◆ Understanding Windows NT networking architecture

◆ Using the Control Panel's Network utility

In Windows NT, Microsoft has fully integrated network services into the operating system. Full Microsoft LAN Manager functionality and (nearly full) interoperability come standard. Extended, or replacement, software from other PC network vendors such as Novell will tie into the same Control Panel management and configuration facility.

Understanding Windows NT and Microsoft LAN Manager

Although Microsoft has achieved a high degree of integration between the operating system and the network under Windows NT, the network interface is based on the LAN Manager model. Naming conventions, management by domains, Workstation and Server components, and the standard NetBEUI transport and Named Pipes IPC all are quite similar to elements of the LAN Manager.

LAN Manager Concepts and Terminology under Windows NT

A Windows NT computer is easily integrated into an existing LAN Manager network, and a Windows NT Advanced Server can act as the domain controller for LAN Manager clients. A Windows NT computer cannot join a LAN Manager domain if it is managed by an OS/2 server, however.

If a Windows NT computer is used in such a domain, you need to specify a workgroup name that is different from the domain name (see the section on using the Control Panel later in this chapter), and the Windows NT computer does not fall under the management of the domain. Provided that there is a domain account for the user name logged on at the Windows NT machine, it can attach to shared resources available on that domain and communicate by using IPC with computers in that domain.

Just how, and how well, a Windows NT computer integrates into a local area network (LAN) that is based on Novell NetWare (or other PC network operating systems) is still unclear. Windows NT is not yet in final release as this book is being written, and only preliminary software of limited functionality has been made available by Novell.

Windows NT Network Resources

The standard network interface for Windows NT is nearly the same as that of Microsoft LAN Manager's interface. Shared network disks or printers on other Windows NT computers or OS/2 LAN Manager computers can be attached to with the familiar NET USE command.

Interprocess communications (IPC) and Universal Naming Convention (UNC) file access use the computer name specified on the top-level screen of the Control Panel Network utility. Workstation and server components exist that you can manage with the NET START and NET STOP commands.

One difference is that there is no NET LOGON; the username and password specified for the current Windows NT session is used. This is a consideration when integrating a Windows NT computer into an existing LAN Manager network. A Windows NT workstation integrates seamlessly into a Windows for Workgroups workgroup by specifying the appropriate workgroup name in the Control Panel.

A variety of IPC interfaces are provided to maximize connectivity with client-server applications. These include Named Pipes; Sockets; DCE-conformant, remote-procedure calls (RPCs); DLC connectivity for SNA access to IBM mainframes; and a Remote Access Service package to enable access to Windows NT–based networks via telephony. Standard TCP/IP utilities also are provided, including ftp, telnet, and rsh.

Peer Networking

Windows NT provides full peer-networking capabilities. This means that it can act as both a server and a workstation on the network. It shares resources with other computers while enabling users to access shared resources on other computers.

Peer networking is not common under DOS and Windows 3.1, for which a distinct separation usually exists between client computers (although Windows for Workgroups has recently provided some of this capability). Under DOS and Windows 95, a distinct separation exists between client computers (which can access but not share remote resources) and server computers (which can share, but not provide access to, resources).

On the other hand, peer networking is a standard feature of Unix workstations, and it is a feature of some OS/2 networking packages, such as Microsoft LAN Manager. Other OS/2 packages, such as the Novell NetWare Requester for OS/2, have only limited peer capabilities. The recent popularity of Windows for Workgroups has rekindled interest in peer networking among PCs.

Understanding NT Networking Architecture

Windows NT has a layered network architecture that enables great flexibility in combining various components. Numerous layered conceptual models exist, such as the ISO and IEEE standards, but for purposes of understanding Windows NT network architecture, it can be simplified to three distinct layers:

◆ A network adapter device driver, which provides the control functions for a specific network card

◆ A transport protocol layer, which provides one of several standardized formats and mechanisms for moving data across the network

◆ Higher-level services, such as the Server and Workstation software, for sharing resources such as disks or printers, IPC mechanisms such as Named Pipes or Sockets, and various network utilities

The power of the layered approach is the capability to "mix and match" among components at the three levels. You can install a variety of network adapters under Windows NT, regardless of the choices at a higher level, because the device drivers running these adapters conform to the NDIS standard first developed for OS/2 LAN Manager.

Similarly, you can use different transport protocols, such as TCP/IP or NetWare IPX. Because these transports are also written to established standards, they can interoperate among versions of the same transport protocol provided by different vendors. These transport protocols are accessed from higher-level network services via the Windows NT Transport Driver Interface.

Transport Protocols

Windows NT has three standard protocols:

◆ **NetBEUI.** This transport protocol, used by LAN Manager, is installed automatically in Windows NT and is a good choice for a departmental LAN. It does not support routing and is not suited for wide area networks (WANs), however.

◆ **TCP/IP.** This protocol is the industry-standard routable transport protocol, and it is provided for full WAN connectivity. TCP/IP also is the standard for Unix computers. You can configure TCP/IP routing options from the Control Panel.

◆ **DLC.** This transport protocol is provided primarily to facilitate connectivity with IBM mainframe computers on SNA networks.

◆ Other standard protocols, such as Novell's IPX, will undoubtedly be made available by third-party vendors.

Under Windows NT, you can install multiple network adapter cards and their device drivers on a single computer. Additionally, you can use multiple transport protocols on a single card, and you can use the same transport protocol on multiple adapter cards. This capability is the essence of the flexibility provided by a layered architecture.

Setting up these connection pathways from adapter driver through transport protocol to network services is known as binding. The next section discusses the way choices are made among options for each of these layers, and the chosen packages are configured and bound together to form a full networking capability.

Using the Control Panel Network Utility

Windows NT network functionality is controlled by using the Network Control Panel utility. To use this utility, you must be logged on as a member of the Administrators group (see fig. 17.1).

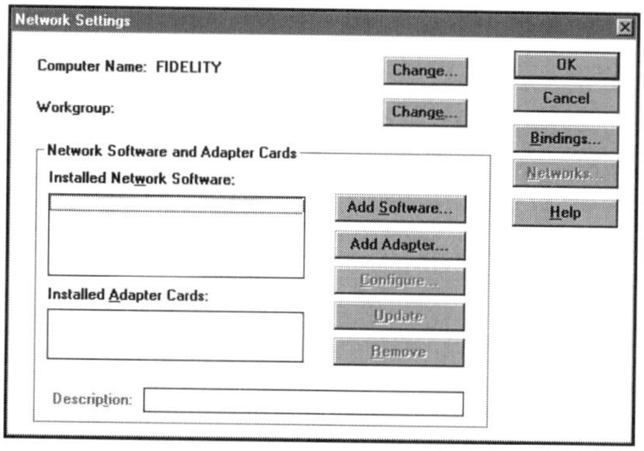

Figure 17.1

The highest-level screen of the Network Neighborhood applet.

Network Name and Domain

The top two lines specify the computer's network name (the name by which it is known on the network) and the workgroup or domain to which the computer belongs.

The computer name must be unique within the workgroup or domain, and it cannot be the same as the workgroup name. Although a workgroup is a group of computers listed together in the Network Browser, a domain is a managed group with a Windows NT Advanced Server that acts as the domain controller.

To join a domain, the computer name being used must have an account on the Windows NT domain controller, or valid information must be entered in the Create Computer Account in Domain dialog box under the Domain Workgroup Settings screen (see fig. 17.2).

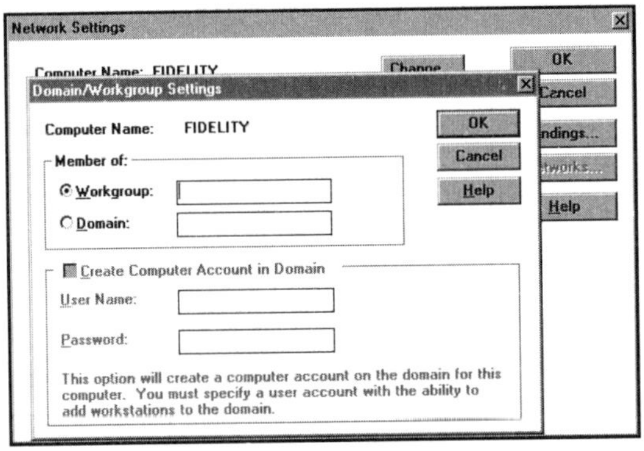

Figure 17.2

*The Domain/
Workgroup
Settings dialog
box.*

If you are using the Windows NT Advanced Server, you must be either a member of, or domain controller for, a domain.

Network Software and Adapter Cards

Also found in the top-level screen are list boxes, showing Installed Network Software and Installed Adapter Cards. You can add new items to these lists by clicking on the Add Software or Add Adapter buttons.

In each case, there is an option to allow new choices not listed to be installed from disk. This is the way you can add a package such as Novell NetWare, or a device driver for a nonstandard network card, to a Windows NT computer. You can delete items in the list boxes by highlighting them and clicking the Remove button.

You specify configuration settings for an adapter by highlighting the adapter card in the Install Adapter Cards list box and clicking on the Configure button. A screen that is specific to the network adapter type appears (see fig. 17.3). More than one network adapter can be installed in a Windows NT computer.

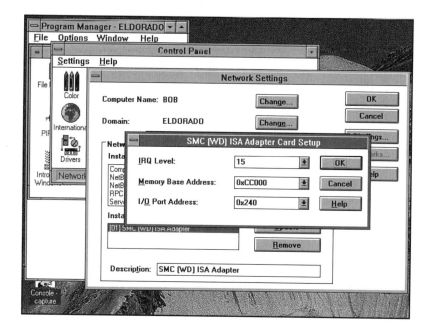

Figure 17.3

A sample Adapter Card Setup dialog box.

If you make incorrect choices for settings such as the adapter card IRQ, the network card might not function. Although Windows NT usually detects such errors and enables the user to make changes, it is still the user's responsibility to make sure that a network adapter has correct jumper settings and that no conflicts exist with other components in the system.

If problems still exist, use the Event Viewer to check the Event Log for relevant system messages.

Similarly, you can set configuration parameters for network software by highlighting the software and selecting Configure. The dialog box for TCP/IP configuration is shown in figure 17.4; this is where parameters such as the computer's IP address, subnet mask, and default name resolution behavior are set. The latter two settings control TCP/IP routing, and they should be set only by a network administrator familiar with TCP/IP.

A variety of other network-related software, including Remote Access Service (RAS), RPC, and DLC links, can be configured from this section also. In most cases, Windows NT will need to be rebooted for system-wide changes to become effective.

Although you can physically put more than one network adapter card into your computer and connect them to unrelated networks, it is not recommended.

Figure 17.4

*The TCP/IP
Configuration
dialog box.*

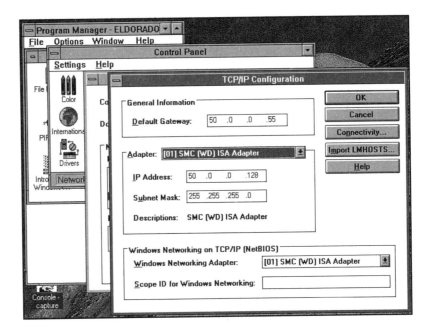

Figure 17.4

*The TCP/IP
Configuration
dialog box.*

Bindings

Binding, the process of linking together software to form pathways through the three conceptual layers, is controlled from a screen brought up by clicking the Bindings button. By default, all possible bindings are set up, and when new network adapters or transports are added, an automatic binding step occurs.

It is possible to disable some bindings if they are not going to be used—for instance, if a Token Ring card is connected to a NetBEUI network only and an Ethernet adapter is connected to a TCP/IP network only. This is seldom necessary, however, and should be done only by a network administrator because incorrect bindings can disable network connectivity. The Bindings screen is chiefly of interest to a network administrator while troubleshooting. An example of the Bindings dialog box is shown in figure 17.5.

Because you can connect a Windows NT computer to more than one network simultaneously, the question arises of which network to search first for a requested resource or service. You can control this from the Network Provider Search Order screen, accessed from the Network Settings screen, which is available on Windows NT computers that have more than one network installed.

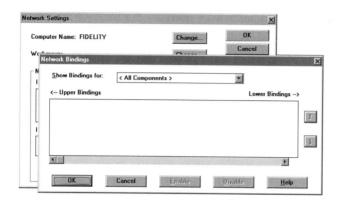

Figure 17.5

The Network Bindings dialog box.

Using Telnet

The Telnet utility enables you to operate your workstation from a remote computer. You cannot open graphical interfaces on remote computers, but you can issue commands from the command line. You can, for example, move, copy, and delete files. You can also run text-based programs, such as a mail program.

A Telnet session consists of the following steps:

1. You use a modem to dial into your NT workstation using an Internet protocol, such as PPP.

2. You log in to your workstation using your username and password.

3. You issue commands just as you would if you were sitting at your workstation.

Windows NT now enables you to capture your Telnet session in a log file. When you turn on the logging feature, every line printed on the screen from the remote computer is also saved in a logging file. After the Telnet session is over, you can open the logging file and, for example, cut and paste from it just as you would with any other text file. This is a handy feature when you retrieve you mail remotely, for example, and then want to reread some of it when you are not connected to the remote computer through the Internet.

To capture a Telnet session, use the following procedure:

1. In the Accessories program group, double-click on the Telnet icon. Windows NT displays the Telnet window.

2. Click on the Start Logging... option in the Terminal menu. Windows NT displays the Open log file window.

3. In the Directories: box, click on file folders until you define the correct pathname to your log file.

4. In the File Name: box, type the name of the log file. By convention, log files use the extension .log. This extension is not mandatory, however.

5. Click on the OK button.

6. Begin the Telnet session by connecting to the remote computer, then choosing the Connect option in the Connect menu.

7. After logging in and conducting your Telnet session (or at any time during the session), terminate logging by selecting the Stop Logging option in the Terminal menu.

Note   If you use the default name for the logging file, telnet.log, more than once, the log data is overwritten in the new logging session. Make sure to save the information to another file if you need to keep it, or define a new log file name for each capture session.

You can turn on and off logging at any time during your Telnet session. You do not have to start logging at the beginning of the Telnet session, and you do not have to stop at the end of the Telnet session. You often might want to start and stop the logging several times in one Telnet session, according to your needs.

Summary

Windows NT provides a powerful and flexible set of network services that are based on the LAN Manager model. Features include full peer networking, support for multiple network adapters and transports, and a complete set of IPC facilities.

Installation and configuration of these components have been unified under a single interface, the Control Panel utility. Windows NT is completely compatible with Windows for Workgroups, and full domain-management facilities are provided in the Windows NT Advanced Server. These features give Windows NT the most fully featured, and yet easy-to-use, network support available under any PC operating system.

Using the Remote Access Service

In a world where the Internet is becoming more and more common, where the technology to support telecommuting is finally in place, it is important to understand how the Remote Access Service can play a part in interconnecting work places.

The RAS service enables users to connect to a remote workstation and network and work just as though they were working directly on the remote workstation in the remote network. You can, for example, run any applications installed on the network from the remote workstation, just as you would if you were connected directly to the network.

You can configure RAS to provide remote access to a single client or to many clients.

RAS enables you to dial into a Windows NT server over telephone lines using a modem. You can also remotely access the network using faster transports, such as ISDN, X.25, or an RS-232C null modem.

Network security is maintained by the Windows NT server. That security includes support for the following features:

◆ Logon user names and passwords

◆ Security hosts

◆ Data encryption

◆ Call back

Call back is the process by which the remote users call into the network, type their user names and passwords, and then terminate the call. The RAS service, in response, calls back the user at the phone number stored for that user in the database. In this way, it is impossible for a computer to access the network unless the computer is connected by a modem to the phone line whose number is stored in the database.

The RAS service supports a variety of clients, including the following:

◆ Windows NT

◆ Windows for Workgroups

◆ MS-DOS

◆ LAN Manager RAS clients

◆ PPP clients

The RAS service supports a variety of wide area network (WAN) protocols, including the following:

◆ PPP

◆ TCP/IP

◆ IPX

◆ NetBEUI

◆ SLIP

The RAS service supports a variety of local area network (LAN) protocols as well, including the following:

◆ IP, which allows access to a TCP/IP network such as the Internet

◆ IPX, which allows access to NetWare servers and printers and NetBIOS applications

◆ NetBEUI

◆ Windows sockets applications

◆ Remote procedure calls (RPC)

◆ LAN Manager

After showing you how to install RAS, this chapter explains how to use it.

Installing RAS

You can install RAS during the Custom Setup of Windows NT or through Express Setup, if a network card is installed. You can also install RAS after installing Windows NT, as long as you are logged on as a member of the Administrators group. This section explains how to install RAS (assuming Windows NT is already installed).

Meeting Hardware Requirements

Using RAS requires a connection to a network. Which network you connect to and the speed of the connection determines the kind of hardware you need. This section lists the various possibilities. After you decide on the type of connection you intend to make to a network, you can buy and install the hardware. Make sure it is working error free before you install RAS.

The different connection possibilities include the following:

◆ A network adapter card, such as an Ethernet card, along with its driver, if you are accessing a network directly

◆ A modem that is supported by Windows NT, if you intend to connect either to the Internet or a specific network using telephone lines

◆ An X.25 smart card, if you intend to connect to an X.25 network

◆ An ISDN adapter card, if you intend to connect to the Internet or a local network using ISDN: a pair of dedicated telephone lines

The fastest connection is in the network adapter card, but probably you will be using one of the other connections if you are working offsite.

Installing the Software

The installation of RAS depends, in part, on the kind of network you are connecting to. Make sure, before you install RAS, that you have successfully installed the network protocol you intend to use, such as TCP/IP or IPX.

Use the following procedure to install RAS:

1. Click on the Network option in the Control Panel application group. Windows NT displays the Network Settings window, as shown in figure 18.1.

Figure 18.1

The Network Settings window.

Network Settings	
Computer Name: FIDELITY Change...	OK
Workgroup: Change...	Cancel
	Bindings...
Network Software and Adapter Cards	Networks...
Installed Network Software:	
	Add Software...
	Add Adapter...
	Configure...
Installed Adapter Cards:	Update
	Remove
Description:	

2. Click on the Add Software button.

3. Scroll through the list of software in the Network Software list and click on the Remote Access Service (RAS) entry.

4. Click on the Continue button.

5. Windows NT now prompts you for the path to the source code. Provide the pathname and click on the OK button.

   Windows NT copies the RAS service to your hard drive.

6. In the list of ports in the Add Port window, click on the port you will use for remote access. If you successfully added any network cards, such as an ISDN card, it should appear in the list of ports.

7. Click on the OK button.

8. Windows NT offers to detect the modem connected to your system. Click on Cancel to specify the modem or click on the OK button to let Windows NT determine the type of modem connected to the system.

  ◆ If Windows NT detects a modem, the name of the modem is highlighted in the Configure Port window. If Windows NT cannot determine the identity of the installed modem, click on the modem in the list of modems.

  ◆ The list of modems contains only those modems supported by Windows NT. If your modem is not listed, you can either try one that is similar to your own, you can call your modem manufacturer to see if they now support Windows NT, or, as a last resort, you need to buy a new modem.

Note   If you have already installed RAS and afterwards installed a new modem, you can click on the Detect button in the Configure Port window to have Windows NT detect the newly added modem.

9. In the Port Usage section of Configure Port window, click on one of the following:

  ◆ Dial out only radio button if you want to use your workstation only as a client of the RAS service.

  ◆ Receive calls only button if you want to use your workstation as a RAS server only.

  ◆ Dial out and Receive calls button if you want your workstation to function both as a client of RAS and a RAS server, but not both at the same time.

10. To configure the port settings for the device, click on its listing in the Attached Device list.

11. Click on the Settings button.

   Windows NT displays the Remote Access Setup window.

12. To change the settings, click on the device in the list of devices and then click on one of the buttons surrounding the list. Table 18.1 describes the functions of the different buttons.

TABLE 18.1
Button Functions in the Remote Access Setup Window

Button	Description
Add	Adds a port that RAS can use.
Remove	Deletes a port that RAS can use.
Configure	Resets the configuration settings for a port, such as whether or not the port is used by RAS to dial out only, receive only, or both.
Clone	Copies the configuration settings of one device to another device.
Continue	Closes this window and accepts the changes.
Cancel	Closes this window and does not accept the changes.
Network	Sets a wide range of network-related configuration settings, including authentication and data encryption options.
Disable Automatic Restoration Of Network Connections At Logon	Uncheck this check box if you do not want to reestablish a previous network connection when you log on. Because this is a time-consuming activity, the box is checked by default.

13. Click on the Continue button in the Remote Access Setup window.

    Windows NT displays RAS Server Configuration windows for each protocol installed.

14. Set the configuration settings for each RAS Server Configuration window.

    Windows NT carries out the configuration settings, creates the Remote Access Service program group, and displays a confirmation message that the installation of RAS was successful.

15. Click on the OK button in the confirmation windows.

    If you have network connections, you might be prompted to confirm their settings.

16. For the configuration of RAS to take effect, you must reboot your computer.

When you reboot your computer, you will see the new program group called Remote Access Service.

Creating a Personal RAS Server

Instead of opening your server up to an Internet of users, you might like to configure your workstation so that you can use it as a server for another, remote computer—perhaps in your home. Or you might like to grant workstation access to a small number of coworkers or clients.

To set up your workstation as a personal RAS server, complete the installation steps up through step 12 in the previous section, then continue with the following procedure.

1. Click on the Network button in the Remote Access Setup window.

2. In the Network Setting window, click on the protocols to be used by the RAS service.

3. Click on an encryption option.

4. If the only clients accessing your server use Microsoft software, click on the Require Microsoft Encrypted authentication.

    If you do not expect the clients to use Microsoft software, click on another option for the clients.

5. For each protocol you choose for the RAS server to support, highlight the protocol and click on the Configure button, one at a time.

    Windows NT displays the RAS Server Protocol Configuration window.

6. Click on the option deciding whether the RAS clients will be given access to the entire network or to only the RAS server.

7. Click on the OK button.

8. To determine the permissions of the users, double-click on the Remote Access Admin icon.

9. Specify that the focus is the personal RAS server.

10. Click on the Permission item in the Users menu.

11. Select the permissions for each individual or group of individuals.

Now you have successfully created a personal RAS server.

Troubleshooting RAS

The major problem that you might run into after you install and run RAS is that some users cannot connect to the service. Solving RAS problems is often not a cut and dry process. It normally takes some creativity to unravel RAS problems. The following list, however, suggests common problems and corrections.

◆ RAS client problems often relate directly to the configuration of the software and hardware. You can look at the error messages and audit logs to get some insight on the problems.

◆ Monitor the ports used by the RAS service. If the port does not show usage equal to the other ports, examine it to see if it is working correctly.

◆ Use the Port Status window to monitor user connection attempts to determine what is wrong.

One way to monitor RAS and help troubleshoot problems is by using RAS logs.

Enabling RAS Logs

Monitoring a user's attempts to access the RAS server is probably the most direct way of solving their RAS-access problem. Real-time monitoring, however, does not always yield the answers you want. In that case, you should enable the logging of RAS-specific log data.

The data in the log files is text that can be read with any text editor, word processor, or at the command line. You cannot, however, read log data using the Event Viewer.

The RAS-specific logs are the PPP log and the device log. The PPP log stores all PPP-related messages in \<systemRoot>\SYSTEM32\RAS\PPP.log.

The device log stores all messages between serial ports and the devices connected to them in \<systemRoot>\SYSTEM32\RAS\DEVICE.LOG. Messages stop only after the device and port are connected and the data is transmitted between them.

You enable these logging facilities by changing two lines in the Registry. To enable the PPP log, change the Logging parameter to 1 in the following line:

```
HKEY_LOCAL_MACHINE\SYSTEM\CurrentControlSet\Services\RasM\PPP
```

To enable the DEVICE log, change the Logging parameter to 1 in the following line:

```
HKEY_LOCAL_MACHINE\SYSTEM\CurrentControlSet\Services\Rasman\Parameters
```

Logs give you valuable insights into the working of the RAS service.

Summary

In this chapter you saw how to set up your workstation to function either as a RAS client, server, or both. You saw how to configure your workstation so that the RAS server could provide access to the entire network, or just to itself. Finally, this chapter looked at some common problems and solutions.

Understanding the System Registry

Anyone who has ever installed a peripheral card or software package on a PC can appreciate the difficulties involved in system configuration. You encounter CONFIG.SYS entries, AUTOEXEC.BAT entries, and WIN.INI entries. Each of these file entries has its own format, is in its own location, and has various ways of interacting with the system.

Multiply the problem by several hundred—or thousand—PCs on a large network, and you can begin to understand the challenge faced by today's corporate information systems departments. Simplifying the process of system configuration is the basic concept behind the Windows NT System Registry.

The System Registry provides a single storage point for configuration information, which controls all the hardware and software on a computer, with a standard structure and interface for access to that information.

In addition, Windows NT permits remote Registry access across the network, enabling the configuration of all of a group's PCs from a single central point.

This chapter discusses the following:

- ◆ Understanding the Registry format

- ◆ Using the Registry

- ◆ Accessing the Registry with REGEDT32

- ◆ Exploring the four root keys

- ◆ Recovering the system with Registry backups

You can control access to the Registry by using Windows NT's security system. Because the entire machine configuration is held in one place, backing up a system (and copying or moving it to another machine) becomes much simpler.

Understanding the Registry Format

The basic structure of the System Registry is similar to the familiar tree structure of a hierarchical file system, such as that found in DOS, OS/2, and Unix.

The file system has the following components:

The *root directory* contains

  some *files*, and

  some *subdirectories*, each containing

  some *files*, and

  some *subdirectories*, each containing...

  and so on.

The System Registry has the following components:

The *root key* contains

  some *values*, and

  some *subkeys*, each containing

  some *values*, and

  some *subkeys*, each containing...

  and so on.

The Windows NT System Registry has four root keys. Following the preceding file-system analogy, you can think of the root keys as equivalent to file-system logical drives C, D, E, and F.

These root keys are referred to in Microsoft's documentation as predefined keys, or first-level keys.

The four root keys are described in table 19.1.

TABLE 19.1
Windows NT Root Keys

Root key	Function
HKEY_LOCAL_MACHINE	Shows information about the hardware and software on the computer. This information includes configuration data for the hardware and software installed on the computer, as well as the basic configuration of the computer itself (processor type, and so on).
HKEY_USERS	Shows information about all users active on the computer. It does not show all user IDs, only those currently active.
HKEY_CURRENT_USER	Actually a subkey of HKEY_USERS, it shows information for the user examining the Registry information.
HKEY_CLASSES_ROOT	Included for Windows NT 3.1 compatibility and OLE support. Associates filename extension with an application package.

Each branching point, or *node*, of the Registry tree is a root key that has a name. As in a file system, the names are unique for all subkeys under a given key, so the full hierarchical name (or *Registry path*) of any node in the tree is unique.

Value names under a specific root key also are unique—both among themselves and among subkey names under that key—just as filenames and subdirectory names are unique within the same directory. The similarity of structure between the Registry and a file system is further emphasized by Microsoft's use of the backslash delimiter for Registry paths.

Any specific value in the Registry has a unique full Registry path name, beginning with the name of one of the root keys, extending through subkey names, and ending in the value name, as in the following example:

```
HKEY_LOCAL_MACHINE\SOFTWARE\Microsoft\Windows NT\CurrentVersion\InstallDate
HKEY_CURRENT_USER\Keyboard Layout\Active
```

Value names consist of the Registry name, which defines the value, a data type, and associated data. There are five predefined value data types, described in table 19.2.

TABLE 19.2
Registry Value Data Types

Value data type	Description
REG_BINARY	Unstructured binary data.
REG_DWORD	A numeric value, stored in a 32-bit integer.
REG_SZ	A NULL-terminated string.
REG_MULTI_SZ	Multiple NULL-terminated strings, concatenated and terminated with a double NULL.
REG_EXPAND_SZ	A NULL-terminated string, meant to be taken as a filename, and which will be expanded when used into a fully qualified path name.

The size of value data for a Registry entry has a large (about 1 MB) limit. The Registry is not intended for storing large data items; you should store large data items in application-specific disk files, with the path name stored in the Registry.

Using the Registry

You can add or remove keys and values from the Registry, or edit value data, by using the Windows NT graphical utility REGEDT32. Microsoft recommends that you not use REGEDT32 to directly alter the Registry, but rather use Windows NT utilities such as Setup and the Control Panel (or an application-installation program) to make any modifications programmatically.

Because all machine-configuration information is stored in the Registry, an incorrect entry can be disastrous. The Windows NT API presents an interface for Registry manipulation, and Microsoft is encouraging software developers and makers of hardware peripherals to use this interface to store configuration data during installation. Until third-party products can correctly make all entries every time, which is unlikely in this imperfect world, those responsible for PC installation or configuration need to be able to use REGEDT32.

Setting the Size of the Registry

The size of the registry determines the maximum number of user and group accounts available in the Windows NT Server domain. To increase the number of user and group accounts, use the following procedure:

1. Click on the System icon in the Control Panel group. Windows NT displays the System window.

2. Click on the Virtual Memory button. Windows NT displays the Virtual Memory window.

3. Type the maximum registry size in the Maximum Registry Size field in the Registry Size portion of the window. The default registry size is 25 percent of the paged pool size. For this change to take effect, you must reboot your system.

You can also change the registry size using the Windows NT Server. Using the Server is the more common way of changing the registry. For more information about the Windows NT Server, see *Inside Windows NT Server* published by New Riders.

Accessing the System Registry with REGEDT32

You can launch REGEDT32 from a Windows NT command line, from the **R**un option in the menu displayed by the Start button. In the following section, REGEDT32 is used to examine some of the basic structures and features of the Registry.

Be careful not to change Registry values if you follow along on your own computer. As noted earlier, entering incorrect information in the Registry can cause serious problems, such as your system not being able to boot.

After you launch REGEDT32 for the first time, you see a window for each of the four root keys (see fig. 19.1).

Within the window for each root key, key entries appear in a graphical tree structure on the left side of the screen, with one key highlighted. Values under the key are listed on the right side of the screen.

Figure 19.1

*Windows of the
four root keys.*

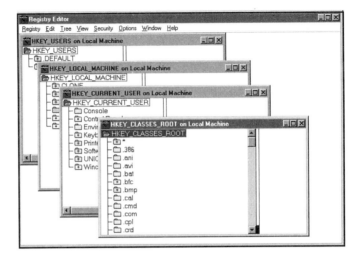

Each key has a file folder icon, which is marked with a + if that key contains further
subkeys (see fig. 19.2).

Figure 19.2

*File folders with
subkeys are
marked with +.*

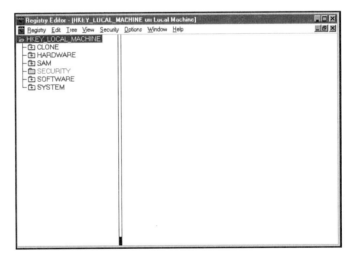

Double-clicking on the key causes the subkey structure to appear, and it replaces the
+ with a - (see fig. 19.3).

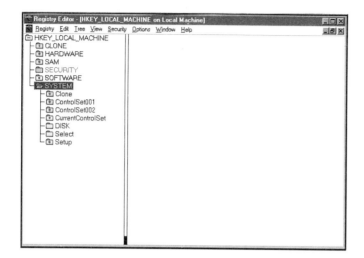

Figure 19.3

Subkey structure for SYSTEM.

Double-clicking on the key again closes the key.

You can edit values by double-clicking on them. If you double-click on a value, a dialog box appears that is specific to the data type for that value (see fig. 19.4).

Figure 19.4

DWORD Editor dialog box.

The Select Computer option under the **R**egistry entry on the menu bar enables you to access the Registry on another Windows NT computer on the network.

You must have the appropriate security privileges to edit values.

Exploring the Four Root Keys

The four root keys contain the most important configuration data in the Registry. Windows NT's four root keys are discussed in the following sections.

The HKEY_LOCAL_MACHINE Key

The HKEY_LOCAL_MACHINE key has the most interesting information in the Registry. It includes the hardware and software configuration for the machine, as well as security information and the default boot configuration.

The HKEY_LOCAL_MACHINE key has five subkeys: HARDWARE, SAM, SECURITY, SOFTWARE, and SYSTEM. (Figure 19.2 shows this structure.) These subkeys are discussed in the following sections.

HARDWARE Subkey

The HARDWARE subkey has information about the hardware installed on the machine: the interrupt and I/O port used by a peripheral card, the video-adapter type present in the machine, and linkages to device drivers. Although some of this information is set during installation, many entries are refreshed at boot time by the hardware-detection program NTDETECT.COM, which is a hidden file in the root directory of the boot drive.

SAM and SECURITY Subkeys

The SAM and SECURITY subkeys have information that controls the security configuration for the computer, including user- and group-account information. You cannot directly change these keys; they can be accessed only in a limited and controlled way. Changes must be made by using the Windows NT security interfaces.

SOFTWARE Subkey

The SOFTWARE subkey has information about software installed on the computer. Applications are arranged under a subkey structure, using the vendor company's name and the name of the software package as its higher-level components.

The information under SOFTWARE is not specific to the individual user logged on; it is global to the machine and affects all users.

SYSTEM Subkey

The SYSTEM subkey is further subdivided into *control sets*. Each control set actually is a set of system parameters, which (with the other Registry entries) can control the operation of the computer. This structure is displayed in figure 19.5.

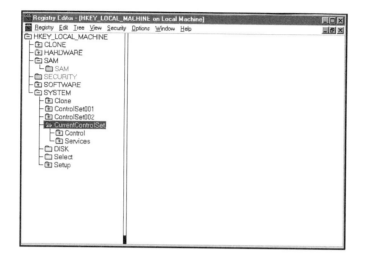

Figure 19.5

The SYSTEM subkey.

The CurrentControlSet subkey holds the information that was used when the computer was last booted. Previous versions of control sets are stored as *ControlSet001*, *ControlSet002*, and so on. If an incorrect entry is made in the Registry, you can restore and use a previous, correct System.

Under CurrentControlSet is the subkey *Services.* In Services, you find a list of the Windows NT services available on the computer. You can configure these special system programs, for instance, to start at boot time.

The HKEY_USERS Key

The HKEY_USERS key contains the actual user account information. Under this key are two subkeys: DEFAULT and another key, the encrypted identifier for the user currently logged on.

Information about Personal Program Groups, desktop preferences that are set by Control Panel, and other user-specific information is kept in this key. The DEFAULT branch holds default information for new users. The HKEY_USERS key is illustrated in figure 19.6.

The HKEY_CURRENT_USER Key

The HKEY_CURRENT_USER key is a duplicate of the branch of the HKEY_USERS key that refers to the currently logged-on user—the encrypted key described previously (see fig. 19.7).

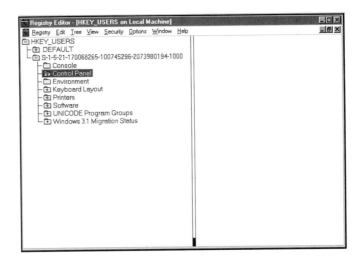

Figure 19.6

The HKEY_USERS tree.

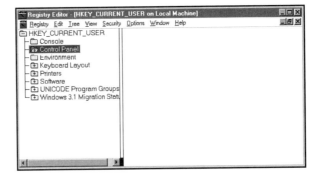

Figure 19.7

The HKEY_CURRENT _USER key.

The HKEY_CLASSES_ROOT Key

The HKEY_CLASSES_ROOT key controls the association of certain file extensions with specific applications (for instance, the DOC extension that is used for Microsoft Word documents, or the TXT extension for Notepad files).

This key also controls certain OLE information, and it has information used to provide compatibility with Windows 3.1 and Windows 95 applications. The HKEY_CLASSES_ROOT key structure is illustrated in figure 19.8.

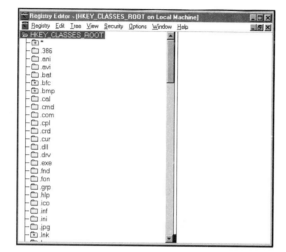

Figure 19.8

The HKEY_CLASSES _ROOT key.

Recovering the System with System Backups

One key use of the Registry is to back up a computer's configuration. During the installation of Windows NT, you are prompted for a blank disk. Windows NT changes it to an emergency repair disk, which you can use later to restore the machine's configuration to its state just after the original installation.

A copy of the contents of the Registry is on the emergency repair disk, which can be restored by Windows NT system services in case of corruption.

It also is wise to back up the Registry at other times (for instance, before you install a major new software or hardware package). If the installation fails, a working configuration can be restored. After the new component is installed and working correctly, another Registry backup saves the new System.

Backing Up the Registry

The Registry files are found in the SYSTEM32\CONFIG directory under the Windows NT system root. (For instance, \WINNT\SYSTEM32\CONFIG is the default installation path of \WINNT).

These files, sometimes referred to as the *hives*, cannot be copied while Windows NT is running because they are locked by the operating system.

To make a backup of the hives, boot the computer under DOS, either from the Windows NT dual-boot manager or from a floppy disk. All files in the CONFIG directory should be copied; this can take several disks, depending on the complexity of the hardware configuration and the number of users defined.

If a previous configuration has to be restored, again boot the computer under another operating system to unlock the files. You then can delete the contents of the CONFIG directory and replace them with the contents of the backup disks.

The **R**egistry menu has an option that restores the Registry, either from a Registry backup or from raw hive files. If the Registry is corrupted, you may not be able to use this facility. The file-copy method described previously was recommended by Microsoft developers.

If the hardware or software configuration has changed since the last backup, some information will be lost. In the worst case, the hardware or software configuration can change so much that the computer does not even run.

It is important to maintain a current copy of the Registry contents. Deleting and restoring the Registry is a last-resort procedure.

Summary

The Windows NT System Registry provides a single storage point for all system-configuration data for a computer. The Registry also acts as a consistent and remotely accessible interface to that information.

The Registry contains all configuration data for the Windows NT operating system and its base hardware, and it is designed to hold configuration information for all other vendor software and hardware installed on that computer.

You can—and should—back up the Registry regularly to capture a current image of a computer's full configuration set.

CHAPTER

20

Exploring the Windows NT Advanced Server

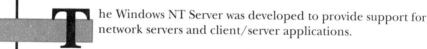

T he Windows NT Server was developed to provide support for network servers and client/server applications.

Several features were specifically designed to provide a powerful and reliable network server platform: a network-aware and extensible security system; enhanced administration capabilities; and advanced storage-management features, such as disk mirroring and support for disk arrays. This chapter discusses the following:

◆ Understanding client-server computing

◆ Understanding the Windows NT Advanced Server

◆ Exploring Windows NT Advanced Server storage-device management

◆ Learning how NT implements disk mirroring and duplexing

◆ Understanding Windows NT Advanced Server security

◆ Exploring Windows NT "impersonation" and IPC management

◆ Understanding remote access service

In this chapter, you examine the Windows NT Advanced Server and other topics related to using Windows NT as a network server.

Understanding Client/Server Computing

The concept of *downsizing*, or the movement of computing resources from centralized mainframes to distributed networks of PCs, is perhaps today's hottest topic in corporate computing.

The enabling software technology behind this downsizing movement is the *client/ server application*, which is a software application that runs partly on a network server and partly on an end user's desktop PC. The separate pieces communicate and interact across the network.

Although this technology is in its early stages—and many an unpleasant surprise has met those on the leading edge of what is sometimes called the "client/server revolution"—it is clearly the future of enterprise computing. The cost-effectiveness of client/server solutions versus their mainframe-based counterparts is undeniable. To better understand the client/server technology, consider the following example of a departmental database.

Enterprise computing can be loosely defined as computing technologies that are applied to handling the information management needs of large and small companies and organizations. The requirements of enterprise computing systems are very different from those of individual, stand-alone computers. Network security, reliability, and throughput are much larger concerns in a business environment than in a single-user situation. As the size of the enterprise system increases (often to several thousand users), these issues grow proportionally.

Under the *centralized model*, a single large computer runs a number of terminal screens, from which the database can be accessed. Not only does the central computer store and retrieve data, it performs all calculations based on the data. It also manages the video screens, keyboards, and other attached devices. The terminals have no processing power, and all users are presented with the same interface and software tools by the central computer.

Under the *distributed model*, a central computer (the *server*) holds the database, storing and retrieving data for end users. In this case, however, a computer on the receiving end (the *client*) can perform calculations on the data received, and it manages the display and attached input devices.

The distributed model enables the server to concentrate on only those tasks needed to run the database, so the same performance presented by the centralized model is possible (with a much smaller and less expensive computer acting as the server).

If the system is properly designed to adhere to standardized access protocols, you can use a variety of different client-based applications to access the database, and you can choose the one best suited for your needs.

This quality of adhering to standards and the consequent capability to mix applications is referred to as an *open-systems design*, which is another important aspect of client/server computing.

To successfully deploy a reliable client/server application, the following components are necessary:

◆ A reliable network

◆ A powerful and secure server platform

◆ A simple means of administering these systems

◆ Extensive client-connectivity possibilities

The rest of this chapter examines the ways in which Windows NT provides each of these components with a successful client/server environment.

Examining the Windows NT Advanced Server

A number of added features are available under the Windows NT Advanced Server that are not available under regular Windows NT. Some of these features are network-aware extensions to utilities that are found in Windows NT.

The network-aware extensions enable these utilities to access certain network services provided by NT. For instance, it might be useful for a printer-server process to send a message via network IPC (interprocess communication) to the application requesting a print job if the printer is off-line or out of paper.

The Print Manager utility is enhanced to provide for the administration of remote printers. Sometimes entirely new utilities are provided, such as the Server Manager and User Profile Editor in the Administrator Tools program group of the Windows NT Advanced Server. You can explore a few of these added capabilities in the following sections.

NT Advanced Server Storage-Device Management

A number of advanced storage-device management features are available through the Disk Manager utility, which is found under the Administrator Tools program group of the Windows NT Advanced Server.

Normal, single-disk access proceeds in a linear fashion. The disk's read/write heads are initially positioned over the first track to be read (see fig. 20.1). As the data is read from the disk, the read/write head is moved incrementally across the disk to succeeding tracks containing data.

Figure 20.1

Normal single-disk access.

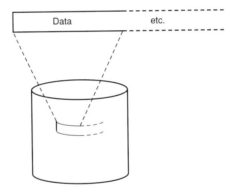

A. Normal Single - Disk Access

Windows NT provides very high-performance disk access through *disk striping*, in which data is broken up and written to several physical disks simultaneously, then recombined when the data is read (see fig. 20.2).

All the data under all the read/write heads is read at one time. Because the read/write head on each disk needs to move only one-fourth as often, the speed with which data is moved to or from the disk is multiplied by a factor of four. You can use the Disk Manager to link as many as 32 disks together.

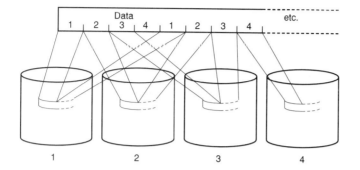

Figure 20.2

Disk striping (four-disk example).

B. Disk Striping (Four - Disk Example)

Fault Tolerance

A major concern in enterprise computing is *fault tolerance*, defined as the capability of the computer to tolerate errors in data transmission, power failures, and other conditions that can lead to data loss. Windows NT Advanced Server utilizes a number of fault-tolerant design features that enhance its suitability as an enterprise-computing operating system.

Disk Striping with Parity

One form of fault tolerance is *disk striping with parity*. As in disk striping, data is written to a number of disks simultaneously. In this case, however, one disk does not receive actual user data; it receives *parity data*, which is information about the contents of the other disks in the array. Thus, if any one of the data disks fail, the missing information can be reconstructed.

You can specify Automatic File Replication of important files to other servers, to be carried out upon notification of a change to one of the files.

Because Windows NT is reading the parity disk at the same time as the other disks in the array, error correction can occur in real time. As Windows NT encounters a disk-parity error, the correction is applied before the data is passed on to the process that requested it.

Disk Mirroring and Duplexing

With *disk mirroring*, a complete duplication of all disk contents is maintained on two disk drives. In the event of a disk failure, one copy of the data is still available.

Disk mirroring is activated by choosing Establish Mirror from the Fault Tolerance menu in the Disk Administrator utility (see figure 20.3).

Figure 20.3

Activating Windows NT disk mirroring.

Disk Administrator	▼ ◆
Partition	Fault Tolerance	Options	Help

Establish Mirror

🖙 **Disk 0**

325 MB

■ Primary partition   ■ Logical drive   ☐ Stripe set   ■ Mirror set   ☐ Volume set

A similar feature, *disk duplexing*, adds the capability to use separate disk controllers to provide fault tolerance for controller or disk failure.

As in regular Windows NT, the Windows NT Advanced Server supplies fault-tolerance features, such as an Uninterruptable Power Supply (UPS) service under the Control Panel, and a full-featured Tape Backup utility under Administration Tools. The UPS option in the Control Panel allows you to specify a command file to run before the operating system shuts down. This command file cannot, however, display a user dialog box. Waiting for user input defeats the purpose of the UPS safety feature. The goal is for the system to shut down gracefully, especially in the advent of a power failure. Waiting for user input might prevent that.

Understanding Security Features

If you move critical data to a networked PC server, the same high security standards should be available that were on the mainframe. (Windows NT has U.S. Department of Defense C2-level security and password encryption to the DES standard used in the banking industry, so it provides such a platform.)

The Windows NT Advanced Server provides an enhanced tool, the User Manager for Domains, to administer security.

Domain Administration

The User Manager for Domains is an enhanced version of the User Manager provided in Windows NT. It is a fully network-aware utility for managing users and groups across multiple Windows NT servers.

This utility enables you to define both global and local groups. A single network logon thus provides access to resources on all servers in the domain.

The User Manager for Domains solves the problem of a user having multiple logon IDs and passwords for various resources on the network.

Among the added features of the User Manager for Domains are a number of predefined groups, such as Account Operators, Backup Operators, and Domain Admins, which facilitate the management of large networks.

The User Manager enables easier management of individual user accounts across the network. It enables a system administrator to make changes to an individual's account from anywhere on the network. The system administrator does not have to log on to the system from the user's workstation or even copy files from the user's computer. All user-account management can be done remotely.

Figure 20.4 shows the User Manager utility screen. All common user-account management tasks (adding new users, assigning to user groups, and so on) are conducted through the User Manager utility.

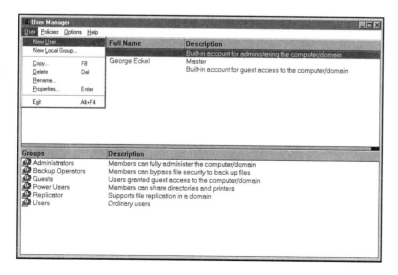

Figure 20.4

The User Manager utility screen.

Impersonation APIs

The Win32 API provides a set of impersonation calls that enable an individual thread of a client/server application to assume the security context of the client who is being served by that thread.

Impersonation enables the control of access to server resources from attached clients. A process thread spawned by an ongoing process has the same security privileges as the parent process. The thread is able to open and modify files, send and receive messages, and behave in the same manner as the parent process.

Impersonation properties can be applied to Named Pipe, RPC, and DDE transactions.

Impersonation sidesteps a lot of daunting security and performance issues. If a process thread had no privileges, the parent process would not be able to spawn independent threads. The parent process would have to perform each and every action requiring security privileges, affecting overall efficiency.

With Windows NT's impersonation calls, a parent process can spawn as many privileged threads as are needed to get the job done efficiently.

Understanding Connectivity

As distributed computing has grown, a number of standards for communications between client and server processes have evolved. Windows NT has been designed to provide the most extensive IPC support available under any current server-based operating system.

IPC (interprocess communication) enables processes to send messages to each other or signal when they are done. When properly managed, IPC greatly enhances the system's performance because processes can start and stop independent of each other.

The Microsoft LAN Manager standard of NetBEUI and Named Pipes is supported. Additionally, TCP/IP support for both Named Pipes and Sockets (the WinSockets API) and support for Novell's IPX/SPX standard are available. There is RPC support compatible with the OSF CE standard and DLC support for IBM SNA connectivity. Interfaces also are available to network-management protocols such as SNMP and SNA/NetView.

Understanding Remote Access Service

The Windows NT *remote access service (RAS)* provides remote access to Windows NT servers via modem for up to 64 simultaneous users.

A RAS user is integrated into the Windows NT network security system. After a RAS user is attached, you can access any server resources that are available to other network clients. You can implement callbacks for additional security, and passwords are encrypted and authenticated upon connection. RAS is optimized for client/server applications, with full IPC support available. A RAS administration utility is provided to control service, monitor usage, and manage access permissions.

Remote access service is initiated through the Remote Access Administration utility. After the Start Remote Access Service option has been selected from the Server menu, remote access to the target workstation is enabled (see fig. 20.5).

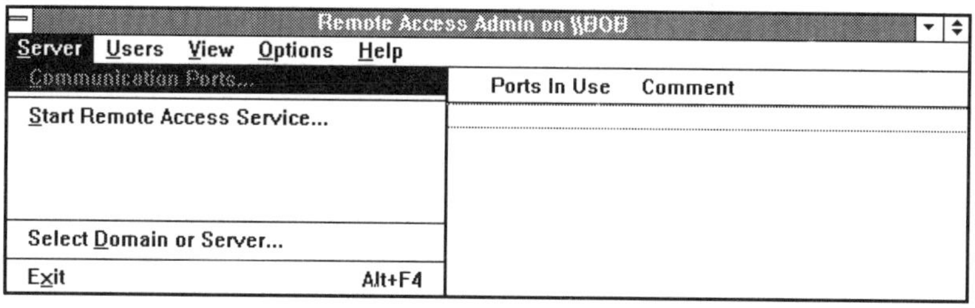

Figure 20.5

Starting remote access service.

For more information about RAS, see Chapter 18, "Using the Remote Access Service."

Macintosh Services

As part of the Windows NT Advanced Server package, Macintosh Services provides for the sharing of printers, files, and applications on the Macintosh (with no new software needed).

This service maintains the Macintosh "look and feel" by presenting AppleTalk file-sharing features such as long filenames and file/type associations. Full, bidirectional sharing of PostScript printers on both AppleTalk networks and Windows NT servers is supported, as well as automatic conversion of Apple PostScript to other printer setups specified on Windows NT servers.

You can manage Macintosh computers as part of the network, and you can connect them to client/server application, such as Microsoft SQL Server. Optional client software on the Macintosh enables DES password encryption.

Summary

This chapter has explored the principles of Windows NT client/server computing. Through its sophisticated security measures, fault-tolerant capabilities, disk striping, and interprocess-communications facilities, Windows NT is ideally suited for enterprise-computing environments.

Most user-account management can be mediated through the User Management utility from any workstation on the network. The remote access services (RAS) must be explicitly activated in the Remote Access Administration utility before dial-up access to the Windows NT system is enabled.

Part V

Appendices

Creating an Answer File

An answer file is just a list of answers to the questions Windows NT asks while users install Windows NT. When you want to perform an unattended Setup, you must specify these answers in an Answer file in the order that Setup asks for them, otherwise, Windows NT waits for user input—not a good thing when you want the installation to run automatically!

Syntax Rules in Answer Files

You can create an Answer file by using any text editor and by using the following rules:

♦ Semicolons (;) must start every comment.

♦ Never delete section names regardless of whether or not they contain information. Section names are marked by brackets, for example, [Unattended].

◆ Keynames (the variables you are setting) should never be changed.

◆ Blank spaces should go before and after equal signs, for example, keyname = value.

◆ Use double quotes to specify an empty value, for example, keyname = "".

◆ In the graphical part of Setup, each keyname is preceded by an exclamation point (!).

Template Answer File

The following Answer file provides a template for you to make your own. Make sure not to change the order of the keynames.

```
[Unattended]
Method = custom | express
; The method keyname determines whether Setup runs in
; custom or express mode. If in express mode, the user
; need not answer any other questions and the answer
; file can end here. The default value is the express
; mode which you can specify in one of two ways:
; Method = express
; or
; Method = " "
ConfirmHardware = yes | no
; The keyname specifies whether you want to confirm the
; mass storage devices found on your system, including
; SCSI hard disk drive and CD-ROM drives. Setup detects
; most hardware automatically. It is hard to run Setup
; unattended if you have to approve NT's detection of
; hardware, so go with the default,
;
; ConfirmHardware = no
NtUpgrade = manual | yes | no | single
;
; NtUpgrade specifies what to do when one or more
; versions of Windows or Windows NT are found on the
; boot drive.
; manual means that the user must specify whether an
;     installed version of Windows NT Workstation or
;     Windows NT Server needs upgrading and where the
```

```
;     upgrade should be installed. This value is not a
;     good choice for unattended installation.
; yes means that Setup should upgrade if a previous
;     version of Windows NT Workstation or Server is
;     found. If more than one version is found in the
;     system, upgrade the first one found (the first one
;     listed in BOOT.INI for x86 systems, or the first
;     one listed in the startup environment for PowerPC,
;     Alpha, and MIPS platforms).
; no means that Setup should not perform the upgrade if
;     a previous version of Windows NT Workstation or
;     Server is found.
; single means that Setup should only perform the
;     upgrade if a single, older version of Windows NT
;     Workstation or Server is found.
Win31Upgrade = yes | no
;
; This keyname specifies whether or not (yes or no,
; respectively) to install Windows NT if a version of
; Windows or Windows for Workgroups is found in the
; system. If you choose "no," the automated
; installation will fail here if Windows or Windows for
; Workgroups is found.
TargetPath = manual | * | <path>
;
; This keyname specifies whether or not the user is
; specifying the file where Windows NT will be
; installed. If you choose "manual," you must also
; specify the full pathname. If you choose "*," Setup
; creates a random, unique name in the target
; partition.
OverwriteOemFilesOnUpgrade = yes | no
;
; This keyname specifies whether or not OEM files of
; the same name as Windows NT files are overwritten by
; the Windows NT files. The default value is "yes."
; Uncomment the following line if you have an X86
; platform.
; [DetectedMassStorage]
; In this section you have the option of listing the
; mass storage devices in your system. The values you
; list in this section must match values in the [SCSI]
```

```
; section of the TXTSETUP.SIF file on the Setup boot
; floppy disks.
;
; If you uncomment the above line but leave the section
; empty, Setup assumes that there are no mass storage
; devices in the system.
;
; If you do not uncomment the line, Setup tries to
; detect the mass storage devices by loading all of
; the drivers included in the software distribution.
;
; If you know that your SCSI device is not supported
; by NT, you must list it here. If your devices are
; listed in the Hardware Compatibility Guide, you can
; let Setup detect them automatically.
;
; ******* GUI MODE *******
[GuiUnattended]
; !UpgradeEnableDhcp = yes | no
;
; This keyname specifies whether DHCP is configured
; automatically during an unattended installation.
; Uncomment this parameter only when upgrading Windows
; NT Server 3.1 with Microsoft TCP/IP installed.
;
; !DetachedProgram = <path>\<filename>
;
; If you have a custom program that should run
; concurrently with Setup, uncomment this line and
; specify the pathname and filename here, for example,
; !DetachedProgram = c:\mt32\mtrun.exe
;
!DetachedProgram = ""
;
; Null is the default value of the keyname.
;
; !Arguments = <path>\<filename>/<argument>
;
; Uncomment this line if your custom program specified
; in the previous keyname requires specific arguments,
; for example,
; !Arguments = c:\mt32\scriptl.pcd/H
```

```
!Arguments = ""
;
; This is the default value of the keyname.
; !SetupNetwork = yes | no
;
; This keyname specifies whether or not the computer
; will be connected to a network. If not, the network
; code is not installed thereby saving a significant
; amount of disk space.
;
!SetupApplications = YES
;
; This is the default value of the keyname.
;
; !AdvServerType = LANMANNT | SERVERNT
;
; This keyname is only used when installing NT Server.
; LANMANNT specifies that the computer will be the
; primary of backup domain controller.
;
; SERVERNT specifies that installation is happening on
; a standalone computer.
;
; !TimeZone = <time zone>
;
; This keyname specifies the time zone the user is in.
; This value must be supplied, otherwise Setup waits
; for user input. The following list shows you the
; possible values for this keyname.
;
;Time Zone List
;   (GMT) Greenwich Mean Time; Dublin, Edinburgh, London
;   (GMT+01:00) Lisbon, Warsaw
;   (GMT+01:00) Paris, Madrid
;   (GMT+01:00) Berlin, Stockholm, Rome, Bern, Brussels, ;       Vienna
;   (GMT+02:00) Eastern Europe
;   (GMT+01:00) Prague
;   (GMT+02:00) Athens, Helsinki, Istanbul
;   (GMT-03:00) Rio de Janeiro
;   (GMT-04:00) Atlantic Time (Canada)
;   (GMT-05:00) Eastern Time (US & Canada)
;   (GMT-06:00) Central Time (US & Canada)
```

```
;   (GMT-07:00) Mountain Time (US & Canada)
;   (GMT-08:00) Pacific Time (US & Canada); Tijuana
;   (GMT-09:00) Alaska
;   (GMT-10:00) Hawaii
;   (GMT-11:00) Midway Island, Samoa
;   (GMT+12:00) Wellington
;   (GMT+10:00) Brisbane, Melbourne, Sydney
;   (GMT+09:30) Adelaide
;   (GMT+09:00) Tokyo, Osaka, Sapporo, Seoul, Yakutsk
;   (GMT+08:00) Hong Kong, Perth, Singapore, Taipei
;   (GMT+07:00) Bangkok, Jakarta, Hanoi
;   (GMT+05:30) Bombay, Calcutta, Madras, New Delhi, ;   Colombo
;   (GMT+04:00) Abu Dhabi, Muscat, Tbilisi, Kazan,
;       Volgograd
;   (GMT+03:30) Tehran
;   (GMT+03:00) Baghdad, Kuwait, Nairobi, Riyadh
;   (GMT+02:00) Israel
;   (GMT-03:30) Newfoundland
;   (GMT-01:00) Azores, Cape Verde Is.
;   (GMT-02:00) Mid-Atlantic
;   (GMT) Monrovia, Casablanca
;   (GMT-03:00) Buenos Aires, Georgetown
;   (GMT-04:00) Caracas, La Paz
;   (GMT-05:00) Indiana (East)
;   (GMT-05:00) Bogota, Lima
;   (GMT-06:00) Saskatchewan
;   (GMT-06:00) Mexico City, Tegucigalpa
;   (GMT-07:00) Arizona
;   (GMT-12:00) Enewetak, Kwajalein
;   (GMT+12:00) Fiji, Kamchatka, Marshall Is.
;   (GMT+11:00) Magadan, Soloman Is., New Caledonia
;   (GMT+10:00) Hobart
;   (GMT+10:00) Guam, Port Moresby, Vladivostok
;   (GMT+09:30) Darwin
;   (GMT+08:00) Beijing, Chongqing, Urumqi
;   (GMT+06:00) Alma Ata, Dhaka
;   (GMT+05:00) Islamabad, Karachi, Sverdlovsk, Tashkent
;   (GMT+04:30) Kabul
;   (GMT+02:00) Cairo
;   (GMT+02:00) Harare, Pretoria
;   (GMT+03:00) Moscow, St. Petersburg
!TimeZone = "(GMT-08:00) Pacific Time (US & Canada); Tijuana"
```

```
[UserData]
!FullName = "Your full name"
;
; This keyname equals your full first and last names.
;
!OrgName = "Your organization name"
;
; This keyname equals your organization's name.
;
!ComputerName = MYCOMPUTER
;
; This keyname equals your computer's name.
;
!ProductId = "123456789012345"
;
; This keyname equals the serial number found on your
; Windows NT CD-ROM package.
[LicenseFilePrintData]
;
; This section pertains to Windows NT Server only, so
; we will skip the discussion in this section.
; !AutoMode = PerSeat | PerServer
; !AutoUsers = 0-999999
;
;
[NetworkAdapterData]
;
; In this section, if your system is connected to a
; network, find the network card it is using in the
; following list of network adapter cards and supply
; any information they require. The network adapter
; cards listed below can install automatically.
;
; When you find your network adapter card in the list
; below, express its value as a decimal not a
; hexidecimal, for example, use 768 not 0x300.
;
; !NetworkAddress = addressis treated as an ASCII.
;
; This keyword is the value of your computer's network
; address. This value must be a hexidecimal. Set this value to that of the
adapter card on
```

```
;
; !AutoNetInterfaceType = buss
;
; Normally, do not uncomment this line unless you have
; more than one bus of the same type and network. If
; your system does have that, you must specify which
; bus has the network adapter card.
;
; The following list gives appropriate settings for
; many network adapter cards. Uncomment the lines
; that match your network adapter card.
;
; !AutoNetOption = DEC100 | DEC101
; 1. DEC100 = "DEC EtherWORKS LC Adapter"
;    DEC101 = "DEC EtherWORKS Turbo/LC Adapter"
;
; [AdapterParameters]
;
; InterruptNumber = __
; IoBaseAddress = 1 | 2
; MemoryMappedBaseAddress = __
;     where IoBaseAddress = 1 -- Primary; 2 -- Secondary
;
; Optional:
;!AutoNetInterfaceType = 0 | 1 | 2 | 3 | ...
;     where 0 = Ms Jazz Internal Bus; 1 = ISA; 2 = EISA; 3 = MCA;
;           4 = TurboChannel; 5 = PCI bus; 6 -- VMEBus; 7 = NuBus;
;           8 = PCMCIABus; 9 = CBus; 10 = MPIBus; 11 =
;               MPSABus
;
; !AutoNetBusNumber = 0 | 1 | ...
;
;
; !AutoNetOption = DECETHERWORKSTURBO
; 2. DECETHERWORKSTURBO = "DEC EtherWORKS Turbo Adapter"
;
; [AdapterParameters]
;
;
; InterruptNumber = __
; IoBaseAddress = 1 | 2
; MemoryMappedBaseAddress = __
```

```
;      where IoBaseAddress = 1 -- Primary; 2 -- Secondary
;
; Optional:
;    !AutoNetInterfaceType = 0 | 1 | 2 | 3 |...
;    !AutoNetBusNumber = 0 | 1 | ...
;
;
; !AutoNetOption = DEC422
; 3. DEC422 = "DEC EtherWORKS Turbo EISA Adapter"
;
;
; !AutoNetOption = DECSTAT
; 4. DECSTAT = "DEC Turbo Channel Ethernet Adapter"
;
; Optional:
;    !AutoNetInterfaceType = 0 | 1 | 2 | 3 |...
;    !AutoNetBusNumber = 0 | 1 | ...
;
;
; !AutoNetOption = DECPC
; 5. DECPC = "DEC EtherWORKS DEPCA"
;
; Optional:
;    !AutoNetInterfaceType = 0 | 1 | 2 | 3 |...
;    !AutoNetBusNumber = 0 | 1 | ...
;
;
;
; !AutoNetOption = ELNK16
; 6. ELNK16 = "3Com Etherlink16/EtherLink16 TP Adapter"
;
; [AdapterParameters]
;
; InterruptNumber = __
; IoBaseAddress = __
; MemoryMappedBaseAddress = __
; MemoryMappedSize = __
; Transceiver = 1 | 2
; ZeroWaitState = 1 | 0
;     where Transceiver   = 1 - External ; 2 - On Board
;           ZeroWaitState = 1 - ON        ; 0 - OFF
;
```

```
; Optional:
;    !AutoNetInterfaceType = 0 | 1 | 2 | 3 |...
;    !AutoNetBusNumber = 0 | 1 | ...
;
;
;
; !AutoNetOption = ELNKII
; 7. ELNKII = "3Com Etherlink II Adapter (also II/16
; and II/16 TP)"
;
; [AdapterParameters]
; InterruptNumber == __
; IOBaseAddress = __
; Transceiver = 1 | 2
; MemoryMapped = 0 | 1
;    where Transceiver = 1 - External; 2 - On Board
;         MemoryMapped = 1 - ON; 0 - OFF
; Optional:
;    !AutoNetInterfaceType = 0 | 1 | 2 ...
;    !AutoNetBusNumber = 0 | 1 | ...
;
;
;
; !AutoNetOption = ELNK3ISA509
; 8. ELNK3ISA509 = "3Com Etherlink III Adapter"
;
; [AdapterParameters]
;
; InterruptNumber = __
; Transceiver = 1 | 2 | 3
; IoBaseAddress = __
;    where Transceiver = 0 — 10 Base T
;                        1 — Thick Net (AUI/DIX)
;                        2 — Thin Net (BNC/COAX)
;
; Optional:
;    !AutoNetInterfaceType = 0 | 1 | 2 | 3 |...
;    !AutoNetBusNumber = 0 | 1 | ...
;
;
;
; !AutoNetOption = ELNK3EISA
```

```
;  9. ELNK3EISA = "3Com Etherlink III EISA Adapter"
;
;
;
;  !AutoNetOption = EE16
;  10. EE16 = "Intel Ether Express 16 LAN Adapter"
;
;  [AdapterParameters]
;
;  InterruptNumber = __
;  IoChannelReady = 1 | 2 | 3
;  Transceiver = 1 | 2 | 3
;  IoBaseAddress = __
;     where IoChannelReady = 1 - Early
;                          = 2 - Late
;                          = 3 - Never
;              Transceiver = 1 -- Thick Net (AUI/DIX)
;                          = 2 -- Thin Net (BNC/COAX)
;                          = 3 -- Twisted-Pair (TPE)
;
;  Optional:
;   !AutoNetInterfaceType = 0 | 1 | 2 | 3 |...
;   !AutoNetBusNumber = 0 | 1 | ...
;
;
;
;  !AutoNetOption = LOOP
;  11. LOOP = "MS Loopback Adapter"
;
;  [AdapterParameters]
;
;  Medium = 0 | 1 | 2
;    where Medium = 0 - 802.3; 1 - 802.5; 2 - Fddi
;
;
;
;  !AutoNetOption = LT200MC
;  12. LT200MC = "DayStar Digital LocalTalk Adapter
;               (MCA)"
;
;
;
;
```

```
; !AutoNetOption = LT200
; 13. LT200 = "DayStar Digital LocalTalk Adapter"
;
; [AdapterParameters]
;
; IOBaseAddress = __
;
; Optional:
;   !AutoNetInterfaceType = 0 | 1 | 2 | 3 |...
;   !AutoNetBusNumber = 0 | 1 | ...
;
;
;
; !AutoNetOption = NE1000
; 14. NE1000 = "Novell NE1000 Adapter"
;
; [AdapterParameters]
;
; InterruptNumber = __
; IOBaseAddress = __
; Optional:
;     !AutoNetInterfaceType = 0 | 1 | 2 | 3 |...
;     !AutoNetBusNumber = 0 | 1 | ...
;
;
;
; !AutoNetOption = NE2000
; 15. NE2000 = "Novell NE2000 Adapter"
;
; [AdapterParameters]
;
; InterruptNumber = __
; IOBaseAddress = __
;
; Optional:
;     !AutoNetInterfaceType = 0 | 1 | 2 | 3 |...
;     !AutoNetBusNumber = 0 | 1 | ...
;
;
;
; !AutoNetOption = NE3200
; 16. NE3200 = "Novell NE3200 EISA Adapter"
```

```
;
;
;
; !AutoNetOption = BONSAI | NETFLX | CPQTOK
; 17. BONSAI = "COMPAQ DualPort Ethernet Controller"
;     NETFLX = "COMPAQ 32-Bit NetFlex/NetFlex-2 Controller"
;     CPQTOK = "COMPAQ 32-Bit DualSpeed Token-Ring Controller"
;
;
;
; !AutoNetOption = NPEISA
; 18. NPEISA = "Network Peripherals FDDI, EISA"
;
;
;
; !AutoNetOption = P1390
; 19. P1390 = "Proteon p1390 Adapter"
;
; [AdapterParameters]
;
; InterruptNumber = __
; IOBaseAddress = __
; DMAChannel = __
; CableType = 1 | 2
; CardSpeed = 4 | 16
; NetworkAddress = __
;   where CableType = 1 -- UTP; 2 -- STP
;
; Optional:
;   !AutoNetInterfaceType = 0 | 1 | 2 | 3 |...
;   !AutoNetBusNumber = 0 | 1 | ...
;
;
;
; !AutoNetOption = P1990
; 20. P1990 = "Proteon p1990 Adapter"
;
; [AdapterParameters]
;
; NetworkAddress = __
;
;
```

```
;
; !AutoNetOption = SONICEISA
; 21. SONICEISA = "SONIC, EISA"
;
;
;
; !AutoNetOption = IBMTOK2ISA
; 22. IBMTOK2ISA = "IBM Token-Ring Network 16/4 ISA Adapter II"
;
; [AdapterParameters]
;
; IOBaseAddress = __
; NetworkAddress = __
;
; Optional:
;    !AutoNetInterfaceType = 0 | 1 | 2 | 3 |...
;    !AutoNetBusNumber = 0 | 1 | ...
;
;
;
; !AutoNetOption = IBMTOK2E
; 23. IBMTOK2E = "IBM Token Ring EISA Adapter"
;
; [AdapterParameters]
;
; NetworkAddress = __
;
;
;
;
; !AutoNetOption = IBMTOK
; 24. IBMTOK = "IBM Token Ring Adapter"
;
; [AdapterParameters]
;
; IOBaseAddress = 1 | 2
; NetworkAddress =
;    where IoBaseAddress = 1 -- Primary; 2 -- Secondary
;
; Optional:
;    !AutoNetInterfaceType = 0 | 1 | 2 | 3 | ...
;    !AutoNetBusNumber = 0 | 1 | ...
```

```
;
;
;
; !AutoNetOption = UBPC | UBPCEOTP
; 25. UBPC = "Ungermann-Bass Ethernet NIUpc Adapter"
;      UBPCEOTP = "Ungermann-Bass Ethernet NIUpc/EOTP Adapter"
;
; [AdapterParameters]
;
; InterruptNumber = __
; IOBaseAddress = __
; MemoryMappedBaseAddress = __
;
; Optional:
;    !AutoNetInterfaceType = 0 | 1 | 2 | 3 |...
;    !AutoNetBusNumber = 0 | 1 | —
;
;
;
; !AutoNetOption = SMCISA
; 26. SMCISA = "SMC (WD) EtherCard"
;
; [AdapterParameters]
;
; InterruptNumber = __
; IOBaseAddress = __
; MemoryMappedBaseAddress = __
;
; Optional:
;    !AutoNetInterfaceType = 0 | 1 | 2 | 3 |...
;    !AutoNetBusNumber = 0 | 1 | ...
;
;
;
; !AutoNetOption = AM1500T | AM1500T1 | AM1500T2
; 27. AM1500T = "Advanced Micro Devices
; AM2100/AM1500T/PCnet Adapter"—X86 specific
; AM1500T1 = "Novell/Anthem NE1500T Adapter"— x86
; specific AM1500T2 = "Novell/Anthem NE2100 Adapter "—
; x86 specific
;
; [AdapterParameters]
```

```
;
; InterruptNumber = __
; IOBaseAddress = __
; DMAChannel = __
;
; Optional:
;   !AutoNetInterfaceType = 0 | 1 | 2 | 3 | ...
;   !AutoNetBusNumber = 0 | 1 | ...
;
;
;
; !AutoNetOption = ELNKMC
; 28. ELNKMC = "3Com 3C523 Etherlink/MC Adapter"-- x86
; specific
;
;
;
; !AutoNetOption = ELNK3MCA
; 29. ELNK3MCA = "3Com Etherlink III MCA Adapter"-- x86
; specific
;
;
;
; !AutoNetOption = NPMCA
; 30. NPMCA = "Network Peripherals FDDI, MCA"-- x86
; specific
;
;
;
; !AutoNetOption = NE2000MCA
; 31. NE2000MCA = "NE/2 and compatible MC Adapter"--
; x86 specific
;
; If the network adapter card is UB NE2000 POS ID =
; 24863 you must also
; specify the following:
;
; [AdapterParameters]
;
; InterruptNumber = __
; IoBaseAddress = __
;
```

```
;
;
;
; !AutoNetOption = IBMTOKMC
; 32. IBMTOKMC = "IBM Token Ring Adapter /A"-- x86
; specific
;
; [AdapterParameters]
;
; NetworkAddress = __
;
;
;
; !AutoNetOption = UBPS
; 33. UBPS = "Ungermann-Bass Ethernet NIUps Adapter "--
; x86 specific
;
;
;
; !AutoNetOption = P189X
; 34. P189X = Proteon ProNET - 4/16 p189X NIC
;
; [AdapterParameters]
;
; CardSpeed = 4 | 16
; PacketSize = 4210 | 17986
; NetworkAddress = __
;  Note: If CardSpeed is 4, PacketSize should be 4210.
;  If CardSpeed is 16, PacketSize should be 17986.
;
;
;
; !AutoNetOption = WD8003EA | WD8003WA | WD8013WPA |
; WD8013EPA
; 35. WD8003EA = "SMC (WD) 8003E /A" -- x86 specific
;     WD8003WA = "SMC (WD) 8003W /A"
;     WD8013WPA = "SMC (WD) 8013WP /A"
;     WD8013EPA = "SMC (WD) 8013EP /A"
;
;
;
; !AutoNetOption = SONIC
```

```
; 36. SONIC = "ARC Built-in Ethernet Adapter"-- MIPS
; specific
;
;
;
; !OEMNetOption = yes
; 37. OEM adapter installation
;
; To specify an OEM network adapter card, you have to
; set the !OEMNetOption equal to YES. The location of
; the OEMSETUP.INF file and the driver files for the
; particular network card must be set using the
; !OEMNetInfFile and OEMNetDrive keys respectively.
; Driver files include the .SYS file and the tag file
; mentioned in the .INF file.
;
; !OEFINetInfFile = b:\oemsetup.inf
; !OEMNetDrive = b:\
; !AutoNetOption = <adapter_card_name> (defined in
; OEMSETUP.INF file)
;
;
; [AdapterParameters]
;
; The actual parameters are defined in the OEM
; installation .INF file.
```

A Network Adapter Card Example Configuration

If you went step by step through the template Answer file, you should now have an Answer file you can use for automatically installing Windows NT Workstation.

The following Answer file is provided by Microsoft as an example. This example uses the following settings:

◆ Network Adapter card = ELNKII

◆ IRQ = 2

◆ Port Address = 0x300

◆ McmoryMapped OFF

◆ Transceiver = External

```
; Example Network Adapter Card Configuration.
;
;     !AutoNetOption = ELNKII
;
;     [AdapterParameters]
;
;     InterruptNumber = 2
;     IOBaseAddress = 768
;     Transceiver = 1
;     MemoryMapped = 0
;
!AutoNetOption = ELNKII
[AdapterParameters]
InterruptNumber = 2
IoBaseAddress = 768
Transceiver = 1
MemoryMapped = 0
[TransportData]
; !InstallNWLink = 1 | 0
; !InstallNetBEUI = 1 | 0
; !InstallTCPIP = 1 | 0
; The specified keys set the IPX transports that should
; be installed on the computer.
; 1 indicates that the specified transport should be
; installed on the computer.
; 0 indicates that the transport should not be
; installed.
; Default:  0
; !AUTONETIPXFRAMETYPE = 255 | 0 | 1 | 2 | 3 | 4
;       Specify the NWLink Frame Type if !InstallNWLink
;            -- 1.
;       where 255 = AutoDetect; 0 = EtherNEt;
;       1 = 802.3; 2 = 802.2; 3 = SNAP; 4 = ARCNET
;
!InstallNWLink = 1
!AUTONETIPXFRAMETYPE = 255
!InstallNetBEUI = 1
```

```
!InstallTCPIP = 1
[DomainData]
; !AutoWorkGroup = <workgroup_name>
;
; The AutoWorkGroup key is used to indicate the name of
; a work group to join.
; !AutoDomain = <domain_name>
; The AutoDomain key is used to indicate the name of
; a domain to join.
; !AutoWorkGroup and AutoDomain are mutually exclusive.
; Specify only one of the two options.
!AutoWorkGroup = MYWORKGROUP
; !AutoPrimary = yes | no
; The !AutoPrimary key is used to indicate whether the
; computer is a primary or backup domain controller.
; Use the key when the !AdvServerType is equal to
; LANMANNT. The !AutoPrimary key is ignored
; when the !AdvServerType equals SERVERNT because the
; computer is a server. The !AutoPrimary key requires
; that a domain name be specified in the !AutoDomain
; key. If errors occur, a Domain/Workgroup Settings
; dialog box is displayed which requires user input.
; Currently, usernames and passwords cannot be passed
; when joining a domain. Therefore, before beginning an
; unattended Setup, a system administrator must create
; machine accounts in the domain using Server Manager.
; Yes indicates that the computer is a primary domain
; controller.
;
; No indicates that the computer is a backup domain
; controller.
; Default:  No
```

Learning How to Perform Basic Tasks with Windows NT

Paradoxically, as operating systems have become much more powerful and architecturally complex, they also have become easier to use. Today's state-of-the-art operating systems (particularly Windows NT and OS/2) are graphical environments, in which you use a pointing device to perform many actions instead of typing arcane instructions at a command prompt. New Windows NT users should take comfort in the fact that the graphical nature of Windows NT makes it easy to navigate and use.

This chapter begins a discussion of the very basic tools you use when you interact with the Windows NT interface. An *interface* is what an operating system uses to interact with a user.

This chapter also talks about the concept of Common User Access (CUA), by which basic commands (such as opening or printing a file) are done similarly across different applications. The following topics are covered:

- ◆ Examining the Windows NT interface

- ◆ Using the mouse

◆ Working with windows and icons

◆ Performing common Windows tasks

◆ Introducing WYSIWYG and MDI

Historically, the interface used in most operating system environments has been the *command-line interface* (CLI), and the operating system is represented by the *command prompt* (C:> on most MS-DOS systems, $ on most Unix systems). You enter commands at the command prompt by typing at the keyboard. The prompt tells you that the computer is ready to receive information. To start a program, type the program's name, and press Enter.

In most operating systems, simple file-manipulation commands consist of two words: a verb followed by a noun, as in the MS-DOS command DELETE MYFILE.TST. Commands can be complex (involving other nouns and options), and the command-line interface can be intimidating to the novice user. Although MS-DOS and OS/2 commands are based on the English language, they can appear cryptic (for example, RD stands for Remove Directory in DOS). Unix commands are famous for being cryptic because most consist of such a two-letter abbreviation.

In Windows NT, this verb-noun process is reversed. First, you select the item to be manipulated, then you indicate the action to be performed. The action can involve moving the mouse and clicking the mouse button, selecting an item from a menu, or entering text from the keyboard. In many cases, especially within applications in which the same item is manipulated a number of times, the item already is selected by Windows NT, and you need to specify only the action; for example, in a word processing program, you might highlight a word and then make it bold, italicized, and underlined. The word remains highlighted after you perform each of these actions.

Using a Graphical Interface

As you have learned, Windows NT is a graphical user interface (GUI) that dramatically changes the way in which users interact with the computer. To become comfortable with the Windows NT environment, you must get used to a different way of doing things. Instead of entering commands at a prompt, you use the keyboard or mouse to manipulate symbols on the screen. This collection of symbols is the heart of the Windows NT environment.

As you enter Windows NT after logging on, you see the Windows NT desktop. The term *desktop* often is used to refer to the entire Windows NT environment. Technically, the desktop is the screen background for Windows NT, but the term is used to signify all the things you see when you look at the Windows NT screen (like the items on an office desktop). Each new task is run within individual display areas called *windows*.

Note Many users who are used to DOS and Unix find multiple windows a curiosity because few DOS or Unix programs have exotic options that give you new ways to look at your documents.

If you use a spreadsheet, for example, you can use one window for the data-input area; another window can show the grand totals for the worksheet. As you enter new numbers, you see the effect in terms of total expenditures on the bottom line, even hundreds of rows below. You even can compare two versions of a letter you are writing, or you can keep an outline in one window while writing the body of your text in another.

Using the Mouse

While in Windows NT, most actions are performed by using a mouse or other pointing device. Although there are keyboard equivalents for most mouse actions, they are cumbersome to use. Even though a mouse is not required to run Windows NT, you need a pointing device to be productive in the graphical environment.

For many users of character-based environments, it is difficult to learn to use the mouse. Typically, these users learned how to use the keyboard to interact with the computer. Now, the action of removing their hands from the keys is foreign to their standard way of working. After they work with a mouse for a short period of time, however, the actions become second nature.

Note A single mouse action can replace several commands that you must type and execute individually at the command prompt.

The location of the mouse is represented on-screen by the *pointer* (sometimes described as the *mouse cursor*). The standard pointer is the arrow, as shown in figure B.1.

The pointer and the mouse move together. By sliding the mouse away from you, you move the pointer up on the display. By pulling the mouse toward you, you move the pointer down on the display. Side-to-side motions move the pointer to the left and right on the display. This activity of changing the location of the mouse pointer is often called *pointing* in Windows NT.

Note Windows NT enables you to choose a custom mouse cursor. Chapter 11, "Configuring and Customizing the Windows NT Desktop," describes ways to customize your mouse cursor.

Figure B.1

*The location of
the mouse,
represented by the
arrow pointer.*

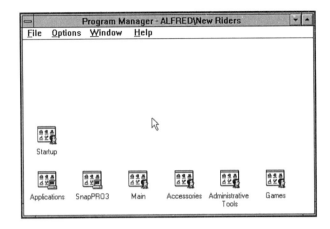

Besides pointing, there are four other mouse actions; each one has an action associated with it that application programs exploit. These mouse actions are described in the following sections.

Clicking with the Mouse

Mouse actions are performed by using the mouse buttons. In a standard Windows NT environment, the left mouse button is the select button. Depressing and releasing the mouse button is referred to as *clicking* the button. In most situations, clicking the mouse button while the pointer is over an object selects that object, causing it to become active. The item actually is selected when the mouse button is first pressed; releasing the button completes the action.

If you click on a menu name, the menu opens and becomes active. If you click on a menu option, the associated command becomes active, and it executes. If you click on an application icon, it becomes active and displays its Control menu. If you click on a window, it becomes the active window. If you click on a window's workspace, you move the insertion point.

In addition to activating objects on-screen, you also can use the click to execute an action. For example, dialog boxes often have OK and Cancel buttons. By clicking the OK button on the Open dialog box, you open the specified file. If you click the Cancel button instead, the dialog box closes without taking any additional action (that is, opening a file).

Note   Because a click action is not performed until you release the mouse button, you can cancel a click action in progress by moving the mouse pointer away from the object before releasing the mouse button.

One mouse click saves you multiple keystrokes when you have to cycle through a list of objects on the screen or move the cursor from the lower-right corner to the upper-left corner. The mouse enables you to be more efficient.

 Note By default, the left mouse button is used to select an object. However, you can change your mouse configuration to enable the right button to act as the select button. Instructions are given in Chapter 11.

Double-Clicking with the Mouse

Double-clicking is pressing the mouse button twice in rapid succession (usually within one-half of a second). Double-clicking has a rhythm to it, so do not be disappointed if it takes some time to get the hang of it. Double-clicking activates an object and causes it to take a predefined action.

If the two clicks are not done within the time limit, the action is seen as two separate clicks rather than as one double-click. The double-click action typically is used to start applications and open new windows.

Double-clicking on an icon, for example, activates the icon and causes it to open and display the associated window (see fig. B.2). Each type of icon opens and displays its window differently. It might launch a new application, for instance, or display information present in memory.

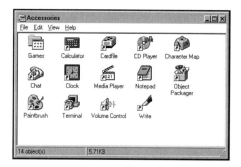

Figure B.2

The result of double-clicking on the Accessories program-item icon.

 Note Double-clicking on the icon on the left side of the title bar selects the **C**lose option in the Control menu. You can exit any window that has an icon in the title bar in this manner.

Dragging an Object

Many actions within the Windows NT environment involve changing the position of an item on-screen by *dragging* the item to a new location. To drag an item, position the pointer over the item, press the mouse button, move the mouse to the new location (while still holding down the mouse button), and then release the mouse button. Each of these steps serves a specific function.

The first item is selected by positioning the pointer over the item and pressing the mouse button. Because the action is not yet completed, the mouse button is not yet released. Moving the mouse moves the items, and when the item is in its new location, the action is completed by releasing the mouse button. Although this combination of actions might seem awkward at first, it quickly becomes a simple task.

Dragging can dramatically affect objects. If you drag the title bar of a window, the entire window moves about on the screen. Dragging a window border changes the window's size. Dragging an icon moves it about on the screen. Dragging the insertion point selects an area of the workspace.

Dragging is like using the arrow-control key combinations in DOS programs. Screen items change position, and you can mark screen blocks for block operations. Using the mouse to perform such actions is faster than using the keyboard, and boosts efficiency. Figure B.3 shows a result of dragging.

Figure B.3

The result of dragging on the workspace.

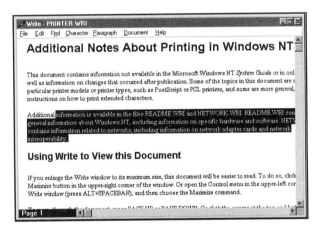

 Note   Dragging in Windows NT is like using the keyboard to mark screen blocks in programs that run under other, nongraphical operating systems.

Dragging-and-Dropping

The final mouse action is called *dragging-and-dropping*. In this action, you drag an object with the mouse as previously described. The goal of dragging the object is not to change its location on the screen, but to take an action on the object. You drag the object over another object—one that is capable of taking action on the object you are dragging. Then you release the mouse button, dropping the dragged object on its destination. The destination object opens and takes a default action on the dropped object.

File Manager is one application in which you can put drag-and-drop to good use. You can, for example, select a text file from the file list and drag-and-drop it on an open Notepad window; this action causes Notepad to open the text file automatically.

You also can drag-and-drop a file name onto a directory icon to move the file from its current path into the chosen directory. Or you can copy a selected file to another drive by dragging-and-dropping the file name onto a drive icon. Thus, in File Manager, dragging-and-dropping automates an open, move, or copy operation. Dragging-and-dropping enables you to perform very complex processes with a fraction of the effort of typing commands at a command prompt. As a result, you gain in productivity.

Use the following exercise to become familiar with basic mouse actions:

1. Click on the Start button and click on the Programs option.

2. Click on the Accessories program group by double-clicking on the icon labeled Accessories.

3. Select the Notepad icon by moving the mouse, placing the pointer over the icon labeled Notepad, and pressing the select button once. This process is known as *clicking* on the item.

4. Select the Write icon by placing the mouse on the icon and clicking it.

5. Double-click on the Notepad icon. This process opens the Notepad program.

6. Place the pointer at the bottom-right corner of Notepad's window so that the pointer changes to a double diagonal arrow.

7. To resize the Notepad window, drag the window by pressing and holding the select button, moving the mouse to make Notepad's window smaller, and then releasing the select button.

8. Double-click on Notepad's title bar, which is located at the top of the program. It shows the name of the application or document.

9. Click on Notepad's minimize button, which is the button with the dash in the upper-right corner of the Notepad window.

You can see that manipulating items in the Windows NT environment is an easy task when you use the mouse.

Windows NT often uses a three-dimensional appearance for buttons and other screen objects. Usually, these 3-D objects "move" when you click on them with the mouse—indicating that the mouse click is seen by Windows NT.

Using the Mouse Pointer

Within the Windows NT environment, the pointer often changes to indicate the type of action being performed. Figure B.4 shows several common Windows NT pointers. These pointers inform the user that Windows NT is ready to perform a special type of task.

Figure B.4

Pointer appearance indicates Windows NT's current function.

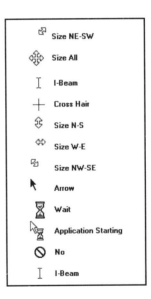

When resizing an object, the pointer changes to a multiheaded arrow. The directions of the arrows indicate the directions that the object can be moved. When moving an object, the pointer changes to a ghost of the object. A *ghost*, within Windows NT, is an object that is represented with a light gray outline or a special picture.

One of the most common (and least loved) pointers is the hourglass, which appears when Windows NT is performing a task that requires you to wait. Although it is annoying to have to wait, the hourglass lets you know that the system still is functioning.

Note Because Windows NT is a multithreaded and multitasking operating system, a new mouse cursor that combines the arrow and the hourglass has been added. It shows you that the system is busy with one application, but that you are free to continue work with others.

Users familiar with Windows 3.1 also know that the hourglass rarely appears over the background layer of the desktop in Windows NT. Usually it appears only while the cursor is over a busy application. One of the advantages of multithreading and multitasking strategies employed in Windows NT is that you can work with other applications even though one application is busy.

When working with text in Windows NT, the standard pointer is replaced with a steadily flashing dark vertical bar called the *insertion point*. This bar indicates the location at which new text is inserted when you start typing. This mouse pointer looks like a capital I.

A related pointer is referred to as the *I-beam pointer* because of its shape. This mouse pointer tells you where you will move the insertion point if you click at the current location of the mouse. The I-beam appears when you move the mouse pointer over a window in which you can insert text, and tells you that the mouse action you would perform by clicking is the relocation of the insertion point. It also tells you that you can select text by dragging.

The following exercise illustrates the way Windows NT changes the pointer according to the current action. Follow these steps:

1. Select the Notepad window by clicking inside it with the mouse.

2. Place the pointer inside the Notepad window and notice the shape of the pointer. It changes to the I-beam pointer.

3. Move the pointer into the title bar. The pointer changes back to the arrow pointer.

4. Place the pointer on the top window border. The pointer changes to an up/down arrow to indicate window resizing.

You see from this exercise that Windows NT gives you visual clues about the function of the pointer as the task changes. Windows NT also uses the shape of the pointer to give you information about your actions, as is the case with the prevent pointer.

Working with Windows and Application Buttons

As its name suggests, the basic element of the Windows NT interface is a *window*, which is a rectangular area on the screen that displays information from a program. A window can be expanded to cover the entire screen. In this state, the window is said to be *maximized*.

If you no longer need to view the information in the window, but you want to keep it active, you can reduce the window to an *application button* (a small button on the Taskbar). Reducing a window to an application button is referred to as *minimizing* a window. To restore the application button to a window, single click on its application button in the Taskbar. Figure B.5 shows several common Windows applications as windows and as application buttons in the Taskbar.

Figure B.5

Program windows and application buttons on the desktop.

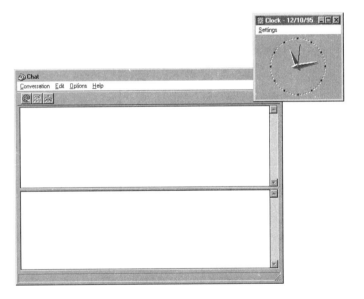

Each Windows NT application has its own window, referred to as a *parent window* or *application window*. The coordination of the parent windows is managed by the Windows NT environment.

Each application may in turn contain windows of its own. These windows, called *child windows* or *document windows*, are managed by the application. The terms *child window* and *parent window* are used when discussing the window's relationships; the terms *application window* and *document window* are used when discussing the window's contents.

Note If an application supports child windows, it is said to have a multiple document interface (MDI). For more information on working with an MDI application, see the discussion later in this chapter.

Individual windows are similar to flexible sheets of paper: you can stack them on top of each other or place them side by side. You can resize windows to display as little or as much of the information as you want. You can change the position or size of the window without changing its content. The view you see through a window is like a landscape being viewed through a video-camera lens; there is a big world out there, but you can see only what is directly in front of the camera.

If you make the view or aperture smaller, you see less of the same view. To see an item that is not in the current view, increase the amount of information in the view (make the view larger). If that does not work, move the camera. If you want to maintain your first view and see another item, get a second camera (open a new window).

Not all of the spreadsheet can be shown within a document window. To view the remainder of the spreadsheet, you can think of moving the window over the part of the spreadsheet that you want to see.

Basic Window Elements

All windows within the Windows NT environment have the same basic set of elements. These elements enable you to manipulate the window's view and its position. Each component is used to perform a specific Windows-management task. As with all actions within Windows NT, each of the tasks associated with managing windows can be accomplished in a number of distinct ways. Figure B.6 shows these window elements.

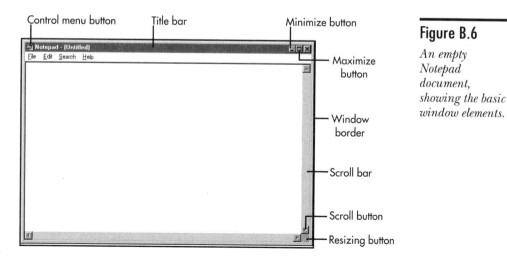

Figure B.6

An empty Notepad document, showing the basic window elements.

The window components are discussed in the following sections.

Window Border

The *border* around each window can be used to change the size and shape of the window. If you grab the side of the window, you can change only the position of that side. By grabbing a corner, you change the dimensions of both neighboring sides. When you place the mouse on the border or corner, the mouse pointer changes into a double-headed arrow, enabling you to drag the window border to enlarge or shrink the window.

 Note The shape of the pointer when it is over a window border indicates the way in which the window can be resized. The pointer changes to a pair of vertical arrows (resize vertically), a pair of horizontal arrows (resize horizontally), or a pair of diagonal arrows (resize diagonally).

The lower-right corner of most windows is an empty square. This square, often called the *resizing button*, also can be used to change the size of the window. Because it is larger than the window border, the resizing button is much easier to grab. You can move the bottom and right sides of the window by dragging the resizing button. When you try to position a window accurately, position the upper-left corner of the window by dragging on the title bar, and then use the resizing button to position the remaining two sides.

 Note Not all Windows NT programs provide a resizing button. The Windows NT applets Write and Notepad, for example, do not; Excel and Word for Windows resize in this manner.

Scroll Bars

If a program contains more information than can fit in a window, vertical and horizontal *scroll bars* appear along the right and bottom sides of the window. If all information is displayed within the current window, scroll bars are not needed (many applications thus do not display them). As shown in figure B.7, Clock does not have scroll bars. Because you can see only one thing inside the window—a clock—you have no need to scroll its window. Notice, however, that the Clock window has all the other window components.

The scroll bar along the bottom shifts the view across the document; the scroll bar along the right side moves up and down through the document. If the document is too large in one direction, only one set of scroll bars appears. A word-processing document, for example, may be too long to be displayed in a single view, so the scroll

bars on the right side appear. If the document is narrow enough to fit in the window, however, the bottom scroll bars may not appear. Figure B.8 shows a long list within a Notepad window.

Figure B.7

Clock's display does not require scroll bars.

Figure B.8

Notepad always displays scroll bars.

The *scroll buttons* are used to move the document view in the indicated direction. By clicking on the scroll button at the bottom of the scroll bar, you move the view down through the document. You can make the view scroll down (or up) the document by pointing to the scroll button and holding down the mouse button.

To move quickly through the document, you also can drag the *scroll box* along the scroll bar. If you know that the text you are looking for is two-thirds of the way down your document, for example, you can drag the scroll box to a position two-thirds down the scroll bar. When you release the mouse button, the view jumps to the new location.

 Note   Besides the scroll bars, most applications allow you to scroll document windows by using the Page Up and Page Down keys.

You can move the view down the document to display the next full window of information by clicking in the scrolling region below the scroll box. Or, by clicking above the scroll box, you move the view up one full window. This technique is recommended for reading through a document. Most programs move slightly less than a full window to enable you to recognize the transition between images.

The Control Menu

On the far left of the title bar is an icon of the application in the window. The icon functions as a button that activates the Control menu, which is a special menu that is a part of both icons and windows. You can click on the Control menu button of a Windows NT application to display the Control menu, as shown in figure B.9.

Figure B.9

All Windows NT applications have the same items on the Control menu.

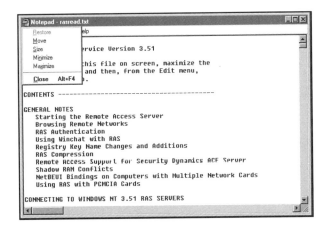

The same Control menu is displayed by clicking on a program icon on the Windows NT desktop. The Control menu is available even when an application is running full-screen. To display the Control menu for a maximized window, press Alt+spacebar or Alt+hyphen.

 Note The Windows NT environment enables you to continue using your MS-DOS and POSIX-compliant Unix application programs. A DOS or POSIX application that runs under the Windows NT environment is said to run within a DOS or POSIX window.

Windows NT enables DOS programs to use graphics mode and text mode when running in a window. Most DOS and POSIX windows have the Control menu, as shown in figure B.10.

Most of the commands on the Control menu are for tasks that can be performed by manipulating the window with the mouse. One of the requirements of the Windows NT user interface is that all tasks also can be performed by using the keyboard. The Control menu provides a way of moving, resizing, and controlling windows by using

the keyboard. These commands appear on all Control menus (whether from an application, document, DOS, or POSIX window).

	PWB
Restore	
Move	
Size	
Minimize	
Maximize	
Close	
Switch To...	Ctrl+Esc
Edit	▶
Settings...	
Fonts...	
Screen Size And Position...	
Screen Colors...	
Hide Mouse Pointer	

Figure B.10

The Control menu.

◆ The **R**estore command is available in Control menus when an application is maximized or minimized. This command is used to return a window to the position and size it was before it was maximized to full-screen or minimized.

◆ The **M**ove command is active only when a window is not full-screen. When you choose it, the mouse pointer changes to a four-arrow pointer. By pressing an arrow key, you can move the current window. You can continue to use the arrow keys to move the window in small increments, or you can move the mouse. The window moves with the mouse without your having to press the mouse button; clicking (or pressing Esc) stops the window's movement and deselects the command. A window also can be moved by dragging the title bar to the new location. Press Enter to end the procedure.

Note Some actions are quicker to perform by using the keyboard. When you use a DOS program in a window and you want to switch to full-screen mode, for example, press Alt+Enter. To perform the same action by using the mouse, you must select the program's control button and choose the Ma**x**imize command.

◆ The **S**ize option is available only when a window is not full-screen. When you choose **S**ize, the pointer changes to a four-arrow mouse pointer (as with the **M**ove command). You can press any arrow key to select a border, and you then can extend or shrink that dimension of the window. If you press the right arrow once, for example, the right border is selected; if you press the right arrow again, the right border expands to enlarge the window. If you press the left arrow, however, the right border shrinks to reduce the window's size.

Note You also can select a corner by first selecting one side and then using the arrow to select one of the adjacent sides. You now can expand the window in two directions. Press Enter to end the procedure.

◆ The Minimize option shrinks the current program to an icon; it is not available when a program already is minimized to an icon.

◆ The Maximize command is available for both icons and windows, enlarging the current window to fill the screen. (These commands perform the same tasks as the minimize and maximize buttons on the right side of the menu bar.)

◆ The Close option is used to close a document window or to quit a program. If the Control menu is for an application, Close quits the program. The same task can be performed by double-clicking on the Control menu button. If you forget to save the contents of a document window before you choose Close, Windows NT asks whether you want to save the document before closing.

◆ Clicking on the Run option displays the Run window, which allows you to display the Clipboard or the Control Panel.

The following exercise takes you through some of the options in a Control menu:

1. Select the Notepad window, then choose the Control menu.

2. Choose Move. The pointer changes to a four-way arrow.

Note Move is grayed out if the window it is in is maximized—there is nowhere to move such a window.

3. Press the right-arrow key on the keyboard a few times.

4. Press Esc.

5. Press Alt+spacebar to open the Control menu again.

6. Choose Minimize. Notepad minimizes to an icon on the Taskbar.

7. Click on the Notepad icon in the task bar with the secondary mouse button. The Control Menu displays.

8. Choose Restore. Notepad restores to a window.

To help you understand the way other commands work in the Control menu, experiment with them. When you are ready to go on, the next section shows you the other types of menus available in a Windows NT program.

Menus

Every Windows NT program, even a simple application such as Clock, has a menu bar. The *menu bar*, which always is located directly below the title bar, has a collection of the most commonly used commands. The menus within the Windows NT environment are drop-down menus. By selecting a menu name from the menu bar, you can view a list of menu items that drop down from the menu bar. The menu bars of Word for Windows are shown in figure B.11.

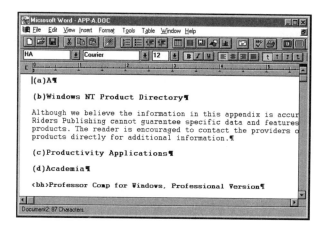

Figure B.11

Menu bars for Word for Windows.

The menu system in Windows NT is very different from that of older DOS and Unix programs. Windows NT's menus and dialog boxes (discussed later) have streamlined the way you interact with programs. A Windows NT menu is designed to tell you which options are available at any level of the Windows NT menu system.

All menus in a Windows NT application appear as names on the menu bar. Whenever possible, the commands and their locations on the menu bar are consistent from program to program. File, for example, always is the first menu choice, and **H**elp always is the last. The **O**pen command always is on the **F**ile menu, and it is used by most programs to open their data files. These common menus are described in the next section.

Common Menus

The **F**ile, **E**dit, and **H**elp menus typically are consistent from one program to another. This consistency is a powerful time-saver for you when you learn a new Windows NT program. After you learn to exit one Windows NT application, for instance, you know how to do it in every other Windows NT program. If you have ever opened a new MS-DOS or Unix program and not known how to quit the program (without finding the computer's on/off switch), you can appreciate a consistent method for such routine operations as quitting applications and opening, saving, and printing documents.

The File Menu

Several commands nearly always are found on the **F**ile menu. The last command on the **F**ile menu, for example, typically is E**x**it, and the first three **F**ile commands usually are **N**ew, **O**pen, and **C**lose. More important, the dialog box generated by selecting the **O**pen command also is similar from program to program. Figure B.12 shows the Open dialog box from Word for Windows 95.

Figure B.12

Open dialog box from Word for Windows.

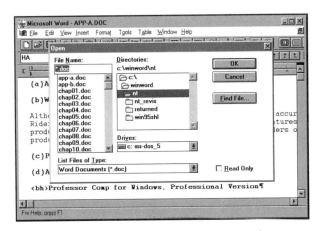

The next pair of commands found on most File menus are those used to save a file—**S**ave and Save **A**s. Not only are the commands the same, but the accelerator keys and shortcut keys (if any) are the same between programs.

The other command commonly found on the menu is the **P**rint command. Depending on the program, a single **P**rint command or a collection of printing menu items (such as **P**rint, Pr**i**nter Setup, and Print Pre**v**iew) can be found here.

The Edit Menu

The **E**dit menu contains commands for moving data between a program and the Windows NT Clipboard, which is a common storage area for data. Data is copied to the Clipboard, and then it is pasted from the Clipboard into the same program or a different program.

The **E**dit menu for most Windows NT programs contains the **U**ndo, Cu**t**, **C**opy, **P**aste, and De**l**ete commands.

The **U**ndo command enables you to cancel your last action; the remaining commands enable you to move data in and out of the Clipboard.

The Cu**t** command removes the selected data (you must select the data prior to cutting it) from the program's window and places it in the Clipboard.

The **C**opy command copies selected data from the program to the Clipboard.

The **P**aste command pastes (copies) data from the Clipboard into the program's window.

The De**l**ete command deletes selected data from the program's window, but it does not place the deleted data in the Clipboard.

Many Windows NT programs also contain other commands in their **E**dit menus. The **E**dit menu for WinGIF, for example, contains a variety of commands for editing a graphics image (see fig. B.13).

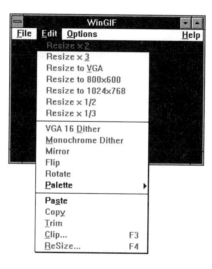

Figure B.13

WinGIF's Edit menu.

Common Menu Actions

As you work with menus, you will find that there are common actions you can perform. These actions are discussed in the following sections.

Selection Methods

The menu system of Windows NT is powerful because of the number of methods it provides to select menu items. The most obvious selection method is to use the mouse. By clicking on a menu name on the menu bar, you display that menu. By clicking on an item in the menu, you activate that item (usually a command). By clicking on another part of the display, you cancel that menu selection. You can close the menu, but leave the menu bar selected, by pressing Esc when a menu appears.

Another way to choose a menu option is to point to the menu name, press the mouse button to display the menu, drag the pointer down the menu until the desired menu item is highlighted, and then release the mouse button. (This method is more familiar for Macintosh users, because this is the way menus work on the Macintosh. In Windows NT, however, you do not have to hold the mouse button down to keep the menu displayed.)

Windows NT menu names on the menu bar contain one underlined character that can be used to select that menu. These characters are referred to as *accelerator keys.* Press Alt (or, in some applications, F10) to activate the menu bar, and then press the letter associated with the desired menu to cause the menu to drop down. When the menu appears, select a command by entering the accelerator key associated with that command. The **F**ile menu, for example, can be activated by pressing Alt+F. When the **F**ile menu appears, press **O** to select the **O**pen command.

Note The menu bar is activated when the Alt key is pressed, not when it is released. Note that you do not have to wait to see the menu before you choose the next letter.

The arrow keys also can be used to select menus and menu items. The menu bar first must be activated by pressing Alt or F10. Use the left- and right-arrow keys to move between menus; use the down-arrow key to display the contents of a menu. After a menu appears, press the up- and down-arrow keys to highlight the menu item you want, and then press Enter to select the highlighted item. Press Esc to close an open menu or to cancel the activation of the menu bar if no menu is displayed.

In the menu shown in figure B.14, notice that some items have keystroke combinations written after the command name. These key combinations are called *shortcut keys* and are an efficient way to use Windows NT menus. A major advantage of the standard Windows NT interface is that the same shortcut keys work in most Windows NT programs.

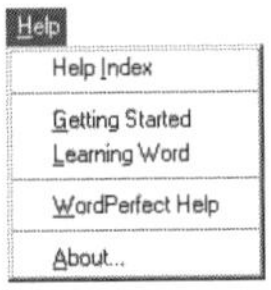

Figure B.14

Many commands on the Edit menu are universal to Windows NT programs.

Because programs share a common interface, learning the shortcuts of the environment can save time. The command to copy information to the Clipboard is always the **C**opy command in the **E**dit menu (select the **E**dit menu, and choose the **C**opy command). You also can press Alt, **E**, and **C** at the same time. Or you can press Alt, and then press **C** after you press **E**.

An even faster way to invoke Copy is with the keyboard shortcut Ctrl+C (or Ctrl+Ins). These methods all work, regardless of your current program. The same process is followed in Excel and Word for Windows, for example.

Note Windows NT features two styles of keyboard shortcuts for cut, copy, and paste: the older Windows standard (Windows 3.0 and earlier) and the new standard for Windows NT/Windows 3.1. These are shown in the following table:

Function	Win 3.0	Win 3.1/NT 3.1 and later
Cut	Shift+Del	Ctrl+X
Copy	Ctrl+Ins	Ctrl+C
Paste	Shift+Ins	Ctrl+V

Menu items within Windows NT are more than a series of commands. Information on the menus changes to provide information about whether commands are available, which options currently are set, and which commands require multiple steps.

Dimmed Options

Windows NT is a "smart" operating environment; it knows, for example, that a maximized window simply cannot be made larger. One of the big advantages of Windows NT over MS-DOS and Unix programs is that you cannot select an option that is inappropriate or unavailable. Thus, if a menu item is unavailable, Windows NT automatically changes the color of the menu item to gray (by default). If you then try to choose the unavailable menu item, the program ignores your request.

Note Dimmed menu items sometimes are referred to as being grayed out.

Menu commands often are unavailable because you still need to select some object or because a previous action is required. The **U**ndo command in the **E**dit menu, for example, is dimmed in all Windows NT programs until you do something that can be undone, such as deleting some text. You cannot cut or copy information from a document until data is selected; these options are dimmed until you make a selection. Likewise, because you cannot paste anything until something has been cut or copied, the **P**aste option is dimmed until information has been placed in the Clipboard.

The following exercise illustrates dimmed menus:

1. Select the Notepad window. Make sure that the README.TXT file is loaded on-screen.

2. Select **E**dit. Note that the **U**ndo, Cu**t**, **C**opy, and De**l**ete commands are dimmed.

3. Select **E**dit, and choose Select **A**ll. The entire document is highlighted.

4. Select **E**dit again. Note that the Cu**t**, **C**opy, and De**l**ete commands are no longer dimmed.

5. Choose the **C**opy command.

6. Select **E**dit. Note that the **P**aste command is no longer dimmed.

7. Press Esc to cancel the menu.

Throughout Windows NT programs, menu items are dimmed (and sometimes removed) if the command does not make sense for the worksheet or document being displayed.

Items with a Solid Arrow

Some applications have an additional level of menus. A solid arrow to the right of a menu item indicates that a second menu appears after you choose that item (see fig. B.15). This type of menu is called a *cascading menu*.

Figure B.15

An example of a cascading menu.

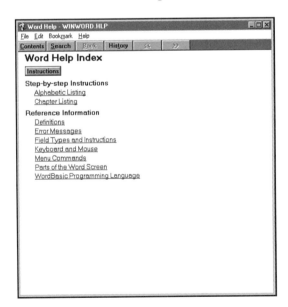

Cascading menus present a series of options or offer a new level of menu choices. If the menu presents a series of options, selecting the value sets the menu item equal to that value. If the cascading menu presents a series of menu items, choosing one of those items is the same as choosing an item from a first-level menu (a drop-down menu from the menu bar).

Items with Check Marks

In some programs, a menu-bar selection actually is a list of options that can be either on or off. If an option is turned on, it has a check mark beside it; if it is turned off, it is not checked. Figure B.16 shows two checked options on the File Manager menu.

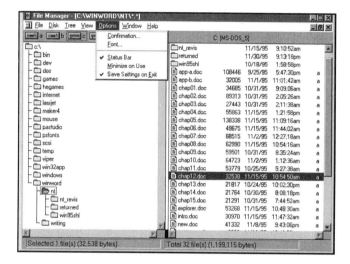

Figure B.16

Active options within File Manager.

This type of menu item is referred to as a *toggle switch.* Just like a light switch, it can move between two settings. Some programs change the name of the item rather than display a check mark, but this method of handling a toggle switch has grown increasingly uncommon among applications.

Items with an Ellipsis

The *ellipsis* symbol (three periods) means "continued." An item on a Windows NT menu that is followed by an ellipsis is continued within a dialog box.

A *dialog box* is used within Windows NT to obtain additional information from the user. When a menu item is followed by an ellipsis, additional information is needed to complete the command. When you choose **F**ind from the **S**earch menu in Notepad, for example, Windows NT produces a dialog box similar to the one in figure B.17. This dialog box asks what you want to search for and how you want to search for it.

The ellipsis provides guidance when you explore a new program and are not sure what is safe to click on. If the menu option has an ellipsis, you can safely click on it and review the box that pops up on-screen without activating any commands. You can press Esc to cancel the dialog box without making any changes.

Figure B.17

Notepad's Find dialog box.

Dialog Boxes

Dialog boxes come in many sizes and flavors, but they all have one thing in common: they gather and contain information that relates to the current action. Although each dialog box is different, they all are composed of a combination of specific items. The controls used in a dialog box are described individually in the following sections.

The information can be entered into the dialog box by using a combination of the mouse and keyboard. You can use the mouse to select an item on the dialog box, including the location in which text is to be entered. Although the mouse can be used to directly select any item, Tab is used to move from one item to another, in a pattern similar to the standard Western reading style (left to right on the first line, and then moving to the next line). Shift+Tab moves you in the opposite direction.

Most items within a dialog box have an accelerator key (underlined letter). To select the item, press the Alt key and the accelerator key.

Text Boxes

A *text box* (sometimes referred to as an *edit box*) is a rectangular box that accepts input from the keyboard. The simplest way to use a text box is to start typing. In most text boxes, any existing text is highlighted automatically and is deleted when you begin typing.

You also can use the mouse (or the arrow keys) to move to a specific point within the text and insert new text. Backspace and Del can remove single characters or blocks of characters when highlighted with the mouse.

Note   To highlight with the keyboard, move to the starting location, hold down Shift, and use the arrow keys to move to the ending location.

Some text boxes, such as the Annotate dialog box shown in figure B.18, accept multiple lines of text. To start a new line in this type of text box, use Ctrl+Enter. To start a new paragraph (skip a line), press Enter (Shift+Enter also works to maintain compatibility with other versions of Windows). Multiple-line text boxes are taller than single-line boxes.

You can use the cut, copy, and paste shortcut keys in a text box.

New Riders Publishing
INSIDE
SERIES

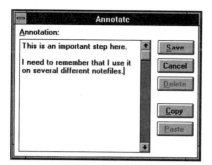

Figure B.18

The Annotate dialog box.

List Boxes

A *list box* shows choices, often sorted alphabetically. You can scroll up and down the list by using vertical scroll bars such as those used to navigate a window's screen display. When the desired item is displayed anywhere in the list box, you can select it with the mouse by clicking on it. If you double-click on an item in the list, the program selects the item and closes the dialog box.

If you do not use a mouse, you can move to the list box (either by using Alt and the accelerator key, or by pressing Tab), and then press the up- and down-arrow keys to make your selection. When the selection has the gray outline, press the spacebar to highlight it, or press Enter to select the item and close the dialog box in a single step. You also can use Page Up and Page Down to move through the list more quickly.

Although most list boxes enable you to select only a single item, some enable you to select multiple items from a single list. To select multiple items with the mouse, hold down Shift while you click on additional items. If you use the keyboard, hold down Ctrl, move the focus with the arrow keys, and press the spacebar for each item you want to add. This type of list box is common in programs that manipulate groups of files, such as the File Manager.

Most list boxes that are sorted also support a technique known as *First Character Goto*. In Excel's Functions list under the Pas**t**e Function command on the Fo**r**mula menu, hundreds of items are available. If you want to select the WEEKDAY function, for example, you must scan more than 100 choices before WEEKDAY scrolls into view. With the First Character Goto technique, press **W**; you are taken to the first entry that begins with the letter W in the list.

Some list boxes and text boxes are linked to form a unit known as a *combination box*, such as the File **N**ame text box and the list box in the File Open dialog box (refer to fig. B.12).

You can access a file by typing its name directly in the text box or by scrolling through the **F**ile Name list box until you find the file you want. The information displayed in the files list box is based on the value shown in the **D**irectories list box (it displays the files contained in the directory specified in the **D**irectories list box). After you choose a filename from the **F**ile Name list box, that filename instantly appears in the text box.

When a list box is connected to a text box like this, selecting an item from the list is the same as having Windows NT do your typing for you with no chance of error. You can elect to do your own typing, however, and enter the same information into the text box directly from the keyboard.

Drop-Down Lists

A normal list box takes up a large amount of space inside a dialog box. In the Files list box in the Open dialog box in the File menu, for example, room for eight filenames exists. A drop-down list is a space-efficient way of combining a text box and a list box, enabling several lists to be included in a single dialog box, as shown in figure B.19.

Figure B.19

Drop-down lists in the Desktop dialog box.

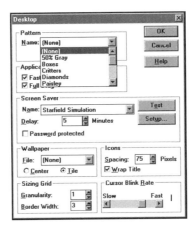

Note   To display the drop-down list in figure B.19, open the Control Panel (double-click on the Control Panel icon). Select Desktop by double-clicking on it. The **N**ame text box in the Pattern box is a drop-down list.

The text box displays the most current selection from the list (or the top item, if no item was selected previously), and it has a pull-down button on the right side. (The *pull-down button* looks like other buttons, but it contains a down arrow.) You can click on the pull-down button to display the other choices available for that item. You then can make your selection as you would in any list box.

For keyboard use, move to the drop-down list by pressing Tab or pressing Alt, followed by the character associated with the drop-down list box. The icon on the drop-down list is an underlined down arrow. The items on the list can be displayed by pressing Alt and the down arrow.

When the list appears, you can press a letter to take you to that portion of the list. If you type **C**, for instance, the highlight bar instantly moves to Critters in the selection list. This is another example of the First Character Goto feature, discussed as part of the standard list box. Finally, if you highlight the text in the top portion of the drop-down list, you can enter text directly as though it were a standard text box.

Tabs

When you use menu items to open child windows, one window often gets lost in the background. Finding hidden windows often requires that you either iconify or move visible windows.

An alternative to layering window upon window is the use of tabs. Tabs are similar to the tabs on file folders. When you look in a file drawer full of file folders, you can pick out the folder you want by looking at the tabs on top of the folders where the name of the folder is written. Tabs in Windows NT work the same way. Although many windows in a tab display are, in effect, on top of one another, you have easy access to any of them by clicking on their tab, which is always visible. Figure B.20 shows you an example of a tab in Windows NT.

Figure B.20

Using tabs in windows.

Notice that all of the tabs remain visible, regardless of which window is on top.

Option Buttons

Option buttons (known in early versions of Windows as *radio buttons*) in a dialog box always are grouped so that only one button in each group can be selected at a time. (When you select a button in a group, any other button that was selected is turned off.) Option buttons are referred to as radio buttons because they resemble the tuning knobs of an old-fashioned radio.

Select an option button by clicking on it with the mouse, or by changing the focus to that group and using the arrow keys on the keyboard to select a particular button. Option buttons sometimes have underlined shortcut keys in their description labels; they can be selected by holding down Alt and pressing the underlined letter key.

The paper Orientation group on the Document Properties dialog box, shown in figure B.21, is an example of a group of option buttons. It contains two choices: **P**ortrait and **L**andscape orientation. The printer's paper can be in only one of these two conditions, so if you choose **L**andscape, the dialog box automatically turns off the **P**ortrait button.

Figure B.21

Only one choice in the Orientation group can be selected.

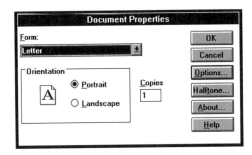

Option buttons are grouped within a named border, called a *group window*. (The option buttons discussed in the Printer Setup dialog box are in the Orientation group.) Option buttons within a group are mutually exclusive: if you select one, all others are deselected.

Check Boxes

A *check box* enables you to specify a preference in the same way you check a box on an order form. When the box is checked, it is considered on or true; when it is empty, it is considered off or false. The Word for Windows Print Options dialog box, shown in figure B.22, for example, has several check box items, including **D**raft Output, **R**everse Print Order, and **U**pdate Fields. You also can include **S**ummary Info, **F**ield Codes, **A**nnotations, and **H**idden Text.

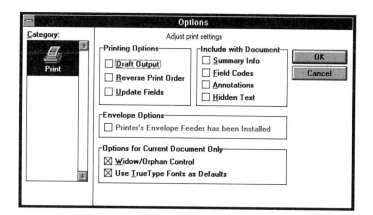

Figure B.22

Any combination of check boxes can be selected.

A check box acts like a toggle switch: clicking on an empty box checks it, and clicking on a checked box clears it. Most check boxes can be accessed by using an accelerator key.

If you use the keyboard, press the spacebar to change the status of a check box from checked to cleared (or from cleared to checked). Check boxes are grouped by the type of action they control, but, unlike option buttons, the grouping is not restrictive: each check box is independent of the other check boxes within the group. You can select one, none, all, or any combination of check boxes within any dialog box.

Command Buttons

The command buttons on a dialog box are used after you complete all necessary information. Two command buttons included on almost every dialog box are OK and Cancel. By clicking on OK, you tell Windows NT to proceed with your selections; clicking on Cancel tells Windows NT that you want to exit without selecting.

The keyboard equivalent of Cancel is always Esc. Enter is a key equivalent for the default command button. (The *default* is the item selected before you make any changes.) In most dialog boxes, the OK button is the default; pressing Enter accepts the changes.

When you use the keyboard and move to a command button, the outer edge of the button becomes darker, meaning that the button is selected. You will notice that the OK button in figure B.21 is selected, whereas the Cancel button is not. You can activate the current button by pressing Enter.

Besides OK and Cancel buttons, another type of button opens a second dialog box on top of the existing one; this *nested dialog box* typically contains related information that cannot fit on the first dialog box or that rarely needs to be changed. (Such a button invariably will be labeled with ellipsis dots to indicate that another dialog box will appear.) When you close a nested dialog box, you generally return to the first-level dialog box.

Note A common example of a nested dialog box is in the Print dialog box of most applications, such as Word for Windows. Select **P**rint from the **F**ile menu to open the Print dialog box. When you click on the **S**etup button, a second dialog box opens, enabling you to specify which printer to use. When you close the Print Setup dialog box by clicking on OK or Cancel, you return to the original Print dialog box.

Icons

Windows NT Explorer, like Windows 95, uses *icons* on the Taskbar to represent active applications. When you start an application, it appears in a window on top of the Root window. At the same time the window displays, the application's icon appears on the Taskbar.

When a window is displayed, the icon on the Taskbar associated with it appears to be pushed down. When a window is minimized, by pushing the dash button on the right side of the Title bar, the icon looks like a button that is raised.

In Windows NT 3.*x*, when you minimized an application, it shrank to an icon at the bottom of the screen. In Windows NT Explorer, when you minimize an application, it disappears from the Root window. All that is left is its icon on the Taskbar.

An icon is a representation of an application or device. Within Windows NT, an icon is a small picture (usually 32×32 screen dots) that represents an application, a file, or an action. Icons can be manipulated by the mouse by clicking on it with the primary mouse button to restore its window, or by clicking on it with the secondary mouse button to display the icon menu. The icon menu has the same options as the Control menu, which was previously described.

Application programs that are minimized to icons still run, and they can perform complex actions. They do not occupy as much memory, however, because they do not need to display their application window. (They often run in the background.) An application shrunk to an icon also presents less clutter on the desktop than if it is left as an application window.

Application Shortcuts

Application Shortcuts are links to application executables. The Shortcut appears as an icon on the Root window. When you double-click on a Shortcut, its application starts. The difference between icons and Shortcuts is that an icon appears on the Taskbar

only when its application is running. A Shortcut appears on the Root window whether its application is running or not.

Using Shortcuts

New in Windows NT is the opportunity for you to store any application as an icon on the Root window. Instead of having to display the Programs to access application icons in version 3.*x*, application icons, called Shortcuts, can be accessed directly. Double-clicking on a Shortcut invokes its application.

 Note   In terms of technical jargon, a Shortcut is really a link. A Shortcut is not a program; it merely represents a program. If you delete a Shortcut, for example, you delete only the reference to the program, not the program itself.

The following example shows you how to create a Shortcut for the clock, but you can use the same procedure for making a Shortcut for any application.

1. Click on the Start button and then click on the Programs option in the Start button menu. In the submenu, click on the Accessories option.

2. Click on the Clock. The clock displays.

3. Click on the Root window with the secondary mouse button to display the Root menu. Place the mouse cursor on the New option in the Root menu and then select Shortcut.

4. In the Shortcut box, browse in the Windows directory to locate the clock executable.

5. Click on Next in the Shortcut box and then the Finish button in the confirmation box. The Clock icon then appears on the Root window.

Application Groups

Application Groups are groups of icons that appear in the Programs menu (under the Start button's menu) and represent application groups. In Windows NT 3.*x*, you arranged icons in application groups in the Programs.

For example, when you installed a Windows application, very often the last action of the install program was to create an application group for the application in the Programs. The application group contained an icon of all of the application executables—including, for example, a readme file, the application itself, and a secondary application, such as a reference manual.

If you carry your CONFIG.SYS and AUTOEXEC.BAT files from Windows 3.*x* or
Windows NT 3.*x* forward in to the latest version of Windows, the application groups
appear in Explorer in the following way. When you click with the primary mouse
button on the Start button, Explorer displays a menu of your application groups
names, as shown in figure B.23.

Figure B.23

The Start Menu.

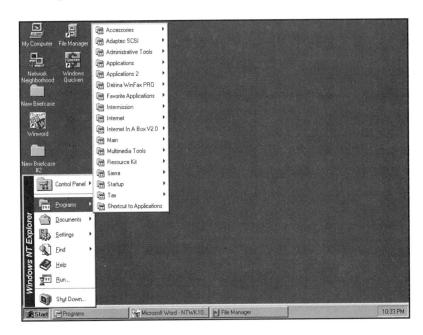

When you click on one of the application group names, another menu displays
showing the names of the applications in the application group. Clicking on one of
the applications starts the application.

Performing Common Windows Tasks

As mentioned earlier in the chapter, Windows NT applications and Windows NT itself
follow strict guidelines regarding the design of the interface of an application.

Note The reason for these guidelines is obvious. In the DOS world, time spent learning
the command structure of one application, such as WordPerfect, does not help you
when you learn another application, such as Lotus 1-2-3. Most DOS applications
have unique command structures, so the steps required to open a file in
WordPerfect are entirely different from those required by Lotus 1-2-3.

In contrast, Windows applications adhere to stricter command structure guidelines known as the *Common User Access* (CUA) standard. The benefit for the user is that after you learn a single Windows application, learning future applications becomes much easier because the basic commands are identical across applications. Therefore, you do not have to worry about whether to use Alt+F or Ctrl+F to open a file because all applications use a single menu action or key sequence. Additionally, you do not need to wonder where the print commands are hidden on the menu, because CUA helps ensure that the **P**rint command is always in the same place.

Windows NT's implementation of the CUA standard makes working with your PC and your programs easier. You can focus on the work at hand and not on figuring out how to use the software.

Basic File Operations

If a Windows NT application works with files, it presents a **F**ile menu as the first menu on the left side of the menu bar. All **F**ile menus in Windows NT applications are the same—they enable you to work with files by using the same command structure, no matter what the files contain. Every **F**ile menu enables you to perform at least four different file operations.

Creating a New File

In any Windows NT application, you can create a new, empty file by selecting the **F**ile menu and then choosing the **N**ew option (see fig. B.24). The application opens a new, empty file and displays it in the workspace.

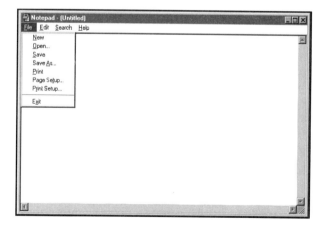

Figure B.24

The File menu.

The Write and Cardfile applications provide examples of ways to use this action to create a variety of files in different applications. In Windows NT Write, the file you create has a format that keeps track of information about fonts, pictures, embedded objects, and text. Select the File menu and choose the New option to bring up a workspace that is ready to accept all information and display properly formatted text (see fig. B.25).

Figure B.25

The New command in Write.

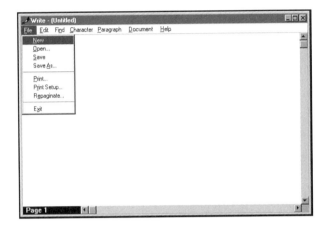

In Windows NT Cardfile, however, you choose the New command in the File menu to create a file that can contain graphical index cards, text, and pictures. The new file is presented as a single blank card in the workspace.

Windows NT Paintbrush presents a file in which you can turn individual pixels on or off. In addition, the file holds information about the color of each pixel. Select File, and then choose New in Paintbrush to create a file that is ready to hold information (see fig. B.26).

Figure B.26

The New command in Paintbrush.

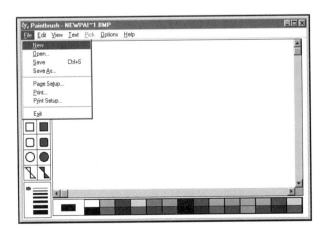

Opening an Existing File

Just as you can create new, empty files in different applications with the same command, you can open existing files in different applications by using the same command sequence.

In Windows NT applications, select the **F**ile menu and then choose the **O**pen option. A dialog box appears for you to select the file you wish to open. After you respond, the application opens the requested file and displays it in the workspace.

The Write and Cardfile programs provide examples of ways the same command is implemented across applications that deal with very different data. When you select **F**ile and then **O**pen in Write, for instance, a document appears in the workspace (see fig. B.27).

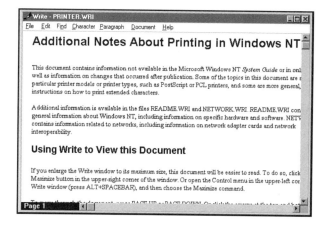

Figure B.27

The result of the Open command in Write's File menu.

When you select **F**ile and then **O**pen in Windows NT Cardfile, on the other hand, a set of index cards in the workspace appears (see fig. B.28).

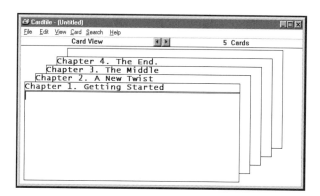

Figure B.28

The result of the Open command in Cardfile's File menu.

Saving a File

Windows NT has the same command structure for saving files in different applications. To save a file, click on the **F**ile menu, and then choose **S**ave in any application. If you have not yet saved the file, a dialog box appears and asks you to type a file name into a text box. After you enter a file name, the application saves the file. If you have previously saved the file, the application saves the file under the same name. If you wish to save the file under a new file name, use the Save **A**s command (covered later in this section).

Note When saving a file, you usually do not need to type the extension, because most applications add their default file extension to your file name automatically (unless you have explicitly typed an alternative extension). Some applications, however, such as Quattro Pro for Windows, do not add an extension.

The Write and Cardfile applications provide examples of ways that the same command is implemented across applications dealing with different data. In Write, select **F**ile and then choose **S**ave to save a file in Windows NT Write file format (see fig. B.29).

Figure B.29

The Save command in Write.

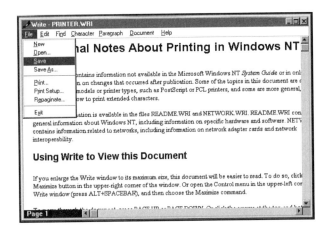

In Cardfile, select **F**ile and then choose **S**ave to save a set of index cards in Cardfile's file format (see fig. B.30).

Paintbrush can accommodate three different file formats; the Save and Open dialog boxes enable you to choose the format you prefer.

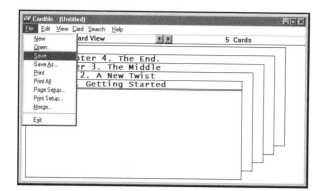

Figure B.30

The Save command in Cardfile.

Note More programs are beginning to standardize shortcut key combinations to make life easier for Windows NT users. Shift+F12, for example, automatically invokes the **S**ave command in the **F**ile menu, whether you are in Word for Windows or Excel. As this trend continues, the investment of learning the standard Windows NT commands yields a greater and greater reward.

Saving a File with a New Name

In Windows NT applications, to save a file under a different name from the one with which you opened it, select the **F**ile menu and then choose Save **A**s.

A dialog box appears (see fig. B.31) and prompts you to type the new file name into a text box.

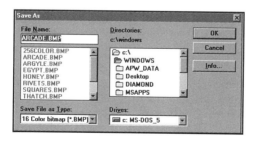

Figure B.31

The Save As dialog box.

Usually you do not have to type the extension, because most applications add the default extension. After you respond to the Save **A**s dialog box, the application saves the file.

Windows Printing

All applications in Windows NT have the same set of commands for printing files. If an application allows you to print, the print commands appear on the File menu.

Printing a File

To print a file in most Windows NT applications, select the File menu and then choose Print. A dialog box appears and prompts you to enter the number of copies or to print only a selected portion of the file (some applications do not offer this option). After you determine the characteristics of your print job by setting the controls in this dialog box, click on the OK button to begin the printing operation.

After the print job begins, a dialog box appears to inform you that the file is printing (see fig. B.32).

Figure B.32

The Print Cancel dialog box in Write.

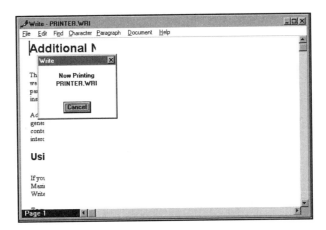

Halt the printing operation by clicking on Cancel in the dialog box or by pressing Esc.

After the Print Cancel dialog box disappears, Windows NT manages the print job, freeing you for other work. You still can control your print job from the Print Manager application if necessary. See Chapter 14 for more information on printing.

Setting Up the Printer

Windows NT applications that enable you to print also enable you to control the printer setup. The actual management of the print job and communication with the printer is performed, not by individual applications, but by Windows NT itself. As part of this management, Windows NT gives application programs access to the installed printers.

You can access a Printer Setup dialog box and specify printer settings in each application. To access the printer setup, select the File menu and then choose the Print Setup option.

As figure B.33 illustrates, the Print Setup dialog box contains a list of the printers attached to the system. Click on the name of the printer you want to use, and then click on the Setup button.

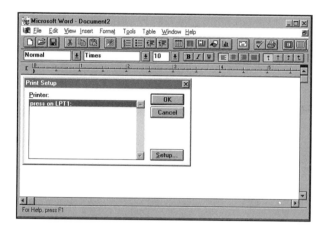

Figure B.33

The Print Setup dialog box in Word.

Another dialog box then appears, which enables you to adjust the printer settings (see fig. B.34). After you adjust the settings, click on the OK button. You return to the Printer Selection dialog box. Click on OK; your printer is set up.

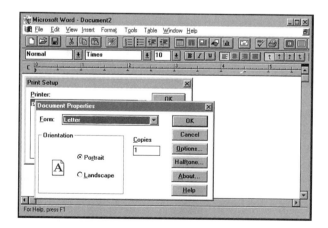

Figure B.34

Document Properties dialog box.

Workspace Searches

Many Windows NT applications (particularly word processors and editors) enable you to search for information in their workspaces (refer to fig. B.17).

Select the appropriate menu name to search for information in the application. A Search dialog box appears and asks you to enter the string to search for (you often are offered the opportunity to enter a replace string as well). Click on the Find button to begin the search.

Views of Your Workspace

Many Windows NT applications enable you to decide how you want to view the data. If the application has this capability, you may find a **V**iew menu, which enables you to display options specific to the data.

File Manager's **V**iew menu enables you to decide ways to sort the listed files and to select which file information appears in the list (see fig. B.35).

Figure B.35

File Manager's View menu.

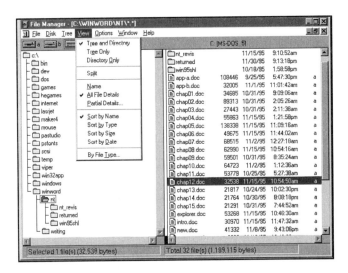

Paintbrush's **V**iew menu enables you to zoom in on a part of the drawing canvas or to zoom out of the canvas. The CD Player's **V**iew menu enables you to choose information about the current CD.

The View menu is less standardized across different Windows applications. Some applications do not provide the capability to change the view of your document or workspace; others place the command elsewhere. For example, Paradox for Windows enables you to change the view of a form or report through the Zoom option on the Properties menu.

Configuring Console Windows

Console windows are character-based and command-prompt windows. A new icon in the Controls Panel window, entitled Console, enables you to change console windows in the following ways:

◆ Specify the size of the cursor, screen buffer, and the position of the window.

◆ Enable or disable QuickEdit and Insert modes.

◆ Specify the background and text colors used in console windows and pop-up menus.

◆ Specify the font and point size of the type used in console windows and pop-up menus.

In earlier versions of Windows NT, you could change the same properties of console windows individually using the Properties command in the Control menu. (You display the Control menu by clicking on the dash button in the upper-left corner of a window.) The Console icon, however, allows you to change the properties of all Console windows at once.

Changing General Settings

When you open the Console Windows Properties window, you see four tabs with the General tab displayed by default. In this tab you can specify the settings for

◆ Cursor size

◆ Buffer size

◆ Window display size

◆ Enabling or disabling QuickEdit and Insert modes

To change the cursor size, use the following procedure:

1. Click on the Control Panel icon in the Main window.

2. Click on the Console icon. The Console Windows Properties window displays, as shown in figure B.36.

3. To change the cursor size, click on the desired size in the Cursor Size portion of the window.

Figure B.36

*The Console
Windows
Properties
window.*

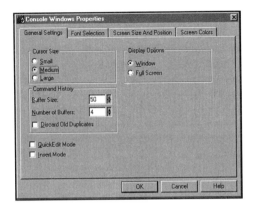

Changing the Command History Size

The Command History buffer records the most recent commands that you use. If you often use commands, you can use the Command History buffer to repeat the commands without retyping them. The default size of the buffer is 50 commands. You can change that size but, remember, the command buffer occupies memory. Setting it at too large a value can needlessly use memory.

You can also use the command buffer to store input for character-based programs that accept buffered input. (Software debuggers, for example, often use buffered input.) You can build a buffer for each program that accepts this kind of input. To do that, you must specify the number of buffers you want to create in the Number of Buffers field. Remember, however, that each buffer occupies memory.

You can display the command history in two ways:

◆ Press the F7 key and then use the up and down arrow to scroll through the list commands. When you find the command you want to reuse, press the Return key.

◆ Type part of the command and then press the F8 key as many times as you need until the command you desire is highlighted. Then press the Return key.

By default, the command history includes the last 50 commands you used regardless of whether or not you repeated commands. If you want to maximize the number of different commands stored in the command history, you can select the Discard Old Duplicates check box. This option removes from the command history any previous instances of a newly used command.

To specify the size of the Command History buffer, type the number of lines you want in the Buffer Size field in the Command History section of the General Settings tab.

Alternately, you can use the up and down arrows associated with the field to increment or decrement the number of commands the Command History buffer holds.

In the Number of Buffers field, type the number of character-based programs that can use buffered input. Alternately, you can use the up and down arrows associated with the field to increment or decrement the number of buffers to associate with character-based programs.

If you would like only one instance of a command in the Command History, click on the Discard Old Duplicates check box. Any time a command is added to the Command History, Windows NT eliminates any previous instance of the command in the Command History. Use this option to maximize the number of different commands that can occupy the Command History buffer.

Enabling QuickEdit and Insert Modes

Enabling QuickEdit allows you to save to a buffer characters highlighted in a document. You use this feature to cut and paste segments of a document without using the Edit menu.

To enable QuickEdit, click on the QuickEdit check box so that it is selected.

Enabling Insert mode enters characters that you type at the cursor. If Insert mode is not enabled, characters you type overwrite existing text.

Changing Display Options

Console panels can either display as a window or full screen. The default setting is window. If you wish to change the setting, however, you can click on the option you desire.

To change a the size of a Console window while it is displayed, type ALT+RETURN to toggle between settings.

RISC-based processors do not support full-screen mode, so the option does not appear to RISC users.

Changing the Default Size and Position of Console Windows

Windows NT allows you to specify the default position and size of Console windows by using the Screen Size and Position tab in the Console Windows Properties window, as shown in figure B.37.

Figure B.37

*Screen Size and
Position tab.*

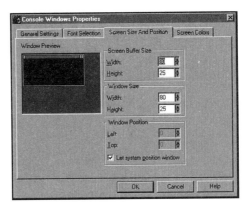

The Screen Buffer Size is the amount of memory, measured in the number of characters wide by the number of characters tall, allocated for each Console window. The Window Size, measured in the number of characters wide by the number of characters tall, is the amount of space taken up by the information on the window. You may not, for example, specify a larger Window Size than Screen Buffer Size. If, however, you specify a smaller Window Size than Screen Buffer Size, Windows NT adds a scroll bar to all console windows. Because a scroll bar is normally not needed with console windows, it is best to keep the Screen Buffer Size and the Windows Size the same.

You can either specify an absolute location on the screen to position all console windows, or you can let Windows NT place the windows directly on top of associated windows. You make that choice in the Windows Position section of the Console Windows Properties window.

To change the size and position of all console windows, use the following procedure:

1. Click on the Screen Size And Position tab in the Console Windows Properties window.

2. Type in the values for the height and width of the screen buffer in the Screen Buffer Size section. Alternately, use the up and down arrows to increment or decrement the screen buffer size, respectively.

3. Type in the values for the height and width of the window size in the Window Size section. Alternately, use the up and down arrows to increment or decrement the window size, respectively. Make sure the values are equal to or less than the values you used in step 2.

4. Choose the position of all console windows in the Window Position section:

  ◆ Click on the Let system position window check box to display console
    windows directly on top of associated windows.

  ◆ Type in the values for the left and top coordinates of the upper left corner
    of the Console window.

Alternately, use the up and down arrows to increment or decrement the coordinates, respectively.

5. Click on the OK button.

Specifying Screen Colors

The final tab in the Console Windows Properties window, Screen Colors, enables you to specify the color of the text and background of Console windows and pop-up windows that are associated with console windows. Pop-up windows are small windows that usually contain little more than text.

To change the colors used in console windows and their associated pop-up windows, use the following procedure:

1. Click on the Screen Colors tab in the Console Windows Properties window.
   Windows NT displays the Screen Colors tab, as shown in figure B.38.

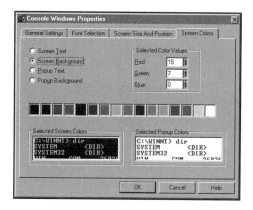

Figure B.38

The Screen Colors tab.

2. Click on the Screen Text radio button.

3. Click on one of the colors displayed in the window. Notice that the color of the text displayed in the Selected Screen Colors section changes according to your color selection. Also notice that the Red, Green, and Blue values change according to your color selection in the Selected Color Values section.

4. Optionally, type in new values in the Red, Green, or Blue fields to change the color of the text. Alternately, use the up and down arrows to increment and decrement the color values, respectively.

5. Click on the Screen Background radio button.

6. Repeat steps 3 and 4 until you arrive at the color of background you like.

7. Click on the Pop-up Text radio button.

8. Repeat steps 3 and 4 until you arrive at the color of pop-up text you like. Notice that as you change the value of the colors of the pop-up text, the color text in the Selected Pop-up Colors changes accordingly.

9. Click on the Pop-up Background radio button.

10. Repeat steps 3 and 4 until you arrive at the color of background you like.

11. Click on the OK button.

Option Selection

Many Windows NT applications have special settings that you can use to customize appearance or behavior. An **O**ptions menu on the menu bar typically indicates this capability (see fig. B.39).

Figure B.39

The Options menu in Paintbrush.

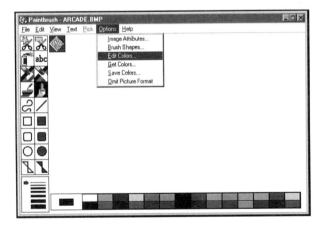

Note The Options menu is another case in which different application vendors have chosen different paths. Although many Microsoft products (such as Word for Windows and Excel) have an Options menu, Borland's Paradox for Windows provides a Properties menu to do essentially the same task.

Various applications enable different degrees of customization. Paintbrush, for instance, enables extensive control of its appearance and features.

File Programs, on the other hand, enables you to control only four aspects, which are found in the **O**ptions and **W**indow menus. These are described as follows:

◆ If you select **A**uto Arrange, icons in a program group rearrange themselves after the program group is resized. The icons move into rows and columns that most efficiently use the available space.

◆ If you select **M**inimize on Use, icons shrink when you launch an application, clearing the screen of clutter and making all desktop space available to the application.

◆ The **S**ave Settings on Exit option saves the position and status of the group windows when you end your Windows session.

◆ The Save Settings Now option enables you to save settings whenever you want.

Font Selection

Windows NT provides a pool of fonts that are available for each application for printing and displaying on-screen. You typically select a font within a given application by choosing a Font option from a menu.

 Note   For more information on fonts, see Chapter 13.

Depending on the application, a dialog box might appear with a list of available fonts. Select the font you want by clicking on a font name. This font is used to write to the screen until you select another one. When you save the file, you save the current font. TrueType font files contain an unlimited number of font sizes because the fonts automatically are scaled to fit the screen.

 Note   Although TrueType renders virtually any point size for a given font, most applications display only those fonts with point sizes between 4–127 points.

You use different menus and commands to select fonts in different applications. The following four figures show different ways to select fonts in various applications.

Paintbrush presents a **T**ext menu on which **F**onts is an option (see fig. B.40).

Figure B.40

Font selection in Paintbrush.

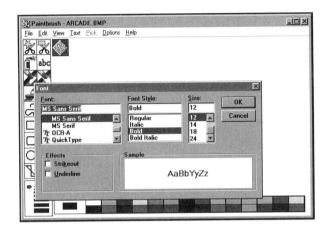

Write presents a **C**haracter menu on which **F**onts is an option (see fig. B.41).

Figure B.41

Font selection in Write.

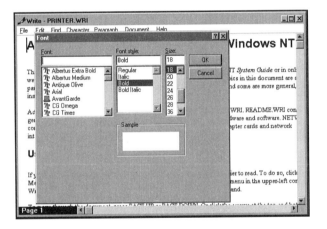

Word for Windows uses two drop-down list boxes that enable you to select the font and its size (see fig. B.42).

Microsoft Excel places the **F**ont option on the Forma**t** menu.

Although applications use different ways to select fonts, Windows NT provides sophisticated fonts and font management for your applications. Because you do not have to install fonts for each separate application, you gain disk space and execution speed.

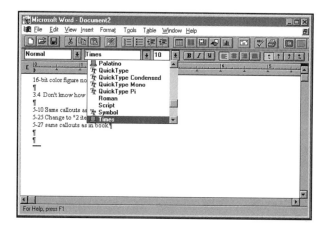

Figure B.42

Font selection in Word for Windows.

Changing Font Settings

The Fonts tab, as shown in figure B.43, enables you to choose the fonts and font size for all Console windows. Changing the size of the fonts makes the window size change correspondingly.

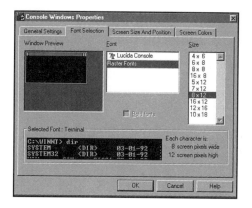

Figure B.43

Fonts tab.

To change the fonts or font size, use the following procedure:

1. Click on the Font Selection tab. Windows NT displays the Font Selection tab.

2. Click on the desired font in the Font box.

3. Click on the desired font size in the Size box.

4. Look at the fonts displayed in the Selected Font:Terminal box. Change your font or font-size selections if necessary.

5. If you want bold fonts, click on the Bold fonts check box.

6. Click on the OK button.

Toolbars

Windows NT applications often offer you the chance to work with a *toolbar*, which is a strip of buttons that typically appears just under the menu bar of an application. You can initiate an action by clicking on a button on the toolbar.

 Note The actual name of the toolbar depends on the software vendor. For example, Microsoft Word for Windows and Excel have toolbars, Borland Paradox for Windows and Quattro Pro for Windows have speed bars, and Lotus 1-2-3 and Ami Pro have SmartIcons. Although the names are different, they are designed to do essentially the same thing—speed up your work.

Every toolbar button has a picture that indicates its function. Normally, a button replaces several or many individual keystrokes or mouse actions. The **S**ave button on the Word for Windows toolbar (see fig. B.44) is equivalent to the **S**ave option under the **F**ile menu.

Figure B.44

The Word for Windows toolbar.

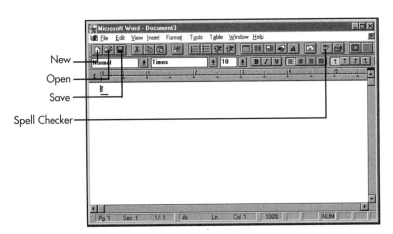

Word for Windows uses a toolbar to provide immediate visual access to 22 common actions in the Word for Windows menu system, as you can see in figure B.44. By clicking on the first button on the left, for example, you can create a new document. The next button opens an existing file.

Note Toolbars are gaining in popularity as the Windows interface becomes more complex. When Apple first introduced a menuing system in the Lisa and early Macs, the actual size of the screen was very small. As a result, using the mouse to select a menu option did not take too much hand movement.

With today's large 1024×768 super-VGA screens and complex menuing systems, selecting a toolbar option requires much less hand movement than the equivalent command found on the menu.

If you want to print, click on the Printer button. If you want to check spelling, click on the Spell checker button. You do not have to remember where the options are on the menus, so you are more efficient and less distracted by the Word for Windows command system.

A *toolbox* (see fig. B.45) is similar to a toolbar. It presents a grid of tools represented by icons. Usually the grid has two columns. To select a tool, click on the corresponding icon in the toolbox. You then can use the tool to take an action in the workspace, such as spray painting in Paintbrush.

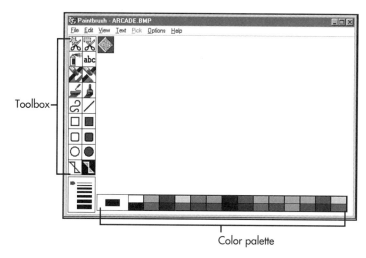

Toolbox—

Color palette

Figure B.45

The Paintbrush toolbox.

The primary difference between a toolbar and a toolbox is the presence of command buttons with actions attached to them. Toolbars use buttons; toolboxes do not. Toolbar buttons initiate actions; toolbox icons select tools to use later. You find both kinds of tool-selection controls in Windows NT applications.

Palettes

A *palette* is similar to a toolbox, but it enables you to select colors. Paintbrush, for example, uses a color palette (refer to figure B.45) to enable you to select the foreground and background colors as you draw.

To select a foreground color in Paintbrush, point to the color and click the left button. To select a background color, point to the color and click the right mouse button.

Other applications use palettes. Control Panel, for instance, uses one palette (see fig. B.46) to enable you to select standard colors, and a separate palette to enable you to create and select custom colors. To see the color palette, activate the Control Panel and click on the Color Palette button.

Figure B.46

The Control Panel color palette.

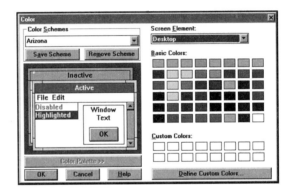

Character Map uses a palette to help you find special characters to use in other applications.

Introducing WYSIWYG

Because of Windows NT's graphical environment and the use of TrueType and related technologies, Windows NT supports the principle of WYSIWYG. *WYSIWYG (What-You-See-Is-What-You-Get)* signifies that what you see on-screen in your application can be printed and look identical on the final output.

Most Windows NT applications can implement a WYSIWYG display because all their display elements are controlled by Windows NT rather than by the application itself. Windows NT renders all graphics and TrueType (and other scalable) fonts you use on-screen exactly as they will print on your printer. Figure B.47 shows a WYSIWYG display.

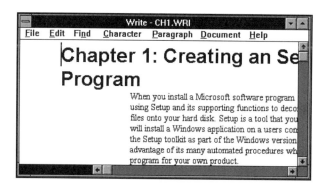

Note WYSIWYG depends on the types of fonts you are using. Bit-mapped fonts (such as MS Sans Serif and MS Serif) do not print exactly as they are viewed on-screen. In contrast, TrueType and ATM (Adobe Type Manager) fonts are WYSIWYG.

Managing the Multiple Document Interface

The Multiple Document Interface (MDI) is another standard to which Windows NT adheres. MDI enables you to open multiple files with a single application window, displaying each in a separate window called a *document window.* Because Windows NT document windows belong to the application window, they appear only in the workspace. Parts of a document window that slide past the workspace border are hidden from view.

MDI enables you to open multiple word processing documents and exchange data among them. You can open several Excel spreadsheets at once, for example, and link cells among them.

Note MDI offers simultaneous views of different drives or directory structures in File Manager.

MDI applications have a special menu, the **W**indow menu, for managing multiple documents in Windows NT. The **W**indow menu appears to the left of the **H**elp menu.

The **N**ew option on the **F**ile menu enables you to open a new document window.

You can enter data and save it in a file from this window. The type of file created by **N**ew depends on the application. Excel, for instance, opens an XLS (Excel spreadsheet) file; Word for Windows opens a DOC (document) file.

The **O**pen option on the **F**ile menu opens an existing document and displays it in an additional window. Any other document window already open remains undisturbed. Normally, you do not have to specify the file extension when you open a file. The application accesses only appropriate file types.

The **N**ew Window option on the **W**indow menu opens another window that displays the same file as the document on-screen. This option enables you to open multiple windows of the same document.

MDI applications provide options on the **W**indow menu for arranging document windows on the workspace. The most common options are **T**ile and **C**ascade.

The **T**ile option arranges the document windows side-by-side like tiles on a wall (see fig. B.48).

Figure B.48

The results of the Tile command.

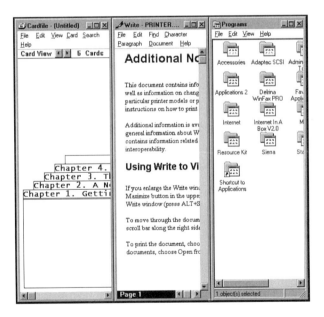

The **C**ascade option tumbles the document windows down the workspace from upper left to lower right (see fig. B.49).

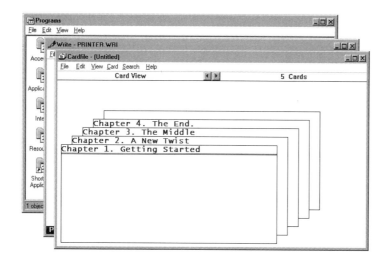

Figure B.49

The results of the Cascade command.

Summary

When users first see Windows NT, their initial impression is how different it looks from the typical DOS, OS/2, or Unix environment. As they begin to use Windows NT, they start to comment on the differences in the way things are done. Windows NT is based on a process of selecting an object to manipulate and then performing an action. Although Windows NT can be used entirely from the keyboard, most users find it easier to use the mouse for performing many tasks. These mouse actions can be used to control the various windows on the screen.

One of the most important aspects of the Windows NT environment is its consistency between applications. The objects that are manipulated within programs are based on a small set of general item types. The most obvious item used for controlling programs is the Windows menu structure. Menu items are selected to perform tasks, to select between settings, and to display dialog boxes.

This consistency is balanced by the fact that Windows NT offers a variety of ways to perform the same task. You can select an item from a menu by using the mouse, the keyboard, or a combination of both. Most menu items (as well as items within a dialog box) have a series of accelerator keys that can be used to select them. In addition, many items have a shortcut-key combination that can be entered with a single keystroke to select the menu item.

This chapter described features that are common to all Windows NT programs. You learned that Windows NT applications have a common set of commands for performing similar tasks, which forms the basis of Windows NT's adherence to the Common User Access (CUA) standard.

These commands make it easier to use applications because you can focus on your working tasks. They also make it easier to use less-familiar applications; you can easily guess the way an application works from having worked on other applications under the same framework.

Index

C

PLUG YOURSELF INTO...

THE MACMILLAN INFORMATION SUPERLIBRARY™

Free information and vast computer resources from the world's leading computer book publisher—online!

FIND THE BOOKS THAT ARE RIGHT FOR YOU!

A complete online catalog, plus sample chapters and tables of contents give you an in-depth look at *all* of our books, including hard-to-find titles. It's the best way to find the books you need!

- STAY INFORMED with the latest computer industry news through our online newsletter, press releases, and customized Information SuperLibrary Reports.

- GET FAST ANSWERS to your questions about MCP books and software.

- VISIT our online bookstore for the latest information and editions!

- COMMUNICATE with our expert authors through e-mail and conferences.

- DOWNLOAD SOFTWARE from the immense MCP library:
    - Source code and files from MCP books
    - The best shareware, freeware, and demos

- DISCOVER HOT SPOTS on other parts of the Internet.

- WIN BOOKS in ongoing contests and giveaways!

INFORMATION?

CHECK OUT THESE RELATED TOPICS OR SEE YOUR LOCAL BOOKSTORE

CAD and 3D Studio

As the number one CAD publisher in the world, and as a Registered Publisher of Autodesk, New Riders Publishing provides unequaled content on this complex topic. Industry-leading products include AutoCAD and 3D Studio.

Networking

As the leading Novell NetWare publisher, New Riders Publishing delivers cutting-edge products for network professionals. We publish books for all levels of users, from those wanting to gain NetWare Certification, to those administering or installing a network. Leading books in this category include *Inside NetWare 3.12*, *CNE Training Guide: Managing NetWare Systems*, *Inside TCP/IP*, and *NetWare: The Professional Reference*.

Graphics

New Riders provides readers with the most comprehensive product tutorials and references available for the graphics market. Best-sellers include *Inside CorelDRAW! 5*, *Inside Photoshop 3*, and *Adobe Photoshop NOW!*

Internet and Communications

As one of the fastest growing publishers in the communications market, New Riders provides unparalleled information and detail on this ever-changing topic area. We publish international best-sellers such as *New Riders' Official Internet Yellow Pages, 2nd Edition*, a directory of over 10,000 listings of Internet sites and resources from around the world, and *Riding the Internet Highway, Deluxe Edition*.

Operating Systems

Expanding off our expertise in technical markets, and driven by the needs of the computing and business professional, New Riders offers comprehensive references for experienced and advanced users of today's most popular operating systems, including *Understanding Windows 95*, *Inside Unix*, *Inside Windows 3.11 Platinum Edition*, *Inside OS/2 Warp Version 3*, and *Inside MS-DOS 6.22*.

Other Markets

Professionals looking to increase productivity and maximize the potential of their software and hardware should spend time discovering our line of products for Word, Excel, and Lotus 1-2-3. These titles include *Inside Word 6 for Windows*, *Inside Excel 5 for Windows*, *Inside 1-2-3 Release 5*, and *Inside WordPerfect for Windows*.

New Riders Publishing   201 West 103rd Street ◆ Indianapolis, Indiana 46290 USA

REGISTRATION CARD

Inside Windows NT Workstation

Name _____ Title _____

Company_____ Type of business _____

Address _____

City/State/ZIP _____

Have you used these types of books before? ☐ yes   ☐ no

If yes, which ones? _____

_____

How many computer books do you purchase each year? ☐ 1–5   ☐ 6 or more

How did you learn about this book? _____

Where did you purchase this book? _____

Which applications do you currently use? _____

_____

Which computer magazines do you subscribe to? _____

_____

What trade shows do you attend? _____

_____

Comments: _____

_____

_____

Would you like to be placed on our preferred mailing list? ☐ yes   ☐ no

☐ **I would like to see my name in print!** You may use my name and quote me in future New Riders products and promotions. My daytime phone number is: _____

New Riders Publishing   201 West 103rd Street ◆ Indianapolis, Indiana 46290 USA

Fax to 317-581-4670

Fold Here

BUSINESS REPLY MAIL
FIRST-CLASS MAIL PERMIT NO. 9918 INDIANAPOLIS IN

POSTAGE WILL BE PAID BY THE ADDRESSEE

NEW RIDERS PUBLISHING
201 W 103RD ST
INDIANAPOLIS IN 46290-9058